Microsoft SQL Server High Availability

Paul Bertucci

SAMS   800 East 96th Street, Indianapolis, Indiana 46240

Microsoft SQL Server High Availability

International Standard Book Number: 0-672-32625-6

Library of Congress Catalog Card Number: 2003098379

Printed in the United States of America

First Printing: October 2004

07 06 05   6 5 4 3

Trademarks

All terms mentioned in this book that are known to be trademarks or service marks have been appropriately capitalized. Sams Publishing cannot attest to the accuracy of this information. Use of a term in this book should not be regarded as affecting the validity of any trademark or service mark.

Warning and Disclaimer

Every effort has been made to make this book as complete and as accurate as possible, but no warranty or fitness is implied. The information provided is on an "as is" basis.

Bulk Sales

Sams Publishing offers excellent discounts on this book when ordered in quantity for bulk purchases or special sales. For more information, please contact

U.S. Corporate and Government Sales

1-800-382-3419

corpsales@pearsontechgroup.com

For sales outside of the U.S., please contact

International Sales

international@pearsoned.com

Associate Publisher
Michael Stephens

Acquisitions Editor
Neil Rowe

Development Editor
Songlin Qiu

Managing Editor
Charlotte Clapp

Project Editor
George E. Nedeff

Production Editor
Benjamin Berg

Proofreader
Eileen Dennie

Indexer
Mandie Frank

Technical Editor
Ray Rankins

Publishing Coordinator
Cindy Teeters

Multimedia Developer
Dan Scherf

Book Designer
Gary Adair

*With each milestone I complete,
with each book that I publish,
with each success that I achieve, I
am that much more sure that it is
due to the influence, guidance,
support, and love from my mother
and father. For this reason, I
dedicate this book to Donald and
Jane Bertucci.*

Contents

Introduction **1**

Five 9s. 1
Who Is This Book's Intended Audience? 3
How This Book Is Organized 3
Conventions Used in This Book 4
Setting Your Goals High! 4

PART I: UNDERSTANDING HIGH AVAILABILITY

Chapter 1   Essential Elements of High Availability **5**

Overview of High Availability 5
Calculating "Availability" 10
    Availability Example—A 24×7×365 Application. 11
Availability Continuum 12
Availability Variables. 15
General Design Approach for Achieving High Availability 18
    Development Methodology with High Availability
      "Built In". 21
    Assessing Existing Applications 22
    Service Level Agreement 24
High Availability Business Scenarios (Applications). 25
    Application Service Provider. 25
    Worldwide Sales and Marketing—Brand Promotion 26
    Investment Portfolio Management 27
    Call Before You Dig 27
Microsoft Technologies that Yield High Availability. 28
Summary 30

PART II: CHOOSING THE RIGHT HIGH AVAILABILITY APPROACHES

Chapter 2   Microsoft High Availability Options 31

What High Availability Options Are There? 31

Fundamental Areas to Start With 32

Fault Tolerant Disk: RAID and Mirroring. 34

Redundant Array of Independent Disks (RAID) 36

Mitigate Risk by Spreading Out Server Instances 42

Building Your HA Solution with One or More of These Options . . . 44

Microsoft Cluster Services (MSCS) 45

SQL Clustering. 46

Data Replication 47

Log Shipping 49

Distributed Transactions 51

Summary. 52

Chapter 3   Choosing High Availability. 53

Moving Toward High Availability. 53

Step 1—Launching a Phase 0 (Zero) HA Assessment. 55

Resources for a Phase 0 HA Assessment 56

The Phase 0 HA Assessment Tasks 56

Step 2—HA Primary Variables Gauge 59

Step 3—Determining the Optimal HA Solution 60

A Hybrid High Availability Selection Method 61

Cost Justification of a Selected High Availability
Solution 86

Adding HA Elements to Your Development Methodology . . . 88

Summary. 89

PART III: IMPLEMENTING HIGH AVAILABILITY

Chapter 4   Microsoft Cluster Services 91

Understanding Microsoft Cluster Services 91

Hardware/Network/OS Requirements for MSCS 93

How Clustering Actually Works 96
   The Disk Controller Configuration 98
   The Disk Configuration 98
   Network Configuration 99
   Considerations at the Operating System Level 101
Installing MSCS 102
   Pre-installation 104
   Installing MSCS—Step 1 106
   Installing MSCS for the Next Node: Step 2 116
   Extending Clustering with Network Load
      Balancing (NLB) 118
Windows 2003 Options for Quorum Disks and Fail-over 120
4-node and 8-node Clustering Topologies 124
Summary 125

Chapter 5   **Microsoft SQL Server Clustering** **127**

Microsoft SQL Clustering Core Capabilities 127
   SQL Clustering Is Built on MSCS 128
   Configuring MS DTC for Use with SQL Clustering 130
   Laying Out a SQL Cluster Configuration 131
Installing SQL Clustering 138
Failure of a Node 148
Removing SQL Clustering 152
Client Test Program for a SQL Cluster 155
A Node Recovery 160
Application Service Provider—Scenario #1 with SQL
   Clustering 161
Summary 164

Chapter 6   **Microsoft SQL Server Log Shipping** **167**

Microsoft Log Shipping Overview 167
   Data Latency and Log Shipping 169
   Design and Administration Implications of Log
      Shipping 170
Setting Up Log Shipping 171
   Before Creating the Log Shipping DB Maintenance
      Plan 172
   Using the DB Maintenance Plan Wizard to Create
      Log Shipping 173

Viewing Log Shipping Properties 184
Changing the Primary Role. 188
Log Shipping System Stored Procedures 189
Call Before You Dig—Scenario #4 with Log Shipping. 191
Summary. 193

Chapter 7   Microsoft SQL Server Data Replication 195

Microsoft SQL Server Data Replication Overview 195
What Is Data Replication? 197
The Publisher, Distributor, and Subscriber Metaphor 199
Publications and Articles 201
Filtering Articles 201
Replication Scenarios 206
Central Publisher. 207
Central Publisher with Remote Distributor 208
Publishing Subscriber 210
Central Subscriber. 210
Multiple Publishers or Multiple Subscribers 211
Updating Subscribers 212
Subscriptions 214
Pull Subscriptions 214
Push Subscriptions 215
Anonymous Subscriptions (Pull Subscriptions) 215
The Distribution Database 216
Replication Agents. 217
The Snapshot Agent 218
The Log Reader Agent 221
The Distribution Agent 222
The Merge Agent 223
The Miscellaneous Agents 224
Planning for SQL Server Data Replication 225
Timing, Latency, and Autonomy of Data 226
Methods of Data Distribution. 227
SQL Server Replication Types. 228
Snapshot Replication 228
Transactional Replication. 229
Merge Replication 230
User Requirements Drive the Replication Design 232

Setting Up Replication 234
    Enable a Distributor. 235
    Enable Publishing/Configure the Publisher. 239
    Creating a Publication 241
    Creating Subscriptions 246
Switching Over to a Warm Standby (Subscriber) 252
    Scenarios That Will Dictate Switching to the
       Warm Standby 252
    Switching Over to a Warm Standby (Subscription). 253
    Turning the Subscriber into a Publisher (if Needed). 254
    Insulate the Client Using an NLB Cluster Configuration. . . 254
Scripting Replication 254
Monitoring Replication 258
    SQL Statements 258
    SQL Enterprise Manager 259
    The Performance Monitor. 261
    Backup and Recovery in a Replication Configuration. 261
    Alternate Synchronization Partners 264
    Worldwide Sales and Marketing—Scenario #2 with
       Data Replication 265
Summary. 268

Chapter 8   **Other Ways to Distribute Data for High
Availability 271**

Alternate Ways to Achieve High Availability 271
    A Distributed Data Approach from the Outset. 272
    Setting Up Access to Remote SQL Servers. 275
    Querying a Linked Server. 279
    Transact-SQL with Linked Servers 280
Distributed Transactions 282
MS DTC Architecture 283
    Two-Phase Commit Protocol. 283
COM+ Applications for HA 291
Summary. 293

Chapter 9   **High Availability Pieced Together. 295**

Achieving Five 9s. 295
Foundation First. 296
Assemble Your HA Assessment Team. 298

Set the HA Assessment Project Schedule/Timeline 299
Doing a Phase 0 High Availability Assessment 300
  Step 1—HA Assessment 301
  Step 2—Primary Variable Gauge Specification 304
  High Availability Tasks Integrated into Your
    Development Life Cycle 306
Selecting the HA Solution 308
Is the HA Solution Cost Effective? 311
Summary 313

Chapter 10 **High Availability Design Issues and**
Considerations 315

Things to Consider for High Availability 315
  Hardware/OS/Network Design Considerations 316
  Remote Mirroring 320
  Microsoft Cluster Services Design Considerations 321
  SQL Server Clustering Design Considerations 322
  Stretch Clustering 325
  SQL Server Data Replication Design Considerations 326
  SQL Server Log Shipping Design Considerations 329
  Distributed Transaction Processing Design
    Considerations 331
General SQL Server File/Device Placement
  Recommendations 333
Database Backup Strategies in Support of High Availability . . . 335
  Two Backup Approaches for High Availability 337
  Parallel Striped Backup 339
  Split-Mirror Backups (Server-less Backups) 340
  Volume Shadow Copy Service (VSS) 342
  Monitoring/Verifying Backups 342
Disaster Recovery Planning 344
  The Overall Disaster Recovery Approach 344
  The Focus for Disaster Recovery 345
  Documenting Environmental Details Using
    SQLDIAG.EXE 349
  Plan and Execute a Complete Disaster Recovery test 351
Software Upgrade Considerations 351
High Availability and MS Analysis Services/OLAP 353
  OLAP Cubes Variations 356
  Recommended MSAS Implementation for High
    Availability 358

Alternative Techniques in Support of High Availability 361

    Data Transformation Service (DTS) Packages

        Used to Achieve HA 361

    Have You Detached a Database Recently? 362

    Third-party Alternatives to High Availability 362

    IBM/DB2 High Availability Example 364

Summary 366

Chapter 11   **High Availability and Security 369**

Security Breakdowns' Effect on High Availability 369

    Using an Object Permissions and Roles Method 371

    Object Protection Using Schema-Bound Views 373

Proper Security in Place for HA Options 378

    MSCS Security Considerations 379

    SQL Clustering Security Considerations 380

    Log Shipping Security Considerations 381

    Data Replication Security Considerations 384

    General Thoughts on Database Backup/Restore,

        Isolating SQL Roles, and Disaster Recovery Security

        Considerations 388

Summary 389

Chapter 12   **Future Directions of High Availability 391**

Microsoft Stepping Up to the Plate 391

What's Coming in Yukon for High Availability? 392

    Enhancements in Fail-over Clustering (SQL Clustering) . . . 393

    Database Mirroring for Fail-over 394

    Combining Fail-over and Scale Out Options 397

Data Access Enhancements for Higher Availability 398

High Availability from the Windows Server Family Side 401

    Microsoft Virtual Server 2005 401

    Virtual Server 2005 and Disaster Recovery 403

Other Industry Trends in High Availability 403

Summary 404

Index 407

About the Author

Paul Bertucci is the founder of Database Architechs (www. dbarchitechs.com) a database consulting firm with offices in the United States and Paris, France. He has more than 24 years of experience doing database design, data architecture, data replication, performance and tuning, distributed data systems, data integration, high availability assessments, and systems integration for numerous Fortune 500 companies including Intel, 3COM, Coca-Cola, Apple, Toshiba, Lockheed, Wells Fargo, Safeway, Texaco, Charles Schwab, Cisco Systems, Sybase, and Honda, to name a few. He has authored numerous articles, standards, and high profile courses such as Sybase's "Performance and Tuning" and "Physical Database Design" courses. Other Sams books that he has authored include the highly popular *Microsoft SQL Server 2000 Unleashed* and *ADO.NET in 24 Hours*. He has deployed numerous systems with MS SQL Server, Sybase, DB2, and Oracle database engines, and has designed/architected several commercially available tools in the database, data modeling, performance and tuning, data integration, and multi-dimensional planning spaces. Paul also serves part time as CTO for a strategic planning software company and part time as chief technical advisor for a data integration server software company. Paul received his formal education in computer science and electrical engineering from UC Berkeley (Go Bears!). He lives in northern California with his wife, Vilay, and five children, Donny, Juliana, Paul Jr., Marissa, and Nina. Paul can be reached at pbertucci@dbarchitechs.com or by phone at 925-674-0000.

Acknowledgments

With any writing effort, there is always a huge sacrifice of time that must be made to properly research, demonstrate, and describe leading edge subject matter. The brunt of the burden usually falls on those many people that are near and very dear to me. With this in mind, I desperately need to thank my family for allowing me to encroach on many months of what should have been my family's "quality time."

However, with sacrifice also comes reward in the form of technical excellence and solid business relationships. Many individuals were involved in this effort, both directly and indirectly. Starting with my technology leaders network of Ray Rankins, Jack McElreath, Walter Kuketz, and John Williams, who offered ideas and comments in the early stages of development. Richard Waymire (of Microsoft) for his early critique on the book proposal itself. Dave Wickert (of Microsoft) and Carl Rabeler (Network Systems One, Inc.) for their review and edits of the high availability ramifications of analysis services. Collaborative Consulting (Boston, MA) contributed hardware and time from their exceptional system infrastructure team of Don Gingras and Bob Germain for some of the cluster services configuration setup. Hewlett Packard, whose hardware worked flawlessly throughout.

Additional thanks must also go to Gary Dunn and Jose Solera of Intel Corporation; Marco Giammarinaro of Gem of the Sea Brewing Company (for technology help, not beer!); Dan Parkinson and Cathy Mygrant of Mygrant Glass Company; Steve Luk, Martin Sommer, and Eugene Vilain; Howard Sardis of Backroads; and MC for technology verification and other support (moral and technical) on this effort. Thanks guys!

Many good suggestions and comments came from the technical and copy editors at Sams Publishing, yielding an outstanding effort. Songlin, George, and Neil sure know how to put an exceptional book on the shelves.

—Paul Bertucci

References:

1. Rankins, Bertucci, Jensen. "Microsoft SQL Server 2000 Unleashed," Second Edition. Sams Publishing, Indianapolis, Indiana, 2002. Ch 19 pp 385-407, Ch 22 pp 477-533, Ch 24 pp 561-572, Ch 32 pp 909-927.

2. Nasi, I. and B. Schneiderman. "Flowchart Techniques for Structured Programming," ACM SIGPLAN Notices, Vol. 8, No. 8 (August 1973), pp. 12-26.

3. Schneyer, Robin. "Modern Structured Programming," Mitchell Publishing, Santa Cruz, California, 1984.

We Want to Hear from You!

As the reader of this book, *you* are our most important critic and commentator. We value your opinion and want to know what we're doing right, what we could do better, what areas you'd like to see us publish in, and any other words of wisdom you're willing to pass our way.

As an associate publisher for Sams Publishing, I welcome your comments. You can email or write me directly to let me know what you did or didn't like about this book—as well as what we can do to make our books better.

Please note that I cannot help you with technical problems related to the topic of this book. We do have a User Services group, however, where I will forward specific technical questions related to the book.

When you write, please be sure to include this book's title and author as well as your name, email address, and phone number. I will carefully review your comments and share them with the author and editors who worked on the book.

Email: **feedback@samspublishing.com**

Mail: Michael Stephens
          Associate Publisher
          Sams Publishing
          800 East 96th Street
          Indianapolis, IN 46240 USA

For more information about this book or another Sams Publishing title, visit our website at www.samspublishing.com. Type the ISBN (0672326256) or the title of a book in the Search field to find the page you're looking for.

Introduction

"If your company's High Availability requirements are well understood, the potential benefits gained by applying the correct High Availability solution can be enormous! Applying the wrong solution or not understanding your company's high availability needs could cause your company to go out of business!" IT Forum, Atlanta, GA—Paul Bertucci [November, 2003]

Five 9s

Downtime (system unavailability) directly translates to loss of profit, productivity, and customer good will—plain and simple. If your current or planned applications are vulnerable to downtime problems—or you are unsure of the potential downtime issues—then this book is aimed at you. Is your business at or nearing a requirement to be "highly available" or "continually available" in order to protect the previously mentioned profit, productivity, and customer good will? Again, this book is aimed at you.

Helping you understand the high availability (HA) solutions available to you and choosing the high availability approach that maximizes benefit and minimizes cost is our primary goal. A roadmap to design and implement these high availability solutions will be described herein. The good news is that software and hardware vendors in general, and Microsoft specifically, have come a long way in supporting high availability needs and will move even further to achieving 99.999% availability (herein referred to as "five 9s") in the near future. For a 24×7 application that aspires to achieve five 9s, that system would only tolerate a yearly total of 5.26 minutes of downtime. Knowing how to design for this will be crucial.

We will even touch on some alternatives for continually available systems (100% availability). These capabilities, coupled with a formal methodology tailored for designing high availability solutions, will allow you to design, install, and maintain systems maximizing availability while minimizing development and platform cost.

The success or failure of your company may well be influenced, if not be driven, by your ability to understand the essential elements that comprise a high availability environment, the business requirements driving the proper high availability approach, and the cost considerations affecting the ROI (return on investment) of a high availability solution. It is likely that a company's more critical applications demand some type of high availability solution—if a global online ordering system goes down and remains down for any length of time, millions of dollars would be lost along with the public's good will toward that company. The stakes are truly high indeed!

This book will outline how you can "design in" high availability for new applications and "upgrade" current applications to improve availability. In all cases, a crucial consideration will be the business drivers influencing a proposed application's uptime requirements, factoring in the dollar cost, productivity cost, and the good-will cost of *NOT* having that system available to the end-users for any period of time.

Current Microsoft capabilities and options allowing you to achieve high availability systems will be highlighted. These include, among others, Microsoft Cluster Services, Microsoft SQL Server 2000 SQL Clustering, Microsoft SQL Server 2000 Data Replication, Microsoft SQL Server 2000 Log Shipping, and Microsoft Distributed Transaction Coordinator capabilities. Many references to the Microsoft .NET Framework will be made since most of the previously mentioned components are deeply embedded in .NET.

Most importantly, a set of business scenarios will be introduced that will reflect actual companies' high availability requirements. We will use these business scenarios to guide you through the design process, determine the high availability approach best suited for a particular business scenario, and specify a roadmap to implement the business scenario with a specific technical solution.

This book will feel more like a cookbook or AAA route suggestion than a typical technical manual—this is the intention. It is one thing to describe technical syntax, but it is much more important to actually explain why you choose a particular approach to meet a particular business or application requirement. This book will focus on the later. The business scenarios introduced and implemented in this book come from live customer implementations. We will not reveal the names of these customers for obvious nondisclosure reasons. However, these business scenarios should allow the reader to correlate their own business requirements to these high availability scenarios. We will also include examples using the infamous Northwind database provided with

Microsoft SQL Server 2000. This will allow you to replicate some of the solutions quickly and easily in your own sandbox.

Several tools, scripts, documents, and references to help you jump-start your next high availability implementation will be made available at the Sams Publishing website.

Who Is This Book's Intended Audience?

This material is intended for an intermediate-to-advanced level user. This would include roles such as system designer/architect, system administrator, data architect, database administrator, SQL programmer, and even managerial types such as chief information officer (CIO) or chief technology officer (CTO). It has been pointed out to me on several occasions that the justifications, alternatives, and ROI considerations might well be beneficial for a chief financial officer (CFO), since many of the issues and ramifications translate into lost profit, productivity, and good will. A motivated CFO who understands the benefits, complexities, and capabilities of achieving high availability can rest easier at night knowing that they are in good hands with their well-designed high availability solution protecting the bottom line ($).

How This Book Is Organized

This book is divided into three main sections:

- Part I, "Understanding High Availability"—This section will establish our definition of high availability, introduce the high availability business scenarios that are typically found in the real world, and describe the various hardware and software options within the Microsoft family of products that directly address high availability.
- Part II, "Choosing the Right High Availability Approaches"— This section will explicitly define a formal design approach to be used as a roadmap to navigate the appropriate high availability solution for each business scenario introduced.
- Part III, "Implementing High Availability"—This section will describe the architecture, design, implementation steps, and techniques needed for each high availability solution. Each business scenario will be driven to their "complete" implementation.

This is a "soup-to-nuts" approach that should yield ample clarity for the reader—from inception of the business requirements to the complete implementation of a high availability solution for the given business and service level requirements.

Conventions Used in This Book

Names of commands and stored procedures are presented in a special monospaced computer typeface. We have tried to be consistent in our use of uppercase and lowercase for keywords and object names. However, because the default installation of SQL Server doesn't make a distinction between upper- and lowercase for SQL keywords or object names and data, you might find some of the examples presented in either upper- or lowercase.

"Design notes" will cover any design or architecture idea that is related to the topic that is being discussed. They are meant to supplement the discussed idea or to help guide design. An example would be to provide some additional insight into what type of disk RAID levels are appropriate for the different type of data accesses a database is used for. This would be considered above and beyond the normal RAID level explanation, but is great to consider when building SQL Server databases.

Setting Your Goals High!

As with any system you have ever touched, it is critical to establish and document the system's availability expectations with your end-users. For systems aspiring to high availability, these expectations must be very precise. The stakes are truly higher in HA systems. A well-grounded and time-tested HA methodology such as the ones described herein balances costs and benefits and reduces the likelihood of poor or uninformed decisions on the high availability options available with current technology. Lots of things must be done right to achieve the proper level of current and future application "high availability." This book—plain and simple—will show you how to understand, cost justify, and achieve these high availability goals and to minimize your company's exposure to downtime. You might also find that this book is a great companion book to Sams *Microsoft SQL Server 2000 Unleashed* (ISBN: 0672319977).

CHAPTER 1

Essential Elements of High Availability

- Understanding the essential elements and terminology of high availability
- Calculating "availability"
- High availability requirements—primary variables
- A general design approach for achieving high availability
- Common high availability business scenarios
- Microsoft technologies that yield high availability

Overview of High Availability

Knowing clearly what essential elements comprise a high availability environment and completely understanding the business requirements that are driving you to think about high availability solutions may well determine the success or failure of your company (or your job with this company). More times than not, a company's most critical application demands some type of high availability solution. In today's competitive marketplace, if a global online ordering system goes down (is unavailable for any reason) and remains down for any length of time, millions of dollars may be lost along with that company's good will. Profit margins are thin enough without having to add your system's downtime into the equation of whether your company makes a profit or not. The impact of unplanned or even planned downtime may be much more than you realize. The results of a "Cost of Downtime" survey recently conducted by Contingency Planning Research (CPR), a division of Eagle Rock, and Contingency Planning & Management Magazine (CPM) indicate a very high per-hour cost of downtime for different industry sectors (http://www.contingencyplanningresearch.com/).

A few examples are (per-hour dollar losses)

- Airline Reservation System—$67,000–$112,000/hour loss
- ATM Service Fees—$12,000–$17,000/hour loss
- Brokerage (Retail)—$5.6–$7.3 million/hour loss

This translates into an average annual cost exceeding hundreds of millions or billions of dollars for downtime globally. Perhaps even more.

The stakes are high in building rock solid applications to run your business. The trick will be to pour your applications into architectures and systems that can fulfill your availability needs from the start. If you are reading this book and you have existing applications that should have been deployed with a high availability solution, you are possibly putting your company at risk and you will need to accelerate getting your high availability solution into place at almost any cost, and as fast as you can go (without making mistakes). If you are building a new application then you need to take into account the proper high availability solution by integrating various high availability considerations into your current development methodology.

This chapter will set out to define many high availability terms, describe an availability percentage calculation, identify the different categories of availability, show you which critical pieces of information are needed for a complete high availability requirement (perhaps YOUR high availability requirement), and describe a few common business scenarios that are high availability candidates. Later chapters will show you how to match your high availability requirements to a particular high availability solution with a focus on Microsoft-based options.

As seen in Figure 1.1, how highly available a system becomes is actually a combination of several elements. This figure aggregates many of your system components into a single stack representation. From a high availability point of view, your application will only be as good as the weakest link in this stack.

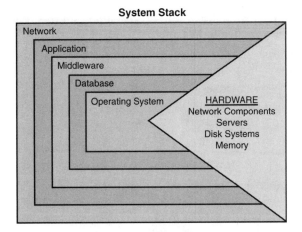

Figure 1.1 System stack—showing each system hardware and software component that can fail.

Each stack component (network, application, middleware, database, and the operating system) has its own vulnerability, and may also affect the other layers of the stack. On the innermost part of this stack is the OS itself. If the OS fails or must be brought down for maintenance, the rest of the stack is affected. In the outermost part of the stack is the network. If the network fails, the application is probably not affected (the application is still running). However, since the application cannot be accessed by a user via the network, it is essentially "down."

Embedded throughout this stack are all of the physical hardware components. These have their own failure issues all to themselves. And, to top things off, there is a human error aspect running through all of these components as well. If you reduce or eliminate human errors (bringing a DB offline accidentally, deleting a table's data in error, and so on), you increase your systems availability greatly. There are standard ways to combat these human error issues, but this is slightly outside the realm of this book.

As the availability tree in Figure 1.2 depicts, continuous application availability (or high availability) adds up to three major variables:

- **Uptime**—The time with which your application is up, running, and available to the end-users.

- **Planned downtime**—The time that IT has made one or more of the system stacks unavailable for planned maintenance, upgrades, so on.

- **Unplanned downtime**—The time that the system becomes unavailable due to failure—human error, hardware failure, software failure.

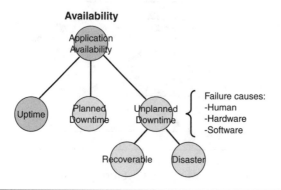

Figure 1.2   Availability tree depicting the different aspects of availability.

As you may already know from your own personal experience, it is the planned downtime that comprises the lion's share of unavailability on most systems. These are things such as hardware upgrades; OS upgrades (from Windows 2000 to Windows 2003); applying service packs to your DB, OS, or applications; and so on. However, there is a steady trend to adopt hardware and software platforms that allow for this element to be minimized. For instance, many vendors offer systems whose hardware components are "hot swappable," such as CPUs, disk drives, and even memory. But, the price of these systems tends to be much higher. We'll talk about the cost and ROI of high availability systems in Chapter 3, "Choosing High Availability."

The uptime variable is what you are typically being measured against. You want this to be constantly moving closer and closer to a "continuously available" level for the applications that require it. Any downtime, planned or unplanned, will be factored into your overall requirements of what *YOU* need for a high availability system. You can "design in" uptime to your overall system stack and application architectures by using basic distributed data techniques, basic backup and recovery practices, and basic application clustering techniques, as well as by leveraging hardware solutions that are almost completely resilient to failures.

As for unplanned downtime, this usually takes the form of memory failures, disk drive failures, database corruptions (both logical and physical), data integrity breakdown, virus breakout, application errors,

OS failures, network failures, and plain and simple human errors. There are basically two types of unplanned downtime:

- Downtime that is "recoverable" by normal recovery mechanisms. This would include downtime caused by things like swapping in a new hard drive to replace a failed one and then bringing the system back up.

- Downtime that is "not recoverable" and that completely makes your system unavailable and unable to be recovered locally. This would be things such as a natural disaster or any other unplanned downtime that affects hardware (for those of us who live in California, we are frequently reminded of things such as earthquakes and forest fires that contribute to many a system's downtime or nonrecoverable failure).

In addition, a good disaster recovery plan is paramount to any company's critical application implementation and should be part of your high availability planning.

If you simply apply a standard high availability technique to all of your applications, you will probably sacrifice something that may turn out to be equally important (such as performance or recovery time). So, be very cautious with a blanket approach to high availability. I found a perfect example of this type of poorly formed blanket high availability approach at a major auto manufacturer (which will remain nameless). Figure 1.3 shows their common SQL Clustering environment for all of their B2C applications.

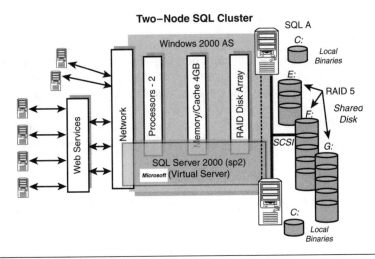

Figure 1.3 Poorly formed high availability blanket approach.

At the outset, they had the right idea (to use SQL clustering), but wondered why some of these applications ran so slowly and why all of them had a fairly long recovery time when failures occurred. Starting with RAID 5 shared storage for all applications was their first mistake. RAID 5 is best suited for "read only" applications, but for typical OLTP applications, twice the number of disk I/Os will be occurring—that directly translates to poorer performance overall. I also found that the only full database backups were being done on a nightly basis and that their OLTP-oriented applications were running "at risk" during the day (no up-to-the-minute recovery). They needed to quickly start doing incremental transaction logging on these volatile data applications. This was just the tip of the iceberg for them.

Calculating "Availability"

Calculating what the availability of a system has been (or needs to be) is actually quite simple. You simply subtract the "time unavailable" from the "meantime between unavailability" and then divide this by the same "meantime between unavailability." Use a common time factor as the basis of this calculation (like minutes). The "time available" is the actual time, if calculating what has already happened, or the estimated time, if doing this for the future—in addition, it is here that you add in all unplanned and planned downtime. The "meantime between unavailability" is the time since the last unavailability occurred.

Design Note

A system that needs to be up 24 hours per day, 7 days a week, 365 days per year would use 100% of the minutes in the year to measure against. A system that is only supposed to be available 18 hours per day, 7 days a week would use 75% of the minutes in the year to measure against. In other words, you measure your availability against the planned hours of operation, not the total number of minutes in a year (except if your planned hours of operation are 24×7×365).

Availability percentage = ((MBU – TU) / MBU) * 100
Where:
MBU is Meantime between unavailability
TU is Time Unavailable (planned/unplanned downtime)

Availability Example—A 24×7×365 Application

This application had an unplanned failure on March 1st that took 38 minutes to recover from (in this example, a database had to be restored from a full database backup due to a application software error). There was planned downtime on April 15th that lasted 68 minutes (to run software upgrades to fix some Microsoft security holes and other server issues). And there was another planned downtime that lasted 442 minutes on April 20th (hardware upgrades of memory and disks). We would calculate this systems availability as follows:

Availability (from Feb 14th through Feb 28th):

> Meantime between unavailability was 20,160 minutes
>
> [MBU =(15 days * 24 hours * 60 minutes)]
>
> Time Unavailable was 38 minutes
>
> [TU = 38 minutes]
>
> The calculation would be
>
> ((MBU – TU) / MBU) * 100 = Availability %
>
> or
>
> ((20,160 minutes – 38 minutes)/20,160 minutes) * 100 = **99.82%**

> Availability (from March 1st through April 15th):
>
> Meantime between unavailability was 66,240 minutes
>
> [MBU = (46 days * 24 hours * 60 minutes)]
>
> The calculation would be
>
> ((MBU – TU) / MBU) * 100 = Availability %
>
> or
>
> ((66,240 minutes – 68 minutes)/ 66,240 minutes) * 100 = **99.89%**

> Availability (from April 16th through April 20th):
>
> Meantime between unavailability was 7,200 minutes
>
> [MBU = (5 days * 24 hours * 60 minutes)]
>
> The calculation would be
>
> ((MBU – TU) / MBU) * 100 = Availability %
>
> or
>
> ((7,200 minutes – 442 minutes)/ 7,200 minutes) * 100 = **93.86%**

Figure 1.4 shows these availability percentages mapped against the time of planned operation by month.

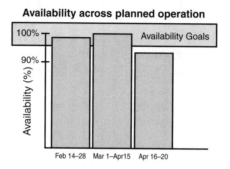

Figure 1.4   Availability percentages across planned operation.

As you can see, the availability goals were being met for February and March, but dipped below these goals in April.

Overall, between Feb 14th and April 20th, the availability averaged 99.42% [(95,640 of planned operation time) and 548 minutes of total downtime yielding an average of 99.42% of availability]. This sustained average may or may not be acceptable depending on the cost of the downtime to the business during those isolated downtime intervals.

Availability Continuum

The continuum in Figure 1.5 shows a general classification of availability based on the amount of downtime an application will tolerate without impacting the business. You would write your service level agreements (SLAs) to support and try to achieve one of these continuum categories.

Topping the chart is a category named "Extreme Availability," so named to indicate that this is the least tolerant category and is essentially a zero (or near zero) downtime requirement (sustained 99.5% to 100% availability). Next is the "High Availability" category, which depicts a minimal tolerance for downtime (sustained 95% to 99.4% availability). I would think that most "critical" applications would fit into this category of availability need. Then comes the "Standard Availability" category with a more normal type of operation (sustained 83% to 94%

availability). The "Acceptable Availability" category is for those applications that are deemed "noncritical" to the business such as online Employee Benefit Package self-service applications. These can tolerate much lower availability ranges (sustained 70% to 82% availability). And lastly, the "Marginal Availability" category are for those "nonproduction" custom applications such as marketing mailing label applications that can tolerate significant downtime (sustained 0% to 69% availability). Again remember, availability is measured by the planned operation times of the application.

Availability Continuum

	Characteristic	Availability Range
Extreme Availability	Near zero downtime!	(99.5% - 100%)
High Availability	Minimal downtime	(95% - 99.4%)
Standard Availability	With some downtime tolerance	(83% - 94%)
Acceptable Availability	Noncritical Applications	(70% - 82%)
Marginal Availability	Nonproduction Applications	(up to 69%)

Availability Range **describes the percentage of time relative to the planned hours of operations**

8,760 hours/year | 168 hours/week | 24 hours/day

525,600 minutes/year | 7,200 minutes/week | 1,440 minutes/day

Figure 1.5   Availability continuum.

Achieving the mythical five 9s (a sustained 99.999% availability) falls directly into the "Extreme Availability" category. In general the computer industry calls this "high availability," but this author pushes this type of near zero downtime requirement into its own "extreme" category all by itself. Most applications can only dream about this level of availability because of the costs involved, the high level of operational support required, the specialized hardware that must be in place, and many other extreme factors.

As you recall, downtime can be either unplanned or planned. Figure 1.6 shows how the availability continuum categories lay out over these aspects.

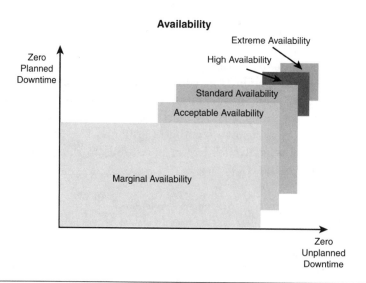

Figure 1.6 Availability planned/unplanned.

As you can see, having "Extreme Availability" places you in the far upper right quadrant of both near zero planned and near zero unplanned downtime.

Figure 1.7 shows the same unplanned/planned availability axis and availability categories, but now includes several common types of applications in the industry and places them in their approximate area of availability need.

Leading the way might be a financial institution's automated teller machine system (ATMs). Having this type of system available 100% of the time can be crucial to a company's customer service perception in this highly competitive industry. A 911 emergency tracking system is another slightly different application that again demands some extreme availability need. In the next plateau, you will find systems such as eCommerce applications (online order systems). These types of systems will tolerate some limited downtime, but clearly need to be very highly available (minimal downtime) because of the potentially high dollar loss if the ordering system is not available to take orders. Other types of applications such as email systems and inventory management tend to only require a standard level of availability, while many human resources and accounting systems can operate just fine in a lower (Acceptable Availability) mode. Marginally available applications are typically those applications such as marketing mailing label runs or other one-off, non-production applications that can be scheduled to run whenever it is convenient or within some predefined range of availability.

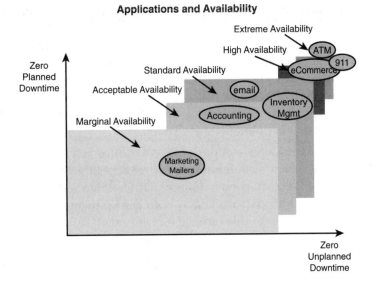

Figure 1.7   Application types and their availability.

Availability Variables

The primary variables to help you determine what high availability path you should be going down are

- Uptime requirement—The goal (from 0% to 100%) of what you require from your application for its planned hours of operation. I would imagine this to be above 95% for a typical highly available application.

- Time to recover—A general indication (from long to short) of the amount of time that can be expended to recover an application and put it back online. This could be in minutes, hours, or just in terms of long, medium, or short amount of time to recover. The more precise the better, though. As an example, a typical time to recover for an OLTP (Online Transaction Processing) application might be 5 minutes. This is fairly short but can be achieved with various techniques.

- Tolerance of recovery time—Describe what the impact might be (from high to low tolerance) of extended recovery times needed to resynchronize data, restore transactions, and so on. This is mostly tied into the time-to-recover variable, but can vary widely depending on who the end-users of the system are. As an example, internal company users of a self-service HR application may have a high tolerance for downtime (because the application doesn't affect their primary work). However, the same end-user might have a very low tolerance for downtime of the conference room scheduling/meeting system.

- Data resiliency—A description of how much data you are willing to lose, and whether it needs to be kept intact (have complete data integrity, even in failure). Often described in terms of from low to high data resiliency. Both hardware and software solutions are in play for this variable—mirrored disk, RAID levels, database backup/recovery options, and so on.

- Application resiliency—An application-oriented description of the behavior you are seeking (from low to high application resiliency). In other words, should your applications (programs) be able to be restarted, switched to other machines without the end-user having to reconnect, and so on? Very often the term *application clustering* is used to describe applications that have been written and designed to fail-over to another machine without the end-user realizing they have been switched. The .NET default of using "optimistic concurrency" combined with SQL clustering often yields this type of end-user experience very easily.

- Degree of distributed access/synchronization—For systems that are geographically distributed or partitioned (as are many global applications), it will be critical to understand how distributed and tightly coupled they must be at all times (indicated from low to high degree of distributed access and synchronization required). A low specification of this variable indicates that the application and data are very loosely coupled and can stand on their own for periods of time. Then, they can be resynchronized at a later date.

- Scheduled maintenance frequency—An indication of the anticipated (or current) rate of scheduled maintenance required for the box, OS, network, application software, and other components in the system stack (from often to never). This may vary greatly. Some applications may undergo upgrades, point releases, or patches very frequently (SAP and Oracle applications come to mind).

- Performance/scalability—A firm requirement of the overall system performance and scalability needed for this application (from low to high performance need). This variable will drive many of the high availability solutions that you end up with since high performance systems often sacrifice many of the other variables mentioned here (like data resilience).

- Cost of downtime ($ lost/hr)—Estimate or calculate the dollar (or euro, yen, and so forth) cost for every minute of downtime (from low to high cost). You will usually find that the cost is not a single number (like an average cost per minute). In reality, short downtimes have lower costs, and the costs (losses) grow exponentially for longer downtimes. In addition, I usually like to try to measure the "good will" cost (or loss) for B2C type of applications. So, this variable might have a subvariable for you to specify.

- Cost to build and maintain the high availability solution ($)—This last variable may not be known initially. However, as you near the design and implementation of a high availability system, the costs come barreling in rapidly and often trump certain decisions (such as throwing out that RAID 10 idea due to the excessive cost of a large number of mirrored disks). This variable will also be used in the cost justification of the high availability solution. So, it must be specified or estimated as early as possible.

As you can see in Figure 1.8, you can think of each of these variables as an oil gauge or temperature gauge. In your early depiction of your high availability requirements, simply place an arrow along the gauge of each variable estimating the approximate "temperature" or level of a particular variable. As you can see, I have specified all of the variables of a system that will fall directly into being highly available. This one is fairly tame, as highly available systems go, because there is a high tolerance for recovery time and application resilience is moderately low. Later in this chapter, four business scenarios will be fully described including a full specification of these primary variables. In addition, starting in Chapter 3, "Choosing High Availability," a return on investment (ROI) calculation will be included that will provide the full cost justification of a particular HA solution.

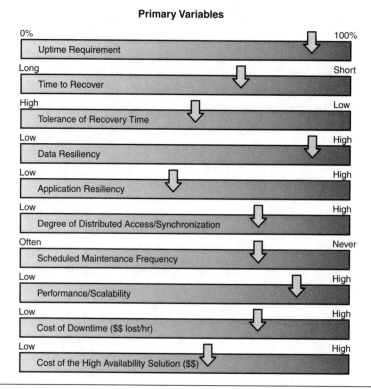

Figure 1.8   Primary variables for understanding availability needs.

General Design Approach for Achieving High Availability

A good overall approach for achieving high availability for any application can be accomplished by

- Shoring up your "software" system stack from the center out (operating system, database, middleware, antivirus, and so on, in this order). This would include upgrading to the latest OS levels and other software component releases, and putting into place all the support service contracts for these (this turns out to be extremely important for being able to get that quick fix for a bug that happened to bring your system down).

- Shoring up your hardware devices (redundant network cards, ECC memory, RAID disk arrays, disk mirroring, clustered servers, and so on). Be careful with the RAID levels since these will vary depending on your applications characteristics.

- Reducing human errors by way of strict system controls, standards, procedures, extensive QA testing, and other application insulation techniques. Human errors account for many a system being unavailable.

- Defining the primary variables of a potential highly available system. This should also include defining your applications' service level requirements along with defining a solid disaster recover plan.

Figure 1.9 depicts a "one-two" punch approach that blends all of these areas into two basic steps that need to be taken to achieve high availability for an application.

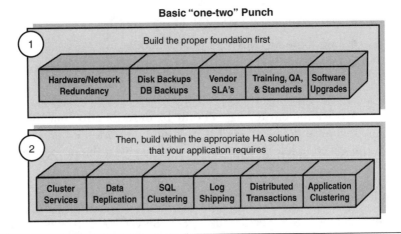

Figure 1.9   "One-Two" punch for achieving high availability.

The basic premise is to (1) "build the proper foundation first" followed by (2) applying the appropriate HA solution that matches your applications' needs.

This proper foundation would consist of

- Building the proper hardware/network redundancies.

- Putting into place all software and upgrades at the highest release levels possible, including antivirus software, and so on.

- Designing/deploying disk backups and DB backups that best service your application platforms.

- Establishing the necessary vendor service level agreements/contracts.

- Comprehensive end-user, administrator, and developer training including extensive QA testing of all applications and rigid programming, system, and database standards.

You must then gather the details of the high availability requirements for your application. Start with the HA primary variables and go from there. Then, based on the software available, the hardware available, and the high availability requirements, you can match and build out the appropriate HA solution on top of this solid foundation.

The types of high availability solutions that will be emphasized in this book are

- Cluster services (MSCS)

- SQL clustering (MS SQL Server 2000)

- Data replication (MS SQL Server 2000)

- Log shipping (MS SQL Server 2000)

- Distributed transactions (MS Distributed Transaction Coordinator)

Application clustering will only be described in concept and not in any technical detail, since it is programming oriented and really would require a complete programming book to give it the proper treatment.

Design Note

As the next release of SQL Server (Yukon/SQL Server 2005) inches its way out of full beta testing, a few other options might enter into the mix; however, most of the mainline options of SQL clustering, data replication, and so forth are here to stay for the long run (in Yukon, log shipping as we know it will evolve to database mirroring and will be great for keeping hot spares around).

Development Methodology with High Availability "Built In"

Figure 1.10 shows a traditional "waterfall" software development methodology. As you can see, understanding and gathering information that will yield the proper high availability designs for your application can start as early as the initial assessment and scoping phase (phase 0).

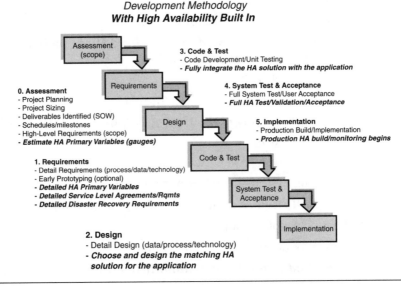

Figure 1.10 Development methodology with high availability "built in."

The general software development phases and the corresponding high availability tasks within each phase are

- Phase 0: Assessment (scope)
    - Project Planning
    - Project Sizing
    - Deliverables Identified (Statement of Work)
    - Schedules/milestones
    - High-Level Requirements (scope)
    - ***Estimate the High Availability Primary Variables (gauges)***

- Phase 1: Requirements
    - Detail Requirements (process/data/technology)
    - Early Prototyping (optional)
    - ***Detailed High Availability Primary Variables***
    - ***Detailed Service Level Agreements/Requirements***
    - ***Detailed Disaster Recovery Requirements***
- Phase 2: Design
    - Detail Design (data/process/technology)
    - ***Choose and design the matching High Availability solution for the application***
- Phase 3: Code & Test
    - Code Development/Unit Testing
    - ***Fully integrate the High Availability solution with the application***
- Phase 4: System Test & Acceptance
    - Full System Test/User Acceptance
    - ***Full High Availability Testing/Validation/Acceptance***
- Phase 5: Implementation
    - Production Build/Implementation
    - ***Production High Availability build/monitoring begins***

For those following a rapid development, "iterative" life cycle (commonly referred to as a rapid/spiral methodology), Figure 1.11 lays out the same type of high availability elements within this iterative development approach.

Assessing Existing Applications

If you haven't integrated high availability into your development methodology, or if you are retrofitting your existing applications for high availability, a more focused mini-assessment project can be launched that will yield all of the right answers and point you to the proper high availability solution that best matches your existing applications' needs. I call this "Phase 0 (zero) high availability assessment" (aka the "weakest link assessment").

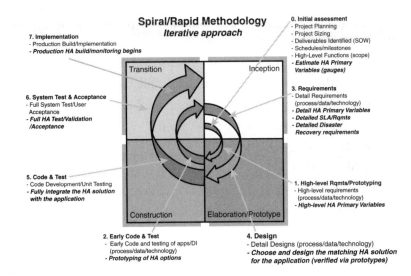

Figure 1.11   Spiral/rapid development methodology.

Essentially, you must quickly understand

- What are the current and future characteristics of your application?
- What are your service level requirements?
- What is the impact (cost) of downtime?
- What are your vulnerabilities (hardware, software, human errors, and so on)?
- What is your timeline for implementing a high availability solution?
- What is your budget for a high availability solution?

These types of assessments can be crunched out in five to seven days. This is an extremely short amount of time considering the potential impact to your company's goodwill and to its bottom line. Completing this type of "Phase 0 high availability" assessment will also provide you with the proper staging platform for the next several steps. These next steps would include defining your formal service level requirements, selecting the right high availability solution, building it, testing it, and implementing it. Oh, and enjoying the comfort of having a rock-solid high available solution in place (that works!).

If you have time, make sure you include as much detail as possible in the following areas:

- Analysis of the current state/future state of the application
- Hardware configuration/options available
- Software configuration/options available
- Backup/recovery procedures used
- Standards/guidelines used
- Testing/QA process employed
- Personnel administering systems assessed
- Personnel developing systems assessed

One deliverable from this assessment should be the complete list of primary variables for high availability. This will be one of your main decision-making tools for choosing which high availability solution matches your application.

Service Level Agreement

Service level agreements (or requirements) have been mentioned over and over in this chapter. Determining what these are and if they are needed is essential to understanding a high availability need.

Basically, a *service level agreement (SLA)* is a contract between the application owner (custodian) and the application user. As an example, an employee of a company is the application user of a self-service benefits application and the HR department is the application owner. The HR department signs up (via an internal SLA) to have this application be available to employees during normal business hours. This is what the HR department is held to (measured against). Then, in turn, the HR department might have its own SLA with the IT department that administers and maintains their application. An SLA will have the following basic elements:

1. Application Owner
2. Application User
3. Application Description
4. Application hours of operation/availability

5. Agreement Terms:
- Duration of agreement (often yearly)
- Response time levels (to failures, application enhancements, so on)
- Procedures/steps to follow
- Penalties if levels not met (very often monetary)

Describing penalties is especially important if you want this kind of agreement to have "teeth," as it should have. Companies such as application service providers (ASPs) probably have the most comprehensive and most severe SLAs on the planet. Of course their livelihood depends on meeting their SLAs, and perhaps they get huge bonuses when they exceed their SLAs as well.

High Availability Business Scenarios (Applications)

Four high availability business scenarios have been hand selected based on their clear need for some type of high availability solution. A short summary of these business scenarios will be described within this section; however, a much more in depth description will follow as each business scenario is identified and matched to a particular high availability solution. This will also include a complete software and system stack depiction, along with the specification of the high availability primary variables (gauge). Your company may have business scenarios similar to these and, at the very least, you should be able to correlate these high availability solutions to ones that will fit your application's high availability needs. All of the business scenarios are Microsoft-based applications with various high availability/fault tolerant hardware configurations in place. Okay, now let's describe these top four business scenarios.

Application Service Provider

The first business scenario/application centers on a very real application service provider (ASP) and their operating model. This ASP houses (and develops) numerous global, web-based online order entry systems for several major beauty and health product companies in the world. Their customer base is truly global (as the earth turns, the user base accessing the system shifts with it). They are headquartered in California (Silicon

Valley—where else?) and this ASP guarantees 99.00% uptime to their customers. In this case, the customers are sales associates and their sales managers. If the ASP achieves these guarantees, they get significant bonuses. If they fall below certain thresholds, they are liable for specific penalties. The processing mix of activity is approximately 65% online order entry and approximately 35% reporting.

Availability:

- 24 hours per day
- 7 days per week
- 365 days per year

Planned Downtime: **.25%** (less than 1%)

Unplanned Downtime: **.25%** (less than 1%) will be tolerable

Availability Possible Category: **Extreme Availability**

The downtime costs and other variables will be fully described as we pick up this business scenario in Chapter 3, "Choosing High Availability" and try to match it with the appropriate high availability solution.

Worldwide Sales and Marketing—Brand Promotion

A major chip manufacturer created a highly successful promotion and branding program that results in billions of dollars in advertising being rebated back to their worldwide sales channel partners. These sales channel partners must enter their complete advertisement copy (whether it is for newspaper, radio, TV, or other media) and be measured against ad compliance and logo usage and placements. If a sales channel partner is in compliance, they will receive up to 50% of the cost of their advertisement back from this chip manufacturer. The dollars being exchanged on a minute-by-minute basis are enormous. There are three major advertising regions: Far East, Europe, and North America. Any other advertisements outside of these first three are lumped into an "Other Regions" bucket. Each region produces a huge daily load of new advertisement information that is processed instantaneously for compliance. Each major region only deals with that region's advertisements, but receives the compliance rules and compliance judgment from the chip manufacturer's headquarters. Application mix is approximately 75% online entry of advertisement events and 25% management and compliance reporting.

Availability:
- 24 hours per day
- 7 days a week
- 365 days a year

Planned Downtime: **3%**

Unplanned Downtime: **2%** will be tolerable

Availability Possible Category: **High Availability**

Investment Portfolio Management

This investment portfolio management application will be housed in a major server farm in the heart of the world's financial center: New York City, NY. Serving North American customers only, this application provides the ability to do full trading of stocks and options in all financial markets (U.S. and international) along with full portfolio holdings assessment, historical performance, and holdings valuation. Primary users are investment managers for their large customers. Stock purchasing/selling comprise 90% of the daytime activity with massive assessment, historical performance, and valuation reporting done after the markets have closed. Three major peaks occur each weekday that are driven by the three major trading markets of the world (U.S., Europe, and the Far East). The weekends are filled with the long-range planning reporting and front-loading stock trades for the coming week.

Availability:
- 20 hours per day
- 7 days per week
- 365 days per year

Planned Downtime: **4%**

Unplanned Downtime: **1%** will be tolerable

Availability Possible Category: **High Availability**

Call Before You Dig

This is a Tri-State Underground Construction Call Center. This application will determine within six inches the likelihood of hitting any underground gas mains, water mains, electrical wiring, phone lines, or cables that might be present on a proposed dig site for construction. Law requires that a call be placed to this center to determine whether it is safe to dig, and to identify the exact location of any underground hazard *BEFORE* any digging has started. This is a "life at risk"-classified application and must be available near 100% of the time during common construction workdays (Monday through Saturday). Each year more than 25 people are killed nationwide digging into unknown underground hazards. Application mix is 95% query only with 5% devoted to updating images, geo-spatial values, and various pipe and cable location information provided by the regional utility companies.

Availability:

- 15 hours per day (5:00am–8:00pm)
- 6 days per week (closed on Sunday)
- 312 days per year

Planned Downtime: **0%**

Unplanned Downtime: **.5%** (less than 1%) will be tolerable

Availability Possible Category: **Extreme Availability**

Several other business scenarios were considered, but these four will demonstrate how you can take a business scenario's requirements and drive this all the way to the proper high availability solution.

Microsoft Technologies that Yield High Availability

As you will see in the coming chapters, there are several mainline technology offerings from Microsoft that will allow you to design a tailored high availability solution that best matches your company's availability needs. As already mentioned earlier, this book will focus on the most viable and production worthy options:

- Cluster services (MSCS)—Available only with Windows Advanced Server and Windows DataCenter Server. Cluster services allow for between two and four machines to be made aware of each other in such a way that if one should fail, the other will take over its resources (like its shared disk, and so on). An application will need to be "cluster aware" for it to take advantage of this capability. An example of a "cluster aware" application is SQL Server. This is considered to be a foundation requirement to many high available solutions such as SQL clustering (described below). This will be described in Chapter 4, "Microsoft Cluster Services."

- SQL clustering (MS SQL Server 2000)—Defines from between two and four SQL Servers running on different machines to act as a point of fail-over should the "active" SQL Server ever fail. Typically run in an Active/Passive mode (but not limited to that), this "cluster aware" capability will guarantee, via the creation of a virtual SQL Server, that a client application can connect to and do work on this virtual SQL Server nearly all of the time. This will be described in Chapter 5, "Microsoft SQL Server Clustering."

- Data replication (MS SQL Server 2000)—SQL Server also offers a highly efficient mechanism to distribute data to other locations for the purpose of maximizing availability and mitigating risk of failures. Data replication identifies a publisher, distributor, and subscriber model to distribute data (replicate it) to another location with full data integrity guarantee. Thus, a separate location can have an exact image of the primary database to be used as a fail-over point or as a location to maximize regional availability. This will be described in Chapter 7, "Microsoft SQL Server Data Replication."

- Log shipping (MS SQL Server 2000)—SQL Server provides a mechanism that will allow the transaction log of a primary database to be applied to a secondary copy of that same database. The end result is that of a hot spare or at least a reasonably "warm" spare (only as hot as the last transaction log that got applied to it). It is available as a potential fail-over point if needed, or as a place to consider isolating read-only processing away from the primary server for performance and availability factors. This will be described in Chapter 6, "Microsoft SQL Server Log Shipping."

- Distributed transactions (MS Distributed Transaction Coordinator)—Building applications that span two or more SQL Server instances will be utilizing the Distributed Transaction Coordinator capabilities. The DTC can allow an application to "design in" a level of application-based redundancy or fail-over to distributed copies of data. In other words, via DTC, you can program applications to use data in distant locations to help mitigate risk of a single point of failure. If one location becomes unavailable, the application has been coded to just reference the other distributed data sources to fulfill their needs. This perhaps is the most complex way to truly implement and tends to be a last resort approach for achieving high availability. But, it is nice to know that it is available if needed. This will be described in Chapter 8, "Other Ways to Distribute Data for High Availability."

Summary

In this chapter we discussed several primary variables of availability that should help to capture your high availability requirements much more cleanly and precisely. These variables included a basic uptime requirement, time to recovery, tolerance of recovery, data resiliency, application resiliency, performance/scalability, and the costs of downtime (loss). You can then take this information, couple it with your hardware/software configurations, several Microsoft-based technology offerings, and your allowable upgrade budget, and determine exactly which high availability solution you should implement that best supports your needs. In addition, a general "one-two" punch approach of establishing a proper high availability foundation in your environment should be done as soon as possible. Once completed, a knock-out punch that matches the proper high availability solution for your application's needs can be administered—getting it right the first time.

CHAPTER 2

Microsoft High Availability Options

THE KEY TOPICS IN THIS CHAPTER ARE

- High Availability options
- Build your foundation first
- Fault tolerant disks: RAID and mirroring
- Redundant hardware components
- Build with one or more HA solutions
- Microsoft Cluster Services
- SQL Server 2000 SQL clustering
- SQL Server 2000 data replication
- SQL Server 2000 log shipping
- Distributed transactions

What High Availability Options Are There?

Understanding your high availability requirements is only the first step in implementing a successful high availability application. Knowing what available technical options exist is equally as important. Then, by following a few basic design guidelines, it will be possible to match your requirements to the "correct" high availability technical solution. This chapter will introduce you to a variety of fundamental HA options such as RAID disk arrays and MSCS clustering, as well as other more high-level options such as SQL clustering and data replication that should lead you to a solid high availability foundation.

Fundamental Areas to Start With

If you remember the hardware/software stack presented in Chapter 1, "Essential Elements of High Availability," it outlined each major component and how if one component fails, the others may also be affected. With this in mind, the best approach for moving into supporting high availability is to work on shoring up the basic foundation components first (as suggested in the one-two punch approach already). Figure 2.1 depicts the initial foundation components to target.

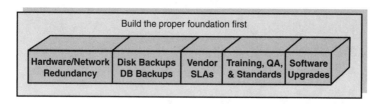

Figure 2.1   Initial foundation components.

By addressing these first, you add a significant amount of stability and high availability capability across your hardware/system stack. In other words, you are moving up to a level where you should be starting from, before you completely jump into a particular high availability solution. If you do nothing further from this point, you will have already achieved a portion of your high availability goals.

- **Hardware**—To get to this foundation level, start by addressing your basic hardware issues for high availability and fault tolerance. This would include redundant power supplies, UPS systems, redundant network connections, and ECC Memory (Error Correcting). Also available are "hot-swappable" components such as disks, CPUs, and memory. And, most servers are now using multiple CPUs, fault tolerant disk systems like RAID disk arrays, mirrored disks, Storage Area Network (SAN), Network Attached Storage (NAS), redundant fans, and so on. Cost may drive the full extent of what you choose to build out. However, start with the following

- Redundant power supplies (and UPS)
- Redundant fan systems
- Fault tolerant disks—RAID disk arrays (1 through 10), preferably "hot swappable"
- ECC memory
- Redundant Ethernet connections

- **Backup**—Next look at the basic techniques and frequency of your disk backups and database backups. Often this is way behind in what it needs to be to guarantee recoverability and even the basic level of high availability. I've lost track of the number of times I've walked into a customer site and found out that the database backups were not being run, were corrupted, or weren't even considered necessary. You would be shocked by the list of fortune 1000 companies where this occurs.

- **Operating System**—Not only do you make sure that all upgrades to your OS are applied, but that the configuration of all options are correct. This would include making sure you have antivirus software installed (if applicable) along with the appropriate firewalls for external facing systems.

- **Vendor Agreements**—Come in the form of software licenses, software support agreements, hardware service agreements, and both hardware and software service level agreements. Essentially, you are trying to make sure you can get all software upgrades and patches for your OS and for your application software at any time, as well as get software support, hardware support agreements, and both software and hardware service level agreements (SLAs) in place that will guarantee a level of service within a defined period of time

Design Note

I was thinking back over the last 10 or 15 years on the number of service agreements I have put into place, and realized that I never lost my job by doing this; however, I know of people who didn't bother to put these type of agreements in place, and who did lose their jobs. This is a good insurance policy to have.

- **Training**—This is multifaceted, in that training can be for software developers to guarantee the code they write is optimal, for system administrators who need to administer your applications, and even for the end-users themselves to make sure they use the system correctly. All play into the ultimate goals of achieving high availability.

- **Quality Assurance**—Testing as much as possible and doing it in a very formal way is a great way to guarantee a system's availability. I've seen dozens of studies over the years that clearly show that the more thoroughly you test (and more formal your QA procedures are), the fewer software problems you will have. To this day I'm not sure why people skimp on testing. It has such a huge impact in system reliability and availability.

- **Standards/Procedures**—This is interlaced heavily with training and QA. Coding standards, code walkthroughs, naming standards, formal system development life cycles, protecting tables from being dropped, use of governors, and so on all contribute to more stable and potentially more highly available systems.

- **Server Instance Isolation**—By design, you may want to isolate applications (SQL Server's applications and their databases, and so on) away from each other in order to mitigate the risk of one of these applications causing the other to fail. Plain and simple, never put other applications in each other's way if you don't have to. The only things that might force you to load up a single server with all of your applications would be expensive licensing costs for each server's software, and perhaps hardware scarcity (strict limitations to the number of servers available for all applications). We will explore more details of this in a bit.

Fault Tolerant Disk: RAID and Mirroring

When it comes to creating a fault tolerant disk subsystem, you can do basic "vanilla" mirroring of a disk or varying RAID disk array configurations. These are tried and true methods, but which one to use is the tricky part. The problem is that there are often significant implementation aspects such as the performance impact, complexity of administration, and cost that must be understood thoroughly. So, let's look at disk mirroring first.

Basically, disk mirroring is a technique that writes data to two duplicate disks simultaneously (or three if doing triple-mirroring) as part of a single logical disk write operation. In other words, when you write a piece of data to a disk that has been mirrored, it is automatically written to the primary disk *AND* to the mirrored (duplicate) disk at the same time. Both disks in the mirror are usually the same size and have the same technical specification. If the primary disk fails, for any reason, the mirrored (duplicate) disk is automatically used as the primary. The application that was using the disk never knows that a failure has occurred, thus enhancing your application's availability greatly. At some point, you can swap in a new disk and re-mirror it, and off you go again without missing a beat. Figure 2.2 illustrates the basic disk-mirroring concept of data being written simultaneously.

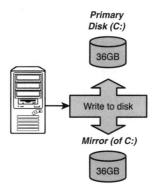

Figure 2.2   Mirrored disk—simultaneous writes.

Of course, the downside of disk mirroring is that the mirrored disk drive(s) are not directly usable, and you are effectively burning up double the amount of disk drives. This can be costly as well, as many servers don't have the sheer space within their physical rack footprint to house numerous mirrored disks. Very often, separate external disk drive rack systems (with separate power supplies) solve this problem.

What should be mirrored? In many high availability systems, the first disk drive that is targeted for mirroring is the one that contains the OS. This one mirroring choice instantly increases the availability of the system by some factor and is considered a fundamental cornerstone for high availability. For non-RAID systems, you can selectively choose critical pieces of your application and its underlying databases as high candidates for mirrored disk. Figure 2.3 illustrates an MS SQL Server

2000–based ERP system that has been laid out within a mirrored disk configuration.

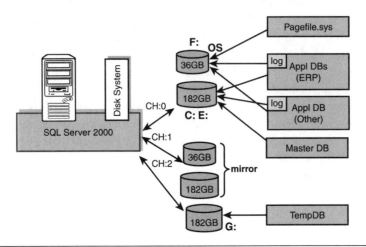

Figure 2.3   ERP System (MS SQL Server 2000 based)—mirrored disk.

The use of disk mirroring has also been integrated into various RAID level configurations. These will be explained in the next section.

Redundant Array of Independent Disks (RAID)

Perhaps the most popular method of increasing system availability is by implementing various RAID disk configurations. This will, by definition, make the underlying disk subsystem much more stable and available with less susceptibility to disk failures. Using certain RAID configurations is another strong tool that you can use as part of your foundation for high availability. Let's look at what RAID really is.

RAID stands for Redundant Array of Independent Disks and has several "levels" of configurations that yield different capabilities. The primary goal of RAID is to decrease disk subsystem failures. Some configurations are highly redundant and incorporate disk mirroring. Some use sophisticated algorithms for spreading data out over several disks so that if any one disk fails, the others can continue processing. In addition, the data that was on the failed disk can be recovered from what is stored on the other disks (RAID 5). This is almost like magic. But, where there is magic there is cost (both in performance and in hardware). Figure 2.4 summarizes the common RAID level configurations.

RAID 0: Striping (without Parity)

RAID 1: Mirroring (with duplexing if available)

RAID 2: Bit-level striping with Hamming code ECC

RAID 3: Byte-level striping with dedicated parity

RAID 4: Block-level striping with dedicated parity

RAID 5: Block-level striping with distributed parity

RAID 6: Block-level striping with dual distributed parity

RAID 7: Asynchronous, cached striping with dedicated parity

RAID 0+1, 01, 0/1: mirrored stripes

RAID 1+0, 10, 1/0: stripe of mirrors

RAID 50, 0/5: Striped Set of RAID 5 Arrays

RAID 53, 3/5: Striped Set of RAID 3 Arrays

Figure 2.4 RAID levels summary.

Disk controller manufacturers and disk drive manufacturers sell various types of disk controllers for these RAID arrays that may also have different amounts of cache (memory) built in. These product offerings give you a great deal of flexibility in regard to defining different RAID level configurations that best suit your needs. Since many of the defined RAID levels are not commercially viable (or available), we will describe only the ones that are best suited for a company's high availability solution (from a cost, management, and fault tolerance point of view). These are RAID levels 0, 1, 5, and 1+0 (10).

- **RAID 0: Striping (without Parity)**—RAID 0 (zero) is simply a disk array that consists of one or more physical disks that have no parity checking (error checking of disk writes/reads) at all. This is really just a series of disk drives sitting on the operating system without any redundancy or error checking whatsoever—no fault tolerance. The disk striping comes from the ability to spread *segments (data blocks)* across more than one physical disk for performance. Figure 2.5 shows this basic RAID level configuration and how data blocks can be striped across multiple disks. A piece of data (A) is broken down into data block A1 (on Disk W) and data block A2 (on Disk X). The payoff comes when you need to retrieve the data. On average, because of the striping, the data is stored more shallowly and is readily retrieved (as compared to normal non-striped data storage retrieval). In other words, you don't have to seek as deep into an individual disk to retrieve a piece of data; it is, on average, located higher up on multiple disks and assembled more quickly. This translates directly into faster retrieval times. For the best performance, you can have one disk drive per controller, or at the very least one disk drive per channel (as seen in Figure 2.5).

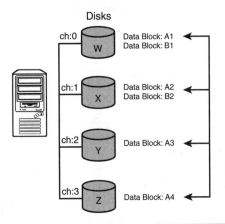

Figure 2.5   RAID level 0.

RAID 0 is often configured to support file access that doesn't need to be protected from failure but does need to be fast (no additional overhead in any way).

You would be surprised at the number of things that meet this type of requirement. RAID 0 is also used in combination with both RAID 1+0 (10) and RAID 0+1 (01) to produce much more robust availability. These will be described shortly.

■ **RAID 1: Mirroring (with duplexing)**—RAID 1 is the first RAID level that handles disk failures and therefore is truly fault tolerant. RAID 1 is mirroring for one or more disks at a time. In other words, if you configure five disks with RAID 1 (mirroring), you will need five additional redundant disks for their mirror. Think of this as "mirrored pairs." As has already been described, when writes occur to this RAID 1 configuration, they are simultaneously written to the redundant (mirrored) disks. If a failure of any primary disk should ever occur, the mirrored disk is instantly activated. Most mirrored configurations may well read from either the mirrored or primary disk for data (it doesn't matter since the disks are identical and this read traffic is managed by the disk controller). However, for every logical disk write, there will be two separate physical disk writes (primary and the mirror). Duplexing is achieved by adding a redundant disk controller card for additional fault tolerance. Figure 2.6 illustrates a RAID 1 configuration.

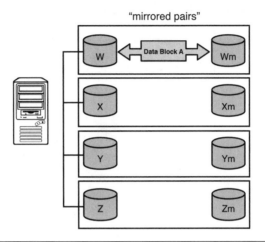

Figure 2.6   RAID level 1.

This RAID configuration offers good results for folks who need a certain level of write fault tolerance but can withstand the slight performance impact of the additional physical writes. To reestablish a mirrored pair (after a disk failure has occurred), you just pop in a replacement disk, re-copy the good disk's data to the new disk, and off you go.

- **RAID 5: Block-level striping with distributed parity**—The notion of parity is first introduced with RAID 3. *Parity* means that there will be a data parity value generated (and stored) for a piece of data (or block of data) when it is written, and this parity is checked when it is read (and corrected if necessary). RAID 5 distributes the parity storage across all the disks in the array in such a way that any piece of data can be recovered from the parity information found on all of the other disks. Figure 2.7 shows this striped, distributed parity technique.

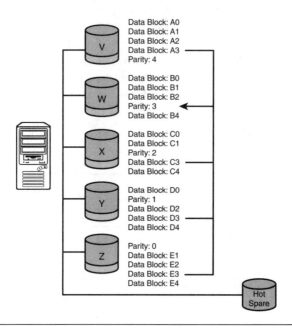

Data Block: A0
Data Block: A1
Data Block: A2
Data Block: A3
Parity: 4

Data Block: B0
Data Block: B1
Data Block: B2
Parity: 3
Data Block: B4

Data Block: C0
Data Block: C1
Parity: 2
Data Block: C3
Data Block: C4

Data Block: D0
Parity: 1
Data Block: D2
Data Block: D3
Data Block: D4

Parity: 0
Data Block: E1
Data Block: E2
Data Block: E3
Data Block: E4

Hot Spare

Figure 2.7   RAID level 5.

To put this another way, if the disk containing data blocks A is lost, the data can be recovered from the parity values that are stored on all of the other disks. Notice that a data block never stores its own parity values. This makes RAID 5 a good fault-tolerant option for those applications that need this type of availability.

In most RAID 5 implementations, a hot spare is kept online that can be used automatically when a failure has occurred. This hot spare gets rebuilt with data blocks (and parity) dynamically from all of the surviving disks. You usually notice this via RAID failure alarms, and there is a huge disk subsystem slowdown during this rebuild. Once completed, you are back in a fault tolerant state. However, RAID 5 configurations cannot sustain two disk failures at one time because this would not allow the complete parity values that are needed to rebuild a single disk's data blocks to be accessed. RAID 5 requires that there be up to four (or more) physical disk writes for every logical write that is done (one write to each parity storage). This translates to poor performance for write and update intensive applications, but ample performance for read intensive applications.

- **RAID 0+1, 01, 0/1: Mirrored stripes**—RAID 0+1 is implemented as a mirrored array (RAID 1) whose segments are RAID 0 arrays. This is not the same as RAID 1+0 (10), as you will see in a bit. RAID 0+1 has the same fault tolerance as RAID level 5. It also has the same overhead for fault tolerance as mirroring alone. Fairly high read/write rates can be sustained due to the multiple stripe segments of the RAID 0 portion.

  The downside of RAID 0+1 is when a single drive fails, the whole array deteriorates to a RAID level 0 array because of the approach used of mixing striping with mirroring this way. Figure 2.8 shows how this mirrored stripe configuration is achieved.

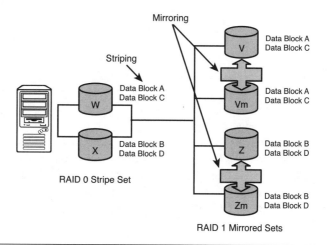

Figure 2.8   RAID Level 0+1 (0/1).

- **RAID 1+0, 10, 1/0: Stripe of Mirrors**—RAID 1+0 is implemented as a striped array (RAID 0) whose segments are mirrored arrays (RAID 1). This is more favorable in regard to failures. Basically, RAID 1+0 has the same fault tolerance as RAID level 1 (mirroring). The failure of a single disk will not put any other mirrored segments in jeopardy. This is considered to be better than RAID 0+1 in this regard. And, to the delight of many a system designer, RAID 1+0 can sustain very high read/write rates because of the striping (the RAID 0). Figure 2.9 shows the subtleties of this RAID 1+0 configuration.

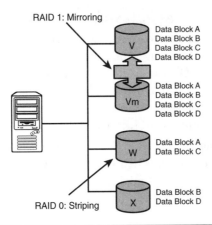

Figure 2.9   RAID Level 1+0 (10).

Design Note

Building your systems/servers with at least RAID 1, RAID 5, and RAID 1+0 is critical to achieving a highly available system along with a high performing system. RAID 5 is better suited for read-only applications that need fault tolerance and high availability while RAID 1 and RAID 1+0 are better suited for OLTP or moderately high volatility applications. RAID 0 by itself can help boost performance for any data allocations that don't need the fault tolerance of the other RAID configurations, but need to be high performing.

Mitigate Risk by Spreading Out Server Instances

Server instance isolation was briefly touched on in a prior section of this chapter, but needs to be expanded on because it is so critical and because application isolation should become a part of your fundamental design principles. As was mentioned, by design, you should try to isolate applications (SQL Server's applications and their associated databases, and so on) away from each other in order to mitigate the risk of one of these applications causing the other to fail. A classic example of this is when a company loads up a single SQL Server instance with between two and eight applications and their associated databases. The only problem is that the applications are sharing memory, CPUs, and internal work areas such as TempDB. Figure 2.10 shows a loaded up SQL Server instance that is being asked to service four major applications (Appl 1 DB thru Appl 4 DB).

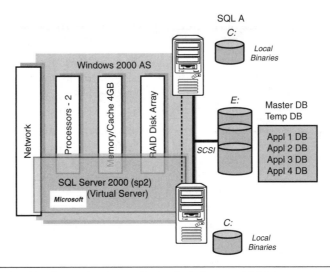

Figure 2.10 Applications sharing a single SQL Server 2000 instance.

This single SQL Server instance is sharing memory (cache) and critical internal working areas such as TempDB with all four major applications. Everything runs along fine until one of these applications submits a runaway query and all other applications being serviced by that SQL Server instance come to a grinding halt. Most of this built-in risk could have been avoided by simply putting each application (or perhaps two applications) onto their own SQL Server instance, as shown in Figure 2.11. This fundamental design approach reduces greatly the risk of one application affecting another.

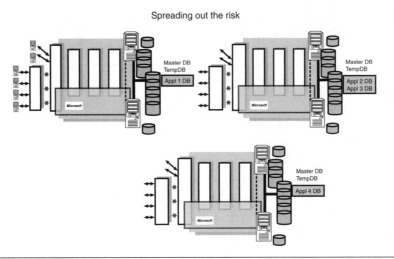

Figure 2.11 Isolating applications away from each other—SQL Server 2000.

I've lost count of the number of companies that have made this very fundamental error. The trouble is they keep adding new applications to their existing server instance without a full understanding of the "shared" resources that underpin the environment. It is very often too late when they finally realize that they are hurting themselves "by design." The readers of this book have now been given proper warning of the risks. If other factors such as cost or hardware availability dictate otherwise, then at least it is a calculated risk that is entered into knowingly (and is properly documented as well).

Building Your HA Solution with One or More of These Options

Once we have the proper foundation in place, we can build a tailored software-driven high availability solution much more easily and "match" one or more high availability options to *YOUR* requirements. Remember, different high availability solutions will yield different results. The focus of this book will be on the Microsoft offerings since they are potentially already available in your company's software stack. Figure 2.12 identifies the current Microsoft options that can be drawn upon together or individually.

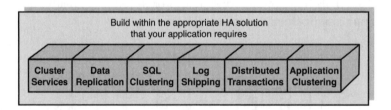

Figure 2.12   Building with various Microsoft high availability options.

With the exception of application clustering (which is available as part of a particular application's capabilities—like with some application server technologies), all are readily available "out-of-the-box" from Microsoft from the Windows Server family of products and from Microsoft SQL Server 2000.

It is important to understand that one or more of these options can be used together, but not all go together. As an example, you would be using Microsoft Cluster Services (MSCS) along with Microsoft SQL Server 2000's SQL Clustering to implement the SQL clustering database configuration. We will get into much more detailed explanations on these in the next few chapters. But, first let's describe a brief overview of each of these options.

Microsoft Cluster Services (MSCS)

Cluster Services could actually be considered a part of the basic foundation components that we described earlier, except that it's possible to build a high availability system without it (one that uses numerous redundant hardware components and disk mirroring or RAID for its disk subsystem, for example). Microsoft has made MSCS the cornerstone of their clustering capabilities, and MSCS is utilized by applications that are "cluster-enabled." The prime example of a cluster-enabled technology is MS SQL Server 2000.

So, what is MSCS anyway?

MSCS is the additional Windows OS configuration information that will define and manage from between two to four servers as "nodes" in a cluster. These nodes are aware of each other and can be set up to take over cluster-aware applications from any node that fails (a failed server). This cluster will also share and control one or more disk subsystems as part of its high availability capability. MSCS is only available within the Microsoft Windows Advanced Server and Data Center operating system (OS) products. It is *NOT* available with standard Windows servers (Win2k Professional, and so on). Don't be alarmed though. If you are looking at a high availability system to begin with, there is a high probability that your applications are already running with these enterprise-level OS versions. Figure 2.13 illustrates a basic two-node MSCS configuration.

In Chapter 4, "Microsoft Cluster Services," we will completely build up a clustered configuration and detail the minimal hardware components that must be present for MSCS. MSCS can be set up in an active/passive or active/active model. Essentially, in an active/passive mode, one server sits idle (is passive) while the other is doing the work (is active). If the active server fails, the passive one takes over the shared disk and the cluster-aware applications instantaneously. I believe some people think this is "magic." We will see exactly how this is done in Chapter 4. And, it's not magic.

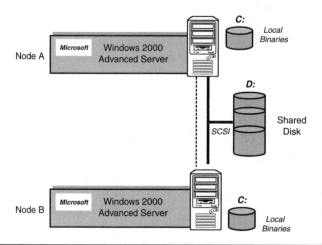

Figure 2.13   MSCS cluster services basic configuration.

SQL Clustering

If you want a SQL Server instance to be clustered for high availability, you are essentially asking that this SQL Server instance (and the database) be completely resilient to a server failure and completely available to the application without the end-user ever even noticing that there was a failure. Microsoft provides this capability through the SQL clustering option within SQL Server 2000. SQL clustering builds on top of cluster services (MSCS) for its underlying detection of a failed server and for its availability of the databases on the shared disk (which is controlled by MSCS). SQL Server is a "cluster aware/enabled" technology. This is done by creating a "virtual" SQL Server that is known to the application (the constant in the equation), and then two physical SQL Servers that share one set of databases. Only one SQL Server is active at a time and just goes along and does its work. If that server fails (and with it the physical SQL Server instance), the passive server (and the physical SQL Server instance on that server) simply takes over instantaneously. This is possible because cluster services also controls the shared disk where the databases are. The end-user (and application) pretty much never know which physical SQL Server instance they are on, or if one failed or not. Figure 2.14 illustrates a typical SQL clustering configuration that is built on top of MSCS.

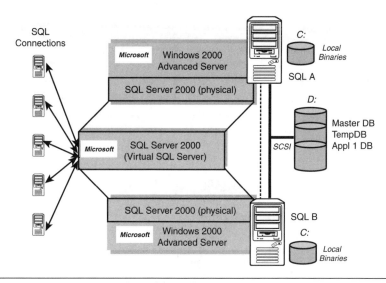

Figure 2.14 SQL clustering basic configuration.

Setup and management of this type of configuration is much easier than you realize. More and more, SQL clustering is the method chosen for most high availability solutions. Later on, you will see that other methods may also be viable for achieving high availability (based on the application's HA requirements). We will fully outline SQL clustering in its own chapter shortly. Extending the clustering model to include network load balancing (NLB) pushes this particular solution even further into higher availability. Figure 2.15 shows a four-host network load balanced (NLB) cluster architecture acting as a virtual server to handle the network traffic.

Each NLB host works together among the four hosts distributing the work efficiently. NLB automatically detects the failure of a server and repartitions client traffic among the remaining servers.

Data Replication

The next technology option that can be utilized to achieve high availability is data replication. Originally data replication was created to off-load processing from a very busy server (such as an OLTP application that must also support a big reporting workload) or to distribute data for different, very distinct user bases (such as worldwide geographic specific applications). As data replication (transactional replication) became more stable and reliable, it started to be used to create "warm," almost "hot" standby SQL Servers that could also be used to fulfill basic report-ing needs. If the primary server ever failed, the reporting users would still be able to work (hence a higher degree of availability achieved for them) and the replicated reporting database could be utilized as a substi-tute for the primary server if needed (hence a warm standby SQL Server). When doing transactional replication in the "instantaneous replication" mode, all data changes are replicated to the replicate servers extremely quickly. This may fit some companies' availability require-ments and also fulfill their distributed reporting requirements as well. Figure 2.16 shows a typical SQL data replication configuration that serves as a basis for high availability and also fulfills a reporting server requirement at the same time.

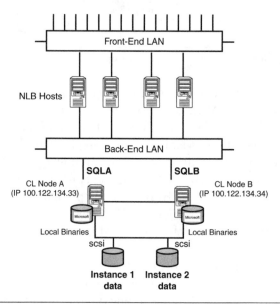

Figure 2.15   An NLB host cluster with a two-node server cluster.

The downside comes into play if ever the replicate is needed to become the primary server (take over the work from the original server). It takes a bit of administration that is *NOT* transparent to the end-user. Connection strings have to be changed, ODBC data sources need to be updated, and so on. But, this may be something that would take minutes as opposed to hours of database recovery time, and may well be tolera-ble to the end-users. In addition, a risk of not having all of the transac-tions from the primary server also exists. But, often, a company is willing to live with this small risk in favor of availability. Remember, this replicated database is a mirror image of the primary database (up to the point of the last update), which makes it very attractive as a warm standby. For databases that are primarily read-only, this is a great way to distribute the load and mitigate risk of any one server failing. More on this in Chapter 7, "Microsoft SQL Server Data Replication."

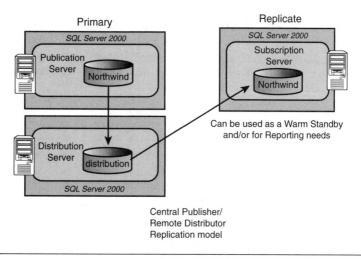

Figure 2.16   Data replication basic configuration for HA.

Log Shipping

Another, more direct method of creating a completely redundant database image is log shipping. Microsoft certifies log shipping as a method of creating an "almost hot" spare. Some folks even use log shipping as an alternative to data replication (it has been referred to as "the poor man's data replication"). Keep in mind that log shipping does three primary things:

- Makes an exact image copy of a database on one server from a database dump
- Creates a copy of that database on one or more other servers from that dump
- Continuously applies transaction log dumps from the original database to the copy

In other words, log shipping effectively replicates the data of one server to one or more other servers via transaction log dumps. Figure 2.17 shows a source/destination SQL Server pair that has been configured for log shipping.

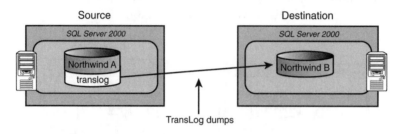

Figure 2.17   Log shipping in support of high availability.

This is a great solution when you have to create one or more failover servers. It turns out that, to some degree, log shipping fits the requirement of creating a read-only subscriber as well. The gating factors for using log shipping as the method of creating and maintaining a redundant database image are

- Data latency—The time that exists between the frequency of the transaction log dumps on the source database and when these dumps get applied to the destination DBs.

- Sources and destinations must be the same SQL Server version.

- Data is read-only on the destination SQL Server until the log shipping pairing is broken (as it should be to guarantee that the translogs can be applied to the destination SQL Server).

The data latency restrictions might quickly disqualify log shipping as a full-proof high availability solution. However, log shipping might be adequate for certain situations. If a failure ever occurs on the primary SQL Server, a destination SQL Server that was created and maintained via Log Shipping can be swapped into use at a moment's notice. It would contain exactly what was on the source SQL Server (right down to every user id, table, index, and file allocation map, except for any changes to the source database that occurred after the last log dump that was applied). This directly achieves a level of high availability. It is still not quite completely transparent though, since the SQL Server instance names are different and the end-user may be required to log in again to the new server instance.

Distributed Transactions

A slightly more complex approach to high availability might be to create a distributed application that is "programmed" to be aware of a failed server (data source). In other words, when data is needed (read only) by an application, it tries its primary data location first, and if that is not available, it tries a secondary data location, and so on. When updates (inserts/deletes/updates) occur at any one of the data locations, a single distributed transaction needs to be used to guarantee the integrity of all data locations (often referred to as two-phase commit). Building applications that span two or more data locations will be utilizing the distributed transaction coordinator (MS DTC).

Each Microsoft SQL Server will have an associated distributed transaction coordinator (MS DTC) on the same machine with it. For that matter, MS DTC is present on your Windows Server regardless of whether you have SQL Server installed or not.

The MS DTC allows applications to extend transactions across two or more instances of MS SQL Server (or other data sources) and participate in transactions managed by transaction managers that comply with the X/Open DTP XA standard. The MS DTC will act as the primary coordinator for these distributed transactions. MS DTC ensures that all updates are made permanent in all data locations (committed), or makes sure that all of the work is undone (rolled back) if it needs to be. Figure 2.18 shows how an application could be developed to do a primary data read request against one location, and if that access fails (because the location has failed), it would try a secondary location that had the same data. Updates to data by the application must be made in both locations at once so that data integrity would be guaranteed.

As you can also see in this figure, MS DTC will provide the update transaction stability to all locations. The application takes on more of the burden of high availability in this case, but provides a reasonably good high availability result. The update capability of the application is lost for a period of time, but the read capability is never lost.

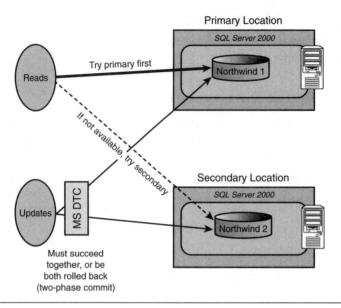

Figure 2.18 A distributed transaction approach.

Summary

Many of the principal high availability options available within the Microsoft software stack and with hardware components have now been introduced. A solid foundation must be created to build your highly available systems on. As you completely define your application's high availability requirements, a matching high availability solution can be made that will serve you well for years to come.

The next chapter outlines the complicated process of matching your high availability requirements to the proper high availability solution (option). Very often, two or more options, used together, must be selected to meet your needs. For this reason, a step-by-step approach (that you can repeat) will be followed that yields the best possible solution.

CHAPTER 3

Choosing High Availability

THE KEY TOPICS IN THIS CHAPTER ARE

- Launching a Phase 0 (zero) High Availability assessment
- A hybrid high availability selection method
- Scenario 1: Application service provider (ASP) assessment
- Scenario 2: Worldwide sales and marketing (brand promotion) assessment
- Scenario 3: Investment portfolio management assessment
- Scenario 4: Call before you dig assessment
- Cost justification of a selected high availability solution—ROI
- High availability considerations embedded in your development methodology

Moving Toward High Availability

Up to this point, we have described most of the essential elements that need to be defined for you to properly assess your application's likeliness of being built utilizing a high availability solution. Formally conducting the Phase 0 (zero) High Availability assessment (and within this, completing the High Availability Primary Variables Gauge) is the primary tool to start this effort with and is geared toward garnering results very quickly.

The mere fact that you are considering a Phase 0 HA assessment for an application points to the likeliness of some type of high availability solution. But, which one? And, which one is the *BEST* one?

In order to make the best possible decision of which high availability solution matches your business requirements, a simple four-step process can be followed. The steps are

- **Step one** calls for a launch of a brief Phase 0 HA assessment effort to gather all the needed information as quickly and as accurately as possible. Or, perhaps not so brief if you can drill down a bit further in each requirement area.

- **Step two** will require that the High Availability Primary Variables Gauge be done as completely and accurately as possible. This gauge is actually a deliverable of the Phase 0 HA assessment, but is more than worth calling out individually as a separate step since it can be used as a high-level depiction of your application's HA requirements and is easily understood by management-level folks in the organization.

- **Step three** will use the assessment and the gauge information to determine the optimal high availability solution that technically matches your business needs. A hybrid decision-tree selection method will be described to help in this step.

- As an added bonus, we will run through a basic Return on Investment (ROI) calculation as an optional **Step four** of this high availability decision process. The ROI calculation is optional because most folks don't bother with it—they are already losing so much money and goodwill during downtime that the return on their investment can be overwhelming. Very often, the ROI cannot be clearly measured and no financial impact can be calculated.

This four-step process is, in effect, a mini-methodology designed to yield a specific high availability answer that best matches your needs.

Design Note

ROI Calculation: We will try to describe a fairly simple and straightforward method of calculating the ROI when deploying a specific high availability solution. Your calculations will vary because ROI is extremely unique for any company. However, in general ROI can be calculated by adding up the incremental costs of the new HA solution and comparing them against the complete cost of downtime for a period of time (I suggest this be a one year time period). This ROI calculation will include

continues

Maintenance Cost (for a one year period):
+ system admin personnel cost (additional time for training of these personnel)
+ software licensing cost (of additional HA components)
Hardware Cost (add +)
+ hardware cost (of additional HW in the new HA solution)
Deployment/Assessment Cost:
+ deployment cost (develop, test, QA, production implementation of the solution)
+ HA assessment cost (be bold and go ahead and throw the cost of the assessment into this to be a complete ROI calculation)
Downtime Cost (for a one year period):
If you kept track of last year's downtime record, use this number; otherwise produce an estimate of planned and unplanned downtime for this calculation.
+ Planned downtime hours × cost of hourly downtime to the company (revenue loss/productivity loss/goodwill loss [optional])
+ Unplanned downtime hours × cost of hourly downtime to the company (revenue loss/productivity loss/goodwill loss [optional])
If the HA costs (above) are more than the downtime costs for one year, then extend it out another year, and then another until you can determine how long it will take to get the ROI.
In reality, most companies will have achieved the ROI within 6 to 9 months of the first year.

Step 1—Launching a Phase 0 (Zero) HA Assessment

The hardest part of getting a Phase 0 HA assessment started is rounding up the right resources to pull it off well. You are going to want to use your best folks for this effort; it is so critical to your company's existence. In addition, timing is everything. It would be nice if you have launched this Phase 0 HA assessment before you have gotten too far down the path on a new system's development. Or, if this is after the fact, put all the attention you can on completing this as accurately and as completely as possible.

Resources for a Phase 0 HA Assessment

A Phase 0 (Zero) HA assessment will require that you assemble between two and three resources (professionals) with the ability to properly understand and capture the technical components of your environment, along with the business drivers behind the application being assessed. Again, these should be some of the best folks you have. If your best folks don't have enough bandwidth to take this on, then get outside help; don't settle for anything less (such as your lower skilled employees). The small amount of time and budget that this assessment will cost will be minimal compared to the far-reaching impact of the results of this assessment. The type of person and their skill set would be

- A system architect/data architect (SA/DA)—Someone with both extensive system design and data design experience who will be able to understand the hardware, software, and database aspects of high availability.

- A very senior business analyst (SBA)—This person must be completely versed in development methodologies and the business requirements that are being targeted by the application (and by the assessment).

- A part-time senior technical lead (STL)—A software engineer type with good overall system development skills so that they can help in assessing the coding standards that are being followed, the completeness of the system testing tasks, and the general software configuration that has been (or will be) implemented.

The Phase 0 HA Assessment Tasks

Once these folks are assembled, the assessment itself will be broken down into several tasks that will yield the different critical pieces of information needed to determine the correct high availability solution. Some tasks are used when you are assessing existing systems. These same tasks might not apply to a system that is brand new.

Nine out of ten Phase 0 assessments that are conducted are for existing systems. What this seems to indicate is that most folks are retrofitting their applications to be more highly available after they have been implemented. Of course, it would have been best to have identified and analyzed the high availability requirements of an application during development in the first place.

A few of the tasks that will be described here may not be needed in determining the correct HA solution. However, we have included them here for the sake of completeness, and they often help form a more complete picture of the environment and processing that is being implemented. Remember, this type of assessment becomes a valuable depiction of what you were trying to achieve based on what you were being asked to support. Salient areas (points) within each task will be outlined as well. Let's dig into these tasks:

- **Task 1**—Describe the current state of the application

  [NOTE: If this is a new application then this task is skipped!]

  - Data (data usage and physical implementation)
  - Process (business processes being supported)
  - Technology (hardware/software platform/configuration)
  - Backup/recovery procedures
  - Standards/guidelines used
  - Testing/QA process employed
  - Service level agreement (SLA) currently defined
  - Level of expertise of personnel administering system
  - Level of expertise of personnel developing/testing system

- **Task 2**—Describe the future state of the application

  - Data (data usage and physical implementation, data volume growth, data resilience)
  - Process (business processes being supported, expanded functionality anticipated, and application resilience)
  - Technology (hardware/software platform/configuration, new technology being acquired)
  - Backup/recovery procedures being planned
  - Standards/guidelines used or being enhanced
  - Testing/QA process being changed or enhanced
  - Service level agreement(SLA) desired (from here on out)
  - Level of expertise of personnel administering system (planned training and hiring)
  - Level of expertise of personnel developing/testing system (planned training and hiring)

- **Task 3**—Describe the unplanned downtime reasons at different intervals (last seven days, last month, last quarter, last six months, last year)

  [NOTE: If this is a new application then this task is an estimate of the future month, quarter, six-month, and one year intervals]

- **Task 4**—Describe the planned downtime reasons at different intervals (last seven days, last month, last quarter, last six months, last year)

  [NOTE: If this is a new application then this task is an estimate of the future month, quarter, six-month, and one-year intervals]

- **Task 5**—Calculate the availability percentage across different time intervals (last seven days, last month, last quarter, last six months, last year). Please refer back to Chapter 1, "Essential Elements of High Availability," for this complete calculation.

  [NOTE: If this is a new application then this task is an estimate of the future month, quarter, six-month, and one-year intervals]

- **Task 6**—Calculate the loss of downtime

  - Revenue loss (per hour of unavailability)—As an example in an online order entry system, look at any peak order entry hour and calculate the total order amounts for that peak hour. This will be your revenue loss per hour value.

  - Productivity dollar loss (per hour of unavailability)—As an example in an internal financial data warehouse that is used for executive decision support, calculate the length of time that this data mart/warehouse was not available within the last month or two and multiply this times the number of executives/managers who were supposed to be querying it during that period. This would be the "productivity effect." Then multiply this by the average salary of these execs/managers. This would be a rough estimate of productivity dollar loss. This does not consider the bad business decisions they might have made without having their data mart/warehouse available and the dollar loss of those bad business decisions. Calculating a productivity dollar loss might be a bit aggressive to be included in this assessment, but there needs to be something to measure against and to help justify the return on investment. For applications that are not productivity applications, this value will not be calculated.

- Goodwill dollar loss (in terms of customers lost per hour of unavailability)—It's extremely important to include this component. Goodwill loss can be measured by taking the average number of customers for a period of time (such as last month's online order customer average) and comparing it with a period of processing following a system failure (where there was a significant amount of downtime). Chances are that there was a drop-off of the same amount that can be rationalized as goodwill loss (the online customer didn't come back to you, they went to the competition). You must then take that percentage drop-off (like 2%) and multiply it by the peak order amount averages for the defined period. This period loss number is like a repeating loss overhead value that should be included in the ROI calculation for every month.

[NOTE: If this is a new application then this task is an estimate of the losses].

This might be a little difficult to calculate but will help in any justification process for purchase of HA-enabling products and in the measurement of ROI.

Once you have completed the above tasks you will be able to complete the HA Primary Variables gauge without much trouble.

Step 2—HA Primary Variables Gauge

It is now time to properly place your arrows (these will be relative value indications) on each of the primary variable gauges. The placement of the assessment arrow on each of the 10 variables should be done as accurately as possible and as rigorously as possible. Each variable continuum should be evenly divided into a scale of some kind and an exact value should be determined or calculated to help place the arrow. As an example, the cost of downtime (per hour) variable could be a scale from $0/hr at the bottom (left) to $500,000/hr at the top (right) for Company X. The $500,000/hr top scale value would represent what might have been the peak order amounts ever taken in by the online order entry system for Company X and thusly would represent the known dollar amount being lost for this period. Remember, everything is relative to the other systems in your company and to the perceived value of each of these variables. In other words, some companies won't place much value on the end-user tolerance of downtime variable if the application is for internal employees. So, adjust accordingly.

For all of the primary variable gauges you will need to

1. Assign relative values to each primary variable (based on your company's characteristics).

2. Place an arrow on the perceived (or estimated) point in each gauge that best reflects the system being assessed.

As another example, let's look at the first HA primary variable of total "uptime requirement percentage." If we are assessing an ATM system, the placement of the assessment arrow would be at a percentage of 98% or higher. Remember that five 9s means a 99.999% uptime percentage. Also remember that this uptime requirement is for the "planned" time of operation, not the total time in a day (or a year)— except, of course, if the system is a 24x7x365 system. Very often the service level agreement that is defined for this application will spell out the uptime percentage requirement. Figure 3.1 shows the placement of the assessment arrow at 99.5% for the ATM application example. This places this application on the bottom edge of what we call "Extreme Availability" (at least from the uptime percentage point of view).

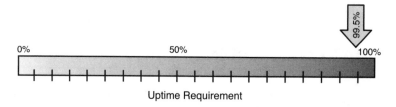

Figure 3.1   HA Primary Variables Gauge—ATM uptime percentage example.

Step 3—Determining the Optimal HA Solution

Once you have completed step 1 and step 2, the hard part is over because you probably have enough information now to make a *VERY* good high availability solution choice. If your information from these two steps was spotty and incomplete, the decision you make will probably be somewhat suspect. But, in general, it may be good enough to get you mostly what you are trying to achieve.

Step 3 will draw on a formal deterministic approach that takes the assessment results and gauge information and will yield the right HA solution for your requirements.

A Hybrid High Availability Selection Method

There are many potential selection methods that could be used to help in selecting the best HA solution. There are scoring methods, decision-tree based methods, and simple estimation methods. We like a hybrid decision-tree based method we have evolved over the past few years that will use the primary variable answers to guide you to an HA solution.

With any selection method for determining an HA solution, there will be several possible high availability answers, one of which will be that *NO* high availability solution is needed. The general cost and administrative complexity of each solution will also be described as well. As new HA solutions are identified in the industry (or by a particular vendor, such as Microsoft), this list can be expanded. But, for now, this book will focus on the following (as seen in Figure 3.2):

- Disk methods—Disk mirroring, RAID, and so on. Characteristics: High $ cost and low administration complexity.

- Other hardware—Redundant power supplies, fans, CPUs, and so on (many of which are hot-swappable). Characteristics: High $ cost and low administration complexity.

- Cluster services—Microsoft Cluster Services allows two (or more) systems to fail-over to each other in a passive/active or active/active mode. Characteristics: High $ cost and moderate administration complexity.

- SQL clustering—Fully enables a Microsoft SQL Server instance to fail-over to another system using MSCS (SQL Server 2000 is cluster aware). Characteristics: High $ cost and moderate administration complexity.

- Data replication—Primarily using "transactional replication," which will redundantly distribute transactions from one SQL Server database to another instantaneously. Both SQL Server databases (on different servers) can be used for workload balancing as well. Some limitations exist but are very manageable. Characteristics: Moderate $ cost and moderate administration complexity.

- Log shipping—The direct application of SQL Server database transaction log entries to a warm standby copy of the same SQL Server database. There are some limitations with this technique. Characteristics: Moderate $ cost and low administration complexity.

- Distributed transactions—Application controlled methods via programming and distributed transaction techniques (potentially using MS-DTC, and two-phase commit approaches) to redundantly create and manage data in alternate (redundant) locations. Any location becomes available if the other should fail. Characteristics: Low $ cost and high administration complexity.

- *NO* high availability solution needed.

Figure 3.2 also illustrates the options that are typically valid together or by themselves. Any options that are diagonally shaded can be used together (disk methods + other HW + MSCS + SQL clustering, and so on). Crosshatched shaded intersections indicate options that must be done together (MSCS + SQL clustering), and vertical-lined intersections indicate that these are *NOT* typically done together (log shipping is typically not done with data replication, and so on).

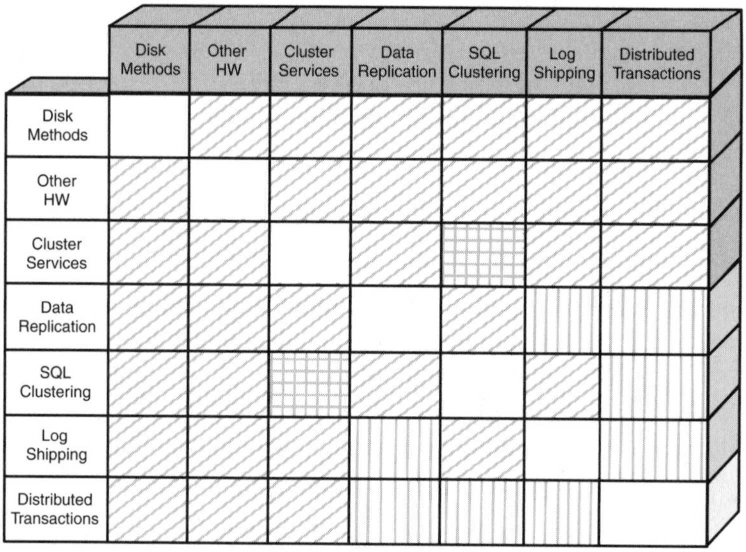

Figure 3.2 Valid high availability options.

As has already been pointed out, some of these possible solutions actually include the other (for example, SQL clustering is built on top of MSCS). This will be factored into the results of the selection.

The Decision-Tree Approach for Choosing an HA Solution

The decision-tree approach will take the high availability information garnered in the Phase 0 assessment and will traverse down a particular path (decision-tree) to an appropriate HA solution. In this case, we have chosen a hybrid decision-tree technique that uses Nassi-Schneiderman charts, which fit well with depicting complex questions and yield very specific results. We won't be using all of the Nassi-Schneiderman chart techniques, only the Conditional/Question part. As Figure 3.3 shows, a Nassi-Schneiderman chart will be in the form of

- **Condition/Question**—For which you need to decide an answer.

- **Cases**—Any number of known cases (answers) that the question might have (Case A, Case B…Case n).

- **Action/Result**—The specific result or action to be followed depending on the case chosen (Result A, Result B…Result n).

Each question will always be considered in context of all questions answered before it. You are essentially navigating your way down a complex tree structure that will yield a definitive HA solution.

The questions will be ordered in a way so that they will clearly flesh out specific needs and push you in a specific high availability direction. Figure 3.4 illustrates an example of a question put into the Nassi-Schneiderman construct. The question is "what percentage of availability must your application have?" (for its scheduled time of operation).

If you have completed enough of the Phase 0 assessment, the answer to this question should be easy to come up with. This will also be a good audit or validation of your Phase 0 assessment.

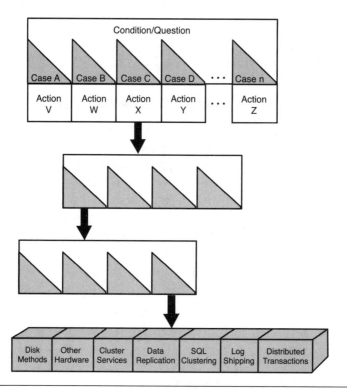

Figure 3.3 Hybrid decision-tree using Nassi-Schneiderman charts.

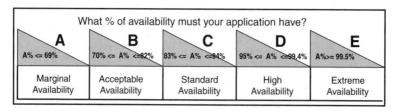

A% = Availability Percentage (for planned hours of operation)

Figure 3.4 Nassi-Schneiderman example question.

In the normal course of events, we will start with the most critical aspects of high availability first. Then, depending on the answer to each question, proceed down a specific path and a new question. As each high availability characteristic is considered, the path (actions followed) will lead you to a specific HA solution. The series of questions that need to be answered are taken from the HA Primary Variables Gauge but are expanded slightly to make them conditional in nature. These are

1. What percentage of time must the application remain up during its scheduled time of operation? (The goal!)

2. How much tolerance does the end-user have when the system is not available (planned or unplanned unavailability)?

3. What is the per hour cost of downtime for this application?

4. How long does it take to get the application back online following a failure (of any kind)? (Worst case!)

5. How much of the application is distributed and will require some type of synchronization with other nodes before all nodes are considered to be 100% available?

6. How much data inconsistency can be tolerated in favor of having the application available?

7. How often is scheduled maintenance required for this application (and environment)?

8. How important is high performance and scalability?

9. How important is it for the application to keep its current connection alive with the end-user?

10. What is the estimated cost of a possible high availability solution? What is your budget?

Design Note

One other important thing that may come into play is the timeline that you have on getting an application to become highly available. If the timeline is very short, then your solution may exclude costs as a barrier and may not even consider hardware solutions that take months to order and install. So, it would be more than appropriate to expand the Primary Variables Gauge to include this question (and any others) as well. This particular question could be "What is your timeline for making your application highly available?"

However, this book will assume that you have a reasonable amount of time to properly assess your application.

It is also assumed that if you have written (or are planning to write) an application that will be "cluster aware," you can leverage MSCS. This would be considered to be an implementation of "application" clustering (an application that is cluster aware). As mentioned before, SQL Server is a cluster aware program. However, we don't consider it to be "application" clustering in the strictest sense; it is "database" clustering.

Scenario 1: Application Service Provider (ASP) Assessment

To drive home the decision-tree method, we will proceed down a complete path (decision-tree) for the application service provider (ASP) business scenario (Scenario #1). We will answer the questions based on an already completed Phase 0 HA assessment for it. As you recall, Scenario #1 centers on a very real ASP and their operating model. This ASP houses (and develops) numerous global, web-based online order entry systems for several major beauty and health product companies in the world. Their customer base is truly global (as the earth turns, the user base accessing the system shifts with it). They are headquartered in California and this ASP guarantees 99.5% uptime to their customers. In this case, the customers are sales associates and their sales managers. If the ASP achieves these guarantees, they get significant bonuses; if they fall below certain thresholds, they are liable for specific penalties. The processing mix of activity is approximately 65% online order entry and approximately 35% reporting.

Availability:

- 24 hours per day
- 7 days per week
- 365 days per year

Planned Downtime: **.25%** (less than 1%)
Unplanned Downtime: **.25%** (less than 1%) will be tolerable

Figure 3.5 depicts the first three questions in the decision tree and their corresponding responses (actions). Remember, these are cumulative. Each new question carries along the responses of the preceding questions. Your responses, taken together, determine the HA solution that best fits. Let's proceed through the ASP business scenario depiction to give you a feel of how this works.

HA Assessment (Decision-Tree):

1. What percentage of time must the application remain up during its scheduled time of operation? (The goal!)

   Response: **E: 99.5%** → Extreme availability goal.

2. How much tolerance does the end-user have when the system is not available (planned or unplanned unavailability)?

   Response: **E: Very low tolerance of downtime** → Extremely Critical.

3. What is the per hour cost of downtime for this application?

   Response: **D: $15K/hour cost of downtime** → High Cost.

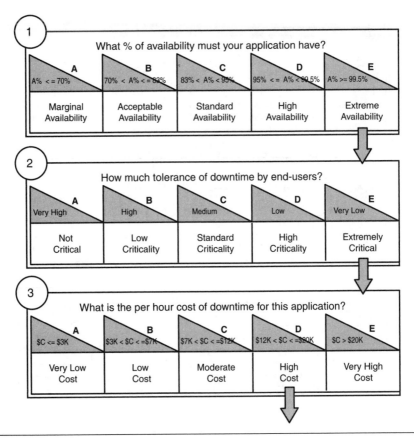

Figure 3.5   Decision-tree: ASP questions 1–3.

Remember, all questions are additive. So, after going through just three questions, we see that this ASP business scenario has a pretty high cost per hour when it is not available (a .5% per hour cost [total gross revenues of $3 billion]). And, coupled with high uptime goals and extremely low end-user tolerance for downtime (because of the nature of the ASP business) will drive this application to a particular type of HA solution very quickly. We could easily just stop now and jump to an HA solution of maximum hardware redundancy, RAID, MSCS, and SQL clustering in order to fulfill the HA requirement goals; however, there are still several aspects of the requirement such as distributed data processing requirements and budget available for the HA solution that could easily change this outcome. You should always complete the entire set of questions for clarity, consistency, completeness, and cost justification purposes.

Figure 3.6 forges ahead with the next set of questions and answers.

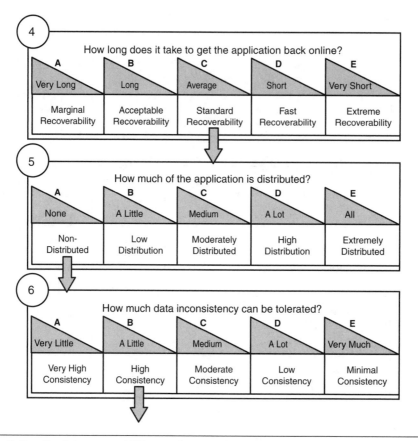

Figure 3.6   Decision-tree: ASP questions 4–6.

4. How long does it take to get the application back online following a failure (of any kind)? (Worst case!)

    Response: **C: Average** → Standard amount of time to recover (to get back online). Accomplished via standard DB recovery mechanisms (incremental transaction log dumps done every 15 minutes). Faster recovery times would be beneficial but data integrity is of huge importance.

5. How much of the application is distributed and will require some type of synchronization with other nodes before all nodes are considered to be 100% available?

    Response: **A: None** → There aren't any components of this application that are distributed (non-distributed). This simplifies the data synchronization aspects to consider, but does not necessarily mean that a distributed HA solution won't better serve the overall application. If the application has a heavy reporting component, some type of data replication architecture could serve it well. This will be addressed in the performance/scalability question later.

6. How much data inconsistency can be tolerated in favor of having the application available?

   Response: **B: A little** → A high degree of data consistency must be maintained at all times. This gives little room for any HA option that would sacrifice data consistency in favor of availability.

   For systems with primarily static data, complete images of the application databases could be kept at numerous locations for instantaneous access any time they needed to get to it, with little danger of having data inconsistent (in administered properly). For systems with a lot of data volatility, the answer on this one question may well dictate the HA option to use. Very often the HA option best suited for high data consistency needs is that of SQL clustering and log shipping, coupled with RAID at the disk subsystem level.

   Another short pause in our path to an HA solution finds us not having to support a complex distributed environment, but having to make sure we keep our data consistent as much as possible. In addition, we can plan on typical recovery times to get the application back on line in case of failures (this was probably stated this way in the ASP's service level agreement). However, if a faster recovery mechanism is possible, it should be considered because it will have a direct impact on the total amount of unplanned downtime, and could potentially allow the ASP to get some uptime bonuses (that might also be in the SLA). Now, let's venture into the next set of questions as illustrated in Figure 3.7. These focus on planned downtime, performance, and application connectivity perception.

7. How often is scheduled maintenance required for this application (and environment)?

   Response: **C: Average** → A reasonable amount of downtime will occur to service operating system patches/upgrades, hardware changes/swapping, and application patches/upgrades. For 24x7 systems, this will cut into the availability time directly. For systems with downtime windows, the pressure is much less in this area.

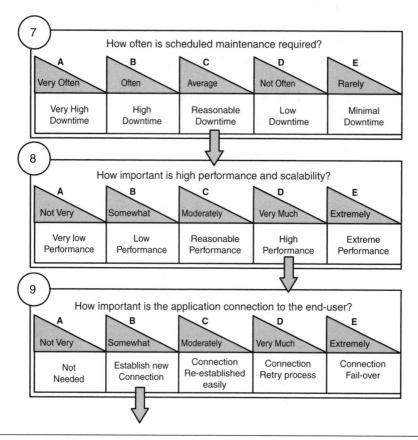

Figure 3.7   Decision-tree: ASP questions 7–9.

8. How important is high performance and scalability?

Response: **D: Very much** → The ASP considers all of its applications to be high-performance systems that must meet strict performance numbers and be able to scale to support large number of users. These performance thresholds would be spelled out clearly in the service level agreement. Any HA solution must therefore be a scalable solution as well.

9. How important is it for the application to keep its current connection alive with the end-user?

Response: **B: Somewhat** → At the very least, the ability to establish a new connection to the application within a short amount of time will be required. No client connection fail-over is required. This was partially made possible by the overall transactional approach of "optimistic concurrency" used by their applications. This approach puts much less pressure on holding a connection for long periods of time (to hold/lock rows).

As you can see in Figure 3.8, the estimated cost of a potential HA solution would be between $100K and $250K. Budget for HA should be estimated to be a couple of full days' worth of downtime cost. For our ASP example, this would be roughly about $720K. The ROI calculation will show how quickly this will be recovered.

A bit later in this chapter, we will work though a complete ROI calculation so that you can fully understand where these values come from.

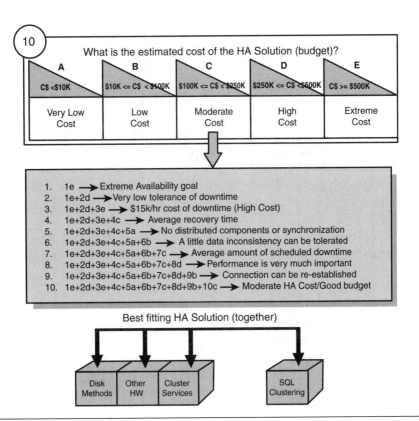

Figure 3.8   Decision-tree: ASP question 10 and HA solution.

10. What is the estimated cost of a possible high availability solution? What is your budget?

Response: **C: $100K <= C$ < $250K** → This is a moderate amount of cost for potentially a huge amount of benefit. They are estimating

- Five new four-way servers with 4GB RAM at $30K per server
- Ten MS Windows 2000 Advanced Server licenses
- Five shared SCSI disk systems with RAID 10 (50 drives)
- Five days of additional training costs for personnel
- No new SQL Server licenses because of the plan to operate in an active/passive clustering mode

The HA Solution for Scenario #1

Figure 3.8 also shows the final selection of hardware redundancy, shared disk RAID arrays, MSCS, and SQL clustering as the best fitting HA solution (all four, together). There is little doubt about the needs being met well by this particular set of HA solutions. It clearly meets all of the most significant requirements of uptime, tolerance, performance, and costs. The lack of distributed data or data synchronization pointed this away from distributed transaction techniques such as data replication or distributed applications. Log shipping might have helped but is not transparent enough to the application. Their SLA allows for brief amounts of downtime to service all OS, hardware, and application upgrades. Figure 3.9 shows the live HA solution technical architecture. Budget allowed for a larger amount of hardware redundancy to be utilized.

Once this HA solution was put into place, the ASP achieved nearly five 9s for extended periods of time (exceeding their original goals of 99.5% uptime). One additional note is that the ASP company also employs a spreading out of the risk solution to further reduce downtime created from application and shared hardware failures. They will only put at most two to three applications on a particular clustered solution (refer back to Figure 2.11 in Chapter 2, "Microsoft High Availability Options," for a more complete depiction of this risk mitigation approach).

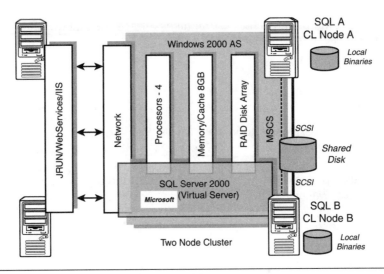

Figure 3.9 ASP HA solution technical architecture.

If you aren't quite getting the idea of how the decision-tree approach works, it can also be illustrated in a slightly different way. Figure 3.10 depicts an abbreviated bubble chart technique of this decision-tree path traversal.

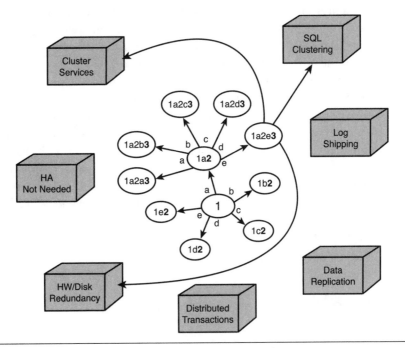

Figure 3.10 Bubble chart decision-tree path traversal.

Remember, each question takes into context all questions before it. The result is a specific HA solution that best meets your business requirements.

Design Note

A full decision-tree explosion (Complete HA Decision-Tree) that has all questions and paths defined is available in MS Excel document form on the Sams Publishing website.

In addition, a blank Nassi-Schneiderman chart and an HA Primary Variables Gauge are also available in a single PowerPoint document.

Scenario 2: Worldwide Sales and Marketing (Brand Promotion) Assessment

As you recall, this scenario is about a major chip manufacturer that has created a highly successful promotion and branding program, which results in billions of dollars in advertising dollars being rebated back to their worldwide sales channel partners. These sales channel partners must enter in their complete advertisements (newspaper, radio, TV, other) and be measured against ad compliance and logo usage and placements. If a sales channel partner is in compliance, they will receive up to 50% of the cost of their advertisement back from this chip manufacturer. There are three major advertising regions: Far East, Europe, and North America. Any other advertisements outside of these first three are lumped into an "Other Regions" bucket. Each region produces a huge daily load of new advertisement information that is processed instantaneously for compliance. Each major region only deals with that region's advertisements, but receives the compliance rules and compliance judgment from the chip manufacturer's headquarters. Application mix is approximately 75% online entry of advertisement events and 25% management and compliance reporting.

Availability:

- 24 hours per day
- 7 days a week
- 365 days a year

Planned Downtime: **3%**
Unplanned Downtime: **2%** will be tolerable
HA Assessment (Decision-Tree):

1. What percentage of time must the application remain up during its scheduled time of operation? (The goal!)

   Response: **D: 95.0%** → High availability goal. This, however, is not a super critical application in terms of keeping the company running (like an order entry system would be).

2. How much tolerance does the end-user have when the system is not available (planned or unplanned unavailability)?

   Response: **C: Medium tolerance of downtime** → Standard criticality.

3. What is the per hour cost of downtime for this application?

   Response: **B: $5K/hour cost of downtime** → Low cost.

   As we can see so far, this sales and marketing application is nice to have available, but it can tolerate some downtime without hurting the company very much. Sales are not lost; work just gets backed up a bit. In addition, the cost of downtime is reasonably low at $5K/hr. This is roughly the rate at which advertisement reimbursements take place.

4. How long does it take to get the application back online following a failure (of any kind)? (Worst case!)

   Response: **C: Average** → Standard amount of time to recover (to get back online). Accomplished via standard DB recovery mechanisms (incremental transaction log dumps done every 15 minutes).

5. How much of the application is distributed and will require some type of synchronization with other nodes before all nodes are considered to be 100% available?

   Response: **D: High Distribution** → This is a global application that relies on data being created and maintained at headquarters from around the world (OLTP activity) but must also support heavy regional reporting (reporting activity) that doesn't interfere with the performance of the OLTP activity.

6. How much data inconsistency can be tolerated in favor of having the application available?

Response: **B: A little** → A high degree of data consistency must be maintained at all times. This gives little room for any HA option that would sacrifice data consistency in favor of availability. This is regionally sensitive, in that when data is being updated by Europe, the Far East doesn't need to get their data updates right away.

7. How often is scheduled maintenance required for this application (and environment)?

   Response: **C: Average** → A reasonable amount of downtime will occur to service operating system patches/upgrades, hardware changes/swapping, and application patches/upgrades.

8. How important is high performance and scalability?

   Response: **D: Very much** → Performance (and scalability) are very important for this application. Ideally, an overall approach of separating the OLTP activity from the reporting activity will pay big dividends towards this.

9. How important is it for the application to keep its current connection alive with the end-user?

   Response: **B: Somewhat** → At the very least, the ability to establish a new connection to the application within a short amount of time will be required. No client connection fail-over is required. In fact, for the worst case scenario of the headquarters database becoming unavailable, the OLTP activity could easily be shifted to any other full copy of the database that is being used for reporting and is being kept current (as will be seen in the HA solution for this scenario).

10. What is the estimated cost of a possible high availability solution? What is your budget?

    Response: **B: $10K <= C$ < $100K** → This is a pretty low amount of cost for potentially a huge amount of benefit. They are estimating

    - Three new two-way servers with 4GB RAM at $10K per server
    - Three new MS Windows 2000 Server licenses
    - Three SCSI disk systems with RAID 10 (15 drives)
    - Two days of additional training costs for personnel
    - Four new SQL Server licenses (remote distributor, three subscribers)

The HA Solution for Scenario #2

Figure 3.11 also shows that a basic hardware/disk redundancy approach on each server should be used along with SQL Server's robust "transactional" data replication implementation to create three regional reporting images of the primary marketing database (MktgDB). These distributed copies will try to alleviate the major reporting burden against the OLTP (primary database) and also can serve as a warm standby copy of the database in the event of a major database problem at headquarters. Overall, this distributed architecture is easy to maintain and keep in sync and is highly scalable, as seen in Figure 3.12.

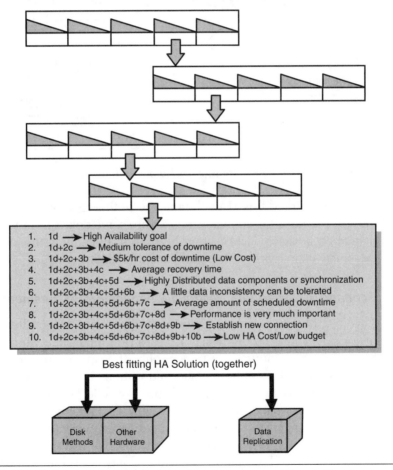

1. 1d ➛ High Availability goal
2. 1d+2c ➛ Medium tolerance of downtime
3. 1d+2c+3b ➛ $5k/hr cost of downtime (Low Cost)
4. 1d+2c+3b+4c ➛ Average recovery time
5. 1d+2c+3b+4c+5d ➛ Highly Distributed data components or synchronization
6. 1d+2c+3b+4c+5d+6b ➛ A little data inconsistency can be tolerated
7. 1d+2c+3b+4c+5d+6b+7c ➛ Average amount of scheduled downtime
8. 1d+2c+3b+4c+5d+6b+7c+8d ➛ Performance is very much important
9. 1d+2c+3b+4c+5d+6b+7c+8d+9b ➛ Establish new connection
10. 1d+2c+3b+4c+5d+6b+7c+8d+9b+10b ➛ Low HA Cost/Low budget

Best fitting HA Solution (together)

Disk Methods   Other Hardware   Data Replication

Figure 3.11   Sales/marketing decision-tree summary + HA solution.

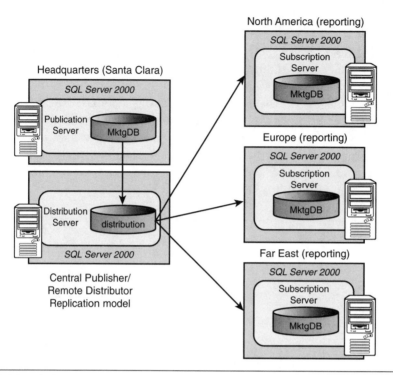

Figure 3.12 Sales/marketing HA solution technical architecture.

After building this HA solution, the uptime goal was achieved for most of the time. Occasionally, there were some delays in resyncing the data at each regional site (subscribers). But, in general, the users were extremely happy with performance and availability.

Scenario 3: Investment Portfolio Management Assessment

This investment portfolio management application will be housed in a major server farm in the heart of the world's financial center: NY, NY. Serving North American customers only, this application provides the ability to do full trading of stocks and options in all financial markets (U.S. and international) along with full portfolio holdings assessment, historical performance, and holdings valuation. Primary users are investment managers for their large customers. Stock purchasing/selling comprise 90% of the daytime activity with massive assessment, historical performance, and valuation reporting done after the markets have closed. Three major peaks occur each weekday that are driven by the three major trading markets of the world (United States, Europe, and the Far East). The weekends are filled with the long range planning reporting and front-loading stock trades for the coming week.

Availability:

- 20 hours per day
- 7 days per week
- 365 days per year

Planned Downtime: **4%**
Unplanned Downtime: **1%** will be tolerable
HA Assessment (Decision-Tree):

1. What percentage of time must the application remain up during its scheduled time of operation? (The goal!)

    Response: **D: 95.0%** → High availability goal. This particular financial institution (one of the largest on the planet) tends to allow for a small percentage of "built-in" downtime (planned or unplanned). A smaller, more nimble financial institution would probably have slightly more aggressive uptime goals (like five 9s). Time is money, you know.

2. How much tolerance does the end-user have when the system is not available (planned or unplanned unavailability)?

    Response: **D: Low tolerance of downtime** → High criticality due to market timings (selling and buying stocks within market windows).

3. What is the per hour cost of downtime for this application?

    Response: **E: $150K/hour cost of downtime** → Very high cost. However, this is the worse case scenario. When the markets are closed, the cost of downtime is marginal.

4. How long does it take to get the application back online following a failure (of any kind)? (Worst case!)

    Response: **E: Very short recovery** → This application's time to recover should be a very short amount of time (to get back online).

5. How much of the application is distributed and will require some type of synchronization with other nodes before all nodes are considered to be 100% available?

    Response: **C: Medium distribution** → This moderately distributed application has a large OLTP processing requirement and a large report processing requirement.

6. How much data inconsistency can be tolerated in favor of having the application available?

   Response: **A: Very little** → A very high degree of data consistency must be maintained at all times. This is financial data.

7. How often is scheduled maintenance required for this application (and environment)?

   Response: **C: Average** → A reasonable amount of downtime will occur to service operating system patches/upgrades, hardware changes/swapping, and application patches/upgrades.

8. How important is high performance and scalability?

   Response: **D: Very much** → Performance (and scalability) are very important for this application.

9. How important is it for the application to keep its current connection alive with the end-user?

   Response: **B: Somewhat** → At the very least, the ability to establish a new connection to the application within a short amount of time will be required. No client connection fail-over is required.

10. What is the estimated cost of a possible high availability solution? What is your budget?

    Response: **C: $100K <= C$ < $250K** → This is a moderate amount of cost for potentially a huge amount of benefit. They are estimating

    - Four new four-way servers with 8GB RAM at $50K per server
    - Four MS Windows 2000 Advanced Server licenses
    - Two shared SCSI disk systems with RAID 10 (30 drives)
    - Twelve days of additional training costs for personnel
    - Four new SQL Server licenses

    From the budget point-of-view, they had budgeted of $1.25 million for all HA costs. A solid HA solution won't even approach those numbers.

Figure 3.13 shows the overall summary of the decision-tree results along with the HA solution for the portfolio management scenario.

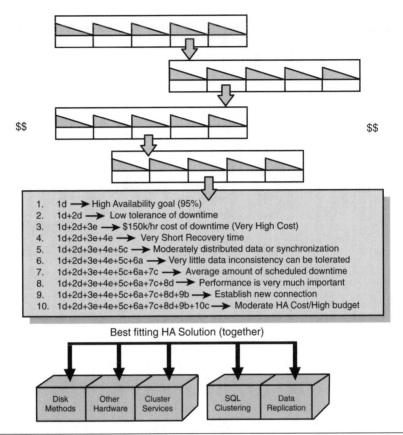

1. 1d ➝ High Availability goal (95%)
2. 1d+2d ➝ Low tolerance of downtime
3. 1d+2d+3e ➝ $150k/hr cost of downtime (Very High Cost)
4. 1d+2d+3e+4e ➝ Very Short Recovery time
5. 1d+2d+3e+4e+5c ➝ Moderately distributed data or synchronization
6. 1d+2d+3e+4e+5c+6a ➝ Very little data inconsistency can be tolerated
7. 1d+2d+3e+4e+5c+6a+7c ➝ Average amount of scheduled downtime
8. 1d+2d+3e+4e+5c+6a+7c+8d ➝ Performance is very much important
9. 1d+2d+3e+4e+5c+6a+7c+8d+9b ➝ Establish new connection
10. 1d+2d+3e+4e+5c+6a+7c+8d+9b+10c ➝ Moderate HA Cost/High budget

Figure 3.13 Portfolio management decision-tree summary + HA solution.

The HA Solution for Scenario #3

As identified in Figure 3.13, we opt for the basic hardware/disk redundancy approach on each server, add on the MS Cluster Services and SQL Clustering for the primary database, then use data replication to offload the reporting load (and risk) to a secondary "reporting" server. There is now plenty of risk mitigation with this technical architecture, but it is not that difficult to maintain (as seen in Figure 3.14).

Once this HA solution was put together, it exceeded the high availability goals on a regular basis. Great performance has also resulted due to the splitting out of the OLTP from the reporting (very often a solid design approach).

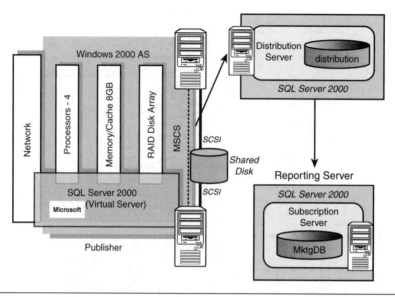

Figure 3.14   Portfolio management HA solution technical architecture.

Scenario 4: Call Before You Dig Assessment

The last scenario is the Tri-State Underground Construction Call Center. This application will determine within 6 inches the likelihood of hitting any underground gas mains, water mains, electrical wiring, phone lines, or cables that might be present on a proposed dig site for construction. Law requires that a call be placed to this center to determine whether or not it is safe to dig and identify the exact location of any underground hazard *BEFORE* any digging has started. This is a "life at risk" classified application and must be available very nearly 100% of the time during common construction workdays (Monday through Saturday). Each year more than 25 people are killed nationwide digging into unknown underground hazards. Application mix is 95% query only with 5% devoted to updating images, geo-spatial values, and various pipe and cable location information provided by the regional utility companies.
   Availability:

- 15 hours per day (5:00 a.m.–8:00 p.m.)
- 6 days per week (closed on Sunday)
- 312 days per year

Planned Downtime: **0%**
Unplanned Downtime: **.5%** (less than 1%) will be tolerable
HA Assessment (Decision-Tree):

1. What percentage of time must the application remain up during its scheduled time of operation? (The goal!)

Response: **E: 99.5%** → Extreme availability goal. This is a "life critical" application. Literally, someone may get killed if information cannot be obtained from this system during its planned time of operation.

2. How much tolerance does the end-user have when the system is not available (planned or unplanned unavailability)?

Response: **E: Very low tolerance of downtime** → In other words, this has extreme criticality from the end-user's point-of-view.

3. What is the per hour cost of downtime for this application?

Response: **A: $2K/hour cost of downtime** → Very low dollar cost. Very high life cost. This one question is very deceiving. There is no limit to the cost of "loss of life." However, we must go with the original dollar costing approach. So, bear with us on this one. Hopefully, the outcome will be the same.

4. How long does it take to get the application back online following a failure (of any kind)? (Worst case!)

Response: **E: Very short recovery** → This application's time to recover should be a very short amount of time (to get back online).

5. How much of the application is distributed and will require some type of synchronization with other nodes before all nodes are considered to be 100% available?

Response: **A: None** → There is no data distribution requirement for this application.

6. How much data inconsistency can be tolerated in favor of having the application available?

Response: **A: Very little** → A very high degree of data consistency must be maintained at all times. This data must be extremely accurate and up to date due to the life-threatening aspects to incorrect information.

7. How often is scheduled maintenance required for this application (and environment)?

   Response: **C: Average** → A reasonable amount of downtime will occur to service operating system patches/upgrades, hardware changes/swapping, and application patches/upgrades. This system has a planned time of operation of 15x6x312. Plenty of time for this type of maintenance. Thus 0% planned downtime but average amount of scheduled maintenance.

8. How important is high performance and scalability?

   Response: **C: Moderate performance** → Performance (and scalability) isn't paramount for this application. The accuracy and availability to the information is most important.

9. How important is it for the application to keep its current connection alive with the end-user?

   Response: **B: Somewhat** → At the very least, the ability to establish a new connection to the application within a short amount of time will be required. No client connection fail-over is required.

10. What is the estimated cost of a possible high availability solution? What is your budget?

    Response: **B: $10K <= C$ < $100K** → This is a pretty low amount of cost.

    They are estimating

    - Three new four-way servers with 4GB RAM at $30K per server
    - Three new MS Windows 2000 Advanced Server licenses
    - One shared SCSI disk system with RAID 5 (10 drives)—this is primarily a read-only system (95% reads)
    - One SCSI disk system RAID 5 (5 drives)
    - Five days of additional training costs for personnel
    - Three new SQL Server licenses

    Budget for the whole HA solution is somewhat limited to under $100K as well.

The HA Solution for Scenario #4

Figure 3.15 summarizes the decision-tree answers for the Call Before You Dig application. As you have seen, this is a very critical system during its planned hours of operation, but has low performance goals, and low cost of downtime (when it is down). Regardless, it is highly desirable for this system to be up and running as much as possible. The HA solution that best fits this particular applications needs is a combination that yields maximum redundancy (hardware, disk, and database) with the additional insurance policy of maintaining a hot standby server (via log shipping) in case the whole SQL cluster configuration fails. This is a pretty extreme attempt at always having a valid application up and running to support the loss of life aspect of this application.

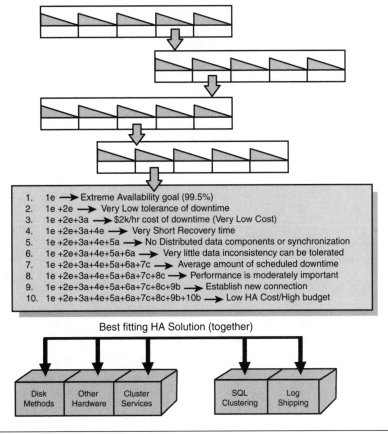

1. 1e ⟶ Extreme Availability goal (99.5%)
2. 1e +2e ⟶ Very Low tolerance of downtime
3. 1e +2e+3a ⟶ $2k/hr cost of downtime (Very Low Cost)
4. 1e +2e+3a+4e ⟶ Very Short Recovery time
5. 1e +2e+3a+4e+5a ⟶ No Distributed data components or synchronization
6. 1e +2e+3a+4e+5a+6a ⟶ Very little data inconsistency can be tolerated
7. 1e +2e+3a+4e+5a+6a+7c ⟶ Average amount of scheduled downtime
8. 1e +2e+3a+4e+5a+6a+7c+8c ⟶ Performance is moderately important
9. 1e +2e+3a+4e+5a+6a+7c+8c+9b ⟶ Establish new connection
10. 1e +2e+3a+4e+5a+6a+7c+8c+9b+10b ⟶ Low HA Cost/High budget

Best fitting HA Solution (together)

Disk Methods | Other Hardware | Cluster Services | SQL Clustering | Log Shipping

Figure 3.15   Call before you dig decision-tree summary + HA solution.

After building this HA solution, the uptime goal was achieved easily. In fact, after three months, the log shipping configuration was disabled. Two days after the log shipping was disabled, the whole SQL cluster configuration failed (Murphy's law). The log shipping was rebuilt and this configuration has remained in place since then. Performance has been exceptional and this application continuously achieves its availability goals! Figure 3.16 shows the technical HA solution employed.

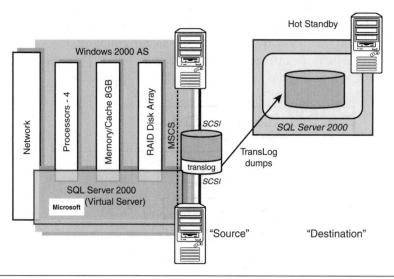

Figure 3.16   Call before you dig HA solution technical architecture.

Cost Justification of a Selected High Availability Solution

As was described earlier, it might be necessary for you to cost justify the high availability solution that you are about to go out and build. This is assuming that money doesn't grow on trees in your organization or that the cost of downtime isn't a huge dollar amount per hour. If you are like most organizations, any new change to a system or application must be evaluated on its value to the organization and a calculation of how soon it will pay for itself must be done. That's what ROI (Return on Investment) calculations serve to provide—the cost justification behind a proposed solution.

ROI Calculation: As was stated earlier, ROI can be calculated by adding up the incremental costs (or estimates) of the new HA solution and comparing them against the complete cost of downtime for a period of time (I suggest this be calculated across a one year time period). We will use the ASP business (Scenario #1) as the basis for our ROI calculation. As you might also recall, we had estimated the costs to be in the range of between **$100K and $250K**, which included

- Five new four-way servers with 4GB RAM at $30K per server
- Ten MS Windows 2000 Advanced Server licenses
- Five shared SCSI disk systems with RAID 10 (50 drives)
- Five days of additional training costs for personnel
- No new SQL Server licenses because of the plan to operate in an active/passive clustering mode

Okay, the incremental costs are

1. Maintenance Cost (for a one year period):
   - $20K (estimate)—System admin personnel cost (additional time for training of these personnel)
   - $35K (estimate)—Software licensing cost (of additional HA components)

2. Hardware Cost:
   - $100K hardware cost (of additional HW in the new HA solution)

3. Deployment/Assessment Cost:
   - $20K deployment cost (develop, test, QA, production implementation of the solution)
   - $10K HA assessment cost (be bold and go ahead and throw the cost of the assessment into this to be a complete ROI calculation)

4. Downtime Cost (for a one year period):
   - If you kept track of last year's downtime record, use this number; otherwise produce an estimate of planned and unplanned downtime for this calculation. We estimated the cost of downtime/hour to be **$15K/hour.**

- Planned downtime cost (revenue loss cost) = Planned downtime hours × cost of hourly downtime to the company:
  - **a.** .25% × 8760 hours in a year = 21.9 hours of planned downtime
  - **b.** 21.9 hours × $15K/hr = $328,500/year cost of planned downtime.
- Unplanned downtime cost (revenue loss cost) = Unplanned downtime hours × cost of hourly downtime to the company:
  - **a.** .25% × 8760 hours in a year = 21.9 hours of unplanned downtime
  - **b.** 21.9 hours × $15K/hr = $328,500/year cost of unplanned downtime.

ROI totals:

- Total of the incremental costs = $185,000 (for the year)
- Total of downtime cost = $656,000 (for the year)

Incremental cost is .28 of the downtime cost for one year. In other words, the investment of the HA solution will pay for itself in .28 of a year or 3.4 months!

In reality, most companies will have achieved the ROI within 6 to 9 months of the first year.

Adding HA Elements to Your Development Methodology

Most of the high availability elements that were identified in the Phase 0 HA assessment process and the Primary Variables Gauge can be cleanly added (extended) to your company's current system development life cycle. By adding the HA-oriented elements to your standard development methodology, you ensure that this information is captured and can readily target new applications to the correct technology solution. Figure 3.17 highlights the high availability tasks that could be added to a typical waterfall development methodology. As you can see, HA starts from early on in the assessment phase, and is present all the way though the implementation phase. Think of this as extending your development capability. It truly guarantees that all your applications get properly evaluated and designed against their high availability needs if they have any.

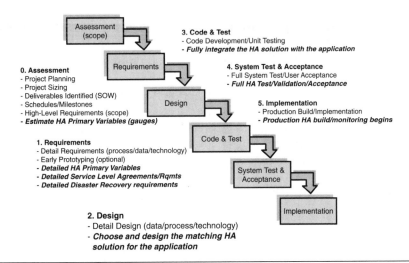

Figure 3.17   Development methodology with high availability built in.

Summary

We have introduced a fairly formal approach to assessing and choosing a high availability solution for your applications. In reality, most folks who are attempting to do this Phase 0 HA assessment are really retrofitting their existing application for high availability. That's okay, since this Phase 0 assessment directly supports the retrofitting process. The key to success is doing as complete a job as you can on the assessment and using some of your best folks to do it. They will interpret the technology and the business needs with the most accuracy. You have so much riding on the proper assessment (potentially your company's existence). If you cannot free up your best folks to do this Phase 0 assessment, then go out and get some professionals that do this every day to do this for you. The relative small cost of this short effort will be retrieved very quickly. It is no small task to understand an application's HA requirement, time to recovery, tolerance of recovery, data resiliency, application resiliency, performance/scalability, and the costs of downtime (loss). Then, you must take this information, and couple it with your hardware/software configurations, several Microsoft-based technology offerings, and your allowable upgrade budget. But, the cost of not doing this will have a much greater impact, and if you are going to move to a high availability solution, getting the right one in place to start with will save tons of time and money in and of itself (and potentially your job).

Chapters 4 through 8 will describe the Microsoft solutions that can comprise a high availability solution (or component) and show you exactly how to implement them. This is intended to be more like a cookbook approach that will take you through the complete setup of something such as MSCS, SQL clustering, log shipping, data replication, or even distributed transaction processing. So, hold on to your hat, here we go.

CHAPTER 4

Microsoft Cluster Services

THE KEY TOPICS IN THIS CHAPTER ARE

- Understanding Microsoft Cluster Services (MSCS)
- Hardware/Network/OS requirements for MSCS
- How clustering actually works
- Installing MSCS
- Extending MSCS with network load balancing (NLB)
- Windows 2003 options for quorum disks and failover
- How MSCS sets the stage for SQL clustering

Understanding Microsoft Cluster Services

A server "cluster" is a group of two or more physically separate servers that are running Microsoft Cluster Services and working collectively as a single system. This server cluster, in turn, provides high availability, scalability, and manageability for resources and applications. In other words, this group of servers is physically connected via communication hardware (network), shares storage (via SCSI or fibreChannel), and uses cluster services software to tie them all together into one managed resource.

Design Note: OS Versions and MSCS

You cannot do clustering with Windows 2000 Professional or lower server versions. Clustering is only available on servers running Windows 2000 Advanced Server (which supports 2-node clusters), Windows 2000 Datacenter Server (which supports up to 4-node clusters), or Windows 2003 Enterprise Edition and Windows 2003 Datacenter Server (which support up to 8-node clusters).

Server clusters can preserve client access to applications and resources during failures and planned outages. If one of the servers in the cluster is unavailable due to failure or maintenance, resources and applications move to another available cluster node.

Clusters use an algorithm to detect a failure, and use failover policies to determine how to handle the work from a failed server. These policies also specify how a server is to be restored to the cluster when it becomes available again.

While clustering doesn't guarantee "continuous" operation, it does provide availability sufficient for most mission-critical applications and is the building blocks of numerous high availability solutions. Cluster services can monitor applications and resources, automatically recognizing and recovering from many failure conditions. This provides greater flexibility in managing the workload within a cluster, and improves overall availability of the system. If you are using a mechanism that is "cluster aware" such as SQL Server, Microsoft Message Queue (MSMQ), or file shares, they have already been programmed to work with MSCS. If you are writing a new application, you will have to factor in the needed "cluster aware" code to take advantage of this capability. There is a "Server Cluster API" that can be harnessed for applications or tools that need to directly interface with MSCS. An application is considered cluster-aware if it uses these server cluster APIs. For more information on the Windows Server clustering APIs, follow this URL link to MSDN at http://msdn.microsoft.com/library/default.asp?url=/library/en-us/mscs.

Design Note: Cluster Aware Applications

Any type of application that has a fault-tolerance requirement may be ripe for leveraging MSCS. If the application is designed (and coded) to be cluster aware, it becomes a "managed resource" within MSCS. Some types of applications that have been made cluster aware are

continues

- Databases—Microsoft SQL Server 7.0, SQL Server 2000, and IBM DB2
- Messaging servers—Microsoft Exchange Server 5.5, Exchange 2000 Server, and Lotus Domino
- Management tools—NetIQ's AppManager
- Disaster recovery tools—NSI Software's DoubleTake 3.0
- ERP applications—SAP, Baan, PeopleSoft, and JD Edwards
- Services—DHCP, WINS, SMTP, and NNTP

Hardware/Network/OS Requirements for MSCS

In the Windows 2000 server family, creating a basic two-node cluster will increase your high availability instantly. In addition, as has already been pointed out, it is possible to have up to four server nodes within a single cluster (which improves your high availability even further—likeliness of a server failure is now mitigated even more). Each node (server) in the cluster doesn't need to have the exact hardware/software configuration as the others; they just have to have a least common denominator configuration. As an example, each node in a cluster must have at least enough RAM memory as the smallest active server—a 4GB RAM server cannot failover to a server that only has 1GB RAM; however, it is highly recommended that you make each node (server) in a cluster as close to the same size as possible (variations in this theme will be discussed later).

In the Windows 2003 server family, you will be able to push this even further with up to eight server nodes in a cluster.

Before we configure our servers with MSCS, let's first examine the basic hardware, network, and operating system configuration requirements. Figure 4.1 shows a basic two-node clustered configuration that will be built with the Microsoft Windows 2000 Advanced Server operating system.

The following lists the typical hardware components in a two-node cluster:

- TWO Servers (as the two cluster nodes—Node "A" and Node "B")

- TWO 800MHz Pentium III Xeon (or greater) processors per node
- Between 4 and 8GB RAM per node
- THREE SCSI Controllers in each node—one controller for local disk storage, the other two for the external "clustered" shared disks (actually, using only one external "clustered" shared disk would work also—if money was tight)
- TWO Shared Storage Units (SCSI storage) typically configured as RAID or at least a mirrored disk configuration (including a separate partition for the Quorum disk)
- TEN to TWENTY SCSI disks (FIVE or TEN per storage unit depending on the RAID/Mirroring desired)
- TWO Ethernet NICs per node (one for communication to the public network, the other for dedicated internal heartbeat communication between the nodes—more on this later)

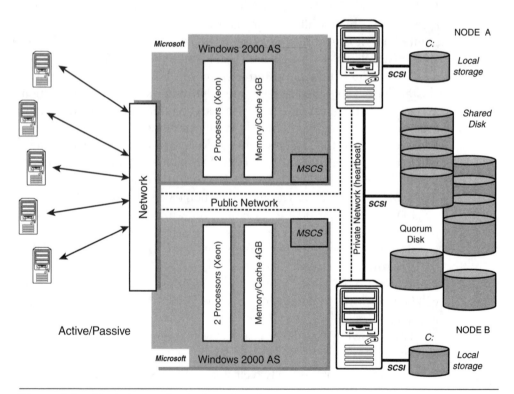

Figure 4.1 Basic two-node cluster—topology.

Then, at the network level

- A Domain Name Server connected to the public network. However, using WINS or HOSTS files is sufficient as long as some sort of name resolution mechanism is in place.
- Network access connecting each node with the domain name server

And, at the operating system level

- TWO Windows 2000 Advanced Server with Service Pack 3 (or Windows 2003 Enterprise Edition) installed.

Microsoft clustering is extremely sensitive to the hardware and network equipment that you put in place. For this reason, it is imperative that you verify your own hardware's compatibility *before* you go any further in deploying MSCS.

NOTE   A quick check to see if your hardware (server, controllers, and storage devices) is listed on Microsoft's HCL will save plenty of headaches later on:

http://www.microsoft.com/windows2000/datacenter/HCL/default.asp

or for Windows 2003 server family at

http://www.microsoft.com/windows/catalog/server/

You might also want to verify the different types of software from Microsoft and third-party software vendors that have been certified with MSCS at

http://www.microsoft.com/windows2000/professional/howtobuy/upgrading/compat/search/software.asp

For Windows 2003, you can go to Windows Hardware Quality Labs (WHQL), which provides Hardware Compatibility Tests (HCTs), support tools, and test procedures for servers and systems that will be running clustering at

http://www.microsoft.com/whdc/hwtest/system/default.mspx

How Clustering Actually Works

A *node* is a server within the cluster. Windows 2000 Advanced Server supports two-node clustering, and Windows 2000 Datacenter Server supports up to four-node clustering. Windows 2003 Enterprise Edition supports up to eight-node clustering.

As you can see in Figure 4.1, the *heartbeat* is a private network set up between the nodes of the cluster that checks to see whether a server is up and running. This occurs at regular intervals known as *time slices*. If the heartbeat is not functioning, a failover is initiated, and another node in the cluster will take over for the failed node. In addition to the heartbeat private network, at least one public network must be enabled so external connections can be made to the cluster.

The *shared disk* array is a collection of physical disks (SCSI RAID or FibreChannel) that is accessed by the cluster. Windows clustering supports "shared nothing" disk arrays. A shared nothing disk array is a setup in which only one node can own a given resource at any given moment. All other nodes are denied access until they own the resource. This protects the data from being overwritten when two computers have access to the same drives concurrently.

The *quorum drive* (as identified separately in Figure 4.1) is a logical drive designated on the shared disk array for Windows clustering. This continuously updated drive contains information about the state of the cluster. If this drive becomes corrupt or damaged, the cluster installation also becomes corrupt or damaged. The MSCS architecture requires there to be a single quorum resource in the cluster that is used as the tie-breaker to avoid split-brain scenarios. A *split-brain scenario* happens when all of the network communication links between two or more cluster nodes fail. In these cases, the cluster may be split into two or more partitions that cannot communicate with each other. The cluster service guarantees that even in these cases, a resource is only brought online on one node. If the different partitions of the cluster each brought a given resource online, it would violate what a cluster guarantees and potentially cause data corruption. When the cluster is partitioned, the quorum resource is used as an arbiter. The partition that owns the quorum resource is allowed to continue. The other partitions of the cluster are said to have lost quorum, and the cluster service and any resources hosted on the nodes not part of the partition that has quorum are terminated.

The quorum resource is a storage-class resource and, in addition to being the arbiter in a split-brain scenario, is used to store the definitive version of the cluster configuration. To ensure that the cluster always has an up-to-date copy of the latest configuration information, the quorum resource should be deployed on a highly available disk configuration (mirroring, triple-mirroring, or RAID 10 at the very least). In a Windows 2000 Server, the quorum device is typically a shared disk or physical disk resource type. In Windows 2003, the quorum may be spread out over multiple nodes (and logical drives). More on this later when majority node sets are discussed.

"Active/passive" versus "active/active" clustering describes the control that you want the cluster configuration to have. A typical *active/passive* 2-node cluster configuration has two servers, one actively serving the applications, the other server sitting there idle. Only one server has control over the shared disk system at a time (controlled by the Quorum disk). In the event of failure, the passive server takes control of the shared disk and picks up processing where the failed server left off.

Active/active clustering describes a configuration where all servers (nodes) are active. Each can take over for the other in the event of a failure, but usually the active nodes are not working with the same disk partitions (or data). The Quorum disk keeps track of what they are working with and when a node fails, another node takes control of the failed nodes' resources. In an active/active configuration, you must be sure to allow enough free CPU and memory on each server to accommodate the load from a failed node.

When a server (node) requires maintenance or upgrades, a manual failover can be performed. Manual failover involves instructing the Cluster service to *move* all resources from one node to another.

Design Note: Four-Node Clustering

Creating a four-node Microsoft cluster can support failover of critical applications or infrastructure services, such as databases, DHCP, WINS, messaging, and file and print services. What this means is that a four-node clustering approach provides protection against three successive hardware failures from happening. Three seems to be the magic number from a "Murphy's law" point-of-view. Statistics have shown that this four-node approach helps greatly to mitigate these types of failures (failures caused by hardware or software failure) from being the cause of downtime almost entirely. Do I hear five 9s?

The Disk Controller Configuration

It is important that the clustered computers have a separate PCI storage adapter (SCSI or FibreChannel) for the shared disks. For MSCS to recognize a disk as a shared disk, the disk should be on a controller that is separate from the adapter of the operating system's boot disk (local storage), as shown in Figure 4.1. However, it is technically possible to have the boot disks and shared disks on separate SCSI channels (if you have a multi-channel adapter available).

The PCI storage host adapters you use in both nodes must be identical to ensure that the adapter BIOS and other firmware in both nodes are 100% compatible.

Each device on the shared SCSI bus must have a unique SCSI ID. Because most SCSI controllers default to SCSI ID 7, you must change the SCSI ID on one controller to a different SCSI ID (for example, SCSI ID 6). If more than one disk is located on the shared SCSI bus, each disk must have a unique SCSI ID. Each SCSI bus segment must have exactly two points of termination, and these points must be located at the two ends of the segment. If you overlook any of these requirements, the bus may not operate properly in the MSCS environment.

The Disk Configuration

The Windows 2000 Advanced Server and Datacenter servers do not provide support for dynamic disks in a server cluster (MSCS) environment. However, you can use things like the Volume Manager for Windows 2000 add-on product from Veritas to add dynamic disk features to a server cluster.

By default, MSCS only fails over disks that it recognizes as physical disks. If your hardware manufacturer requires that you configure the shared disks as virtual disks, you need to install their drivers before you install the cluster service. In this way, the virtual disks will appear to be physical disks from MSCS's point-of-view.

CAUTION You have to partition and format all disks you are using with MSCS *before* you run MSCS Setup, and you must format all partitions that you are using as a cluster resource with NTFS.

The disk resources on the shared SCSI bus must have the same drive letter on both nodes. Because computers vary in the way they assign drive letters and because MSCS makes all drive assignments permanent during Setup, assign drive letters to all disk resources on the shared SCSI bus before you install MSCS. Keep in mind that the drive letters that you assign should be higher letters (Q, R, and so on). In addition, a best practice is to avoid having a single extended partition on a logical disk.

CAUTION   Make sure that MSCS is installed and running on one node before you start another node. If you start an operating system on other nodes before you install, configure, and run the cluster service on at least one node, the cluster disks may be damaged.

Network Configuration

Microsoft requires that you have two PCI network adapters in each node of the cluster. These must also be certified (as verified on the Hardware Compatibility List). On each node, you will configure one of the network adapters with a static Internet Protocol (IP) address that is for your public network access for this node. You will configure the other network adapter (on each node) with another IP address on a separate network for private cluster communication only. All network cards on the public network need to be on the same logical network (same subnet) regardless of their physical location.

It is recommended that you put the private network adapter in one of the following private network ranges:

- 10.0.0.0 through 10.255.255.255 (Class A)
- 172.16.0.0 through 172.31.255.255 (Class B)
- 192.168.0.0 through 192.168.255.255 (Class C)

Because the cluster service is not capable of detecting more than one network adapter per node in a particular network, plan your network addresses carefully. Microsoft does not recommend that you use network teaming on a cluster. However, if you do use manufacturer-specific network adapter teaming software, it must be seamless to the cluster and must reside only on the public network.

As you can see in Figure 4.1, the private network adapters (being used for the cluster heartbeat) should be on a standard network adapter and connected with a separate crossover cable (or to a hub). Each network adapter used can have one of four roles in a cluster:

- Only node-to-node communication (like for a heartbeat)
- Only client-to-cluster communication
- Both node-to-node communication and client-to-cluster communication
- No cluster-related communication

The default configuration during installation is to configure your public network adapter for "All Communications" and the private (heartbeat) network adapter for "Internal Cluster Communications Only." Microsoft recommends that you keep this default configuration. For your cluster to install and function properly, you must configure at least one of the networks for "Internal Cluster Communications Only" or "All Communications" as shown in Figure 4.2.

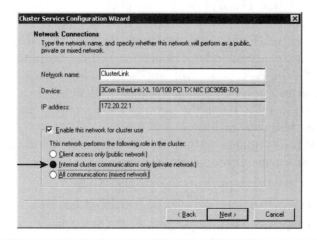

Figure 4.2   Example of a private network configuration for clustering.

The example shows "ClusterLink" as the name for the internal cluster communication network that we will need, and uses a private network IP address in the 172.xxx.xxx.xxx (Class B) range.

CAUTION   MSCS does not support the use of IP addresses assigned from a Dynamic Host Configuration Protocol (DHCP) server for the cluster administration address (which is associated with the cluster name) or any IP address resources. Strictly speaking, Microsoft recommends that you use static IP addresses for your node's public network adapters. However, you can use IP addresses "permanently" leased from a DHCP server for the Windows 2000 public network configuration on each node.

MSCS requires a dynamic name method such as Windows Internet Naming Service (WINS) on your network to function properly. With static entries, you cannot connect to a resource after failover to the other node in the cluster. The public network adapter should have WINS and/or dynamic DNS servers configured in its TCP/IP properties. To prevent a WINS server from registering the cluster's private network adapter as a multi-homed entry, ensure that the WINS TCP/IP client bindings are disabled on your private network adapter. In Windows 2000, you need to disable NetBIOS on the private network adapter.

Considerations at the Operating System Level

From the operating system level, you will have to identify and be given visibility to several cluster resources:

- You will identify a *cluster name* that the Windows 2000/2003 external connections use to refer to the cluster itself.
- You will define a *cluster IP address* that all external connections use to reach the failover cluster itself.
- You will also define a *cluster administrator account* that is used to administer and own the failover cluster. A cluster administrator account must be created at the domain level and must be an administrator of all nodes in the cluster.

Cluster resources include any services, software, or hardware that can be configured within a cluster. These include

- DHCP servers
- File shares
- Generic applications
- Generic services, Internet protocols
- Network names, physical disks, print spoolers
- WINS

A *cluster group* is a collection of logically grouped cluster resources, and may contain cluster-aware application services such as SQL Server

2000. A cluster group is sort of like a folder that has all the things you need to keep together (in this case, for managing cluster resources).

Design Note

Understanding the notion of a virtual server is key to understanding failover clustering and how it provides high availability. To a client or application, a virtual server is simply the server name or IP address used for access. The connection from the client to the virtual server does not need to know which node within a cluster is currently hosting the virtual server. In other words, a clustered SQL Server is known as a SQL Server virtual server, and the physical node that it is running on is never known by the clients that access it. The clients simply reference the SQL Server virtual server name (or IP address).

Installing MSCS

Identifying all of the names of the cluster components, types of networks to configure, and values the network requires (IP addresses) ahead of time will make your installation process go very cleanly (and be repeatable). Also be sure to have the proper hardware in place beforehand. To provide complete documentation for this installation process, you should create a small Excel spreadsheet that contains these values and that organizes (groups) the information to correspond to the MSCS clustering configuration setup process (as shown in Figure 4.3). (This small Excel spreadsheet will also be available for download at the Sams website.) Figure 4.3 depicts the needed values and names for a typical 2-node cluster installation.

Basically, all of the cluster components for each node and for the cluster itself are listed in the spreadsheet. Your values will vary depending on server naming conventions, IP address and domain name availability, and user ID conventions. Once you have specified all values in this spreadsheet, you will find it very easy to walk through the MSCS installation wizard for each node in your cluster. You should always start with the first active server in your cluster. We will assume that your system admin has

- Already built the physical servers (to specification)
- Intalled Windows 2000 Advanced Server (or Datacenter) on each node
- Named each physical server (like COLTST1 and COLTST3)
- Identified (or defined) a domain for the node to be a member of (like the domain COLTEST) or configured all nodes to be domain controllers
- Created a domain account that will be used by cluster services (like a domain account of "cluster")
- Formatted both the local SCSI drive (where the OS lives) and the shared SCSI disks with NTFS
- Identified a pool of IP addresses to be used by MSCS

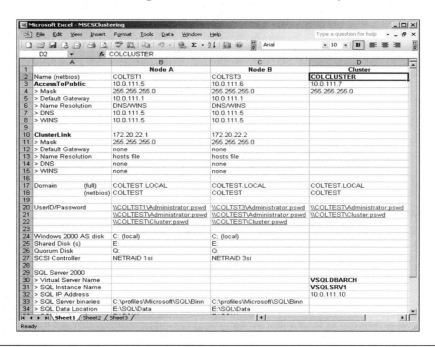

	Node A	Node B	Cluster
Name (netbios)	COLTST1	COLTST3	COLCLUSTER
AccessToPublic	10.0.111.5	10.0.111.6	10.0.111.7
> Mask	255.255.255.0	255.255.255.0	255.255.255.0
> Default Gateway	10.0.111.1	10.0.111.1	
> Name Resolution	DNS/WINS	DNS/WINS	
> DNS	10.0.111.5	10.0.111.5	
> WINS	10.0.111.5	10.0.111.5	
ClusterLink	172.20.22.1	172.20.22.2	
> Mask	255.255.255.0	255.255.255.0	
> Default Gateway	none	none	
> Name Resolution	hosts file	hosts file	
> DNS	none	none	
> WINS	none	none	
Domain (full)	COLTEST.LOCAL	COLTEST.LOCAL	COLTEST.LOCAL
(netbios)	COLTEST	COLTEST	COLTEST
UserID/Password	\\COLTST1\Administrator:pswd	\\COLTST3\Administrator:pswd	\\COLTEST\Administrator:pswd
	\\COLTEST\Administrator:pswd	\\COLTEST\Administrator:pswd	\\COLTEST\Cluster:pswd
	\\COLTEST\Cluster:pswd	\\COLTEST\Cluster:pswd	
Windows 2000 AS disk	C: (local)	C: (local)	
Shared Disk (s)	E:	E:	
Quorum Disk	Q:	Q:	
SCSI Controller	NETRAID 1si	NETRAID 3si	
SQL Server 2000			
> Virtual Server Name			VSQLDBARCH
> SQL Instance Name			VSQLSRV1
> SQL IP Address			10.0.111.10
> SQL Server binaries	C:\profiles\Microsoft\SQL\Binn	C:\profiles\Microsoft\SQL\Binn	
> SQL Data Location	E:\SQL\Data	E:\SQL\Data	

Figure 4.3   MSCS installation spreadsheet example.

Design Note

To configure the cluster service on a Windows server, the account you use must have administrative permissions on each node. All nodes must be member servers, or all nodes must be domain controllers within the same domain. It is not acceptable to have a mix of domain controllers and member servers in a cluster. All nodes in the cluster must be members of the same domain and able to access a domain controller and a DNS server. They can be configured as member servers or domain controllers. If you decide to configure one node as a domain controller, you should configure all other nodes as domain controllers in the same domain as well. In this example, all nodes are configured as domain controllers.

In addition, it is optimal to have defined the quorum disk on a separate physical drive other than that of the primary shared disks. You should also make this disk as fault-tolerant as possible (with at least RAID 5 or RAID 10). If the quorum disk is not available to the cluster, the shared disk is unusable. If you decide not to isolate the quorum disk to a separate drive, a warning will appear during the installation of MSCS (it's only a warning, and will not prevent you from building the installing MSCS).

Pre-installation

Before you start the MSCS installation, take the time to fill out the MSCS clustering Excel spreadsheet (as seen in Figure 4.3) in its entirety. All prompts and questions in the MSCS Setup Wizard can then be taken directly from this spreadsheet.

Design Note

It is also a good idea to check the system logs (event viewer) and make sure that there are no system level errors related to baseline services that are needed by or managed by MSCS such as distributed transaction coordinator (MS DTC) or logical disk manager services errors, and so on. Make sure that all devices and storage are in complete operational status (via Computer Management). This only takes a moment to verify by viewing the properties of each of these components (disk drives, network controllers, storage, and so on).

Figure 4.4 shows the system properties of our first server (COLTST1), its full computer name as it is known in our COLTEST domain (coltst1.coltest.local), the user account profiles that are set up for this computer (COLTEST\Administrator and COLTEST\Cluster), and the system date and time. The time turns out to be pretty important because each node in a cluster has to have its date and time synchronized. Once a node joins a cluster, its time will be automatically synchronized with the other nodes, but if the date/time is out of kilter to start with, a system error (event) will be encountered and a clustering configuration error will occur.

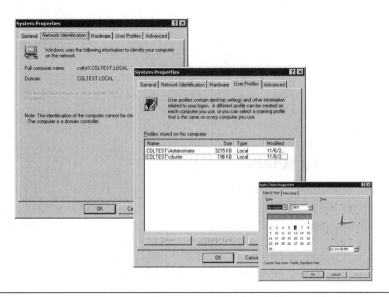

Figure 4.4   System Properties of the first server in the cluster (COLTST1).

In addition, you should take a quick look at the local disk devices that will contain the operating system and the shared disk devices that will contain the application, which is easily done via the SCSI device properties. As you can see in Figure 4.5, both the local and shared SCSI drives are working properly (both the MEGARAID SCSI device and the HP SCSI device). If there are problems with the shared SCSI drives, they will show up here. Please note that the write cache enabled option has been disabled (clustering requires that this be turned off).

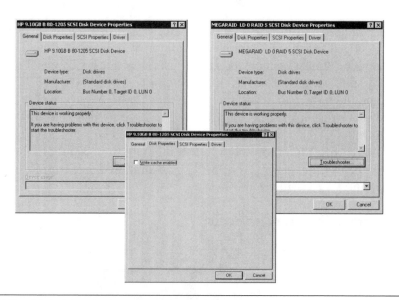

Figure 4.5 Disk drive device properties (SCSI).

Installing MSCS—Step 1

In order to start installing MSCS, you must turn off all servers that will be in the cluster except the primary one (COLTST1 in this example) and the shared disk. Figure 4.6 illustrates the complete MSCS clustering topology for a two-node cluster on a Windows 2000 Advanced Server platform. This will be an active/passive cluster. We will use this clustering example for both the MSCS installation and for the SQL Server clustering installation (in Chapter 5, "Microsoft SQL Server Clustering").

From the Configure Your Server menu (under Administrative tools), you will see the Advanced\Cluster Service option down in the left corner of this menu. This initiates the MSCS wizard, as seen in Figure 4.7.

CAUTION If the OS install files for clustering are not preloaded on the hard drive, you'll need to have your Install CD handy before you'll see the Cluster Service Configuration Wizard welcome screen.

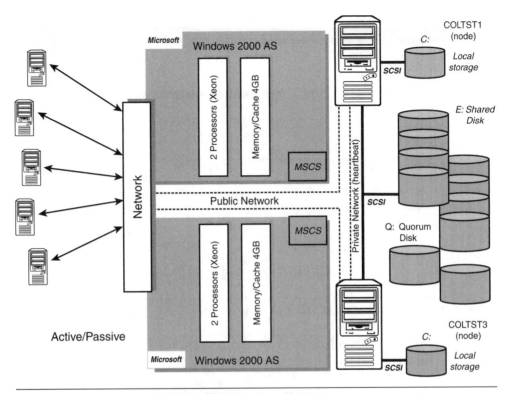

Figure 4.6   Two-node clustering topology—example.

Figure 4.7   Initial MSCS Setup Wizard welcome.

Once past the initial MSCS wizard dialog, you will be gently reminded to make sure you have validated your hardware against the Microsoft HCL (Hardware Compatibility List) that we discussed earlier.

You are about to create a new cluster, since this is the first node in the cluster. When you are presented with the dialog box as seen in Figure 4.8, choose the First Node in the Cluster server option.

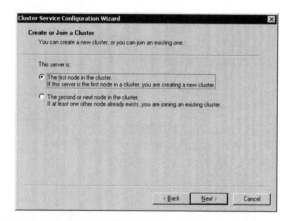

Figure 4.8   MSCS—First node in the cluster.

You will then have to name this new cluster. In Figure 4.9, we have named our sample cluster COLCLUSTER.

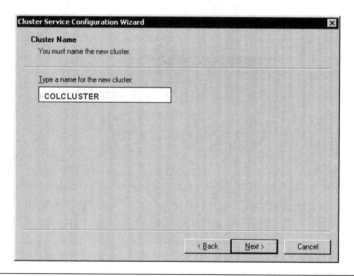

Figure 4.9   MSCS—Naming the cluster to be created.

You will now be asked to identify a user name and domain which will be the domain account that you set up to use with this new cluster. In our example, we had identified a domain user account of Cluster for this purpose. Figure 4.10 shows the dialog box that specifies the user name, password and domain name to use for this new cluster. This domain user account will be given special security privileges on each node in the cluster.

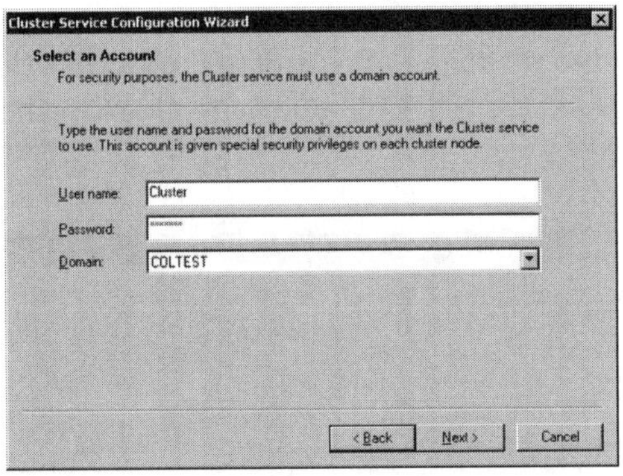

Figure 4.10 MSCS—domain account to use for this cluster.

Next you will identify the shared disks that are to be managed by the cluster. Any unmanaged disks not yet part of a cluster will be listed on the left side of this dialog. You must identify the ones you want by moving them to the right side (managed side) of this dialog box. Figure 4.11 shows the set of disks that are to be managed by this new cluster.

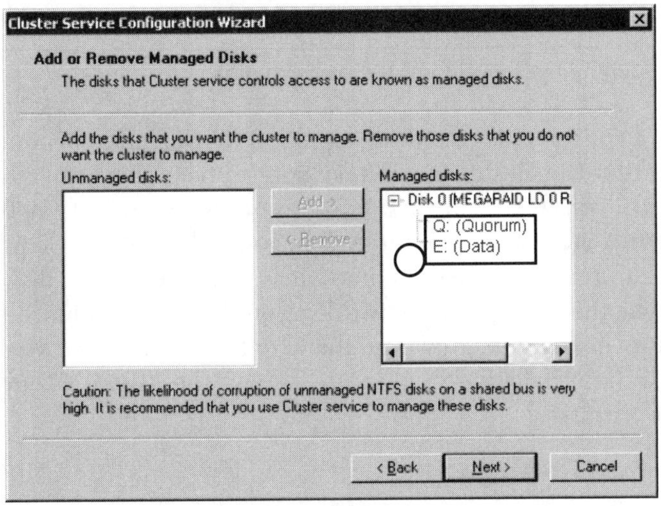

Figure 4.11 MSCS—which shared disks to be managed by the cluster.

In this example, only one shared disk (RAID disk array) is going to be used. This shared disk has been partitioned into a Q: drive (for the quorum disk) and an E: drive (for application use). Once you have selected the disks to be managed by the cluster, you will have to specify the quorum disk location.

Remember, the quorum disk is where the cluster checkpoint and log files needed to manage the cluster are kept; this disk should be at least 100MB in size. Figure 4.12 shows the Q: Drive being selected for this purpose.

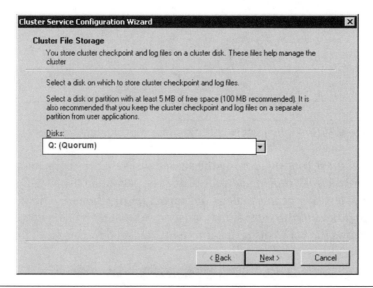

Figure 4.12   Identify the location of the quorum disk.

In our sample clustering topology, we will have only one private network for the cluster communication (to be named ClusterLink). The wizard will warn you that if you use only one private network for this internal heartbeat communication, you will have a single point of failure if that private network becomes unavailable. Use your discretion to create another, redundant network if you desire to minimize this point-of-failure even more. However, this is only a warning and you can proceed with the installation. Figure 4.13 shows the MSCS wizard dialog with this warning.

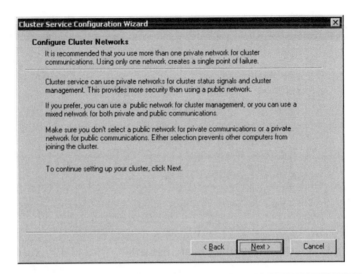

Figure 4.13 MSCS—private network warning.

You now identify the private network that you want to use for the internal communication between the two nodes in the cluster. We have named this private network ClusterLink, as seen in Figure 4.14. Be sure to check the Enable this Network for Cluster Use box and specify that this network is to be for Internal Cluster Communication only (private network). We could have also chosen to use the All Communications (mixed network) option for this network connection role. Either role works (however, private network is recommended for this). You should also be able to see the device name of the network adapter (3Com EtherLink XL 10/100 PCI TX NIC (3C9058-TX)) that is dedicated to this private network along with the IP address (172.20.22.1 in this example) that is associated with this network adapter (you can manage IP addresses via the TCP/IP properties of the network adapter).

Next will be the specification of the public network that all client connections will use to access the server. A different device name (HP NetServer 10/100TX) will now appear in the dialog box along with its IP address (10.0.111.5). As you can see in Figure 4.15, you must specify a network name for this network connection, check the box to Enable this network for cluster use, and specify All communications (mixed network) role for this network connection. In our example, we have named the public network AccessToPublic. Okay, this is a bit boring, but it is also very clear as to its use.

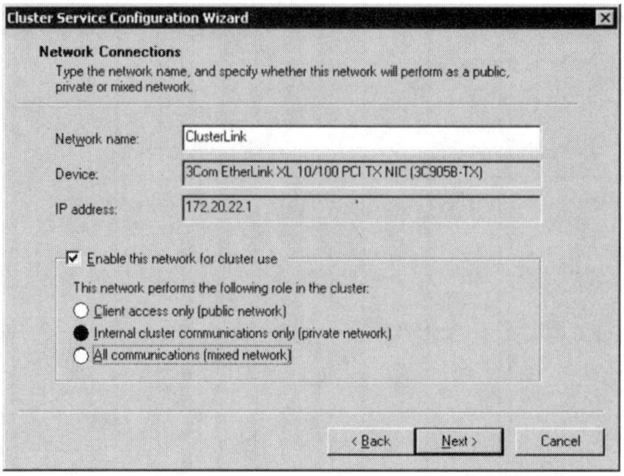

Figure 4.14 MSCS—identifying the private network.

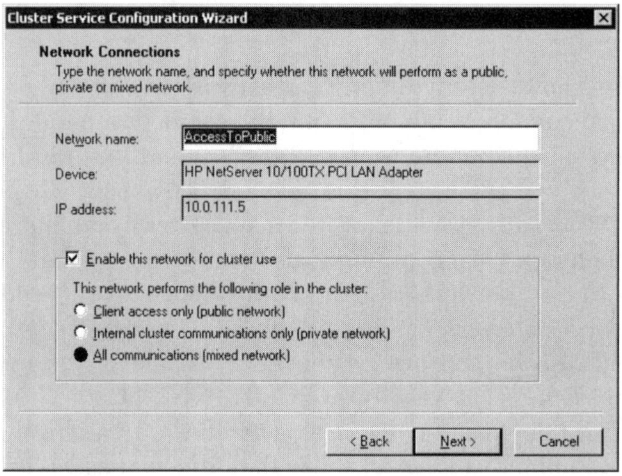

Figure 4.15 MSCS—identifying the public network.

You must specify the internal order that you want the cluster manager to use for communicating across private networks. Remember, you have one network that is private only, and the other that is mixed mode (both public and private). For this reason, both networks should be listed here. This is an ordering specification, so make sure that the private only network is at the top of this list (from top to bottom). In Figure 4.16, our private network named ClusterLink has been moved to be first in line to be used by the cluster manager for internal communication.

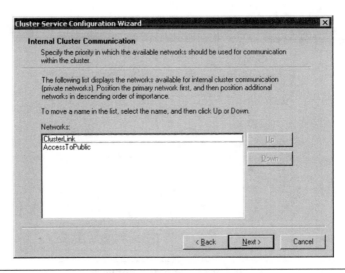

Figure 4.16 MSCS—specifying the internal network communication order.

Now the magic happens: The next dialog box is the place where you specify the cluster IP address (for our cluster named COLCLUSTER). This IP address will be what the cluster is known by for use by any application that is cluster aware (like SQL Server) instead of a physical network address that is tied to a specific network adapter. In fact, as you can see in Figure 4.17, you will also specify a subnet mask and the public network name from which clients (applications) will gain access to the cluster. If we look to our MSCS spreadsheet, we see that we want the cluster COLCLUSTER to have the IP address of 10.0.111.7; we will take the default subnet mask of 255.255.255.0, and specify the AccessToPublic network name for the public network access for the cluster. This is the software/hardware glue point that masks the physical network adapter addresses from the logical cluster address.

Now, the Windows Components Wizard will finish the cluster configuration. Several things are being done here, such as setting up a cluster service (in services), enabling the cluster network communication, and creating a cluster administrator account (to manage the cluster), as seen in Figure 4.18.

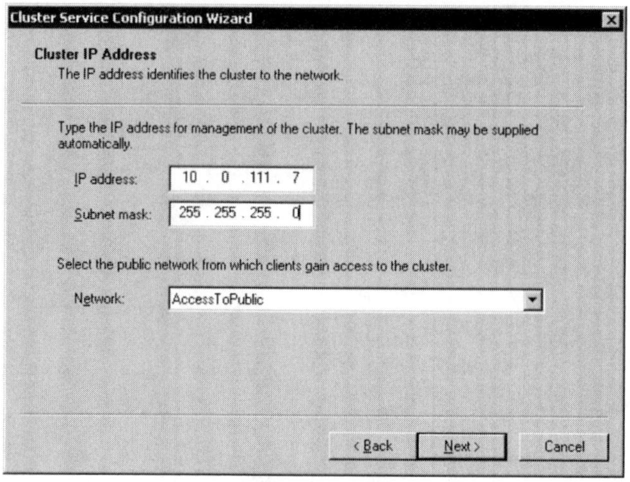

Figure 4.17 MSCS—the cluster IP address and network.

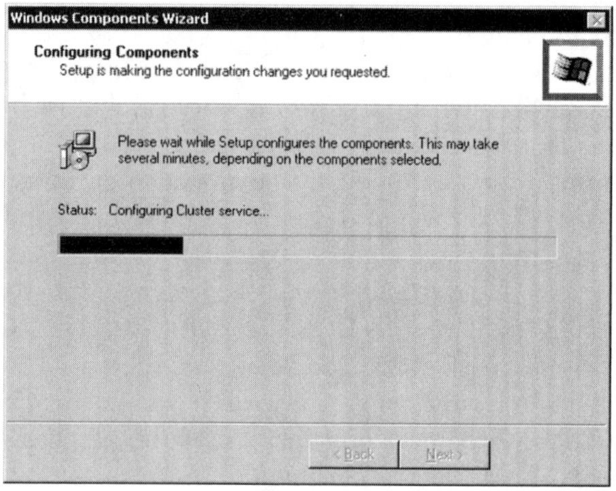

Figure 4.18 MSCS—configuring the cluster components.

Once this is complete, the cluster administrator can be invoked to view or change the cluster configuration. It is now an available program group on your server. In Chapter 5, we will explore more of the capabilities of managing a cluster with the cluster manager. Figure 4.19 shows how the cluster administrator displays the new cluster we just created (COLCLUSTER). If you click on Cluster Resources and expand Networks (as you can see in the box in the left corner of Figure 4.19), both of the networks that are being used by the cluster will be listed (which we just defined).

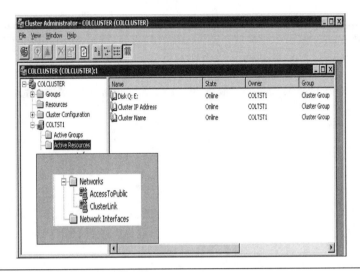

Figure 4.19   MSCS—Cluster Administrator—COLCLUSTER.

As you can see in Figure 4.20, a Cluster Service that is logged in as COLTEST\cluster is added to your local server (COLTST1) and is set to automatically start each time the server is booted.

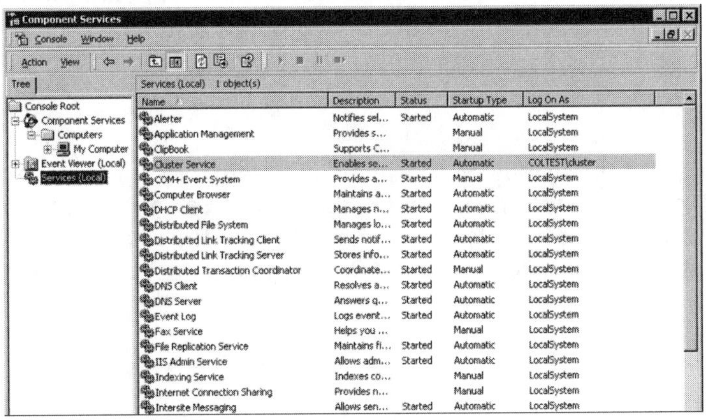

Figure 4.20   MSCS—Cluster Service (services).

When the cluster service is started, several system event messages are generated that provide you with the status of the cluster itself. Figure 4.21 shows an example of event ID 1128 that shows the status of the cluster networks (our private network named ClusterLink and our public network named AccessToPublic). In this example, both are operational and all available cluster nodes can communicate using them. It is also here where you will see problems (errors). In debugging a failed cluster, I always start here first.

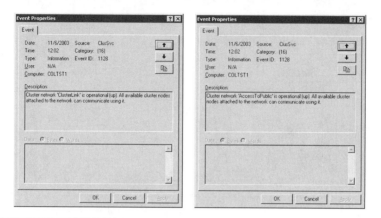

Figure 4.21 MSCS event properties for the private network named "ClusterLink" (dialog box on the left) and event properties for the public network named "AccessToPublic" (dialog box on the right).

Okay, all has gone smoothly in this configuration and now it is time to configure the other node in our two-node cluster.

Design Note

If you cancel out of the Cluster Configuration Wizard for some reason and need to restart it, you can't do it via the Configure Your Server menu anymore. You have to go to Add/Remove Programs and click on the Add/Remove Windows Components to get back to the Cluster Configuration.

Installing MSCS for the Next Node: Step 2

Repeat the same process for the second node in the cluster (and all subsequent nodes if more than two nodes are being set up). You must have the first node up and running and the shared disk available (and connected to this second node). From that new node, as you can see in Figure 4.22, instead of creating a new cluster, you will simply join an existing one by specifying that this server is "The second or next node in the cluster."

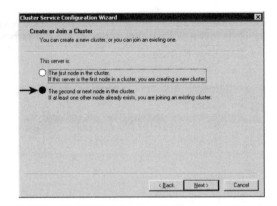

Figure 4.22 MSCS—joining an existing cluster.

Once the second node is created, both cluster nodes will appear in the Cluster Administrator, as seen in Figure 4.23.

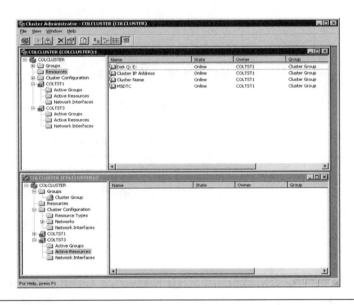

Figure 4.23 MSCS—two-node cluster (Cluster Administrator).

You can see both servers in the cluster administrator (COLTST1 and COLTST3). Currently, COLTST1 is the active server (owns the resources). COLTST3's resources are empty. You can also see these resources are online.

If you click on the Network Interfaces program groups under the Cluster Configuration group, you will see all the details associated with the network and the defined interfaces, including the specified network names, state (UP or DOWN), the network adapters being used, and the IP addresses. See Figure 4.24.

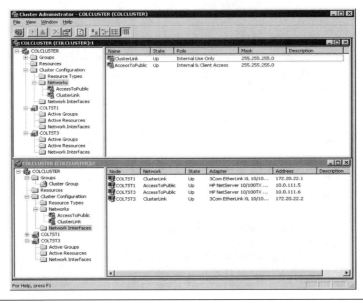

Figure 4.24   MSCS—network interfaces of the cluster.

You can easily test a failover from COLTST1 to COLTST3 by right-clicking on COLTST1's Active Groups program group and choosing the Move Group option. By default, as shown in Figure 4.25, this will take the resources for this cluster group offline from COLTST1 and bring them online to COLTST3.

Congratulations, you have successfully installed and tested a two-node cluster.

Extending Clustering with Network Load Balancing (NLB)

A second clustering technology, called network load balancing (NLB), is used to make sure a server is always available to handle requests. NLB works by spreading incoming client requests among a number of servers that are linked together to support a particular application. A typical example is to use NLB to process incoming visitors to your website. As more visitors come to your site, you can incrementally increase capacity by adding servers. This type of expansion is often referred to as software scaling or *scaling out*. Figure 4.26 illustrates this extended clustering architecture with NLB.

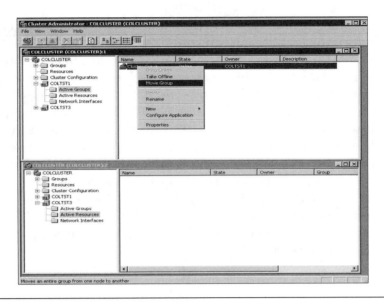

Figure 4.25   MSCS—failing over a cluster.

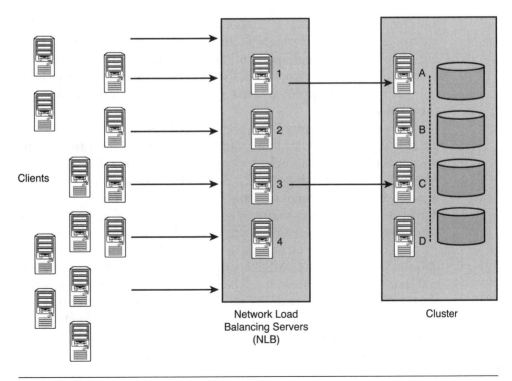

Figure 4.26   MSCS with network load balancing (NLB).

Using both MSCS and NLB clustering technologies together, you can create an n-tier infrastructure. For instance, create an n-tiered e-commerce application by deploying NLB across a front-end web server farm and use MSCS clustering on the back-end for your line-of-business applications such as clustering your SQL Server databases. This gives you the benefits of near-linear scalability without server or application-based single points of failure. This, combined with industry-standard best practices for designing high-availability networking infrastructures, can ensure your Windows 2000[en]based, Internet-enabled business will be online all the time and can quickly scale to meet demand. There are other tiers that could be added to the topology, such as an application center tier that uses component load balancing (CLB). This further extends the clustering and scalability reach for candidate applications that can benefit from this type of architecture.

Windows 2003 Options for Quorum Disks and Fail-over

Starting with Windows 2003, a more durable approach of managing the quorum disks with clustering was created called *majority note set*. It all but eliminates the single-point-of-failure weakness in the traditional quorum disk configuration that exists with Windows 2000 servers. However, even this new approach won't always be the best option for many clustered scenarios.

The notion of "quorum" as a single shared disk resource means that the storage subsystem has to interact with the cluster infrastructure to provide the illusion of a single storage device with very strict semantics. Although the quorum disk itself can be made highly available via RAID or mirroring, the controller port may be a single point of failure. In addition, if an application inadvertently corrupts the quorum disk or an operator takes down the quorum disk, the cluster becomes unavailable.

This can be solved by using a "majority node set" option as a single quorum resource from an MSCS perspective. In this set, the cluster log and configuration information will be stored on multiple disks across the cluster. A new majority node set resource takes care to ensure that the cluster configuration data stored on the majority node set is kept consistent across the different disks.

The disks that make up the majority node set could, in principle, be local disks physically attached to the nodes themselves or disks on a shared storage fabric (collection of centralized shared SAN devices that are connected over a switched-fabric or fibre-channel arbitrated loop storage area network [SAN]). In the majority node set implementation that is provided as part of MSCS in Windows Server 2003, every node in the cluster uses a directory on its own local system disk to store the quorum data. If the configuration of the cluster changes, that change is reflected across the different disks. The change is only considered to have been committed (made persistent) if that change is made to a majority of the nodes (that is [Number of nodes configured in the cluster]/2) + 1). In this way, a majority of the nodes have an up-to-date copy of the data. The cluster service itself will only start up if a majority of the nodes currently configured as part of the cluster are up and running as part of the cluster service.

If there are fewer nodes, the cluster is said *not* to have quorum and therefore the cluster service waits (trying to restart) until more nodes try to join. Only when a majority (or quorum) of nodes is available will the cluster service start up and bring the resources online. This way, since the up-to-date configuration is written to a majority of the nodes, regardless of node failures, the cluster will always guarantee that it starts up with the latest and most up-to-date configuration.

In the case of a failure or split-brain, all resources hosted on the partition of a cluster that has lost quorum are terminated to preserve the clusters' guarantee of only bringing a resource online on one node.

If a cluster becomes partitioned, (for example, if there is a communications failure between two sets of nodes in the cluster), then any partitions that do not have a majority of the configured nodes (less than [n/2]+1 nodes) are said to have lost quorum. The cluster service and all resources hosted on the nodes of partitions that do not have a majority are terminated. This ensures that if there is a partition running that contains a majority of the nodes, it can safely start up any resources that are not running on that partition.

In a typical MSCS cluster, a cluster can continue as long as one of the nodes owns the Quorum disk. Any nodes that can communicate (via heartbeats) with the quorum owner are part of the cluster and can host resources. Any other nodes that are configured to be in the cluster, but that cannot communicate with the quorum owner, are said to have lost quorum, and thus any resources that they are hosting are terminated.

Design Note

The differences between a traditional MSCS cluster quorum and the majority node set approach are vast. The traditional MSCS cluster can continue even if only one node out of the configured set of nodes is up and running as long as that node owns the quorum disk. A cluster running with a majority node set quorum resource will only start up or continue running if a majority of the nodes configured for the cluster are up and running and can all communicate with each other. The failure semantics of the cluster are different than a traditional MSCS cluster. Because of this difference in how the cluster behaves on node failures and partitioned or split-brain scenarios, care must be taken when deciding whether to choose a traditional MSCS cluster using a physical disk resource or a cluster that uses a majority node set as a quorum resource.

The majority node set resource is an optional quorum resource that Microsoft ships with the MSCS. By default, the physical disk resource is set up as a quorum resource.

CAUTION   Because the semantics of a cluster using majority node set are different than a cluster using the standard quorum resource(s), a cluster cannot be converted from one type to another dynamically. The decision on whether to use a traditional quorum resource or the majority node set resource must be made upfront. It cannot be changed later by simply switching cluster quorum resources.

A majority node set is created by first creating a single node cluster. This can be done using the standard cluster setup mechanisms. In the event that the cluster has no shared disks, the cluster configuration wizard will create a single node with a local quorum disk cluster by default. When using shared disks, the cluster configuration wizard will create a single node cluster with a physical disk selected as the quorum resource.

Once a single node cluster is set up, the quorum resource can be switched to the majority node set resource using cluster administrator. You simply open Cluster Administrator and connect to the appropriate cluster. You then create a new resource of type Majority node set. Change the cluster quorum resource to the newly created majority node set resource. The Quorum tab on the cluster properties shows the current quorum resource, and it can be modified by selecting the appropriate resource.

Once a single node cluster is set up using the majority node set resource, other nodes can be added to the cluster. As each node is joined, the quorum calculation is updated. In other words, if two nodes are added to build a 3-node cluster, quorum is adjusted so that two out of the three nodes must be running for the cluster to be considered to have quorum.

The majority node set quorum resource ensures that the quorum data is kept consistent across all nodes of the cluster and it is responsible for making changes to the quorum data stored on all nodes in the cluster.

CAUTION Each node in the cluster stores its quorum data in the following directory on the system disk:

%SystemRoot%\Cluster\QoN.%ResourceGUID%$\%ResourceGUID%$\
MSCS

The contents of this directory should not be modified; this directory contains cluster configuration information. Modifying the data in this directory may mean that the cluster service cannot start on the node.

The quorum resource accesses the data on the other nodes in the cluster using a network share. When a node is added to a cluster using the majority node set resource, a file share is created to expose the cluster quorum data to the majority node set resource. The share name is defined as follows:

```
\\%NodeName%\%ResourceGUID%$
```

The share is created with local system access. Since the cluster service is running under a domain account that is also a member of the local system group, the majority node set resource has access to the share.

The majority node set resource uses the private cluster connection between nodes to transfer data to the shares.

Figure 4.27 shows how the Quorum disk is spread out over multiple nodes as part of the majority set quorum configuration.

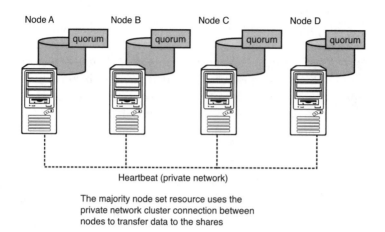

Heartbeat (private network)

The majority node set resource uses the
private network cluster connection between
nodes to transfer data to the shares

Figure 4.27   MSCS Windows 2003 Quorum disk option.

4-node and 8-node Clustering Topologies

Figure 4.28 illustrates multi-node clustering topologies that are possible in both the Windows 2000 family and the Windows 2003 family of servers.

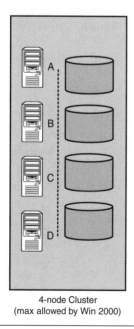

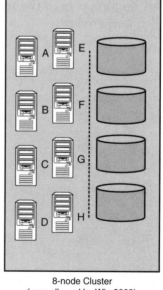

Figure 4.28   4-node and 8-node clustering.

4-node clusters are the maximum allowed for Windows 2000, while up to 8-node clusters are allowed in Windows 2003. As pointed out earlier in the chapter, there can be some subtleties associated with quorum disks and failure policies for the more advanced topologies on the Windows 2003 servers. The size and uptime requirements will drive you to how many nodes you need in a cluster. The more uptime you require, the more nodes you might want to have (mitigating failures by spreading out the risk).

Summary

Building out your company's infrastructure architecture with clustering technology at the heart is a huge step toward achieving the end-game of five 9s. Now, by definition, every application, system component, or database you deploy on this architecture has this added element of resilience. And, in many cases, the application or system component changes needed to take advantage of these clustering technologies are completely transparent! Utilizing a combination of both network load balancing (NLB) and cluster services (MSCS) allows you to not only failover applications but to scale for increasing network capacity. The flexibility that Microsoft has built into these clustering offerings and the extended offerings from other hardware and software vendors put you in a much more desirable position as far as managing this type of infrastructure and achieving your high availability goals. You should have no hesitation in moving forward with these technologies as quickly as you can.

In Chapter 5, we will be installing SQL Server 2000, using its SQL clustering option with MSCS. This will enable us to make SQL Server highly available. As part of this process, we will also be incorporating Microsoft Distributed Transaction Coordinator (MS DTC) as a resource that needs to be managed by the cluster (and is used by SQL Server for distributed transactions). More on this subject in Chapter 5.

CHAPTER 5

Microsoft SQL Server Clustering

THE KEY TOPICS IN THIS CHAPTER ARE

- How Microsoft SQL Server fail-over clustering works
- Installing SQL clustering
- Removing SQL clustering
- SQL Server database disk configurations
- HA client test program
- Things to watch out for when building up SQL clustering
- Scenario #1 using SQL clustering
- An ROI calculation example with SQL clustering

Microsoft SQL Clustering Core Capabilities

SQL Server allows fail-over and fail-back to or from another node in a cluster. In an "active/passive" configuration, an instance of SQL Server will be actively servicing database requests from one of the nodes in a SQL cluster (active node). Another node will be idle until, for whatever reason, a fail-over occurs (passive node). With a fail-over situation, the secondary node (the passive node) will take over all SQL resources (databases and MS DTC) without the end-user ever knowing that a fail-over has occurred. The end-user might experience some type of brief transactional interruption because SQL clustering cannot take over "in flight" transactions. However, from the end-user's point-of-view, they are still just talking to a single (virtual) SQL Server and truly won't know which node is fulfilling their requests. This type of application transparency is a highly desirable feature that is making SQL clustering more and more popular as a high availability option.

In an "active/active" configuration, SQL Server runs multiple servers simultaneously with different databases, allowing for organizations with more constrained hardware requirements (that is, no designated secondary systems) to enable fail-over to or from any node without having to set aside (idle) hardware.

By taking advantage of the clustering capabilities of Windows 2000 Advanced Server, SQL Server 2000 provides the high availability and reliability required of an enterprise class database management system. You can install up to 16 instances of Microsoft SQL Server 2000 in a Microsoft cluster service.

SQL Clustering Is Built on MSCS

As you already have seen in Chapter 4, "Microsoft Cluster Services," MSCS is capable of detecting hardware or software failures and automatically shifting control of the server to a healthy node. SQL Server 2000 implements fail-over clustering based on the clustering features of the Microsoft Clustering Service. In other words, SQL Server is a fully "cluster aware" application. Windows 2000 Advanced Server would normally handle up to two servers, whereas Windows 2000 Datacenter can handle up to four servers in a single cluster. The fail-over cluster shares a common set of cluster resources (or cluster groups) such as clustered (shared) disk drives. You can install SQL Server on as many nodes as you want; this is only limited by the operating system limitations. Each node must be running the same version of MSCS as well.

Figure 5.1 shows a typical two-node clustering configuration that has been configured in an active/passive mode. COLTST1 and all of the highlighted cluster group resources of COLTST1 is the "active" node. COLTST3 is the "passive" node. In the event that COLTST1 should fail, COLTST3 (via MSCS) will pick up control of these cluster group resources. So, the first step in creating a SQL Server clustering configuration entails installing the MSCS feature.

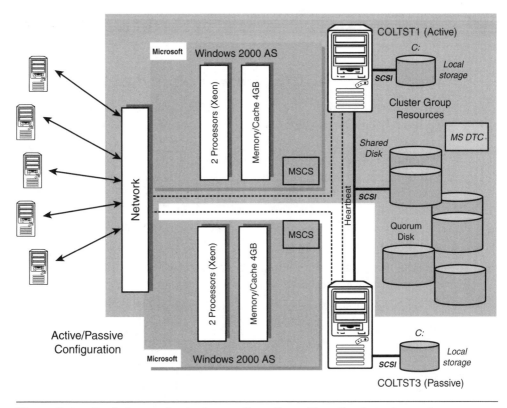

Figure 5.1 Basic two-node cluster configuration with active/passive nodes.

The short list of resources controlled by the cluster will be

- Physical Disks (Q:—Quorum disk, E:—Shared disks, F:, so on)
- Cluster IP Address
- Cluster Name (Network Name)
- MS DTC
- SQL Server Virtual IP Address
- SQL Server Virtual Name (Network Name)
- SQL Server
- SQL Agent
- SQL Full Text Service Instance (if installed)

In Chapter 4, we created the first three cluster group resources (Physical Disks, Cluster IP Address, and Cluster Name). We must now add MS DTC (Microsoft Distributed Transaction Coordinator) and the

SQL Server resources to the cluster to complete the installation of SQL clustering.

Configuring MS DTC for Use with SQL Clustering

MS DTC is required in a cluster for distributed queries and two-phase commit transactions. SQL Server relies on MS DTC heavily in this regard. After you have installed MS Cluster Services (as outlined in Chapter 4) please verify that MS DTC has been installed as well.

On each node of the cluster, check your "services" to see if Distributed Transaction Coordinator is there. If not, you will have to do this now by running DTCSetup.exe on each node in the cluster. DTCSetup.exe can be found in the Windows/System32 folder of each node. Follow these simple steps:

1. Verify that node A has control of the clusters resource groups (via the cluster administrator).

2. Then, first from node A, run the following from a DOS prompt:

```
C:\Windows\System32> DTCSetup.exe
```

This will copy the needed files to the system32 folder.

3. Check the event viewer to make sure that the install was successful on this node. If this fails, you will have to start over, or even have to undo entries in the registry.

4. You might also be prompted to run DTCSetup.exe on the second node. [Do so, only if prompted.]

Once the installation of MS DTC is completed, you can now configure it to be a resource within cluster services. This is done by running the comclust.exe program on each node which will configure MS DTC to run in clustered mode. Make sure you do this on both nodes, *one at a time*.

1. Again, from a DOS command prompt, run comclust.exe on node A. This will configure MS DTC for use with cluster services.

```
C:\Windows\System32> comclust.exe
```

2. After this step completes on the first node, repeat this step on node B.

3. Verify that the DTCLOG folder has been created on the cluster shared disk. NOTE: By default, the MSDTC service will start with a local system account. This local system account must be given full permissions to the DTCLOG folder.

In the top portion of Figure 5.2, the Cluster Administrator window shows that MS DTC is not listed as a resource yet. Once you configure MS DTC as a resource (via comclust.exe), it will appear as a resource in the cluster group (as you can see in the bottom Cluster Administrator window of Figure 5.2).

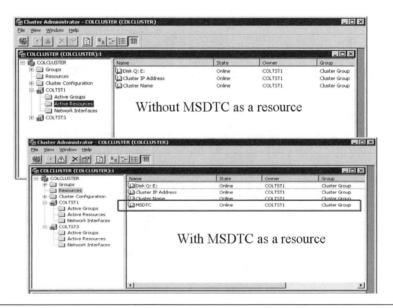

Figure 5.2   Cluster Administrator—MS DTC as a resource.

Laying Out a SQL Cluster Configuration

When you install SQL Server in a clustered server configuration, you create it as a "virtual" SQL Server. In other words, a virtual SQL Server will not be tied to a specific physical server. Figure 5.3 shows the same two-node cluster configuration with all of the SQL Server components identified. This virtual SQL Server will be the only thing the end-user will ever see. As you can also see in Figure 5.3, the virtual server name is VSQLDBARCH and the SQL Server Instance name is VSQLSRV1.

From the network's point of view the fully qualified SQL Server instance will be "VSQLDBARCH\VSQLSRV1." Figure 5.3 also shows the other cluster group resources that will be part of your SQL clustering configuration. These, of course, are MS DTC (as we configured earlier), SQL Agent, and the shared disk where your databases will live. A SQL Agent will be installed as part of the SQL Server installation process and is associated with the SQL Server instance it is installed for. Same is true for MS DTC; it will be associated with the particular SQL Server instance that it is installed to work with (VSQLSRV1 in this case).

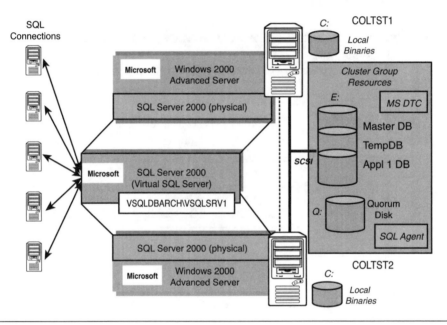

Figure 5.3   The SQL clustering topology and the cluster group resources.

Now, before we go too much further, it would be a good time to talk about how you should lay out a SQL Server implementation on the shared disks that are managed by the cluster. The overall usage intent of a particular SQL Server instance dictates how you might choose to have configured your shared disk and how it might be best configured for scalability and availability.

Figure 5.4 shows the typical RAID levels used in a high availability disk configuration, the fault tolerance to expect, the number of logical I/Os per read, the physical I/Os per read, number of logical I/Os for a write operation, and the number of physical I/Os per writes. In general,

RAID 0 is great for storage that doesn't need fault tolerance; RAID 1 or 10 is great for storage that needs fault tolerance, but doesn't have to sacrifice too much performance (like with most Online Transaction Processing Systems—OLTP); and RAID 5 is great for storage that needs fault tolerance, but whose data doesn't change that much (low data volatility as in many DSS/Read Only systems).

RAID Level	Fault Tolerance	Logical Reads	Physical IOs per Read	Logical Writes	Physical I/Os per Write
RAID 0	None	1	1	1	1
RAID 1 or 10	Best (Optimal for OLTP)	1	1	1	2 writes
RAID 5	Moderate (Optimal for mostly READ ONLY systems)	1	1	1	2 reads + 2 writes (that's 4 per write!)

Figure 5.4   Different I/O costs of the typical RAID level configurations used in HA.

What this all translates to is that there is a time and place to use the different fault tolerant disk configurations. Figure 5.5 provides a very good "rule of thumb" to follow for deciding which SQL Server database file types should be placed on which RAID level disk configuration. This would be true regardless of whether the RAID disk array was a part of a SQL cluster or not.

The Quorum Drive

As part of this high availability disk configuration, the quorum drive should be isolated to a drive all by itself and be mirrored to guarantee that it is available to the cluster at all times. Without it, the cluster won't come up at all and you won't be able to access your SQL databases.

SQL Server Database Files

One or more physically separate shared disk arrays can house your SQL Server managed database files. In a SQL Server database, it is highly desirable to isolate your data files away from your transaction log files for any database that has volatility (like with OLTP systems). In addition, perhaps one of the most critical databases in a SQL Server instance is the internal shared database of TempDB. TempDB should be isolated away from your other databases and perhaps placed on some high performing disk configuration such as RAID 10. SQL Server requires that TempDB be allocated at server startup time, so the location of TempDB should be protected rigorously. Do not place TempDB on a RAID 5 disk array! The write overhead is far too much for this internally used (and shared) database. In general, put your OLTP SQL Server database data/transaction log files on RAID 10 (including Master DB, Model DB, and MSDB) and your DSS/Read Only data/transaction log files on RAID 5.

	Description	Fault Tolerance
Quorum Drive	The quorum drive used with MSCS should be isolated to a drive by itself (very often mirrored as well for maximum availability).	RAID 1 or RAID 10
SQL Server Database files (OLTP)	For OLTP (online transaction processing) systems, the database data/index files should be placed on a RAID 10 disk system.	RAID 10
SQL Server Database files (DSS)	For DSS (Decision Support Systems) systems that are primarily READ ONLY, the database data/index files should be placed on a RAID 5 disk system.	RAID 5
Temp DB	Highly volatile disk I/O (when not able to do all it's work in cache).	RAID 10
SQL Server Transaction Log files	The SQL transaction log files should be on their own mirrored volume for both performance and database protection (for DSS systems, this could be RAID 5 also).	RAID 10 or RAID 1

Figure 5.5   SQL Server/SQL clustering disk fault tolerance.

Design Note

Another good practice is to balance these configurations across disk arrays (controllers). In other words, if you have two (or more) separate shared disk arrays (both RAID 10) available within your cluster group resources, put the data file of database 1 on the first cluster group disk resource (say DiskRAID10-A), and its transaction log on the second cluster group disk resource (say DiskRaid10-B); then put the data file of database 2 on the second cluster group disk resource of DiskRAID10-B, and its transaction log on the first cluster group disk resource of DiskRAID10-A. You have now staggered these allocations and in general have balanced the overall RAID controller usage minimizing any potential bottlenecks that might have occurred on one disk controller.

Figure 5.6 shows an example of a typical production SQL Server instance that has three application databases on it and how all of these database files might be laid out over a shared multi-disk configuration. Master DB and the DSS (read only) database were crated on the E: Drive (a RAID 5 disk array); TempDB database was isolated to the F: Drive (a RAID 10 disk array). The other two OLTP databases were spread out over the G: and H: drives (also RAID 10 disk array), and the Q: drive was reserved for the quorum files for MSCS (a RAID 1 or RAID 10 disk array).

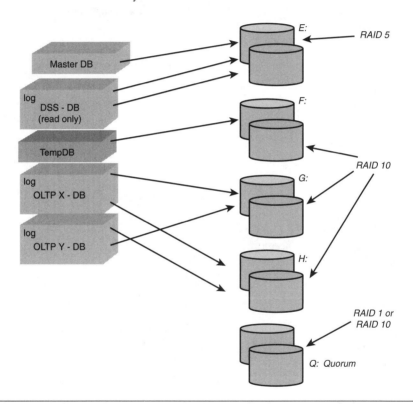

Figure 5.6 Sample SQL Server/SQL clustering database file allocations across multiple shared disks.

Network Interfaces

As you can see in Figure 5.7, one final glance with Cluster Administrator shows that both COLTST1 and COLTST3 nodes and their private and public network interfaces are completely specified and their state (status) is "up." If you like, you should double-check these IP addresses and network names with the Excel spreadsheet that was created for this cluster specification.

Figure 5.7   The state of the cluster network interfaces and their correspondence to our Excel spreadsheet specification.

Cluster Service

As you can see in Figure 5.8, the Cluster Service is running and has been started by the cluster login account for the COLTEST domain as was required.

> **CAUTION**   If Cluster Service is not started, and won't start, you will not be able to install SQL clustering. You will have to remove and then re-install MSCS from scratch. A little extra advice is to browse the Event Viewer to familiarize yourself with the types of warnings and errors that start appearing with Cluster Service.

As you add more things to be managed by the cluster (such as SQL Server), you will want to be able to distinguish the new events from the old (normal) events. Looking at Figure 5.9, you can see the major events that describe the state of the cluster. These are all ClusSvc event sources. The event IDs to focus on are Event ID 1128, 1125, 1061, and 1122.

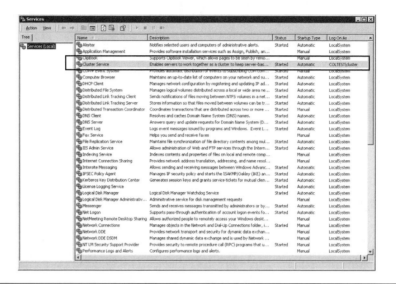

Figure 5.8 Make sure Cluster Service is running and started by the cluster account for the domain.

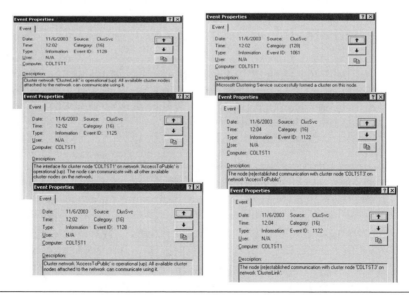

Figure 5.9 Cluster Service event states.

Event ID 1128 shows the cluster network state (the public network and the private network that has been defined in the cluster). For example: Cluster Network "ClusterLink" is operational.

Event ID 1125 shows the interface state (the machine and which network is being used). For example: COLTST1 on "AccessToPublic" network is operational.

Event ID 1122 shows the node communication state for the cluster node. For example: COLTST3 successfully established communication on the "AccessToPublic" network with the cluster.

Okay, the cluster is intact, all services are intact, and the needed resource groups are being managed by the cluster. You will now be able to build up the two-node SQL cluster.

Installing SQL Clustering

To install SQL Server 2000's SQL clustering you must install a new SQL Server "within" the cluster. SQL Server is not something that is moved from a non-clustered configuration to a clustered configuration. With all resources running and in the online state, run the SQL Server setup program from the node that is online (like COLTST1). Figure 5.10 shows the SQL Server setup wizard and the initial dialog box where you will be able to specify the creation of a new "virtual" server (named VSQLDBARCH).

CAUTION Installing SQL clustering is only available with SQL Server 2000 Enterprise Edition. It is not available on Standard Edition. Sorry, but this may require an upgrade of your license with Microsoft. This small upgrade cost will pay for itself over and over.

It is this virtual server that the client applications will see and to which they will connect. When an application attempts to connect to an instance of SQL Server 2000 that is running on a fail-over cluster, the application must specify both the virtual server name and the instance name, such as VSQLDBARCH\VSQLSRV1. The application does not have to specify an instance name if the instance associated with the virtual server is a default instance because it has no name. Additionally, you cannot access the SQL Server by specifying the machine name (COLTST1) and instance name (VSQLSRV1) because the SQL Server is not listening on the IP address of this local server. It is listening on the clustered IP addresses created during the setup of a virtual server. Figure 5.11 shows the dialog boxes for the user information and the licensing agreement with Microsoft.

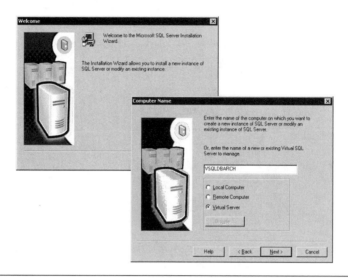

Figure 5.10   SQL Server Setup Wizard and virtual server specification.

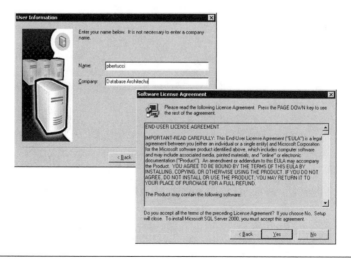

Figure 5.11   Specify the user information and the licensing agreement.

The next thing that must be done for this new virtual server specification will be to identify an IP address and which network it should use.

In our example, we had reserved an IP address for this purpose and had defined the "AccessToPublic" network for the general access. As you can see in Figure 5.12, you simply type in the IP address (for example: 10.0.111.10) that is to be the IP address for this virtual SQL Server and identify which network to use (for example, "AccessToPublic"). Then you click on the Add button. This specification now should appear in the lower window of this dialog box. If the IP address that is being specified is already in use, an error will occur (Figure 5.12 also shows the error message box that will appear for this error).

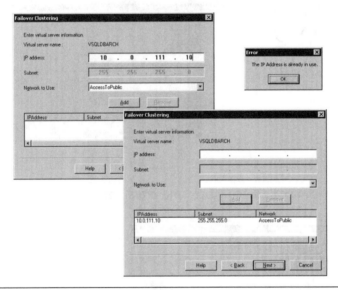

Figure 5.12　Specifying the virtual SQL Server IP address and the dialog box if this IP address is already in use.

Design Note

Keep in mind that we will use a separate IP address for the virtual SQL Server that is completely different from the cluster IP addresses. In a non-clustered installation of SQL Server, SQL server can be referenced by the machines IP address. In a clustered configuration, the IP addresses of the servers themselves will not be referenced, but rather this separately assigned IP address for the virtual SQL Server itself.

Next, you will identify the cluster-managed disk(s) for the database files for SQL Server. For this current example, Figure 5.13 shows the cluster group disk that is available. It contains an E: drive (that we want SQL Server to use) and a Q: drive that is being used for the quorum files (do not select the Q: drive!). Simply select the available drive(s) that you want to put your SQL database files on (E: drive in this example). If the quorum resource is in the cluster group that you have selected, a warning message will be issued (as also shown in Figure 5.13) that informs you of this fact. A general rule of thumb is to isolate the quorum resource to a separate cluster group if it is possible.

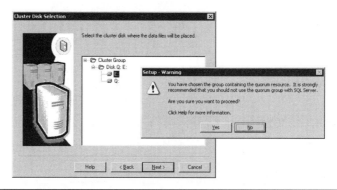

Figure 5.13   Select the disks for use with SQL Server.

Identify the nodes available to run SQL Server. This allows any identified node to take over in the event of a hardware failure. The dialog box in the left of Figure 5.14 shows the configured nodes that will be part of this SQL cluster (COLTST1 and COLTST3). As you can see in the dialog box on the right of this same figure, you must also be ready to specify a domain account that is an administrator account for all nodes in the cluster. If you are not sure, use "Administrator" to be safe.

You will then be prompted to specify a SQL Server instance name or use no instance name (the default). I always specify an instance name because I might choose to add another SQL Server instance to the cluster (since a single cluster can have up to 16 SQL Server instances). This also helps to see the instance name in the Cluster Administrator. Figure 5.15 shows this SQL Server instance name of VSQLSRV1.

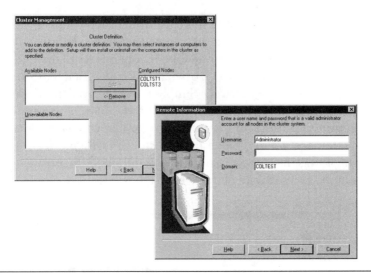

Figure 5.14   Select nodes to be used in the SQL cluster.

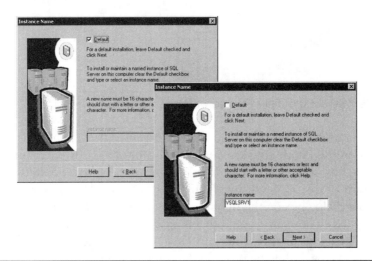

Figure 5.15   Identify a SQL Server instance name (or default with no instance name).

Design Note

As a naming convention note, preface all virtual SQL Server names and virtual SQL Server instance names with a *V* for clarity. This will allow you to easily identify which SQL Servers that may be on your network are clustered or not. Our examples have used VSQLDBARCH as a virtual SQL Server name and VSQL-SRV1 as an instance name.

Specify the destination folders for both the SQL Server program files (binaries) and the database file (for Master DB, so on). Figure 5.16 shows this specification. Basically, the setup process will install SQL Server binaries locally on each node in the cluster (in this case, in C:\Program Files\Microsoft SQL Server directory). The database files for Master DB, Model DB, Temp DB, and MSDB will be placed on the E: drive (in this example). This is the shared disk location that must be available to all nodes in the SQL cluster. In addition, you must be prepared to identify the user account that will be starting the services associated with SQL Server (SQL Server itself, SQL Agent, SQL Full Text Search service). We have specified that this be the same administrator account within this domain. You can use Administrator or better yet, a designated account (like "Cluster" or "ClusterAdmin") that has administrator rights within the domain and on each server (member of the Administrators local group on any node in the cluster). You will also have to specify the type of authentication mode you want for SQL Server access, Windows authentication for mixed mode (Windows Authentication and SQL Server Authentication).

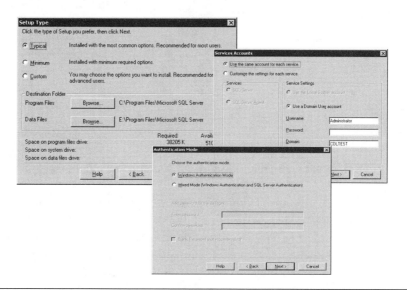

Figure 5.16   Indicate the destination folders for SQL Server, the user account for the new services, and the authentication mode for SQL Server access.

And, lastly, you will be prompted for the SQL Server licensing option information. The SQL Setup wizard now has enough information to do the complete installation of the SQL cluster with the identified nodes. Figure 5.17 shows this intermediate dialog box indicating that the setup is being done on the cluster nodes. This can take a while because quite a lot of things are being done. In particular, binaries are being installed locally, databases are being created on the shared disks, services are being created on each node for SQL Server, and SQL resources are being created and brought online within the cluster group. Eventually, you will see the dialog box indicating that the virtual server resources have been installed (Setup is complete).

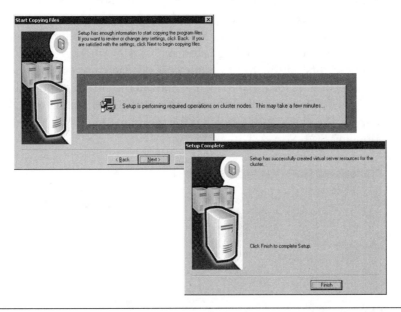

Figure 5.17   Setup has enough information to install on all cluster nodes.

WAIT! You aren't done yet. You now need to apply the latest SQL Server service pack to this installation. Do it now. This is important because any time you take to apply this service pack application in the future counts against you for planned downtime and lowers your high availability percentage. If you haven't done so already, download this service pack from Microsoft and run the setup program. As of this book writing, we downloaded Service Pack 3 and installed it without a hitch. Figure 5.18 shows these steps. Remember, you must specify the virtual SQL Server name here, not a physical SQL Server name.

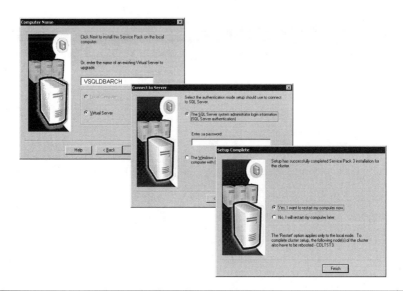

Figure 5.18   Apply the latest service pack to the "virtual" SQL Server.

As you can see from Figure 5.19, SQL Server has been successfully installed on the cluster, and Cluster Administrator is showing these newly added "active" resources within the cluster group.
The SQL Server resource entries are

1. SQL Server Virtual IP Address (for VSQLDBARCH SQL Server)
2. SQL Server Virtual Name (of VSQLDBARCH)
3. SQL Server (VSQLSRV1 instance)
4. SQL Agent (for the VSQLSRV1 instance)
5. SQL Fulltext Service (for the VSQLSRV1 instance)

Each should show that they are ONLINE and owned by the same node (COLTST1 in this example).

You should now verify that the correct services were set up by displaying the services selection (via control panel: administrative tools) for the current node that you are on (COLTST1). Figure 5.20 shows the SQL Server service entry for the new SQL Server instance (MSSQL$VSQLSRV1) and the SQL Agent entry (SQLAgent$VSQLSRV1) for this new instance. Both also have startup type of "manual" because Cluster Service is what is used to start them up.

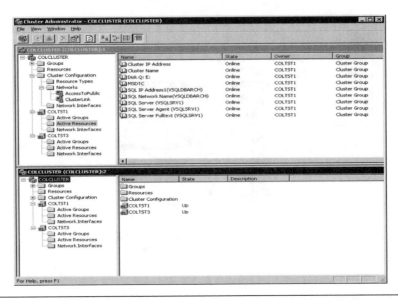

Figure 5.19 Cluster Administrator and the SQL Server resource entries.

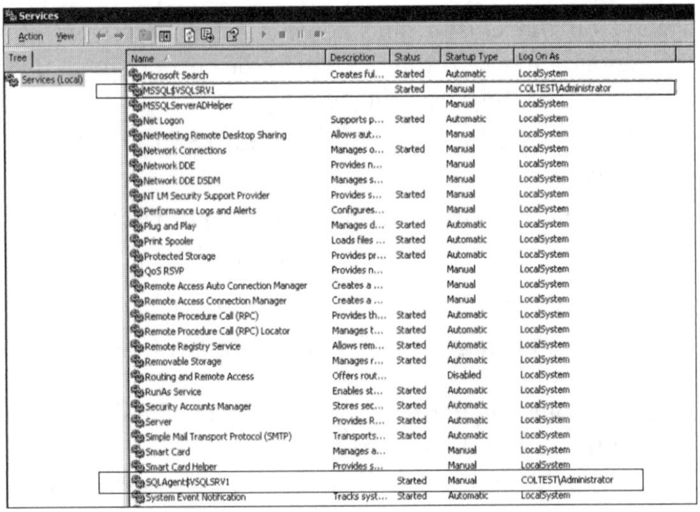

Figure 5.20 New SQL Server "services" entries.

From the Cluster Administrator, you can easily view the properties of each of the new SQL resources by right-clicking on a particular SQL resource and selecting Properties. Figure 5.21 shows the properties of the SQL IP Address resource for the new created virtual SQL Server.

The Parameters tab indicates the IP address (10.0.111.10) that it will have on the network, the subnet mask (255.255.255.0), and the network that it will use ("AccessToPublic" network). It is here where you will change these parameters if and when you need to.

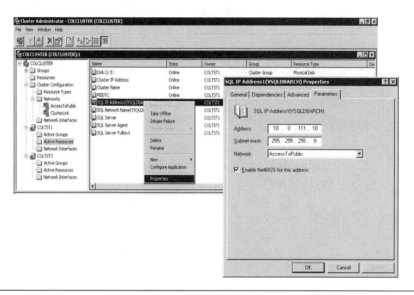

Figure 5.21   Properties of the SQL resources.

As you can also see in Figure 5.21, you can also take the resource "offline" or "initiate a failure" as well. This must be done sometimes when trying to fix or test a SQL clustering configuration. However, when initiating full SQL Server fail-over to another node (like from COLTST1 to COLTST3), you will typically use the "Move" cluster group technique since you want all of the resources for the cluster group to fail-over and not just one resource. Figure 5.22 shows how you can do this easily from the Active Groups item in Cluster Administrator.

Many SQL Server 2000 installations still like to use the SQL Server service manager to see the state of SQL Server, MS DTC, and SQL Agent. Microsoft has been told to not install the service manager in the future. This was considered to be too evasive. So, starting with Yukon (SQL Server 2005), the SQL Server service manager will not be automatically installed. As you can see from Figure 5.23, the service manager entries reflect the virtual SQL Server instance names (as they should).

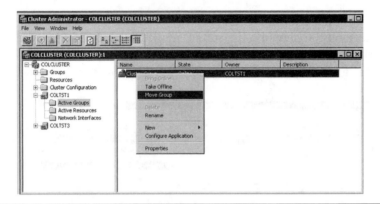

Figure 5.22 Using Move Group to fail-over to the other node in you cluster.

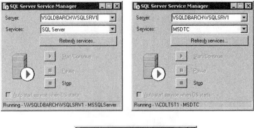

Figure 5.23 SQL Server service manager showing the virtual SQL Server instance, MS DTC, and SQL Agent.

Failure of a Node

As you can see in Figure 5.24 one of the nodes in the SQL cluster has failed (COLTST3 in this case). As you can also see in Cluster Administrator, the COLTST3 node item group has a "red X" on it to indicate this failure. Also note that the state of the resources on COLTST1 are

"Online Pending"! In other words, these resources are in the middle of failing over to this node. As they come up successfully, the "Online Pending" turns to "Online."

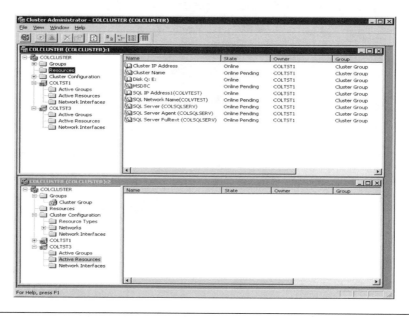

Figure 5.24   Failed node—Cluster Administrator.

In addition, the failure of a node (for any reason) is also written to the system event log.

Figure 5.25 shows the event ID 1069 "Cluster resource 'SQL WERVER (VSQLSRV1)' failed" indicating that there was a cluster resource failure. You would then want to backtrack all of the system events that lead up to this failure.

In this particular case, I intentionally initiated a failure of the SQL Server instance (VSQLSRV1) via the cluster administrator. SQL clustering did the right thing by failing over to the other node. This also served to verify that SQL clustering is working properly. The Client Test Program for a SQL cluster section later on in this chapter shows you how this failure scenario might look from the client application's point of view.

If the cluster itself doesn't come up due to the shared disk not being available, the cluster service not being started, or any number of other reasons, the Cluster Administrator will not function either. Figure 5.26

shows the Cluster Administrator and the error message it generates when it cannot connect to the cluster.

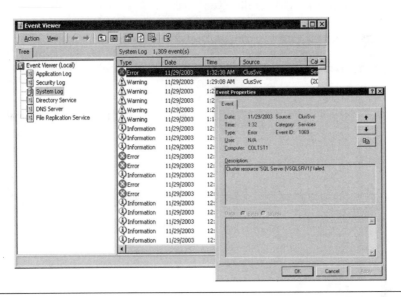

Figure 5.25   System Event Log and Event details for the failed cluster resource.

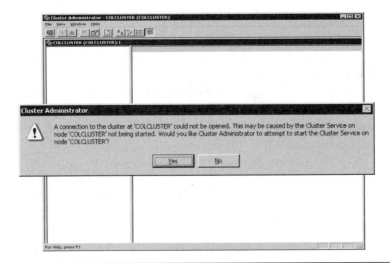

Figure 5.26   Cluster Administrator failing to connect to the cluster.

The SQL resources that are now managed by the cluster can also be adjusted to better serve your needs. Figure 5.27 shows the properties of the primary SQL resources in SQL clustering (SQL Server, SQL Server Agent, and Distributed Transaction Coordinator). In particular, you can modify the poll intervals from the possible owners of the resource. In this case, COLTST1 and COLTST3 are the possible owners of these SQL resources.

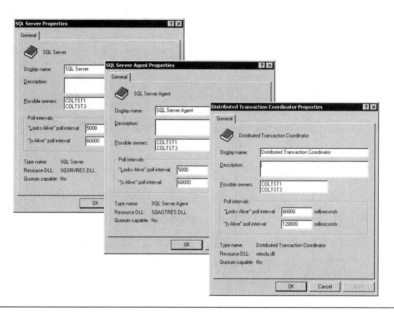

Figure 5.27   Adjusting the polling intervals of the SQL resources.

The "Looks Alive" polling interval for the SQL Server resource defaults to 5000 milliseconds (SQL Server and SQL Server Agent). This is the frequency of the polling by cluster services of SQL Server to see if it appears to be alive. If it has failed for any reason (like it is not available from the network any more), it would *not* appear to be alive and a fail-over would be automatically initiated. The default "Looks Alive" polling interval for the Distributed Transaction Coordinator resource is 60,000 milliseconds since it is not as critical as the server itself.

The "Is Alive" polling interval reflects how often you want Cluster Service to actually check that the resource is "active." This can usually be a much longer interval time than the Look Alive interval. These defaults are fine to start with, but as you define your service level agreements more precisely, you might want to adjust these polling intervals.

Congratulations! You are now up and running with your SQL Server cluster intact and should now be able to start achieving significantly higher availability for your end-users. As you can see in Figure 5.28, it is very easy to register this new virtual SQL Server (VSQLD-BARCH\VSQLSRV1) within SQL Server Enterprise Manager and completely manage it as you would any other SQL Server instance.

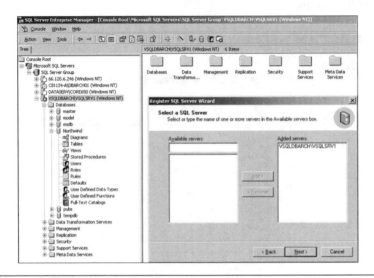

Figure 5.28   Managing the virtual SQL Server from Enterprise Manager.

Removing SQL Clustering

There will be a need to remove your SQL Server 2000 installation from the cluster if you are changing the location of your virtual SQL Server or are just want to reconfigure your existing implementation. This process is fairly easy to do.

CAUTION   This section shows you how to remove SQL Server from the cluster. And, if you follow these steps, it will be removed. Later in this chapter a Client Test Program for a SQL cluster is provided that will require a valid SQL cluster to push against. So, you might not want to remove it just yet if you intend to play with this client test program. It's up to you.

Remember, SQL Server has been installed as a resource that is managed by the cluster. That is where it lives, within the cluster, not on just one node of the cluster. Figure 5.29 shows the SQL Setup wizard dialog and the specification of the virtual server that you are trying to remove from the cluster. Run this from the current active node (COLTST1 as an example). We would want to specify VSQLDBARCH as the virtual SQL Server that we want to remove.

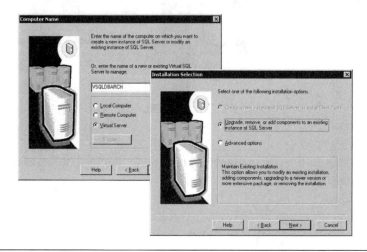

Figure 5.29   SQL Setup wizard for removing SQL Server from a cluster.

The next dialog box (also shown in Figure 5.29) shows the selection to upgrade, remove, or add components to an existing SQL Server instance.

Figure 5.30 shows the instance name that you intend to remove (VSQLSRV1 in this case) along with the Uninstall Your Existing Installation and Administrator Account dialog prompts.

From this point, Setup will perform all necessary tasks to remove SQL Server locally from each node in the cluster and remove all SQL Resources from MSCS. Figure 5.31 shows the messages you will see during this process and the final message of "Successfully uninstalled the instance from the cluster" when it is done.

At the bottom of Figure 5.31, you can see that the cluster group no longer contains the SQL resources. In other words, these have been completely removed and are no longer being managed by the cluster.

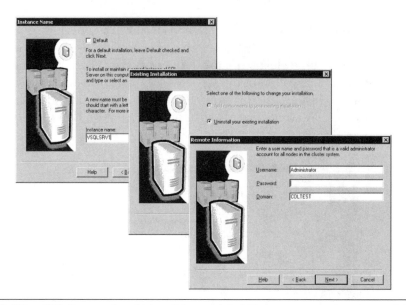

Figure 5.30 SQL Setup wizard identifying which SQL instance to remove and the administrator account to use.

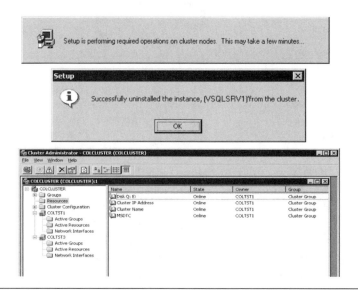

Figure 5.31 Final removal steps for removing SQL Server from the cluster.

Client Test Program for a SQL Cluster

To help in visualizing exactly what effect a SQL Server failure and subsequent fail-over may have on an end-user application, we have created a small test program using Visual Studio .NET 2003. This small C# (pronounced C-sharp) test program accesses the Northwind database that is included with SQL Server, and was created in about 10 minutes. It will display a few columns of data along with a couple of system variables that show connection information. This includes

- CustomerID and CustomerName—A simple two-column display of data from the customer table that meets the selection criteria
- ServerName—The SQL Server name that the client is connected to
- SHOWDATETIME—The date and time (to the millisecond) of the data access
- SPID—The SQL SPID that reflects the connection ID to SQL Server itself by the client application

This type of small program is very useful because the connection that it makes will always be to the virtual SQL Server. This will enable you to see what effect a fail-over will have with your client applications.

To populate this display grid, we will execute the following SQL Statement:

```
SELECT CustomerID, CompanyName, CONVERT (varchar(32),
GETDATE(), 9)
AS SHOWDATETIME, @@SERVERNAME AS servername, @@SPID AS spid
FROM Customers WHERE (CustomerID LIKE 'BERG%')
```

From Visual Studio .NET's point of view, we would simply set up a simple form like the one in Figure 5.32, build a simple button that will retrieve the data from the SQL Server database on the virtual server, and also show the date, time, server name, and SPID information for each access invocation. Figure 5.32 also shows three inset dialog boxes that would appear when setting up the data adapter and SQL Select statement to populate the form.

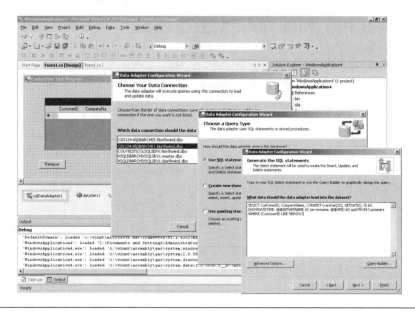

Figure 5.32 Visual Studio .NET 2003 and creating the data adapter to the virtual SQL Server.

As is illustrated in Figure 5.32, you can create a SQL adapter to the virtual SQL Server via the SQL Server Configuration wizard. In our example, the new virtual SQL Server instance will appear in the Choose Your Data Connection dialog box. Select the virtual server that you want this application to connect to (VSQLDBARCH\VSQLSRV1 in this case). Specify that you want to use SQL statements of your own for this SQL adapter connection (second dialog box). Then, drop in the following SELECT statement, and click on the Finish button (as seen in the third dialog box in Figure 5.32). The proper SQL adapter will be generated along with all the C# code needed to invoke and handle errors for this data access.

```
SELECT CustomerID, CompanyName, Convert(varchar(32),
GETDATE(),9) AS SHOWDATETIME,
@@SERVERNAME AS servername, @@SPID AS spid
FROM Customers WHERE (CustomerID LIKE 'BERG%')
```

If you highlight the newly created `sqlConnection` icon at the bottom of the Design panel and right-mouse click, you can view the full properties of this SQL Server connection. Figure 5.33 shows the properties of the `sqlDataAdapter` and the `sqlConnection`. In particular, the `sqlConnection` properties should reflect the correct connection to the new virtual SQL server (data source).

```
workstation id="C81124-A";packet size=4096;user id=sa;
    data source="VSQLDBARCH\VSQLSRV1";
persist security info=False;initial catalog=Northwind
```

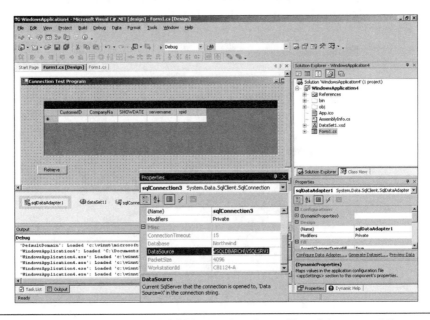

Figure 5.33 Visual Studio .NET 2003 showing the sqlDataAdapter and the sqlConnection properties to the virtual SQL Server.

Now, to verify that your SQL adapter will actually return data to you, simply right-click on the sqlAdapter1 icon and choose the Preview Data option. Figure 5.34 shows this Data Adapter Preview screen for the `sqlAdapter1`. Simply click on the Fill Dataset button on this screen and the result rows should appear in the Results window (only one data row in this case). As you can also see in Figure 5.34, we show you the SQL statement that is being executed that returns the desired result set.

The complete Client Test Program Visual Studio .NET project files will also be available on the Sams website for this title. It is called "WindowsApplication4.csproj" "HAClientTest4" Visual Studio .NET project.

Now, to see this client test program in action, simply hit the F5 key (build and execute) from within Visual Studio .NET, or double-click on the application's executable. At the top of Figure 5.35, you can see the first execution of the client test program. If you click on the Retrieve button, it will update the data grid with a new data access to the virtual SQL Server (as you can see in the servername column), show you the detail datetime information of the data access (in the SHOWDATE-TIME column), and also display the SQL Server process id that it is using for the data access (SPID column). Great; you are now executing a typical C# program against the virtual SQL Server.

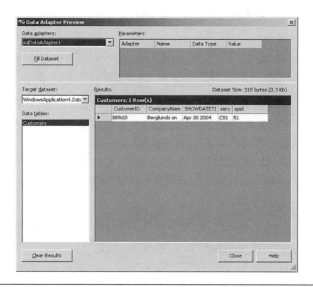

Figure 5.34   Executing the Data Adapter Preview for a `sqlAdapter` within Visual Studio .NET 2003.

Now we want to demonstrate how this high availability approach works, from the client application point-of-view. In order to simulate the failure of the active node, we simply turned off the machine (COLTST1 in this case). We figured this would be the best (and most severe) test case of them all. Once you have simulated a failure, click on the Retrieve button in the client test program again, an unhandled exception occurs (shown in the middle of Figure.5.35). You can view the details of the error message, choose to quit the application, or choose to continue. Just choose Continue for now.

What has happened is the application can no longer connect to the failed SQL Server (because we turned COLTST1 off) and it is still in the middle of failing over to COLTST3. A fail-over will take a short amount of time. This will vary depending on the power and speed of the servers you have implemented and the number of "in-flight" transactions that need to be rolled back or forward at the time of the failure. In our test lab, we usually get a complete SQL fail-over to occur in about 30 to 45 seconds. This is very minor and well within most service level agreements and HA goals. We then simply clicked on the Retrieve button again in the client test program and we're talking to SQL Server again, but now owned by COLTST3. As you can see in the bottom of Figure 5.35, the data connection has returned the customer data, the SHOW-DATETIME has been updated, and the servername still shows the same virtual SQL server name that the application needs to connect to, but the SPID has changed from 57 to 55. This is due to the new connection of the client test program to the newly owned (failed-over) SQL Server. The client test program has simply connected to the newly started SQL Server instance on COLTST3. The unhandled exception (error) goes away and the end-user never knows a complete fail-over occurred. They simply keep processing as usual. Better error handling can be programmed that would not show the "unhandled exception" error. You may want to display a simple error message: "database momentarily unavailable—please try again" would be much more user friendly. That's it for the test program. You can modify this a bit more for your own purposes if you desire.

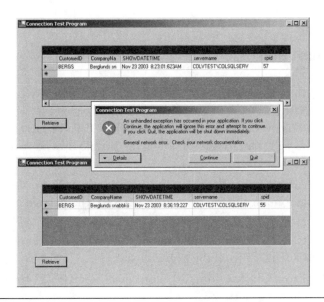

Figure 5.35   Executing the client test program with a real fail-over.

Things to Watch Out For

Many potential issues can arise during setup and configuration for SQL clustering. The following items are some things for you to watch out for:

1. SQL Server service accounts and passwords should be kept the same on all nodes or the node will not be able to restart a SQL Server service. You can use administrator or a designated account (like "cluster") that has administrator rights within the domain and on each server.

2. Drive letters for the cluster disks must be the same on all nodes (servers). Otherwise, you might not be able to access a clustered disk.

3. You might have to create an alternative method to connect to SQL Server if the network name is offline and you cannot connect using TCP/IP. The method is to use named pipes specified as `\\.\pipe\$$\SQLA\sql\query`.

4. Very often, you will run into trouble getting MSCS to install due to hardware incompatibility. Be sure to check Microsoft's hardware compatibility list *before* you venture into this install.

A Node Recovery

Using the same SQL Server clustering example (two-node cluster of COLTST1 and COLTST3), if any failure is caused by a hardware problem on one of the nodes (for example, if COLTST1 has a bad SCSI card) then you will want to use the following simple procedures to resolve this issue:

1. After COLTST1 (the active node) fails, SQL Server 2000 should automatically fail-over to COLTST3 (the passive node).

2. Once you have determined that there is a hardware problem on COLTST1, you should run SQL Server Setup and remove COLTST1 from the SQL Cluster.

3. From Cluster Administrator, "evict" COLTST1 from MSCS (the cluster group).

4. Now, you can install new hardware to replace the failed hardware on COLTST1 and bring it back up.

5. Run MSCS and join (rejoin) the existing cluster.

6. Run the SQL Server Setup on COLTST3 and add COLTST1 back to the SQL cluster (fail-over cluster).

You have done all of these tasks before when you did the initial installation of SQL clustering and MSCS (that we stepped through in Chapter 4 and earlier in this chapter), except for evicting a node from the cluster. There is nothing difficult about evicting a node, though. It simply removes this node from the owner's list of the cluster allowing you to do whatever you need to fix the problem without affecting the availability of your application.

Application Service Provider—Scenario #1 with SQL Clustering

As you may recall from Chapter 3, "Choosing High Availability," the application service provider (ASP) business scenario (scenario #1) yielded a high availability selection of hardware redundancy, shared disk RAID arrays, MSCS, and SQL clustering. Having these four options together clearly met all of their requirements of uptime, tolerance, performance, and costs. The ASP's service level agreement with their customers also allows for brief amounts of downtime to deal with OS upgrades or fixes, hardware upgrades, and application upgrades. The ASP's budget was enough for a larger amount of hardware redundancy to be utilized.

The ASP planned and implemented three separate clusters in order to support their eight major customer applications that are using SQL Server 2000. Each SQL cluster was a two-node cluster configured in the active/passive mode. There customers wanted to make sure that if a failure of a node ever occurred, performance would not be effected. One way to guarantee this is to use the active/passive mode. In other words, since a failed node is not failing over to an active node, there would not be any current processing burden to compete with (that would exist in an active/active configuration). As illustrated in Figure 5.36, each two-node SQL cluster can support between one and three separate customer applications. The ASP established a guideline of never exceeding three applications per SQL cluster to help them mitigate risk overall (and, all of their customers agreed to this approach of minimizing risk). The primary customer application depicted in Figure 5.36 is an online (Internet) health products order entry and distribution system. The HOE database is the main order entry database with between 50 and 150 concurrent SQL Connections. When the ASP someday reaches their tenth major customer application, they will simply create a new 2-node cluster. This is proving to be a very scalable, high-performance, risk mitigating, and cost-effective architecture for them.

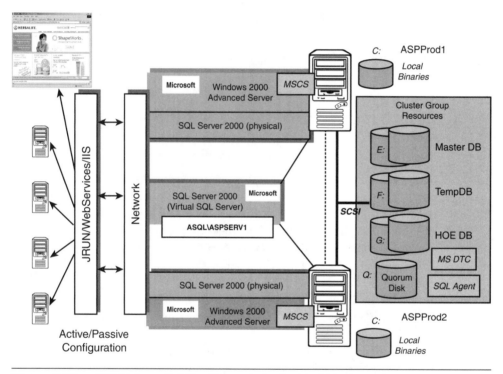

Figure 5.36   ASP high availability "live solution" with SQL clustering.

From an ROI point of view, ROI can be calculated by adding up the incremental costs (or estimates) of the new HA solution and comparing them against the complete cost of downtime for a period of time (one year in our example).

We had previously estimated the total incremental costs to be in the range of between **$100K and $250K**, which included

- Five new four-way servers (with 4GB RAM, local SCSI disk system RAID 10, 2 ethernet NICs, additional SCSI controllers [for shared disk]) at $30K per server

- Five MS Windows 2000 Advanced Server licenses ≈ $3K per server (Windows 2003 Enterprise Edition $4K per server)
- Eighteen SCSI disk systems with RAID 10 (minimum of 6 drives per SCSI disk system, 4 shared SCSI disk systems per cluster— 72 drives in total) ≈ $55K
- Five–seven days of additional training costs for system admin personnel ≈ $15K
- Two new SQL Server licenses (SQL Server 2000, Enterprise Edition) at $5K per server.

Total incremental costs to upgrade to this SQL clustering high availability solution are approximately $245,000 (approximately $81,666 per two-node cluster).

Now, let's work through the complete ROI calculation with these incremental costs along with the cost of downtime:

1. Maintenance cost (for a one year period):
   - $15K (estimate)—yearly system admin personnel cost (additional time for training of these personnel)
   - $25K (estimate)—recurring software licensing cost (of additional HA components; [5]OS + [2]SQL Server 2000)

2. Hardware Cost:
   - $205K hardware cost (of additional HW in the new HA solution)

3. Deployment/Assessment Cost:
   - $20K deployment cost (develop, test, QA, production implementation of the solution)
   - $10K HA Assessment cost

4. Downtime Cost (for a one year period):
   - If you kept track of last year's downtime record, use this number; otherwise produce an estimate of planned and unplanned downtime for this calculation. We estimated the cost of downtime/hour to be **$15K/Hour** for this ASP.
   - Planned downtime cost (revenue loss cost) = Planned downtime hours × cost of hourly downtime to the company:
     a. .25% (estimate of planned downtime percentage in one year) × 8760 hours in a year = 21.9 hours of planned downtime

    b. 21.9 hours (planned downtime) $\times$ $15K/hr (hourly cost of downtime) = $328,500/year cost of planned downtime.

- Unplanned downtime cost (revenue loss cost) = Unplanned downtime hours $\times$ cost of hourly downtime to the company:

    a. .25% (estimate of unplanned downtime percentage in one year) $\times$ 8760 hours in a year = 21.9 hours of unplanned downtime

    b. 21.9 hours $\times$ $15K/hr (hourly cost of downtime) = $328,500/year cost of unplanned downtime.

ROI Totals:

- Total costs to get on this HA solution = $285,000 (for the year—slightly higher than the stated immediate incremental costs)
- Total of downtime cost = $656,000 (for the year)

The incremental cost is 43% of the downtime cost for one year. In other words, the investment of the HA solution will pay for itself in .43 of a year or approximately 5 months! We can see why this ASP didn't blink and eye to get into this HA solution as rapidly as they could.

Summary

We have shown you how easy it is to configure and install both MSCS and SQL Server 2000 for SQL clustering. The 2-node, active/passive node is one of the most common SQL Clustering configurations used. As you become more familiar with SQL clustering and your high availability requirements changed (get closer to five 9s), other more advanced configurations might need to be put into place, such as 4-node SQL clusters and/or data center class clusters (of up to 8-node SQL clusters and active/active variations). If you follow the basic guidelines of disk configurations and database allocations across these disk configurations, as covered in this chapter, you will guarantee yourself a certain level of stability, performance, and scalability. We know money drives many alternatives, so the added exercise of calculating an ROI will help you better understand the impact of your chosen HA solution. For SQL clustering, it is one of the best, cost-effective solutions that is literally "out of the box" with SQL Server and the Windows family of servers.

Also remember, SQL Server 2000 supports other concepts for high availability such as data replication and log shipping. The next two chapters will drill down into these techniques and will highlight when these might be used as opposed to using SQL clustering.

CHAPTER 6

Microsoft SQL Server Log Shipping

THE KEY TOPICS IN THIS CHAPTER ARE

- How Microsoft log shipping works
- Scenario #3 using log shipping
- An ROI calculation example with log shipping

Microsoft Log Shipping Overview

Another, more direct method of creating a completely redundant database image is to use log shipping. Microsoft certifies log shipping as a method of creating an "almost" hot spare. Some folks even use log shipping as an alternative to data replication. Log shipping used to be referred to as "poor man's replication" when replication was an add-on product. Now that they are both included in the box, neither one is really any more expensive to implement than the other. Actually, replication can be cheaper to implement, as it is available in the Standard Edition, while log shipping officially is only available in the Enterprise Edition. Log shipping is comprised of three primary functions:

- Makes an exact image copy of a database on one server (the source server) from a database dump
- Creates a copy of that database on one or more other servers from that dump (these are called destinations)

- Continuously applies transaction log dumps from that source database to the destination databases (dump, copy, restore sequence)

In other words, log shipping effectively replicates the data of one server (the source) to one or more other servers (the destinations) via transaction log dumps. Destination servers are read only. Figure 6.1 shows a typical log shipping configuration with two destination pairs. A destination pair is any unique source/destination combination. You can have any number of source/destination pairs. This means that you can have from 1 to N replicated images of a database using log shipping. Then, if the source server should fail, you can upgrade one of the destination servers to become the source server.

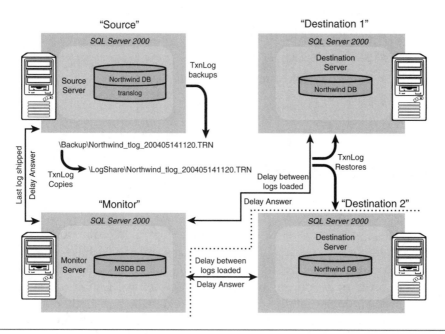

Figure 6.1   Log shipping with two "read only" destination servers and a separate monitor server.

As you can see in Figure 6.1, log shipping also uses a monitor server to help keep track of the current state of the log shipping. The monitor server is another SQL Server instance. A couple of jobs will be created under the SQL Server Agent on the monitor server. In addition, several tables in the MSDB database are used exclusively for keeping the log shipping information (these tables all begin with "log_shipping_"). The monitor server will keep track of when the last log was shipped from the source database to the destinations, keep track of the delays between the logs that get loaded on the destinations, and provide the answer of whether the delays are being exceeded or not.

Data Latency and Log Shipping

Determining the right delays to specify depends on the data latency you can tolerate and how quickly you need to be notified when log shipping breaks down. Your high availability service level agreement will dictate this to you. If there is a breakdown in log shipping, such as the loads on the destination are not being done or are taking longer than what has been set up, the monitor server will generate alerts. It is a good general practice to isolate the monitor server to a separate server by itself so that this critical monitoring of log shipping is not affected if the source server or any destination servers fail (as also seen in Figure 6.1).

Design Note

You can set up log shipping to work entirely within a single SQL Server instance if you wish or between SQL Server instances on the same server. In this case, the source, destination, and monitor server could all reside on the same server machine. I'm not sure what purpose this would serve from a high availability or fail-over point of view; however, there is no restriction in this respect.

The amount of data latency that exists between the source and destination database images is the main determining factor in understanding the state of your recoverability and fail-over capabilities. You will need to set up these data latency (delay) values as part of the log shipping configuration.

However, the gating factors for using log shipping as the method of creating and maintaining a redundant database image are

- Data latency—The time that exists between the frequency of the transaction log dumps on the source database and when these dumps get applied to the destination DBs.
- Sources and destinations must be the same SQL Server version (and must be Enterprise Editions).

- Data is read-only on the destination SQL Server until the log shipping pairing is broken (as it should be to guarantee that the translogs can be applied to the destination SQL Server).

The data latency restrictions might quickly disqualify log shipping as a fool-proof high availability solution though. However, log shipping might be adequate for certain HA situations. If a failure ever occurs on the primary SQL Server, a destination SQL Server that was created and maintained via log shipping can be swapped into use at a moment's notice. It would contain exactly what was on the source SQL Server (right down to every user id, table, index, and file allocation map, except for any changes to the source database that occurred after the last log dump that was applied). This directly achieves a level of high availability. It is still not quite completely transparent, though, since the SQL Server instance names are different and the end-user may be required to log in again to the new SQL Server instance. But, unavailability is usually minimal.

Design and Administration Implications of Log Shipping

From a design and administration point of view, you need to consider some important aspects associated with log shipping:

- User IDs and their associated permissions will be copied as part of log shipping. They will be the same at all servers, which might or might not be what you want. If you are going to create the database on the destination servers first you can use the special Data Transformation Services (DTS) task to transfer logins from the source server to the destination server.
- Log shipping has no filtering. You cannot vertically or horizontally limit the data that will be log shipped.
- Log shipping has no data transformation. No summarizations, format changes, or things like this are possible as part of the log shipping mechanism.
- Data latency will exist. The amount of latency is dependent upon the frequency of transaction log dumps being performed at the source and when they can be applied to the destination copies.
- Sources and destinations must be the same SQL Server version.
- All tables, views, stored procedures, functions, and so on will be copied.

- Indexes cannot be tuned in the copies to support the read-only reporting requirements.
- Data is read-only (until log shipping is turned off).

If these restrictions are not going to cause you any trouble and your high availability requirements dictate a log shipping solution, then you can proceed with confidence in leveraging this Microsoft capability.

Design Note

Log shipping in MS SQL Server 2000 is pretty stable now, but it will eventually be deprecated (dropped from SQL Server). It will still be available in Yukon (SQL Server 2005). In addition, a new option will be introduced called Database Mirroring (once called Real Time Log Shipping [RTLS]). Database Mirroring will dynamically, without latency, apply all source database changes to any destination databases as part of a single managed transaction. This effectively guarantees that any destination database is an up-to-date exact image of the source database and can be used as a complete fail-over option. This will be a true "hot spare." This type of high availability option is headed into a new level of capability! But rest assured, for those of you who choose log shipping now, it will serve you well for years to come (until which time it is deprecated), so don't hesitate in getting into the log shipping business right now. It works well.

Setting Up Log Shipping

In order to use log shipping for a high availability solution, you should plan on having at least three separate servers available. One server is the "source" SQL Server from which you will identify a database to log ship from. Another server will be the "destination" SQL Server that is the target of the log shipping and will be your secondary server for fail-over. And finally, the third server will be the "monitor" SQL Server that keeps track of the log shipping tasks and timeliness. We are assuming that you are using the FULL recovery model (or BULK-LOGGED) for database backup, since this creates transactions in the transaction log that will be the source of log shipping. If you choose the SIMPLE recovery model, there would be nothing to log ship, since the transaction log would be truncated on a regular basis. In fact, the log shipping option would not even be available for any database that has chosen this recovery model.

Before Creating the Log Shipping DB Maintenance Plan

As part of setting up log shipping from Enterprise Manager, we must first register all SQL Server instances that will be used in the log shipping model. It should be noted that if you want to use Enterprise Manager to do the log shipping setup, it can only be used to log ship to disks. Log shipping can be setup to ship to tape as well (backup-to-tape option), but this must be done via manual scripts for copying and restoring the transaction logs (and isn't done much these days anyways).

Design Note

When you configure a database for log shipping, a database maintenance plan is created and a row is inserted in the "msdb..sysdbmaintplans" system table. Then, the following jobs are created:

- A job for database backup (if you have specified one on the source server).
- A job for transaction log backups (on the source server).
- Two jobs for log shipping alerts (on the monitor server).
- Two jobs are created on the destination server for copying and loading the transaction log.
- The entries for these jobs are made in the "msdb..sysjobs" system table. On the destination server there will be a transaction log backup job, but it is disabled until you execute a role change (make the destination the source server).

You should also make sure that each SQL Server instance has its corresponding SQL Server Agent running, since tasks will be created on each SQL Server instance and won't get executed unless the SQL Server Agent is running. The login that you use to start the MS SQL Server and SQL Server Agent services must have administrative access to the log shipping plan jobs, the source server, and the destination server. The user who sets up log shipping must be a member of the SYSADMIN server role, which gives them permission to modify the database to do log shipping.

Next, you will need to create a network share on the primary server where the transaction log backups will be stored. This is done so that the transaction log backups can be accessed by the log shipping jobs (tasks). This is especially important if you use a directory that is different from the default backup location. This would take the form

```
"\\SourceServerXX\NetworkSharename"
```

Using the DB Maintenance Plan Wizard to Create Log Shipping

Now you are ready to begin the log shipping setup process. Microsoft has placed this capability within the database maintenance plan feature. As you can see in Figure 6.2, to create a maintenance plan that includes log shipping, you will have to right-click on the database that will become the "source" of the log shipping, choose the All Tasks option, and then the Maintenance Plan item. This initiates the Database Maintenance Plan Wizard.

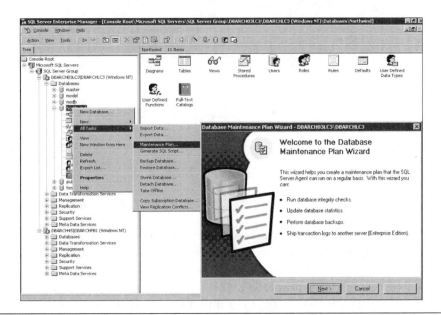

Figure 6.2   Initiating the Database Maintenance Plan Wizard from Enterprise Manager.

Setting Up Log Shipping Using Northwind Database

For simplicity, we will create a maintenance plan for the Northwind database that is shipped with SQL Server 2000. This will also allow you to replicate this example very easily. Be sure to set the Northwind databases recovery model to be "Full" so that the Ship the Transaction Logs check box will be available.

As you can see in Figure 6.3, you will have to identify the database that you wish to create a maintenance plan for (Northwind) and specify if you will be using log shipping. Once you select the log shipping option, you will be presented with many different log shipping related dialogs to complete. These are very different from the usual maintenance plan dialogs that you are probably used to seeing.

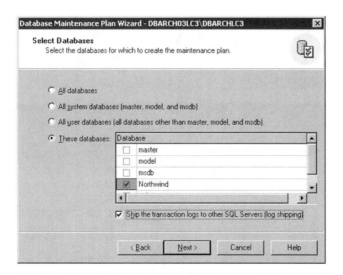

Figure 6.3   Indicate that you will be doing log shipping for this database.

Since this is a database maintenance plan, the next few dialogs are for the usual maintenance plan items. You might already have an existing database maintenance plan for your production database. If this is the case, we would recommend that you create a separate (new) one that is dedicated to doing log shipping only. If this is the only database maintenance plan for this database, go ahead and specify the normal backup options as you would for any production database. Then, there are a few other dialogs that are for specifying the data optimization update options, the database integrity checking options, a regularly scheduled database backup, and the location for the database backups (BACKUP directory is the default). In addition, you will be prompted to specify the location of the transaction log backups as part of this database maintenance plan. If you use a directory that is different from the default backup location, you must share that directory so that it can be accessed by the log shipping jobs.

Long Shipping and Disk Space

This may affect high availability. The directory location you specify for your transaction log dumps should be large enough to accommodate a very long period of dump activity. You may want to consider using the *Remove Files Older Than* option, which will delete backup files from the source servers transaction log directory after a specified amount of time has elapsed. But, remember, disk space is not endless. This will fill up eventually unless you specify something for this option.

Specifying the Network Share Location for Log Shipping

Up to this point, all of the dialogs are the standard dialogs for any database maintenance plan. Figure 6.4 shows the first new dialog for log shipping that requires you to identify a network share location where the transaction logs will be created (stored). This should be that network share location that was previously set up (in the form of "\\SourceServerXX\NetworkSharename").

Identifying the Destination Database for Log Shipping

The next set of dialogs in the maintenance plan wizard specify the destination server (or servers if you intend to create more than one log shipping destination). The initial Log Shipping Destinations dialog (as seen in Figure 6.5 upper left) starts out with no destination servers identified. You simply click on the Add button at the bottom of this dialog and you will be presented with a full screen Add Destination Database dialog (as seen in Figure 6.5 right).

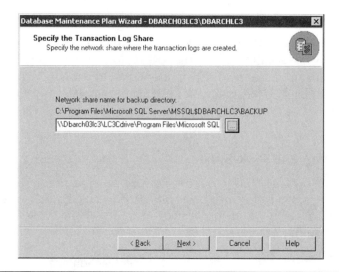

Figure 6.4   Identify the network share name for the transaction log dumps that are to be used by log shipping.

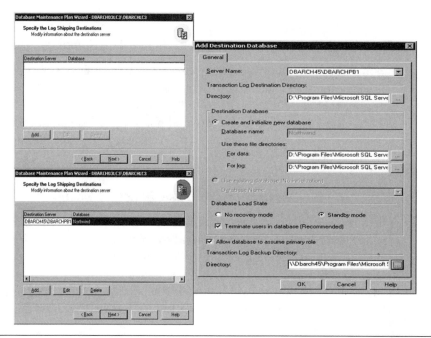

Figure 6.5   Specifying the destination server and database for log shipping.

You start by specifying the server name and SQL Server instance that will be the target of the log shipping (DBARCH45\DBARCHPB1 SQL Server instance in this example). Next, you must identify the transaction log directory on the destination side. This can be the default BACKUP directory on that destination server or any other destination server specific subdirectory. When the destination database is initialized, you can have the wizard fully create the database or use an existing database that you have created manually (for this example, you need to drop the Northwind database on the destination server side first, since you will be having the wizard create a new database with that name). If you have the wizard create the database, remember that this may take a while if the database is large. In the case of a very large database (greater than a terabyte), you should use a full database dump and incremental transaction log dumps to restore to a point in time for this initialization. As you can see in Figure 6.5, we have clicked on the radio button to have the wizard create and initialize a new database for us. As part of this specification, we need to specify valid data and log file directories that correspond to your production file location standards (if you have standards). In our example this will be the SQL Server default locations.

In the case of large databases (or if you just prefer to manually create the destination database yourself), you choose the "existing" database option (this is greyed out in Figure 6.5). When choosing this existing database option, the destination database must be already in standby mode and must be an exact image of the source database from a schema and user id's point of view.

Specifying the Database Load State for Log Shipping

The database load state identifies how a destination database (the target of the log shipping process) is to be managed during data loads.

- NORECOVERY mode indicates that this destination database is not available for use. The destination database will be in NORECOVERY mode as the result of either the RESTORE LOG or RESTORE WITH NORECOVERY operations. When and if the source server fails, the mode for this destination database will be changed so that it can be used.

- STANDBY mode is the indication that this destination database is available for use, but in read-only mode. The destination database will be placed in STANDBY mode as the result of either the RESTORE LOG or RESTORE DATABASE WITH STANDBY operations.

Our example will allow for read-only access to this destination database by specifying the "standby" mode option. You should also specify the "terminate users in database" option, since any restore operation (of transaction logs) will fail if any users are connected to the destination database. This might seem a bit abrupt, but it is critical to keeping the database intact and an exact image of the source database. The users can re-establish their connection to this destination database once the restore process is completed (which is usually very quickly). As we specify the frequency of these restores, the usage of this destination database as a secondary data access point will need to be considered (like for reporting, and so on).

Will This Destination Database Assume the Primary Role?

If you intend to use this destination database as a fail-over database, you must specify that it can assume the role of the source database (the primary). Once you have selected this option, you must indicate the destination server transaction log share name which will be used to store the transaction logs that will be created once this secondary server becomes the source server (has assumed the primary role). Again, this share should be in the form of

```
"\\DestinationServerXX\NetworkSharename"
```

Initializing the Destination Database for Log Shipping

Since we have chosen to create the destination database from scratch, a database dump will be used as the method to create the destination database. As you can see in Figure 6.6 (in the upper left), the Initialize the Destination Databases dialog prompts you to select either to perform a database dump right now, or to use an existing database dump that was done recently for this destination database initialization. In our example, we will specify that a dump be done immediately. If you had chosen to use an existing database backup, the wizard would only list the backups that were done on the current source server. And, when you use an existing database backup, the database backup file must reside in a directory other than the one you are using to store the log shipping backup.

Log Shipping Schedule

After the initialization of the database information is specified, the log shipping schedule has to be established based on your particular needs (your high availability requirements). The default backup schedule is every day, every 15 minutes, as also seen in Figure 6.6 (the dialog on the right is the summary of the log shipping schedule; the dialog on the bottom is the detail job schedule specification that you will see if you need to change the schedule values).

The default backup schedule might not be what you want. If you are using the destination database for reporting purposes, you should adjust this backup schedule (and the associated copy/load frequency, load delay, and file retention period) to reflect your reporting needs.

Design Note

If you are going to use the destination database for reporting, you might want to decrease the frequency of these backups and copy/loads, since the reporting requirements may well tolerate something less frequent.

If the destination server is to be a "hot spare" for fail-over, you might even want to increase the frequency to a few minutes apart for both the backups and the copy/loads.

The default of the load delay is always zero (0). But this too can be adjusted to meet your requirements. Zero delay simply means that the destination server should immediately restore any transaction log backups after they are copied. The *file retention period* is the length of time that the transaction logs are retained on the destination server before they are deleted. The length of time you specify should consider the available disk space. Watch out: These directories fill up rather quickly. And, we already showed you how you can use the Remove Files Older Than option (which deletes backup files from the primary server after a specified amount of time has elapsed).

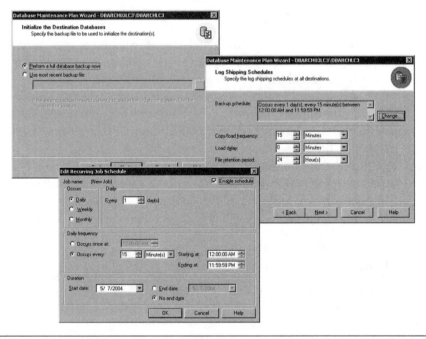

Figure 6.6   Initializing the destination database and specifying the log shipping
schedule values.

Setting Up the Monitor Server and Alerts for Log Shipping

After the destination database schedule has been specified, it is now
time to provide the information for monitoring and alerts. In particular,
you must identify the log shipping thresholds for the Backup Alerts and
for the Out of Sync Alerts. The monitor server will own these jobs
(tasks). The Backup Alert threshold is the maximum elapsed time since
the last transaction log backup occurred on the source server. In other
words, an alert will be generated if the monitor server detects that no
transaction log backup has occurred on the source server within the
threshold value. This makes the most sense to monitor, since these transaction log backups drive the entire log shipping model. As you can see in
Figure 6.7, the default is 45 minutes, but adjust this to fit your monitoring needs. The Out of Sync Alert threshold is the maximum elapsed time
between the last transaction log backup on the source server and the last
transaction log restore on the destination server. In other words, if the
subsequent restore on the destination server side has not happened

within the specified threshold, there is likely a problem on the destination server side. Both alerts are written to the Windows event log and to the SQL Server error logs.

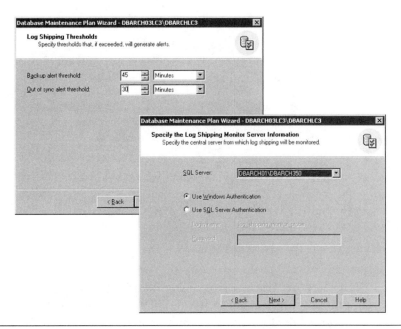

Figure 6.7   Log shipping alert thresholds and monitor server information.

You must now specify the log shipping monitor server information. As previously recommended, use a separate server and SQL Server instance to be your monitor server for risk mitigation purposes. If your source server (primary) fails for any reason, you want to make sure that monitoring is being done by this other (monitor) server. Then, the monitoring alerts will be generated when these failures start occurring (thresholds are exceeded). If you had put the monitor server on the same server as the source server (which is allowed), you would not receive these alerts if the source server failed. As you can also see in Figure 6.7, you can use either Microsoft Windows authentication or SQL Server authentication depending on the security configuration for your server; however, Microsoft recommends that you use Windows authentication. If you use SQL Server authentication, you can only use the `log_shipping_monitor_probe` login to monitor log shipping. If you use the `log_shipping_monitor_probe` login for other database maintenance plans, you must use the same password. If this is the first time you are using the `log_shipping_monitor_probe` login, you will specify a new password.

Design Note

What is actually happening is the `log_shipping_monitor_probe` login (or Windows Authentication) is used by the source and destination servers to update two log shipping tables in the MSDB database. These tables, `msdb.dbo.log_shipping_primaries` and `msdb.dbo.log_shipping_secondaries`, are continuously being updated when the transaction log is backed up, copied, or restored. You can also directly query these tables yourself if you like. It is as easy as the following select statements:

```
SELECT * from msdb..log_shipping_primaries
WHERE primary_database_name like 'yoursourcedb%'

SELECT * from msdb..log_shipping_secondaries
WHERE secondary_database_name like 'yourdestinationdb%'
```

The Reports to Generate dialog identifies where the maintenance plan's text reports are to be written. These reports will include a text description of the log shipping issues or alerts that may have occurred. It is also possible to have these reports sent to an email address. If you choose to have reports generated, specify to delete text reports older than some time period (like four weeks).

Then, as you can see in Figure 6.8 (top left), the Maintenance Plan History dialog prompts you for how and where you want the maintenance plan records to be stored. In keeping with the risk mitigation approach for high availability, we always choose to have the maintenance records written to a remote server in addition to the local server. In this example, it would be the monitor server (DBARCH01\DBARCH350). All maintenance plan records are inserted into the `msdb..sysdbmaintplan_history` table. After you have specified the Maintenance Plan History values, a summary of all plan steps will be shown (Figure 6.8 top right) that describes what will be done with which database on which SQL Server instance in your log shipping configuration, and you will be able to name the maintenance plan (for future reference). Figure 6.8 bottom left shows the status of each step that will be executed to fully initialize log shipping. This includes the initial database backup, the creation of the destination database, and all database plan creations. Once this has completed, log shipping should be active. A quick look at the database properties of the Northwind database on the source server should show you the log shipping role and monitor server that was configured to monitor for this log shipping pair (as seen in Figure 6.8 bottom right).

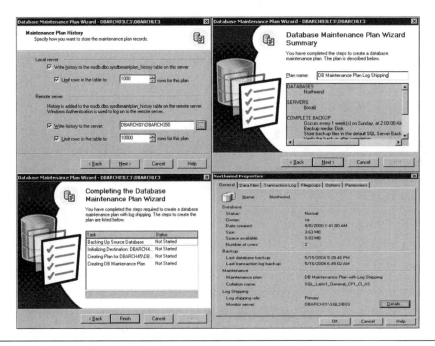

Figure 6.8 Log shipping maintenance plan history (left top), maintenance plan summary (right top), completing the wizard (left bottom), and database properties of a fully configured database with log shipping (right bottom).

Completing Setup of Log Shipping and a Few Potential Issues

If the log shipping source database is a large database, the database initialization will take a while. Once the final process steps have completed, a successfully created maintenance plan dialog box appears. If there were problems on any of these steps, you will see these now. The most common errors are usually related to the copy and restore operations. Very often, the network share becomes unavailable or disconnected. This will result in a copy error to the destination transaction log backup directory (share). After you have re-established this share, everything will work fine. If the maintenance plan tasks end without success because of one or more errors, you may have to "clean up" some of the MSDB log shipping table entries manually. If you simply back up in the wizard and start over, many of the log shipping entries in the log shipping tables will not have been removed. Use the queries identified previously to look to see what needs to be cleaned up and delete the appropriate rows (only the ones that related to the current plan being created). These tables are

```
log_shipping_databases
log_shipping_monitor
log_shipping_plan_databases
log_shipping_plan_history
log_shipping_plans
log_shipping_primaries
log_shipping_secondaries
```

You will not find entries in all tables in all SQL Servers in your topology. Only the tables that are needed by each servers functions will have rows. So, don't be alarmed.

During the setup steps, SQL Server and the SQL Agent must be running under a user account that has permissions to use the network shares. If the setup attempt failed because the SQL Server service account that you are using didn't have access to the share name on the source server, you won't get a chance to back up in the wizard and fix it. The wizard exits and you will have to start all over.

Viewing Log Shipping Properties

Once the maintenance plan wizard has finished and the database maintenance plan has been created successfully (which we just completed in the prior section), you will be able to see the destination database and its new log shipping related properties. Figure 6.9 (top left) shows the Enterprise Manager view of the newly created destination database in its "Read-Only" state. If you try to access this database and if a log restore operation is still in progress, you will get an error message telling you of this failed access attempt. Remember, we specified to have all database connections terminated during these transaction log loads.

Once these are completed, you can freely access all tables in this new, log shipped, destination database. If you right-click on this new database, you will see the added properties of log shipping at the bottom of the General tab (as illustrated in the middle dialog box of Figure 6.9). This identifies the role that this database is serving (secondary server role in this case), which server is the monitor server, and that this database is in the StandBy status. If you click on the Details button in the Log Shipping section of this dialog box, you will see the connection information being used for the monitor server and the detail information of the log shipping role (Figure 6.9 right dialog box).

As you can also see in the Log Shipping Details dialog box of Figure 6.9, you can remove this database from log shipping by clicking on the Remove Log Shipping button. One place this comes into play is when you need to delete the entire maintenance plan that you just created (which contains log shipping). You will have to remove the destination databases from log shipping first. Then, and only then, can you delete the maintenance plan.

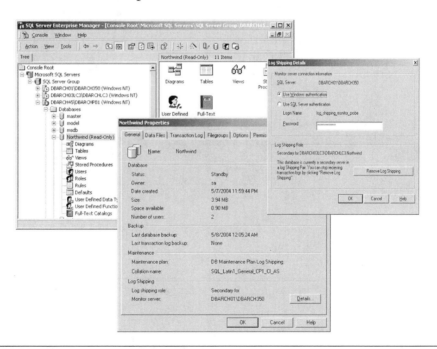

Figure 6.9 The destination database from Enterprise Manager and its log shipping properties.

Monitor Server Properties

From the monitor server's point of view, it now shows a new branch under the Management options called Log Shipping Monitor. Any source/destination pair that this monitor server is monitoring will appear here. In our example, this was a separate monitor server (SQL Server). Figure 6.10 shows this new branch and the current source/destination pair. In addition, you can see the current history of both the backups and the restores by simply choosing either of the view options. As you can also see, the current log shipping pair is "in sync". This means that there are no failures and the pair is busily log shipping to each other. Remember, a log shipping pair is assigned for each source and destination database that you define log shipping for. If you use log shipping to send the source database to two destination databases, there will be two log shipping pairs.

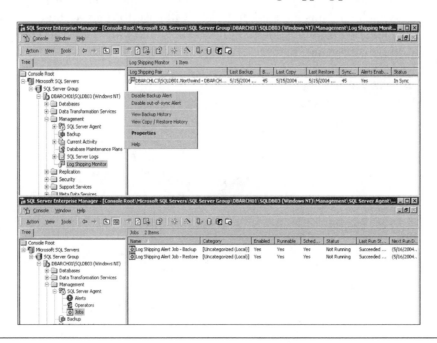

Figure 6.10 Monitor server source/destination pairs and the SQL Server Agent Backup/Restore Alert Jobs.

Figure 6.10 also shows the SQL Server Agent jobs that got created on the monitor server (and, as you remember, the monitor server is just a SQL Server instance that is being used to monitor log shipping). These are the jobs that are managing the Backup and Copy/Load Alert thresholds. If any of these thresholds are exceeded, these jobs will notify the system of these failures via event logs, emails, and so on.

Deleting Log Shipping

If you want to delete log shipping from the maintenance plan, you can go to the properties of the maintenance plan and select the Log Shipping tab. Select the destination server you want to remove from log shipping and click the Delete Log Shipping button.

To see which databases are associated with which maintenance plans, you can run this query:

```
SELECT b.database_name, a.plan_name
FROM msdb..sysdbmaintplans as a,
    msdb..log_shipping_databases as b
WHERE b.maintenance_plan_id  = a.plan_id
```

On this properties dialog you can also update log shipping information like schedules, user accounts, and so on for a destination server/database, as well as add new destination server/database entries. Figure 6.11 shows a complete history view of the transaction log backups that are being generated on the source server side. As you can also see in Figure 6.11, each transaction log backup execution is posted to the system event log (event ID 17055).

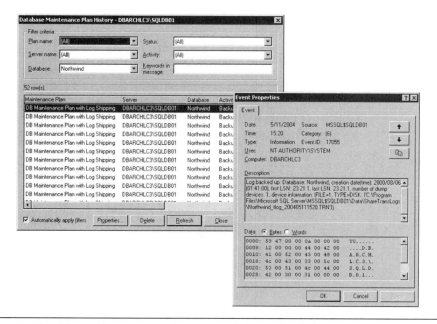

Figure 6.11   View of transaction log backup history (top) and Event Viewer (bottom)—Event ID 17055.

Changing the Primary Role

If you had selected to allow your database to assume the primary role and your source (primary) server/database fails, you can easily upgrade your destination (secondary) server to be the current source (primary) server. This is truly an upgrade. You will be upgrading the destination server to a source server (primary).

1. Make sure your logins/user ids are defined in the destination server. Normally, if you intend the destination to act as a fail-over database, you will be regularly synchronizing the SQL Server logins and user IDs anyway. The special Data Transformation Services (DTS) task to transfer logins from a source server to a destination server should be used. Double-check that each login has the proper role that was present in the source database. This is probably the place that causes the most headaches during a primary role change (getting the logins sync'd, that is).

2. If the source SQL Server is still functioning, issue the following command to start the role change:

```
EXEC msdb..sp_change_primary_role
@db_name = 'sourcedbnamexxx',
@backup_log = 1, -- backup the log
@terminate = 0,  -- do not terminate user
@final_state = 1, -- recovery state
@access_level = 1 -- multi-user
```

This essentially informs the primary server that the source database is not going to be the primary any longer. If it is not available because it has failed, then proceed to the destination server side.

3. On the destination server (the secondary), you must run the following commands to upgrade it to become the source server (primary):

```
EXEC msdb..sp_change_secondary_role
@db_name = 'destinationdbnamexxx',
@do_load = 1, -- load available trans logs before switch
@force_load = 1, -- Load everything and ignore
➡the load_delay
@final_state = 1, -- recovery state
@terminate = 1,  -- terminate user
@access_level = 1, -- multi-user
@keep_replication = 0, -- false
@stopat = null -- valid datetime if needed
```

4. Now, just run this last command on the monitor server to tell it what the changes are:

```
EXEC msdb..sp_change_monitor_role
@primary_server = 'source serverxxx', -- old server name
@secondary_server = 'destination serverxxx', -- new
➥server name
@database = 'databasenamexx', -- database name
@new_source = 'new source share' -- new source share name
```

CAUTION   Remember, when you indicated that the destination server could be used as a primary, you had to specify a share name for the destination server's transaction logs (to be used in this event).

Okay, now the original destination server should be functioning as the current source server (primary). The old source server (primary) is no longer part of the log shipping topology.

Log Shipping System Stored Procedures

The system stored procedures that relate to log shipping are

- `sp_add_log_shipping_database`—Add a new log shipping database.
- `sp_delete_log_shipping_database`—Delete an existing database from log shipping.
- `sp_add_log_shipping_plan`—Add a log shipping plan.
- `sp_delete_log_shipping_plan`—Delete an existing log shipping plan.
- `sp_add_log_shipping_plan_database`—Add a database to the log shipping plan.
- `sp_delete_log_shipping_plan_database`—Delete an existing database from a log shipping plan.
- `sp_add_log_shipping_primary`—Identify (add) the log shipping primary server.
- `sp_delete_log_shipping_primary`—Delete an existing log shipping primary server.
- `sp_add_log_shipping_secondary`—Identify (add) the log shipping secondary server (the destination).

- `sp_delete_log_shipping_secondary`—Delete an existing secondary server.

- `sp_can_tlog_be_applied`—Verify whether the transaction logs can be applied to a destination.

- `sp_get_log_shipping_monitor_info`—Find out the log shipping status for a source/destination pair.

- `sp_change_monitor_role`—Performs the role change on the monitor server of the current secondary to the primary role.

- `sp_remove_log_shipping_monitor`—Removes the existing monitor server for log shipping.

- `sp_change_primary_role`—Removes the current primary server from the log shipping plan.

- `sp_resolve_logins`—Resolves logins from a login file (filename). This can be used as part of the primary role change.

- `sp_change_secondary_role`—Changes the role of the secondary (destination) server to the primary (source) server.

- `sp_update_log_shipping_monitor_info`—Updates the monitoring information for a source/destination pair.

- `sp_create_log_shipping_monitor_account`—Specifies the creation of the `log_shipping_monitor_probe` account.

- `sp_update_log_shipping_plan`—Updates log shipping plan information.

- `sp_define_log_shipping_monitor`—Sets up the log shipping monitor account on the monitor server.

- `sp_update_log_shipping_plan_database`—Updates an existing database that is part of a log shipping plan.

It is possible to add log shipping to an existing database maintenance plan entirely via these system stored procedures. The easiest way to get a template skeleton is to turn profiler on and run through one full database maintenance wizard with log shipping. Then, save these as a manual backup for creating log shipping via scripts. The trickiest part is the plan IDs, since they are unique IDs that are assigned at creation time.

Call Before You Dig—Scenario #4 with Log Shipping

As you saw in Chapter 3, "Choosing High Availability," the call before you dig business scenario (scenario #4) combined hardware redundancy, shared disk RAID arrays, MSCS, SQL clustering, and log shipping. This is a very critical system during its planned hours of operation, but has low performance goals, and low cost of downtime (when it is down). Regardless, it is highly desirable for this system to be up and running as much as possible. Having that warm standby with log shipping provides just enough of an insurance policy in case the whole SQL cluster configuration fails. After building this HA solution, the uptime goal was achieved easily. In fact, after three months, the log shipping configuration was disabled. Two days after the log shipping was disabled, the whole SQL cluster configuration failed (Murphy's law). The log shipping was rebuilt and this configuration has remained in place since then. Performance has been exceptional and this application continuously achieves its availability goals! Figure 6.12 shows the current HA solution with log shipping. The availability that this application requires is

- 15 hours per day (5:00 a.m.–8:00 p.m.)
- 6 days per week (closed on Sunday)
- 312 days per year.

Planned Downtime: **0%**
Unplanned Downtime: **.5%** (less than 1%) will be tolerable
The ROI for the call before you dig scenario is calculated as follows:
We had previously estimated the total incremental costs to be in the range of between **$10K and $100K**, which included

- Three new four-way servers (with 4GB RAM, local SCSI disk system RAID 10, two ethernet NICs, additional SCSI controller [for shared disk]) at $25K per server
- Two MS Windows 2000 Advanced Server licenses ~ $3K per server (Windows 2003 Enterprise Edition $4K per server)
- One Shared SCSI disk system with RAID 5 (minimum of 10 drives per SCSI disk system) ~ $5K
- Four–five days of additional training costs for system admin personnel ~ $12K
- Two new SQL Server licenses (SQL Server 2000, Enterprise Edition) at $5K per server

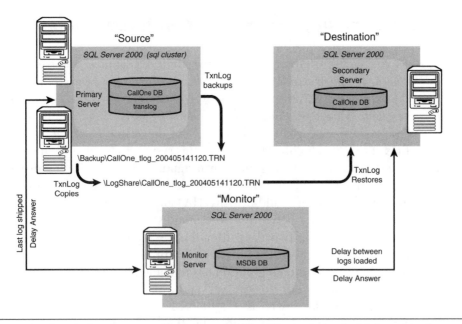

Figure 6.12 Call before you dig high availability "live solution" with log shipping.

Total incremental costs to upgrade to this SQL clustering with log shipping high availability solution is approximately $108,000. Just slightly over the earlier estimates.

Now, let's work through the complete ROI calculation with these incremental costs along with the cost of downtime:

1. Maintenance cost (for a one-year period):
   - $12K (estimate)—yearly system admin personnel cost (additional time for training of these personnel)
   - $16K (estimate)—recurring software licensing cost (of additional HA components; (2) OS + (2) SQL Server 2000)

2. Hardware cost:
   - $80K hardware cost (of additional HW in the new HA solution)

3. Deployment/assessment cost:
   - $20K deployment cost (develop, test, QA, production implementation of the solution)
   - $10K HA assessment cost

4. Downtime cost (for a one-year period):

- If you kept track of last year's downtime record, use this number; otherwise produce an estimate of planned and unplanned downtime for this calculation. We estimated the cost of downtime/hour to be **$2K/Hour.**

- Planned downtime cost (revenue loss cost) = planned downtime hours × cost of hourly downtime to the company. **Should be $0.**

- Unplanned downtime cost (revenue loss cost) = unplanned downtime hours × cost of hourly downtime to the company:

  a. .5% (estimate of unplanned downtime percentage in one year) × 8760 hours in a year = 43.8 hours of unplanned downtime

  b. 43.8 hours × $2K/hr (hourly cost of downtime) = $87,600/year cost of unplanned downtime.

ROI totals:

- Total costs to get on this HA solution = $128,000 (for the year—slightly higher than the immediate incremental costs stated above)

- Total of downtime cost = $87,600 (for the year)

  The incremental cost is about 123% of the downtime cost for one year. In other words, the investment of the HA solution will pay for itself in one year and three months! This is well within the ROI payback they were looking for. And provided a solid HA solution for years to come.

Summary

Log shipping is fairly easy to configure in contrast to data replication or SQL clustering. It also doesn't have many hardware or operating system restrictions other than requiring Enterprise Edition of SQL Server. Log shipping is a good option because it not only provides high availability, but also ensures your data against hardware failures. In other words, if one of the disks on the source (primary) server stops responding, you can still restore the saved transaction logs on the destination (secondary) server and upgrade it to a primary server, with little or no loss of work. Additionally, log shipping does not require that the servers be in close proximity. And, as added benefits, log shipping supports sending transaction logs to more than one secondary server and enables you to offload some of the query processing and reporting needs to these secondary servers.

As indicated earlier, log shipping is not as transparent as things like fail-over clustering because the end-user will not be able to connect to the database for a period of time and users must update the connection information to the new server when it becomes available. And remember, from a data synchronization point of view, you are only able to recover the database up to the last valid transaction log backup, which means that your users may have to redo some of the work that was already performed on the primary server. It is possible to combine log shipping with replication and/or fail-over clustering to overcome some of these disadvantages. Your particular HA requirements may be very well supported with a log shipping model.

CHAPTER 7

Microsoft SQL Server Data Replication

THE KEY TOPICS IN THIS CHAPTER ARE

- Data replication and high availabiltiy
- The publisher, distributor, and subscriber metaphor
- Replication scenarios for high availability
- SQL Server replication types
- Planning for SQL Server data replication
- Building up replication
- Scripting replication
- Failing over to a warm standby subscriber
- HA scenario and replication

Microsoft SQL Server Data Replication Overview

Yes, you can use data replication as a high availability solution! It depends on your HA requirements, though (as usual). Originally Microsoft's SQL Server implementation of data replication was created to offload processing from a very busy server such as an online transaction processing (OLTP) application. Data replication enabled big chunks of processing (like that of reporting) to be isolated "away from" the primary OLTP without having to sacrifice performance. It also was well suited to support naturally distributed data that has very distinct users (such as a geographically oriented order entry system). As data replication became more stable and reliable (post MS SQL Server 6.5's implementation), it could be used to create "warm," almost "hot" standby SQL Servers. If failures ever occurred with the primary server in a replication topology, the secondary (replicate) server would still be able to be used for work. When the failed server was brought back up, the replication of data that had changed would catch up and all of the data could be resynchronized. When doing transactional replication in the "instantaneous replication" mode, data changes on the primary server (publisher) are replicated to one or more secondary servers (subscribers) extremely quickly. This type of replication can essentially create a "warm standby" SQL Server that is as fresh as the last transaction log entries that made it through the distribution server mechanism to the subscriber. And, along the way, there are numerous side benefits such as achieving higher degrees of scalability and mitigating failure risk. Figure 7.1 shows a typical SQL Server data replication configuration that can serve as a basis for high availability and which also fulfills a reporting server requirement (at the same time).

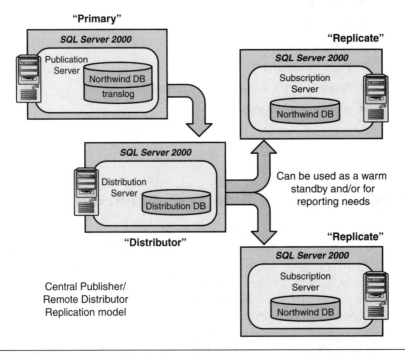

Figure 7.1 Data replication basic configuration for HA.

This particular data replication configuration is a "central publisher, remote distributor" replication model. It maximizes on isolating processing away from the primary server (publisher) including the data distribution mechanism (the distribution server) part of the replication model.

There are a few things to deal with if ever the "replicate" is needed to become the primary server (take over the work from the primary server). Essentially, it takes a bit of administration that is *NOT* transparent to the end-user. Connection strings have to be changed, ODBC data sources need to be updated, and so on. But, this may be something that would take minutes as opposed to hours of potential database recovery time, and may well be tolerable to the end-users. There also exists a risk of not having all of the transactions from the primary server make it over to the replicate (subscriber). Remember, the replicated database will only be as fresh as the last updates that were distributed to it. Often, however, a company is willing to live with this small risk in favor of availability. For databases that are primarily read-only with low to medium data and schema volatility, this is a great way to distribute the load and mitigate risk of failure thus achieving high availability.

What Is Data Replication?

In its classic definition, data replication is based on the "store and forward" data distribution model, as shown in Figure 7.2. Data that is stored in one location (inserted) is automatically "forwarded" to one or more distributed locations.

Of course, a more complete data distribution model would address updates, deletes, data latency, and autonomy for data and schemas. It is this data distribution model that Microsoft's data replication facility serves to implement. There are three primary scenarios for using data replication:

- The first, as you can see in Figure 7.3, is for when you need to offload the processing from the primary server for reporting purposes to a separate reporting server. This server is typically in read-only mode, and contains all the data that is needed to satisfy report requirements.

- Another is for when you need to provide vertical or horizontal subsets of the primary server's data to other servers so that they are working (updating) only their own data. The primary server should contain everyone's data, though. This can directly support high availability. This is common when you need to have your European and Asian users using their own data but corporate headquarters is continuously fed their changes.

- And finally, you could be replicating all data on a server to another server so that if the primary server crashes, users can switch to this fail-over server quickly and continue to work with little downtime or data loss.

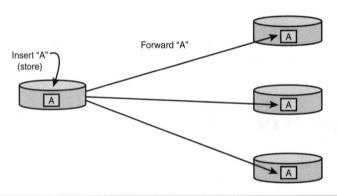

Figure 7.2   Store and forward distribution model.

Each one of these scenarios supports parts (or all) of a high availability solution.

You can use data replication for many reasons. First, however, you need to understand some of the common terms and metaphors used by Microsoft in data replication (as will be described in this chapter).

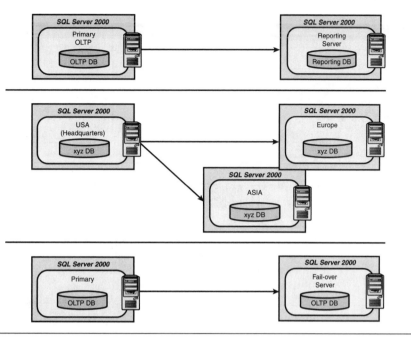

Figure 7.3   Data replication primary scenarios.

The Publisher, Distributor, and Subscriber Metaphor

Any SQL Server can play up to three distinct roles in a data replication environment:

- As a Publication server (the publisher of data)
- As a Distribution server (the distributor of data)
- And, as a Subscription server (the subscriber to the data being published)

The *publication server* contains the database or databases that are going to be published. This is the source of the data that is to be replicated to other servers. In Figure 7.4, the Customers table in the Northwind database is the data to be published. To publish data, the database that contains the data must first be "enabled" for publishing. Full publishing configuration requirements will be discussed later in this chapter in the "Setting Up Replication" section.

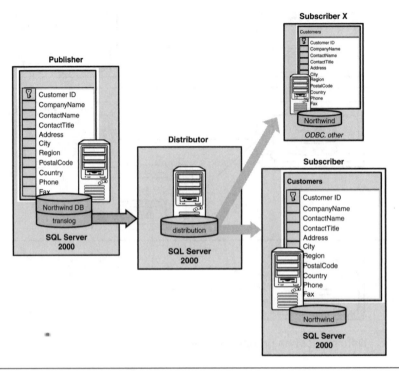

Figure 7.4   The publisher, distributor, and subscriber.

The *distribution server* (distributor) can either be on the same server as the publication server or on a different server—in this case, a remote distribution server. This server will contain the distribution database. This database, also called the store-and-forward database, holds all the data changes that are to be forwarded from the published database to any subscription servers that subscribe to the data. A single distribution server can support several publication servers. The distribution server is truly the workhorse of data replication.

The *subscription server* contains a copy of the database or portions of the database that are being published. The distribution server sends any changes made to a table in a published database to the subscription server's copy of that table. There can be one or more subscribers. SQL Server 2000 also supports heterogeneous subscribers. Pretty much any ODBC or OLE compliant database (such as Oracle) can be a subscriber to data replication.

In early days of SQL Server, data replication would only send the data to the subscription server and then the data would be treated as read-only. In SQL Server 2000, subscribers can make updates, which are then returned to the publisher—known as the updating subscriber. It is important to note that an updating subscriber is not the same as a publisher and requires a special replication configuration.

Along with these distinct server roles, Microsoft utilizes a few more metaphors. These are publications and articles. A *publication* is a group of one or more articles, and is the basic unit of data replication. An *article* is simply a pointer to a single table, or a subset of rows or columns out of a table, that will be made available for replication.

Publications and Articles

A single database can contain more than one publication. You can publish data from tables, database objects, the execution of stored procedures, and even schema objects, such as referential integrity constraints, clustered indexes, non-clustered indexes, user triggers, extended properties, and collation. Regardless of what you plan to replicate, all articles in a publication are synchronized at the same time. Figure 7.5 depicts a typical publication with two articles. You can choose to replicate whole tables, or just parts of tables via filtering.

Filtering Articles

You can create articles on SQL Server in several different ways. The basic way to create an article is to publish all of the columns and rows that are contained in a table. Although this is the easiest way to create articles, your business needs might require that you publish only certain columns or rows out of a table. This is referred to as filtering vertically or horizontally. Vertical filtering filters only specific columns, whereas horizontal filtering filters only specific rows. In addition, SQL Server 2000 provides the added functionality of join filters and dynamic filters. We discuss filtering here because depending on what type of high availability requirements you have, you may need to employ one or more of these techniques within data replication.

As you can see in Figure 7.6, you might only need to replicate a customer's customer ID, company name, and phone number to various subscribing servers around your company (vertical filtering). For this application, the Address data is restricted information and should not be replicated. You can create an article for data replication which contains a subset of the Customers table that will be replicated to these other locations.

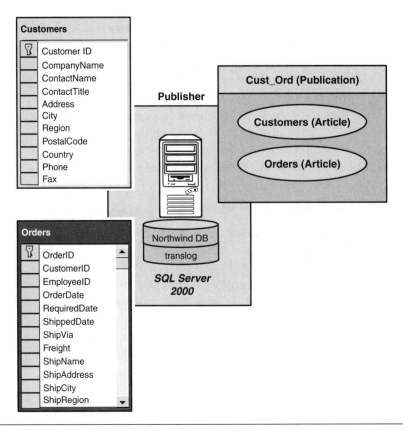

Figure 7.5   Cust_Ord publication (Northwind DB).

In another example, you might need to publish only the Customers table data that is in a specific region, requiring you to geographically partition the data. This process, as shown in Figure 7.7, is known as horizontal filtering.

It is possible for you to combine both horizontal and vertical filtering, as shown in Figure 7.8. This allows you to pare out unneeded columns and rows that aren't required for replication. In our example, we might only need the "west" Region data and only require CustomerID and CompanyName data to be published.

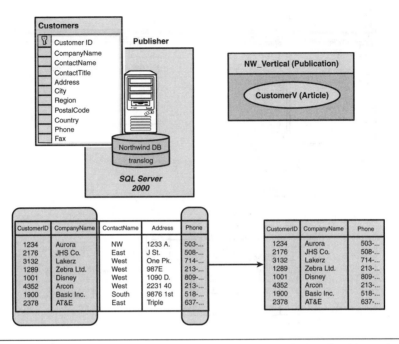

Figure 7.6 Vertical filtering is the process of creating a subset of columns from a table to be replicated to subscribers.

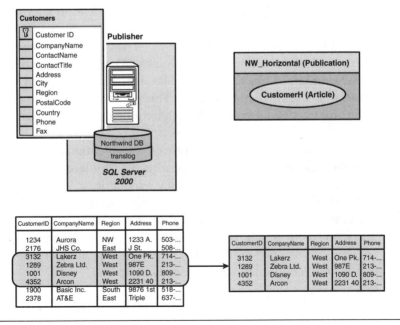

Figure 7.7 Horizontal filtering is the process of creating a subset of rows from a table to be replicated to subscribers.

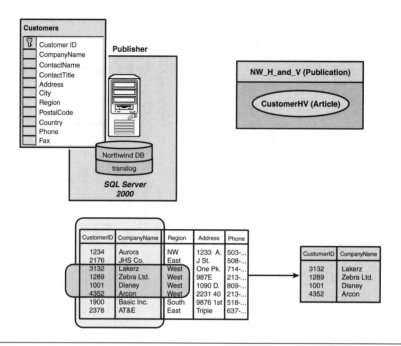

Figure 7.8   Combining horizontal and vertical filtering allows you to pare down the information in an article to only the important information.

As mentioned earlier, it is now possible for you to have join filters. *Join filters* enable you to go one step further for a particular filter created on a table to another. In other words, if you are publishing the Customers table data based on the Region (west), you can extend filtering to the Orders and Order Details tables for the west region customers orders only, as shown in Figure 7.9. This way, you will only be replicating orders for customers in the west to a location that only needs to see that specific data. This can be very efficient if it is done well.

You also can publish "stored procedure executions" as articles, along with their parameters. This can be either a standard procedure execution article or a serializable procedure execution article. The difference is that the latter is executed as a serializable transaction and the other is not. A serializable transaction is a transaction that is being executed with the serializable isolation level, which will place a range lock on the affected data set, preventing other users from updating or inserting rows into the data set until the transaction is complete.

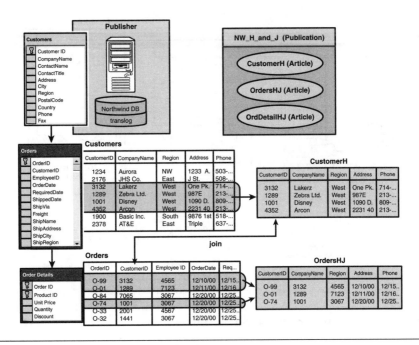

Figure 7.9   Horizontal and join publication.

What publishing stored procedure executions as articles buys you is a major reduction of mass SQL statements being replicated across your network. For instance, if you wanted to update the Customers table for every customer between customerID = 1 and customerID = 5000, the Customers table updates would be replicated as a large multi-step transaction involving 5,000 separate update statements. This would significantly bog down your network. However, with stored procedure execution articles, only the execution of the stored procedure is replicated to the subscription server, and the stored procedure is executed on that subscription server. Figure 7.10 illustrates the difference in execution described earlier. Some subtleties when utilizing this type of data replication processing can't be overlooked, such as making sure that the published stored procedure behaves the same on the subscribing server side. Just to be safe, you should have abbreviated testing scripts that can be run on the subscriber whose results will be verified with the same results on the publisher.

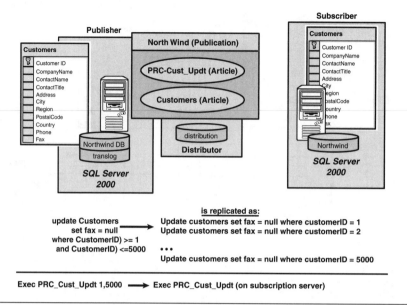

Figure 7.10   Stored procedure execution comparison.

Now, it is essential to learn about the different types of replication scenarios that can be built, and the reasons why any one of these would be desired over the other. It also is worth noting that Microsoft SQL Server 2000 supports replication to and from many different "heterogeneous" data sources. In other words, OLE DB or ODBC data sources can subscribe to SQL Server publications, as well as publish data. This includes a number of data sources, including Microsoft Exchange, Microsoft Access, Oracle, and DB2.

Replication Scenarios

In general, depending on your business requirements, one of several different data replication scenario models can be implemented. These include the following:

- Central publisher
- Central publisher with a remote distributor
- Publishing subscriber
- Central subscriber

- Multiple publishers or multiple subscribers
- Updating subscribers

Central Publisher

The central publisher replication model, as shown in Figure 7.11, is Microsoft's default scenario. In this scenario, one SQL Server performs the function of both publisher and distributor. The publisher/distributor can have any number of subscribers. These subscribers can come in many different varieties, such as SQL Server 2000, SQL Server 7.0, and Oracle.

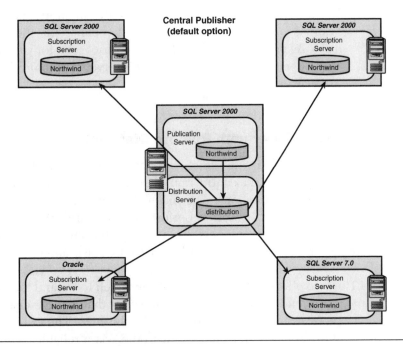

Figure 7.11 The central publisher scenario is a simple and most often used scenario.

The central publisher scenario can be used in the following situations:

- Creation of a copy of a database for ad hoc queries and report generation (classic use)
- Publication of master lists to remote locations, such as master customer lists or master price lists

- Maintenance of a remote copy of an online transaction processing database (OLTP) that could be used by the remote sites during communication outages

- Maintenance of a "spare" copy of an online transaction processing (OLTP) database that could be used as a "hot spare" in case of server failure

However, it's important to consider the following for this scenario:

- If your OLTP server's activity is substantial and affects greater than 10% of your total data per day, then this central publisher scenario is not for you. Other replication configuration scenarios will better fit your needs.

- If your OLTP server is maximized on CPU, memory, and disk utilization, you also should consider another data replication scenario. Again, the central publisher scenario is not for you either. There would be no bandwidth on this server to support the replication overhead.

Central Publisher with Remote Distributor

The central publisher with remote distributor scenario, as shown in Figure 7.12, is similar to the central publisher scenario and would be used in the same general situations. The major difference between the two is that a second server is used to perform the role of distributor. This is highly desirable when you need to free the publishing server from having to perform the distribution task from a CPU, disk, and memory point of view.

This also offers the best scenario from which to expand the number of publishers and subscribers. Also remember that a single distribution server can distribute changes for several publishers. The publisher and distributor must be connected to each other via a reliable, high-speed data link. This remote distributor scenario is proving to be one of the best data replication approaches due to minimal impact on the publication server and maximum distribution capability to any number of subscribers.

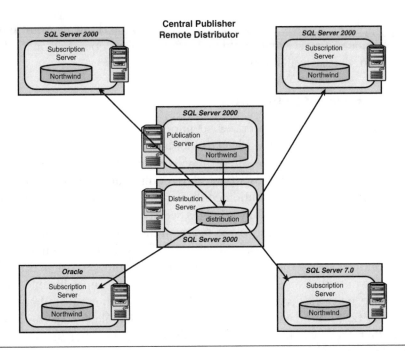

Figure 7.12 The central publisher with remote distributor is used when the role of distributor is removed from the publishing server.

As mentioned previously, the central publisher remote distributor approach can be used for all of the same purposes as the central publisher scenario, but it also provides the added benefit of having minimal resource impact on your publication servers. If your OLTP server's activity affects greater than 10% of your total data per day, this scenario can usually handle it without much issue. If your OLTP server has overburdened its CPU, memory, and disk utilization, you easily have solved this issue as well.

As high availability goes, this data replication model is probably the best, hands down! It not only reduces the workload on the publication server (helping performance and scalability), but it also keeps the distribution mechanism isolated away from the publisher in the event of publisher failures. The distribution server can still be pumping updates to a subscriber even though the publisher has failed (until the distribution queue is empty). You can now easily switch your client applications over to use a subscriber for as long as your publisher remains down (which could be for a long time depending on the failure). Your overall availability has just increased.

Publishing Subscriber

In the publishing subscriber scenario, as shown in Figure 7.13, the publication server also will have to act as a distribution server to one subscriber. This subscriber, in turn, will immediately publish this data to any number of other subscribers. The configuration depicted here is not using a remote distribution configuration option, but is serving the same distribution model purpose. This scenario is best used when a slow or expensive network link exists between the original publishing server and all of the other potential subscribers. This will allow the initial (critical) publication of the data to be distributed from the original publishing server to that single subscriber across that slow, unpredictable, or expensive network line. Then, each of the many other subscribers can subscribe to the data using faster, more predictable, "local" network lines that they will have with the publishing subscriber server. A classic example of this would be that of a company whose main office is in San Francisco and has several branch offices in Europe. Instead of replicating changes to all the branch offices in Europe, the updates are replicated to a single publishing subscriber server in Paris. This publishing subscriber server in Paris then replicates the updates to all other subscriber servers around Europe. Voilà!

Central Subscriber

In the central subscriber scenario, as shown in Figure 7.14, several publishers replicate data to a single, central subscriber. Basically, this supports the concept of consolidating data at a central site. An example of this might be that of consolidating all new orders from regional sales offices to company headquarters. Remember, you now will have several publishers of the Orders table; you need to take some form of precaution, such as filtering by region to prevent one publisher from updating another region's orders.

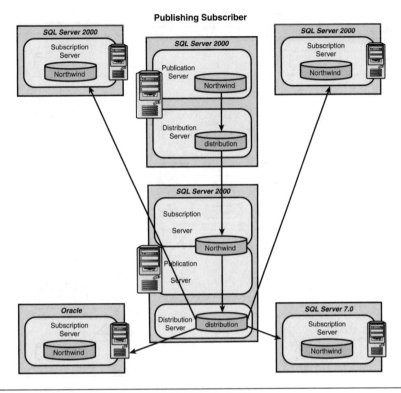

Figure 7.13 The publishing subscriber scenario works well when dealing with slow, unpredictable, or expensive network links in diverse geographic situations.

Multiple Publishers or Multiple Subscribers

In the multiple publishers or multiple subscribers scenario, as shown in Figure 7.15, a common table (such as the Customers table) is maintained on every server participating in the scenario. Each server publishes a particular set of rows that pertain to it—usually via filtering on something that identifies that site to the data rows it owns—and subscribes to the rows that all the other servers are publishing. The result is that each server has all the data at all times, and can make changes to its data only. You must be careful when implementing this scenario to ensure that all sites remain synchronized. The most frequently used applications of this configuration are regional order processing systems and reservation tracking systems. When setting up this configuration, make sure that only local users update local data. This check can be implemented through the use of stored procedures, restrictive views, or a check constraint.

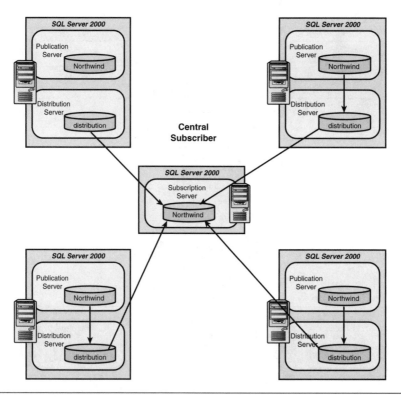

Figure 7.14   When using the central subscriber scenario, several publishers send data to a single, central subscriber.

Updating Subscribers

SQL Server 2000 has built-in functionality that allows the subscriber to update data in a table to which it subscribes, and have those updates automatically pushed back to the publisher through either immediate or queued updates. This model, called "updating subscribers," utilizes a two-phase commit process to update the publishing server as the changes are made on the subscribing server. These updates then are replicated to any other subscribers, but not to the subscriber that made the update.

Immediate updating allows subscribers to update data only if the publisher will accept them immediately. If the changes are accepted at the publisher, they will be propagated to the other subscribers. The subscribers must be continuously and reliably connected to the publisher to make changes at the subscriber.

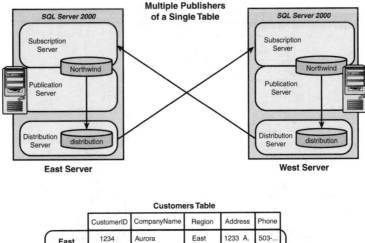

Figure 7.15 In the multiple publishers of a single table scenario, every server in the scenario maintains a common table.

Queued updating allows subscribers to update data and then store those updates in a queue while disconnected from the publisher. When the subscriber reconnects to the publisher, the updates are propagated to the publisher. Subscribers with the queued updating option can use either a Microsoft SQL Server 2000 queue or Microsoft Message Queuing version 2.0 on Microsoft Windows 2000 Server as the queuing mechanism. When selecting queued updating, the default is a SQL Server 2000 queue, which is available to all instances of SQL Server.

A combination of immediate updating with queued updating allows the subscriber to use immediate updating, but switch to queued updating if a connection cannot be maintained between the publisher and subscribers. After switching to queued updating, reconnecting to the publisher, and emptying the queue, the subscriber can switch back to immediate updating mode. An updating subscriber is shown in Figure 7.16.

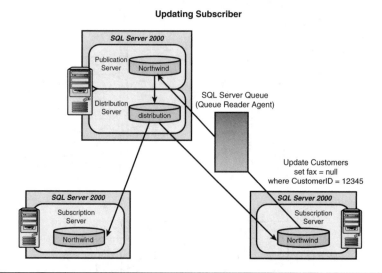

Figure 7.16 Updating subscriber replication topology with the SQL Server Queue mechanism.

Subscriptions

A subscription is essentially a formal request and registration of that request for data that is being published. By default, you will subscribe to all articles of a publication.

When this formal request (the subscription) is being set up, you will have the option of either having the data pushed to the subscriber server, or pulling the data to the subscription server when it is needed. This is referred to as either a *push subscription* or a *pull subscription*.

Pull Subscriptions

As depicted in Figure 7.17, a pull subscription is set up and managed by the subscription server. The biggest advantage here is that pull subscriptions allow the system administrators of the subscription servers to choose what publications they will receive and when they will be received. With pull subscriptions, publishing and subscribing are separate acts and are not necessarily performed by the same user. In general, pull subscriptions are best when the publication does not require high security, or if subscribing is done intermittently when the subscriber's data needs to be periodically brought up to date.

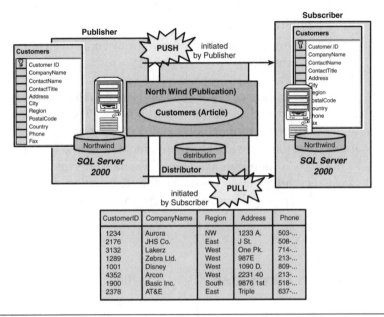

Figure 7.17   Push subscription intiatiated by publisher, and pull subscription initiated by subscriber.

Push Subscriptions

A push subscription is created and managed by the publication server. In effect, the publication server is pushing the publication to the subscription server. The advantage of using push subscriptions is that all of the administration takes place in a central location. In addition, publishing and subscribing happen at the same time, and many subscribers can be set up at once. This also is recommended when dealing with heterogeneous subscribers because of the lack of pull capability on the subscription server side. Use the push subscription approach for your high availability configuration that will be used in a fail-over scenario.

Anonymous Subscriptions (Pull Subscriptions)

It is also possible to have what are called "anonymous" subscriptions. An anonymous subscription is a special type of pull subscription that can be used in the following circumstances:

- You are publishing data to the Internet
- You have a huge number of subscribers
- You don't want the overhead of maintaining extra information at the publisher or distributor
- All the rules of your pull subscriptions apply to all of your anonymous subscribers

Normally, information about all of the subscribers, including performance data, is stored on the distribution server. Therefore, if you have a large number of subscribers, or you do not want to track detailed information about the subscribers, you might want to allow anonymous subscriptions to a publication. Then less subscription metadata and performance information is kept at the distribution server, but it then becomes the responsibility of the subscriber to initiate the subscription and to keep synchronized.

The Distribution Database

The distribution database is a special type of database installed on the distribution server. This database is known as a store-and-forward database and holds all transactions waiting to be distributed to any subscribers. This database receives transactions from any published databases that have designated it as their distributor. The transactions will be held here until they are sent to the subscribers successfully. After a period of time, these transactions will be purged from the distribution database. In some special situations, the transactions might not be purged for a longer period, enabling anonymous subscribers ample time in which to synchronize. The distribution database is the "heart" of the data replication facility. As you can see in Figure 7.18, the distribution database has several "MS" tables, such as Msrepl_transactions. These tables contain all necessary information for the distribution server to fulfill the distribution role. These tables include the following:

- All the different publishers who will use it, such as MSpublisher_databases and MSpublication_access
- The publications and articles that it will distribute, such as MSpublications, MSarticles
- The complete information for all the agents to perform their tasks, such as MSdistribution_agents

- The complete information of the executions of these agents, such as MSdistribution_history
- The subscribers, such as MSsubscriber_info, MSsubscriptions, and so on
- Any errors that occur during replication and synchronization states, such as MSrepl_errors, MSsync_state, and so on
- The commands and transactions that are to be replicated, such as MSrepl_commands and MSrepl_transactions

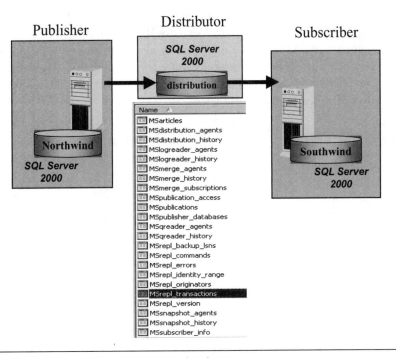

Publisher · Distributor · Subscriber

Figure 7.18 Tables of the distribution database.

Replication Agents

SQL Server utilizes replication agents to do different tasks during the replication process. These agents are constantly waking up at some frequency and fulfilling specific jobs. Let's look at the main ones.

The Snapshot Agent

The snapshot agent is responsible for preparing the schema and initial data files of published tables and stored procedures, storing the snapshot on the distribution server and recording information about the synchronization status in the distribution database. Each publication will have its own snapshot agent that runs on the distribution server. It will take on the name of the publication within the publishing database, within the machine on which it executes ([Machine][Publishing database][Publication Name]).

Figure 7.19 shows what this snapshot agent looks like under the SQL Server Agent (Management, SQL Server Agent, Jobs) branch in Enterprise Manager. In addition, it also can be referenced from the Replication Monitor option (within the Replication Monitor, Agents, Snapshot Agents branch). You probably most often will use the Replication Monitor path to these agents!

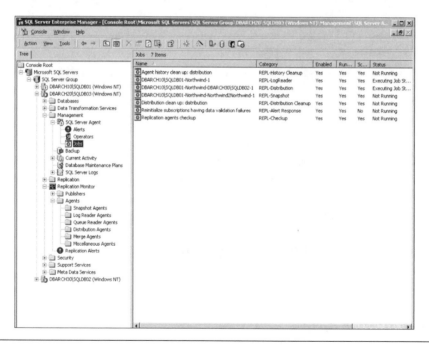

Figure 7.19 The various agent jobs used in replication.

It's worth noting that the snapshot agent might not even be used if the initialization of the subscriber's schema and data is done manually.

The Snapshot Agent Synchronization Process

The snapshot agent will invoke the processing that ensures that both databases start on an even playing field. This process is known as *synchronization*. The synchronization process is performed whenever a publication has a new subscriber. Synchronization happens only one time for each new subscriber and ensures that database schema and data are exact replicas on both servers. After the initial synchronization, all updates are made via replication.

When a new server subscribes to a publication, synchronization is performed. When synchronization begins, a copy of the table schema is copied to a file with an .SCH extension. This file contains all the information necessary to create the tables and any indexes on the tables, if they are requested. Next, a copy is made of the data in the table to be synchronized and written to a file with a .BCP extension. The data file is a BCP, or bulk copy file. Both files are stored in the temporary working directory on the distribution server (defaults to the REPLDATA directory within the SQL Server Instance—C:\Program Files\Microsoft SQL Server\MSSQL$xyz\REPLDATA).

CAUTION   After a synchronization process has started and the data files have been created, any inserts, updates, and deletes that occur on the publisher database are stored in the distribution database. However, these changes will not be replicated to the subscription database until the synchronization process is complete.

In addition, when the synchronization process starts, only new subscribers will get to take advantage of the synchronization results. Any subscriber that has been synchronized already and has been receiving modifications is unaffected. The synchronization set is applied to all servers that are waiting for initial synchronization only. After the schema and data have been re-created, all transactions that have been stored in the distribution server are sent to the subscriber.

When you set up a subscription, it is possible to manually load the initial snapshot onto the server. This is known as manual synchronization. For extremely large databases, it is frequently easier to dump the database to tape and then reload the database on the subscription server. If you load the snapshot this way, SQL Server will assume that the databases already are synchronized and automatically will begin sending data modifications.

The Snapshot Agent Processing

Figure 7.20 shows the details of the snapshot agent execution for a typical push subscription. As you can see, there are numerous bulk copy snapshot steps—two steps for each table/article in the publication.

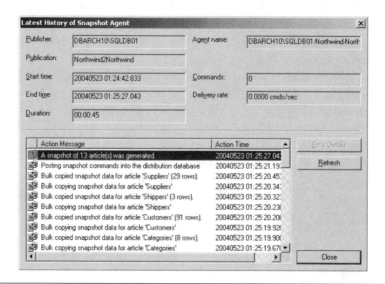

Figure 7.20 Snapshot agent tasks execution showing BCP copies of each table, and final article creation (last task executed is on the top of the history display).

The following is the sequence of tasks that are carried out by the snapshot agent:

1. The snapshot agent is initialized. This initialization can be immediate or at a designated time in your company's nightly processing window.

2. The agent will then connect to the publisher.

3. The agent then generates schema files with an .SCH file extension for each article in the publication. These schema files are written to a temporary working directory on the distribution server. These are the Create Table statements, and such, that will be used to create all objects needed on the subscription server side. They will only exist for the duration of the snapshot processing!

4. All the tables in the publication are then locked (held). The lock is required to ensure that no data modifications are made during the snapshot process.

5. The agent extracts a copy of the data in the publication and writes it into the temporary working directory on the distribution server. If all the subscribers are SQL Servers, then the data will be written using a SQL Server native format with a .BCP file extension. If you are replicating to databases other than SQL Server, the data will be stored in standard text files with the .TXT file extension. The .SCH file and the .TXT files/.BCP files are known as a synchronization set. Every table or article will have a synchronization set.

6. The agent will then execute the object creations and bulk copy processing at the subscription server side in the order that they were generated (or skip the object creation part if the objects have already been created on the subscription server side and you have indicated this during setup). This will take a while. For this reason, it is best to do this during an off time so as not to impact the normal processing day. Network connectivity is critical here. Snapshots often fail at this point.

7. The snapshot agent will then post the fact that a snapshot has occurred and what articles/publications were part of the snapshot to the distribution database. This will be the only thing that is sent to the distribution database.

8. When all the synchronization sets have finished being executed, the agent releases the locks on all of the tables of this publication. The snapshot is now considered finished.

CAUTION   Make sure that you have enough disk space on the drive that contains the temporary working directory (the snapshot folder). The snapshot data files will potentially be huge, which might be the most common reason for snapshot failure. This also directly affects high availability. If you fill up a disk, this will translate to some additional "unplanned" downtime. You've been warned!

The Log Reader Agent

The log reader agent is responsible for moving transactions marked for replication from the transaction log of the published database to the distribution database. Each database published using transactional replication has its own log reader agent that runs on the distribution server. It will be easy to find because it takes on the name of the publishing database whose transaction log it is reading [Machine name][Publishing DB name] and REPL-LogReader category. If you go back and look at Figure 7.19, you will also see a Log Reader agent job (REPL-LogReader category) for the Northwind database named DBARCH10\SQLDB01-Northwind-1.

After initial synchronization has taken place, the log reader agent begins to move transactions from the publication server to the distribution server. All actions that modify data in a database are logged in the transaction log in that database. Not only is this log used in the automatic recovery process, but it also is used in the replication process. When an article is created for publication and the subscription is activated, all entries about that article are marked in the transaction log. For each publication in a database, a log reader agent reads the transaction log and looks for any marked transactions. When the log reader agent finds a change in the log, it reads the changes and converts them to SQL statements that correspond to the action that was taken in the article. The SQL statements then are stored in a table on the distribution server waiting to be distributed to subscribers.

Because replication is based on the transaction log, several changes are made in the way the transaction log works. During normal processing, any transaction that has either been successfully completed or rolled back is marked inactive. When you are performing replication, completed transactions are not marked inactive until the log reader process has read them and sent them to the distribution server.

It should be noted that truncating and fast bulk-copying into a table are non-logged processes. In tables marked for publication, you will not be able to perform non-logged operations unless you, temporarily, turn off replication on that table. Then, you will need to re-sync the table on the subscriber before you re-enable replication.

The Distribution Agent

A distribution agent moves transactions and snapshots held in the distribution database out to the subscribers. This agent won't be created until a push subscription is defined. This distribution agent will take on the name of what the publication database is along with the subscriber information [machine name][publication DB name][subscriber machine name]. Again, looking back at Figure 7.19 you will see a distribution agent job (REPL-Distribution category) for the Northwind database named DBARCH10\SQLDB01-Northwind-DBARCH30\SQLDB02-1.

Subscribers not set up for immediate synchronization share a distribution agent that runs on the distribution server. Pull subscriptions, to either snapshot or transactional publications, have a distribution agent that runs on the subscriber. Merge publications do not have a distribution agent at all. Rather, they rely on the merge agent, discussed next.

In transactional replication, the transactions have been moved into the distribution database, and the distribution agent either pushes out the changes to the subscribers or pulls them from the distributor, depending on how the servers were set up. All actions that change data on the publishing server are applied to the subscribing servers in the same order they were incurred. Figure 7.21 shows the latest history of the distribution agent and the successful delivery of transactions (including the initial setup of the schema to the subscriber).

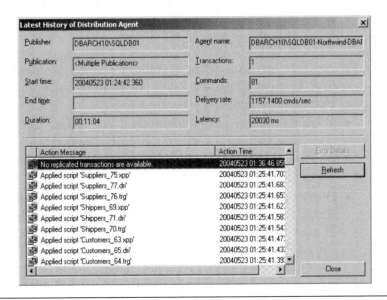

Figure 7.21   Distribution agent activity.

The Merge Agent

When dealing with merge publications, the merge agent moves and reconciles incremental data changes that occurred after the initial snapshot was created. Each merge publication has a merge agent that connects to the publishing server and the subscribing server and updates both as changes are made. In a full merge scenario, the agent first uploads all changes from the subscriber where the generation is 0, or the generation is greater than the last generation sent to the publisher. The agent gathers the rows in which changes were made, and those rows without conflicts are applied to the publishing database.

A "conflict" can arise when changes are made at both the publishing server and the subscription server to a particular row(s) of data. A conflict resolver handles these conflicts. Conflict resolvers are associated with an article in the publication definition. These conflict resolvers are sets of rules or custom scripts that can handle any complex conflict situation that might occur. The agent then reverses the process by downloading any changes from the publisher to the subscriber. Push subscriptions have merge agents that run on the publication server, whereas pull subscriptions have merge agents that run on the subscription server. Snapshot and transactional publications do not use merge agents.

The Miscellaneous Agents

In Figure 7.22, you can see that several miscellaneous agents have been set up to do house cleaning around the replication configuration. These agents include the following:

- Agent History Clean Up: distribution—Clears out agent history from the distribution database every 10 minutes (by default). Depending on the size of the distribution, you might want to vary the frequency of this agent.

- Distribution Clean Up: distribution—Clears out replicated transactions from the distribution database every 72 hours by default. This agent is used for snapshot and transactional publications only. If the volume of transactions is high, the frequency of this agent's execution should be adjusted upward so you don't have too large of a distribution database. And, you will need to adjust the frequency of synchronization with the subscribers as well.

- Expired Subscription Clean Up—Detects and removes expired subscriptions from the published databases. As part of the subscription setup, an expiration date will be set. This agent usually runs once per day by default. You won't need to change this.

- Reinitialize Subscriptions Having Data Validation Failures—This agent is manually invoked. It is not on a schedule, but it could be.

It automatically will detect the subscriptions that failed data validation and mark them for re-initialization. This can then potentially lead to a new snapshot being applied to a subscriber that had data validation failures.

■ Replication Agents Checkup—Detects replication agents that are not actively logging history. This is critical because debugging replication errors is often dependent on an agent's history that has been logged.

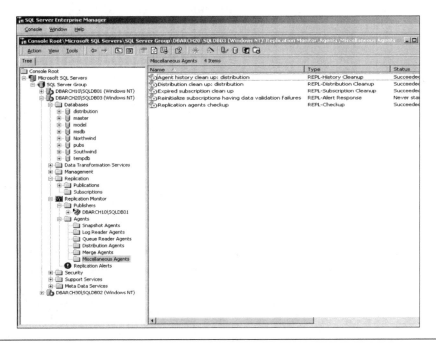

Figure 7.22   Miscellaneous agent job for replication cleanup, failure alert responses (if enabled), and replication checkup.

Planning for SQL Server Data Replication

You must consider many factors when choosing a method to distribute data. Your business requirements will determine which is the right method for you. In general, you will need to understand the timing and latency of your data, its independence at each site, and your specific need to filter or partition the data.

Timing, Latency, and Autonomy of Data

Distributed data implementations can be accomplished using a few different facilities in Microsoft. These are Data Transformation Services (DTS), Distributed Transaction Coordinator (DTC), and Data Replication. The trick is to match the right facility to the type of data distribution that you need to get done.

In some applications, such as online transaction processing and inventory control systems, data must be synchronized at all times. This requirement, called *immediate transactional consistency*, was known as tight consistency in previous versions of SQL Server.

SQL Server implements immediate transactional consistency data distribution in the form of two-phase commit processing. A *two-phase commit*, sometimes known as *2PC*, ensures that transactions are committed on all servers, or the transaction is rolled back on all servers. This ensures that all data on all servers is 100% in sync at all times. One of the main drawbacks of immediate transactional consistency is that it requires a high-speed LAN to work. This type of solution might not be feasible for large environments with many servers because occasional network outages can occur and if the network connection is lost, you cannot perform any updates in a 2PC configuration. These types of implementations can be built with DTC and DTS.

In other applications, such as decision support and report generation systems, 100% data synchronization all of the time is not as important. This requirement, called *latent transactional consistency*, was known as loose consistency in previous versions of SQL Server.

Latent transactional consistency is implemented in SQL Server via data replication. Replication allows data to be updated on all servers, but the process is not a simultaneous one. The result is "real-enough time" data. This is known as real-enough time data, or latent transactional consistency, because a lag exists between the data updated on the main server and the replicated data. In this scenario, if you could stop all data modifications from occurring on all servers, then all of the servers would eventually have the same data. Unlike the two-phase commit model, replication works over both LANs and WANs, as well as slow or fast links and can handle network outages, while 2PC cannot.

When planning a distributed application, you must consider the effect of one site's operation on another. This is known as *site autonomy*. A site with complete autonomy can continue to function without being connected to any other site. A site with no autonomy cannot function without being connected to all other sites. For example, applications that utilize two-phase commits, or 2PC, rely on all other sites being able to immediately accept changes that are sent to them. In the event that any one site is unavailable, no transactions on any server can be committed. In contrast, sites using data replication can be completely disconnected from all other sites and continue to work effectively, though not guaranteeing data consistency. Luckily, some solutions combine both high data consistency and site autonomy.

Methods of Data Distribution

After you have determined the amount of transactional latency and site autonomy based on your business requirements, it is important to select the data distribution method that corresponds. Each different type of data distribution has a different amount of site autonomy and latency. With these distributed data systems, you can choose from several methods:

- Distributed transactions—Distributed transactions ensure that all sites have the same data at all times. This method requires a certain amount of overhead cost to maintain this consistency. We will not be discussing this non-data replication method here.

- Transactional replication with updating subscribers—Users can change data at the local location, and those changes are applied to the source database at the same time. The changes are then eventually replicated to other sites. This type of data distribution combines replication and distributed transactions because data is changed at both the local site and source database.

- Transactional replication—With transactional replication, data is changed only at the source location and is sent out to the subscribers. Because data is only changed at a single location, conflicts cannot occur.

- Snapshot replication with updating subscribers—This method is much like transactional replication with updating subscribers; users can change data at the local location, and those changes are applied to the source database at the same time (or later if the publisher is unavailable). The entire changed publication is then replicated to all subscribers. This type of replication provides a higher autonomy than transactional replication.

- Snapshot replication—A complete copy of the publication is sent out to all subscribers. This includes both changed and unchanged data.

- Merge replication—All sites make changes to local data independently and then update the publisher. It is possible for conflicts to occur, but they will be resolved (using a default conflict resolution rule or by a custom conflict resolution rule). There is always a winner and a loser to a conflict. You can use the Conflict Viewer to review these conflicts and change the outcome of the conflict (make the winner the loser and have it propagated accordingly).

SQL Server Replication Types

Microsoft has narrowed the field to three major types of data replication approaches within SQL Server: snapshot, transactional, and merge. Each replication type applies only to a single publication. However, it is possible to have multiple types of replication per database.

Snapshot Replication

Snapshot replication makes an image of all the tables in a publication at a single moment in time, and then moves that entire image to the subscribers. Little overhead on the server is incurred because snapshot replication does not track data modifications like the other forms of replication do. It is possible, however, for snapshot replication to require large amounts of network bandwidth, especially if the articles being replicated are large. Snapshot replication is the easiest form of replication to set up and is used primarily with smaller tables for which subscribers do not have to perform updates. An example of this might be a phone list that is to be replicated to many subscribers. This phone list is not considered to be critical data, and the reduced frequency of it being refreshed is more than enough to satisfy all its users.

AGENTS USED: snapshot agent and the distribution agent primarily.

The snapshot agent creates files that contain the schema of the publication and the data. The files are temporarily stored in the snapshot folder of the distribution server, and then the distribution jobs are recorded in the distribution database.

The distribution agent is responsible for moving the schema and data from the distributor to the subscribers.

A few other agents also are used that deal with other needed tasks for replication, such as cleanup of files and history. In snapshot replication, after the snapshot has been delivered to all the subscribers, these agents will delete the associated .BCP and .SCH files from the distributor's working directory.

Transactional Replication

Transactional replication is the process of capturing transactions from the transaction log of the published database and applying them to the subscription databases. With SQL Server transactional replication, you can publish all or part of a table, views, or one or more stored procedures as an article. All data updates are then stored in the distribution database and sent and applied to any number of subscribing servers. Obtaining these updates from the publishing database's transaction log is extremely efficient. No direct reading of tables is required except during initial snapshot, and only the minimal amount of traffic is generated over the network. This has made transactional replication the most often used method.

As data changes are made, they are propagated to the other sites at nearly real time—you determine the frequency of this propagation. Because changes are usually made only at the publishing server, data conflicts are avoided for the most part. As an example, push subscribers usually receive updates from the publisher in a minute or less, depending on the speed and availability of the network. Subscribers also can be set up for pull subscriptions. This is useful for disconnected users who are not connected to the network at all times.

AGENTS USED: snapshot agent, log agent, and the distribution agent primarily.

The snapshot agent creates files that contain the schema of the publication and the data. The files are stored in the snapshot folder of the distribution server, and then the distribution jobs are recorded in the distribution database.

The log reader agent monitors the transaction log of the database that it is set up to service. Each database published has its own log reader agent set up for replication and will copy the transactions from the transaction log of that published database into the distribution database.

The distribution agent is responsible for moving the schema and data from the distributor to the subscribers for the initial synchronization and then moving all of the subsequent transactions from the published database to each subscriber as they come in. These transactions are stored in the distribution database for a certain length of time and eventually purged.

As always, a few other agents are used that deal with the other housekeeping issues surrounding data replication, such as schema files cleanup, history cleanup, and transaction cleanup.

Merge Replication

Merge replication involves getting the publisher and all subscribers initialized and then allowing data to be changed at all sites involved in the merge replication at the publisher and at all subscribers. All these changes to the data are subsequently merged at certain intervals so that again, all copies of the database have identical data.

Occasionally, data conflicts will have to be resolved. The publisher will not always win in a conflict resolution. Instead, the winner is determined by whatever criteria you establish.

AGENTS USED: snapshot agent and the merge agent primarily.

The snapshot agent creates files that contain the schema of the publication and the data. The files are stored in the snapshot folder of the distribution server, and then, the distribution jobs are recorded in the distribution database. This is essentially the same behavior as all other types of replication methods.

The merge agent takes the initial snapshot and applies it to all of the subscribers. It then reconciles all changes made on all the servers based on the rules that you configure.

Preparing for Merge Replication

When you set up a table for merge replication, SQL Server performs three schema changes to your database:

- First, SQL Server must either identify or create a unique column for every row that is going to be replicated. This column is used to identify the different rows across all of the different copies of the table. If the table already contains a column with the ROWGUIDCOL property, SQL Server will automatically use that column for the row identifier. If not, SQL Server will add a column called rowguid to the table. SQL Server also will place an index on this rowguid column.

- Next, SQL Server adds triggers to the table to track changes that occur to the data in the table and record them in the merge system tables. The triggers can track changes at either the row or the column level, depending on how you set it up. SQL Server will support multiple triggers of the same type on a table, so merge triggers will not interfere with user-defined triggers on the table.

- Last, SQL Server adds new system tables to the database that contains the replicated tables. These tables (MSMerge_contents and MSMerge_tombstone tables) contain information about updated and deleted data rows for the replicated tables. These tables rely on the rowguid to track which rows have actually been changed.

Merge Agent Behavior

The merge agent is responsible for moving changed data from the site where it was changed to all other sites in the replication scenario. When a row is updated, the triggers that were added by SQL Server fire off and update the new system tables, setting the generation column equal to 0 for the corresponding rowguid. When the merge agent runs, it collects the data from the rows where the generation column is 0, and then resets the generation values to values higher than the previous generation numbers. This allows the merge agent to look for data that has already been shared with other sites without having to look through all the data. The merge agent then sends the changed data to the other sites.

When the data reaches the other sites, the data is merged with existing data according to rules that you have defined. These rules are flexible and highly extensible. The merge agent evaluates existing and new data and resolves conflicts based on priorities or which data was changed first. Another available option is that you can create custom resolution strategies using the component object model (COM) and custom stored procedures. After conflicts have been handled, synchronization occurs to ensure that all sites have the same data.

Merge Replication Conflict Resolution

The merge agent identifies conflicts using the MSMerge_contents table. In this table, a column called lineage is used to track the history of changes to a row. The agent updates the lineage value whenever a user makes changes to the data in a row. The entry into this column is a combination of a site identifier and the last version of the row created at the site. As the merge agent is merging all the changes that have occurred, it examines each site's information to see whether a conflict has occurred. If a conflict has occurred, the agent initiates conflict resolution based on the criteria mentioned earlier.

User Requirements Drive the Replication Design

As mentioned before, the business requirements will really drive your replication configuration and method. The phase zero (0) high availability assessment results will provide you with the answers to most of the detail questions that are needed to pick the right type of replication to use. The answers you gave and the path that was followed through the HA decision tree got you to this point to begin with. However, adding more thoroughness in requirements gathering is highly recommended to get a prototype up and running as quickly as possible. This will allow you to measure the effectiveness of one replication approach over the other.

Figure 7.23 depicts the factors that contribute to replication designs and the possible data replication configuration that would best be used. It is only a partial table because of the numerous factors and the many replication configuration options that are available.

The last option in Figure 7.23 depicts a "hot spare" requirement that will be used for fail-over and will likely be done using the central publisher/remote distributor model.

Data Access	Latency	Autonomy	Sites (locations)	Frequency	Network	Machines	Owner	Other	REPLICATION
Read Only Reporting	short	high	many	high	fast/ stable	1 server/site	1 QLTP site	Each site only needs regional data	Central Publisher Transactional repl filter by region
Read Only Reporting	long	high	many	low	fast/ stable	1 server/site	1 QLTP site	Each site only needs regional data	Central Publisher Snapshot repl filter by region
Read Mostly A few updates	short	high	< 10	medium	fast/ stable	1 server/site	1 QLTP site	Regional updates on one table	Central Publisher Transactional repl Updating Subs
Read Mostly A few updates	medium	high	< 10	medium	slow/ unreliab	1 server/site	All update	Regional update all tables	Central Publisher Merge repl
• • •									
Inserts (new orders)	short	high	many	high	fast/ stable	1 server/site	1 report site	Each site only needs regional data	Central Subscriber Transactional repl
Hot/Warm Spare	Very short	high	< 2	high	fast/ stable	1 server/site	1 QLTP site	Fail-over	Central Publisher Remote Distributor Transactional repl

Figure 7.23   Replication design factors.

Design Note

If you have triggers on your tables and you want them to be replicated along with your table, you might want to revisit them and add a line of code reading NOT FOR REPLICATION so that the trigger code isn't executed redundantly on the subscriber side! So, for a trigger (insert, update, or delete trigger) on the subscriber, you would use the NOT FOR REPLICATION statement for the whole trigger (placed before the AS statement of the trigger). If you want to be selective on a part of the trigger code (FOR INSERT, FOR UPDATE, FOR DELETE) you will put the NOT FOR REPLICATION immediately following the ones you don't want to execute and put nothing on the ones you do want to execute.

If you are using IDENTITY columns to automatically generate column values or to help partition your data you should use the NOT FOR REPLICATION option to keep these values intact during replication. SQL Server will replicate these identity values as they were created on the publisher if you have defined the column on the subscriber to use the NOT FOR REPLICATION statement. If new rows are inserted to subscriber tables with IDENTITY columns, SQL Server increments the identity value in the normal way (because the insert to the subscriber isn't via replication agent, it is via a normal user connection).

continues

You can also use the NOT FOR REPLICATION option if you are using IDENTITY columns in tables and you are implementing ranges of identity values in a partitioned environment (one range of values on one publisher, another range of values on another publisher—and both subscribe and publish to each other). The following create table statements establish the identity value seed and increment for each publisher that owns a set of customerID values (like West Coast publisher and East Coast publisher):

```
-- Publisher Westcoast (range of custid between 1 and 1,000,000)
CREATE TABLE Customers ( CustID INT IDENTITY (1, 1)
NOT FOR REPLICATION PRIMARY KEY,
....)


-- Publisher Eastcoast (range of custid between 1,000,001 and above)
CREATE TABLE Customers ( CustID INT IDENTITY (1000001, 1)
NOT FOR REPLICATION PRIMARY KEY,
....)
```

It is best to use the NOT FOR REPLICATION option along with the CHECK constraint to ensure that the identity values being assigned are within the allowed range. For example

```
CREATE TABLE Customers
(CustID INT IDENTITY(1000001, 1)
    NOT FOR REPLICATION
    CHECK NOT FOR REPLICATION (CustID <= 2000000),
    ...,
    CONSTRAINT valid_range_pk PRIMARY KEY (CustID)
)
```

One caveat is the case when you are using transactional replication with immediate-updating subscribers and only one publisher. You should not use the IDENTITY and NOT FOR REPLICATION approach described here. Instead, use the IDENTITY column at the publisher only, and have the Subscriber use INT(data type) for that column. In this way the next identity value is always generated at the publisher and only the publisher.

Setting Up Replication

In general, SQL Server 2000 data replication is exceptionally easy to set up via Enterprise Manager and wizards. However, please be warned: If you use the wizards, be sure to generate SQL scripts for every phase of replication configuration. In a production environment, you most likely will rely heavily on scripts and will not have the luxury of having much time to set up and break down production replication configurations via wizards.

You always will have to define any data replication configuration in the following order:

1. Create or enable a distributor to enable publishing.

2. Enable/configure publishing. (A distributor must be designated for a publisher.)

3. Create a publication and define articles within the publication.

4. Define subscribers and subscribe to a publication.

Enable a Distributor

Before setting up a publisher, you will have to designate a distribution server to be used by that publisher. As has already been discussed, you can either configure the local server as the distribution server (the Microsoft default), or choose a remote server as the distributor. This is done via the Configure Publishing, Subscribers, and Distribution Wizard. Since any high availability configuration using data replication is best served with a remote distributor, this is what will be shown here. Oh, and you must be a member of the sysadmin server role to use this wizard.

Use the following steps to configure a remote server as a distributor:

1. From Enterprise Manager and with the remote SQL Server (registered server) that will be the distributor highlighted, choose the Tools, Replication, Configure Publishing, Subscribers, and Distribution selection. In our example, this is the DBARCH20\ SQLDB03 SQL Server (the remote distributor). As you can see in Figure 7.24 (upper left), this will start you through the wizard to accomplish two primary tasks:

   - Specify and create a distributor (as seen in the upper right of Figure 7.24).

   - Configure the properties of the distribution server including the name and the file locations of the distribution database, and the location of the snapshot folder.

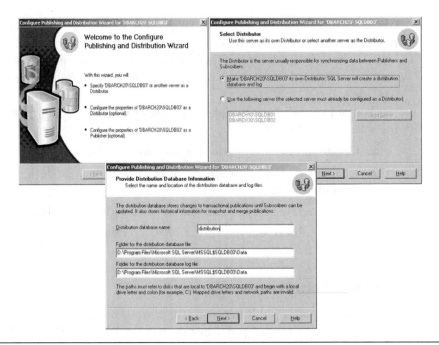

Figure 7.24 Configuring a SQL Server as a distributor for a publisher.

You are not going to enable this remote SQL Server as a publisher, only as a distributor. Figure 7.24 (bottom) also shows the full specification of the physical file location for the new distribution database that will be created and used by the distribution server. These wizard steps will create a few SQL agent tasks as well.

2. Next, as seen in Figure 7.25 (upper left), you'll be asked to specify a snapshot folder. Give it the proper network full pathname. Remember: Tons of data will be moving through this snapshot folder, so it should be on a drive that can support the snapshot concept without filling up the drive.

3. You are then asked to customize the configuration using the default settings or your own settings. Because we are configuring a remote distribution server, we will choose Yes to making a customized configuration. Looking back at Figure 7.25 (bottom right), you can see all of the items that will be configured using this setting option.

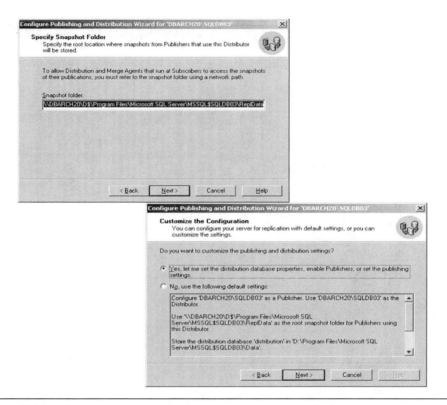

Figure 7.25   Specify the snapshot folder and choose Yes for customizing the configuration.

4. As you now see in Figure 7.26, you are prompted for information regarding which servers this distribution server will distribute for. In our example, we will select DBARCH10\SQLDB01 as the SQL Server that this distributor will be used to distribute data for. This is our publisher. If you click the properties button (the ellipsis button just to the right of the Distribution DB entry for DBARCH10\SQLDB01), you will see the full configuration that this publisher will use during distribution (upper right hand publisher properties dialog in Figure 7.26). This even includes what login the replication agents will use to communicate with the publisher.

Oh, by the way, a distributor can distribute for more than one publisher!

Once all properties are specified, a summary dialog of what the wizard is about to do is shown (bottom left of Figure 7.26). When this is executed, you will be presented with a message indicating that this server has been "enabled for distribution" (final dialog in the lower right of Figure 7.26).

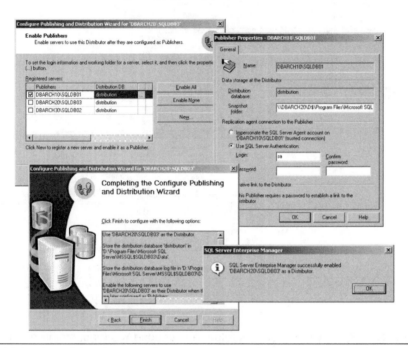

Figure 7.26   Specifying the publisher to distribute data for and completing the distribution server configuration summary.

5. The end result will yield a distribution database being created, the distribution server set up, Replication Monitor being added to Enterprise Manager, and publishing enabled for our publication server (just enabled, nothing more). If you look closely at Figure 7.27, you will see four replication agents being set up as a byproduct of this wizard completing its tasks and the message dialog letting you know that the Replication Monitor has been added to Enterprise Manager.

Now, you can get to the business of creating a publisher and publications.

Figure 7.27 The four replication agents created during the distribution server setup and a note that a Replication Monitor branch has been added to Enterprise Manager under the distribution server.

Design Note

If you haven't noticed by now, being able to completely configure data replication from a single enterprise manager console location is extremely convenient. The methods used by Microsoft to allow us this ability are understated. This is not easy to do. So, I'm going to have to praise Microsoft for this capability. It has made my life a lot easier. In addition, a complete build up and break down of replication can be done using scripts. This is what you will create for your production deployment and can be generated easily from enterprise manager.

Enable Publishing/Configure the Publisher

Because we have created a remote distributor, we only need to "configure" a publisher and create the publications that are to be published. We already enabled the publisher as the last part of the prior step.

Use the following steps to configure a server as a publisher:

1. From Enterprise Manager, highlight the SQL Server (registered server) that will be the publisher, and then choose the Tools, Replication, Configure Publishing, Subscribers, and Distribution selection. In our example, this is the DBARCH10\SQLDB01

SQL Server. As you can see in Figure 7.28, this invokes the same configuration wizard we used before, but this time we will focus on the publisher configuration only. As part of this wizard's invocation, Enterprise Manager looks at what account is defined to start the SQL Server Agent service. You might need to change this account so that replication won't fail (this warning message is also shown in the bottom right of Figure 7.28).

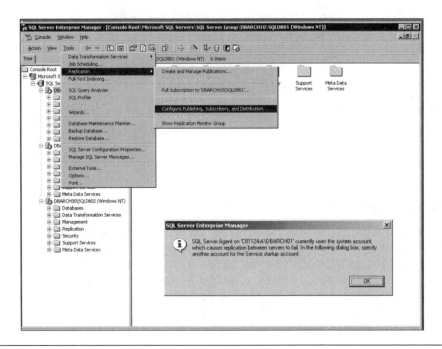

Figure 7.28 Replication, Configure Publishing, Subscribers, and Distributors.

2. The initial wizard dialog describes the configuration options that are possible (upper left of Figure 7.29). First up is the selection of the distributor for this publisher (as seen in the upper right of Figure 7.29). In our case, we will select the remote distributor of DBARCH20/SQLDB03 that we have already enabled for distribution.

3. The next dialog provides us with an opportunity to customize this configuration or not (as seen in the lower left of Figure 7.29). We will just select No and take the defaults for Customize the Configuration dialog since it will correctly configure DBARCH10/SQLDB01 as the publisher and use DBARCH20\SQLDB03 as the distributor.

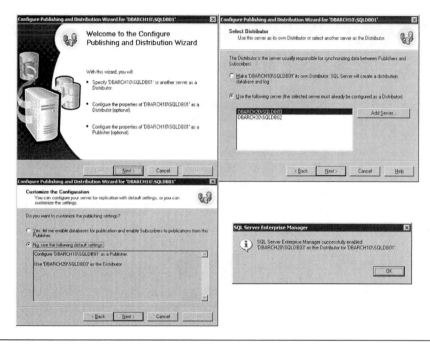

Figure 7.29   Select the remote distributor for this publisher and don't use any customized configuration for the publisher.

4. You will then complete the wizard and be given a message indicating that you have successfully enabled your distributor for this publisher (as you can see in the lower right of Figure 7.29).

Great! Now you are ready to create a publication!

Creating a Publication

Now that the distribution database has been created and publishing has been enabled and configured, you can create and configure a publication. From your publisher, select the Replication option from the Tools menu (as shown in Figure 7.30):

1. From Enterprise Monitor, choose the Tools, Replication, Create and Manage Publications selection.

2. You will be immediately prompted to select the database you are going to set up a publication for (also shown in Figure 7.30). We chose the Northwind database. This immediately launches the Create Publication Wizard dialogs.

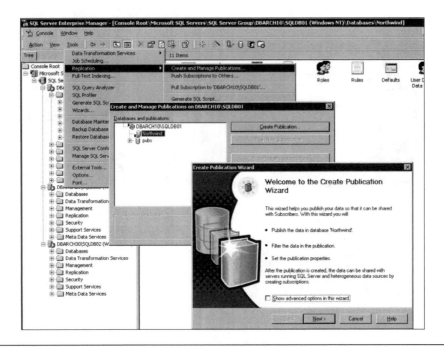

Figure 7.30   Choose the publication database.

3. We will then be prompted to, again, identify the database that you are creating the publication for (top left dialog in Figure 7.31) and asked to specify the type of replication method for this publication (middle dialog in Figure 7.31). This will be either snapshot replication, transactional replication, or merge replication. We have selected transactional replication. And, identify what server type (like SQL Server 2000, SQL Server 7.0, or other heterogeneous server types) the subscriber will be (bottom right of Figure 7.31).

4. From the Specify Articles dialog, you are prompted to identify articles in your publication (see top middle of Figure 7.32). You must include at least one article in your publication. These can be tables, views, or stored procedures. After you select an article, a button with an ellipsis ([el]) appears after the article name. If you click this button, you are presented the article properties dialog and can specify options for your article. In our example we selected to see the properties of the Customers (table) article. The General tab of the Table Article Properties for Customers

shows both the source table name and the destination table name (lower left of Figure 7.32). For snapshot and transactional replication, you can determine how the snapshot portion of the replication will occur (as seen in the Snapshot tab of the Table Article Properties in the lower right of Figure 7.32). The default snapshot approach (taken by the wizard) will be to drop the existing table (on the destination side), to only create its indexes (clustered/non-clustered indexes), and to convert user defined datatypes to base datatypes. In our example, we will want this table and all of its objects created at the subscriber (referential integrity, clustered indexes, non-clustered indexes, and so on). Remember, we are trying to create an exact image of the publisher to use as a warm standby and it must have all objects included. If your table has triggers, you may elect to leave this item unchecked and then run a script on the subscription side with the trigger code that contains the NOT FOR REPLICATION option (as discussed earlier in this chapter).

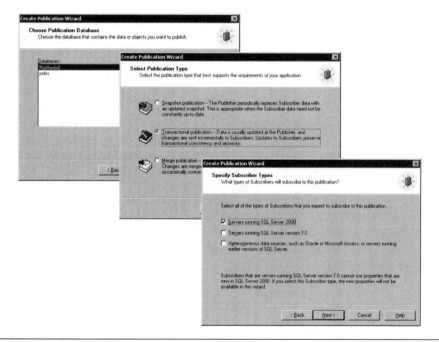

Figure 7.31   Choose the publication database, specify the publication type, and identify what server type the subscribers will be.

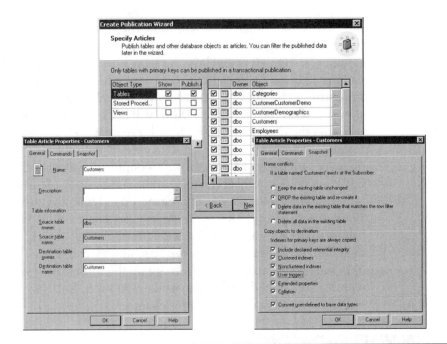

Figure 7.32 The Specify Articles screen allows you to choose which tables you want to publish and see each article's properties.

5. If any article issues exist, they will be presented to you here. Identity columns might be an issue because of the way they will be treated in replication. In addition, you can choose to see an article's properties and alter the defaults that are being set up.

CAUTION If the publication is to be used to create a warm standby for high availability, you need to define a custom script for SQL Server to run when applying the snapshot to create the tables with the `IDENTITY` property and the `NOT FOR REPLICATION` option set (which was described earlier in this chapter).

---

6. You can now name your publication something meaningful. In our example we name it "Northwind2Northwind" because we are creating an exact image of the Northwind database on our subscription (fail-over) server.

7. You are given a chance to customize the properties of the publication. This includes adding data filters and allowing anonymous subscribers. If you select that you do want to create anonymous subscribers, SQL Server will allow any server to connect to and receive data from your publication.

8. As you finish this wizard, it displays what it is doing in a nice dialog box. When this finishes, you will have a valid publication that simply needs to be subscribed to.

As you can see from Enterprise Manager in Figure 7.33, after the publication has been defined, the snapshot agent (REPL-SnapShot) is created along with the log reader agent (REPL-LogReader—because we chose transactional replication).

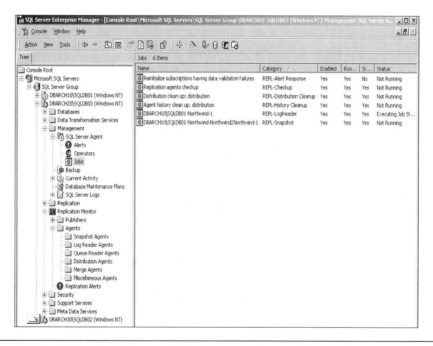

Figure 7.33 Enterprise Manager with new snapshot and log reader agents.

Now that you have installed and configured the remote distributor, enabled publishing, and created a publication, you need to create a subscription.

Creating Subscriptions

Remember that two types of subscriptions can be created: push and pull. Pull subscriptions allow remote sites to subscribe to any publication that they are allowed to, but you must be confident that the administrators at the other sites have properly configured the subscriptions at their sites. Push subscriptions are easier to create because all of the subscription processes are performed and administered from one machine. This also makes them the most common approach taken. Since we are creating this subscriber to be a fail-over server, we will always choose to use the push subscription approach. Following are the steps to create a push subscription:

1. From Enterprise Manager, choose the Tools, Replication, Create and Manage Publications selection. The Push New Subscription option is now active (because a publication exists now). This will allow you to

   - Enable the subscriber

   - Select one or more subscribers to publish to

   - Specify the database that the data is to be replicated into for each subscriber

   - Set/configure the initialization and synchronization process schedule so that they happen when they need to

2. First, make sure you have enabled the subscriber. This can be done from Enterprise Manager by choosing the Tools, Replication, and the Configure Publishing, Subscribers, and Distribution selection. You will be presented with the Publisher and Distributor Properties box. Go to the Subscribers tab and enable the desired SQL Server as a subscriber, as shown in the upper left of Figure 7.34 (by selecting the SQL Server instance and clicking Apply and then close the properties box). Now you can create a subscription to this subscriber.

3. Creating a push subscription can be done by first selecting the publishing server and then choosing the Tools, Replication, and the Create and Manage Publications selection. Now, go ahead and drill down to the publication that has been created for the Northwind database (the one we named Northwind2Northwind). Once you highlight this publication, the Push New Subscription button becomes active. Select this now. You will then specify the subscriber from the list that has been registered in Enterprise

Manager (upper right of Figure 7.34) and has been enabled for subscribing (from what we just enabled up in step 2).

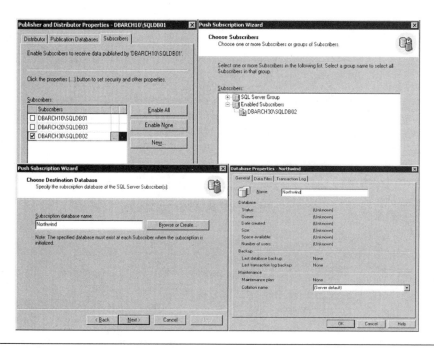

Figure 7.34 Enabling subscribers via publisher and distributor properties, creating a push subscription, and choosing the destination database (at the subscriber).

4. From the Choose Destination Database screen (lower left of Figure 7.34), you are prompted to identify the subscription database that you will publish to. If you click the Browse Database button, you can see a list of all the databases on the destination server (the new subscribing server). If you want to create a new database on the destination server, click the Create New button. In our example, we want this subscription process to create a new, complete image of the Northwind database. This will entail naming the database and specifying the proper data and transaction file location properties for this database on the subscriber (as seen in the lower right of Figure 7.34).

5. As you can see in Figure 7.35 (the dialog in the upper left), we will configure how the distribution agent will run. If you want to provide the shortest latency, select the Run Continuously option (the default). This would most likely be the option if you are configuring replication as your high availability solution.

6. You are then prompted to set the initialization of the database schema and data (middle of Figure 7.35). You will have an option to create the schema and data at the subscriber (and also to do it immediately) or to skip this initialization altogether because you have already created the schema and loaded the data manually. We choose to have the initialization create the schema and initialize the data immediately.

7. The next part of the process, the Start Required Services dialog box, checks whether the required services are running on the server (as you can also see in the lower right of Figure 7.35).

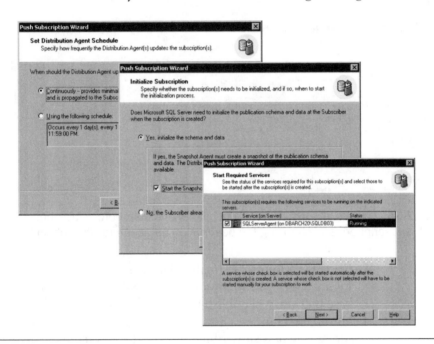

Figure 7.35   Setting the distribution agent schedule, initializing the schema and data, and making sure the SQL Server Agent is started on the subscriber.

Now replication is set up, and the only thing left to do is wait. If you have specified that the schema and data are to be created immediately, things will start happening quickly.

If you head over to the Replication Monitor item in Enterprise Manager and drill down to the Snapshot agent (under the Agents item), you will first see the snapshot agent start up and begin creating schema files (.SCHs), extracting the data into .BCP files (.BCPs), and putting everything in the snapshot folder on the distribution server. You read these latest history windows from the bottom up. What's on top is the last thing to have completed. In Figure 7.36, the upper left shows the initialization steps (the start of the snapshot processing) and the final steps of the snapshot are shown in the bottom right.

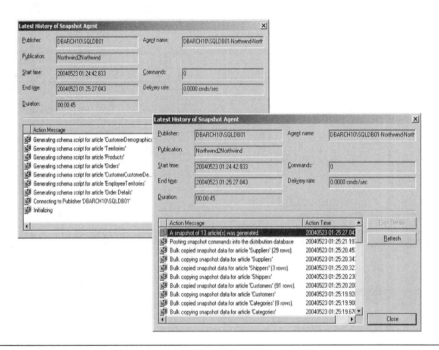

Figure 7.36   Snapshot task details.

In addition, in Figure 7.37, we took a quick peek, via Windows Explorer, at the contents of the snapshot working directory to see all of our .SCHs and .BCPs being created. This is often where trouble is encountered because of the lack of space on the disk drive.

Taking a quick look at the upper left of Figure 7.38, you can see the snapshot agent has succeeded. And, now, the distribution agent finishes the job. As you can also see in the Latest History details for the distribution agent (in the bottom right of Figure 7.38), the distribution agent applies the schemas to the subscriber. The bulk copying of the data into the tables on the subscriber side will follow accordingly. After this bulk copying is done, the initialization step is completed and active replication begins.

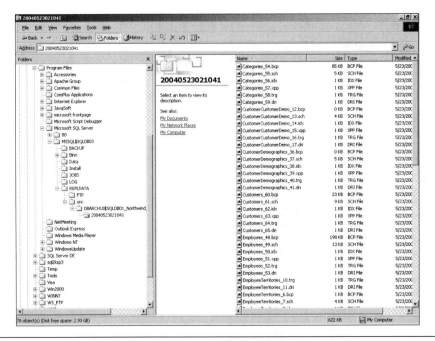

Figure 7.37   Snapshot folder as the schema and data files are being created and used.

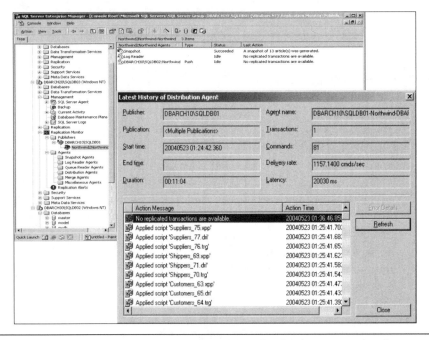

Figure 7.38   The snapshot agent status and the distribution agent detail steps of applying schemas and initializing data at the subscriber.

That's it! You are now in active replication. As any change is made to the publisher, it is continuously replicated to the subscriber. In most cases, this is within a few seconds.

If the publisher fails for any reason, and cannot be recovered normally, the subscriber server can be put into service by pointing all the client applications to this new server.

1. You would first want to stop the log reader agent because it will be in a "retrying" mode and will experience a failure since it cannot connect to the publisher. Figure 7.39 shows the Log Reader in retrying mode.

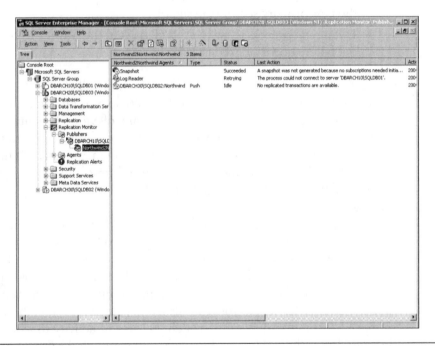

Figure 7.39   Log reader agent retrying due to failure to connect to the publisher.

2. You then want to check to see whether the last transactions were successfully distributed to the subscriber by looking at the history of the distribution agent on the distributor. One point of this high availability is that we isolated the distributor to its own machine for just this reason.

Switching Over to a Warm Standby (Subscriber)

If done properly, failing over to a warm standby (subscriber) in a replication configuration can be done in less than two minutes if the failure is detected early. There will be a few main areas to consider:

- Knowing what has failed. Has the publisher failed only? Have the most recent transactions been replicated to the subscriber?
- Define the process that must be run to make the subscriber the primary server.
- Define the process that must be followed to point the client to the new primary server (the standby).
- Define the process to switch this all back to the way it was before the failure occurred (if desired).

Just as a precaution, you should always keep all the SQL Server instances that are a part of your replication topology as up to date as possible from a SQL Server service packs point of view. Executing the `sp_vupgrade_replication` system stored procedure *before* you are forced to use a subscriber as a warm standby for high availability is highly advised. In particular, the metadata and stored procedures for replication should be kept at the same service pack level across your replication topology.

`SP_vupgrade_replication` will upgrade schema and system data as needed to support replication at the current product level. This stored procedure creates new replication system objects in system and user databases (such as the distribution and msdb databases). This stored procedure should be executed at the server instance where the replication upgrade is to occur. You can also use your warm standby (subscriber) as a temporary place to switch your client activity to while you do upgrades on the publisher. Once these are completed, you can switch back to the publisher (that has been upgraded) and then repeat the upgrade for the subscriber (warm standby server), thus increasing overall availability of your system.

Scenarios That Will Dictate Switching to the Warm Standby

The main reason why we are building a warm standby configuration with replication is so that we can fail-over to it when the primary server fails.

In other words, it does not come back up after automatic SQL Server recovery has attempted to bring it back online. Your database is basically completely unavailable and unusable for any number of reasons (failed disk, failed memory, and so on). When using replication configurations the basic failure scenarios to deal with are

- Publisher fails, distributor alive, subscriber alive—You can use the subscriber for your client connections once the distributor has distributed all published transactions to the subscriber.

- Publisher fails, distributor fails, subscriber alive—You can use the subscriber for your client connections once you have renamed the SQL Server instance (to the publisher's name). Some data loss will potentially have occurred.

Switching Over to a Warm Standby (Subscription)

Assuming that the primary server (publisher) is not available for any number of reasons and won't be available for the foreseeable future, you must now make your warm standby the primary server.

1. Verify that the last set of transactions that made it to the distributor have been replicated to the subscriber by reviewing the history of the distribution agent. This should be up to the minute (if not to the second).

2. Remove replication from the subscriber by executing the system stored procedure `sp_removedbreplication` at the subscriber.

3. Disable all replication agents (Log Reader Agent, Distribution Agent, and so on). Don't delete them, just disable them. We will clean up later.

4. If you are not using Network Load Balancing (NLB) to insulate your client connection from having to change, you may need to rename the subscription server to the name of the old primary server (the one that failed). This is pretty severe and if it is easier to change the client connection string to point to the new server location, pursue that approach. If there are too many clients to do this with, go ahead and rename the server (`sp_dropserver`, followed by `sp_addserver`). In addition, this will require that you start and stop SQL Server so that it will come up under the new server name and be known to the network under this new name.

Before the standby database is made available to the clients for use, be sure you have set the recovery mode to "full" if it was previously set to "simple" or "bulkcopy." Then, you will want to run your backup/recovery scripts to initiate database backups and transaction log backups immediately.

Turning the Subscriber into a Publisher (if Needed)

Most importantly, if you have to use a subscriber as your fail-over SQL Server instance, you need to be prepared to turn this subscriber into a publisher (if needed). This would be the scenario of the subscriber taking over the publisher's job permanently (until it fails and a switch back needs to occur). We strongly advise that you keep all replication configurations in script form. This would include a version of replication scripts that can enable the subscriber as a publisher and start publishing. As a reminder, make sure you have kept your SQL logins/users synchronized and up to date in both the publisher and the subscriber SQL Server instances.

Insulate the Client Using an NLB Cluster Configuration

You can also use the Network Load Balancing cluster configuration to help insulate your clients from having to change their connection information when reconnecting after a failure or from having to wait to have the subscriber renamed to the publisher instance name. The client application only has to worry about the NLB cluster name for its connection. Using NLB within a high availability topology was described in Chapter 5, "Microsoft SQL Server Clustering."

Scripting Replication

Earlier, it was suggested that you generate SQL scripts for all that you do because going through wizards every time you have to configure replication is no way to run a production environment. The easiest way to get to SQL scripting is by right-clicking on either the replication or publications folder and choosing Generate SQL Script. This Generate SQL Script dialog is shown in Figure 7.40. Use this option!

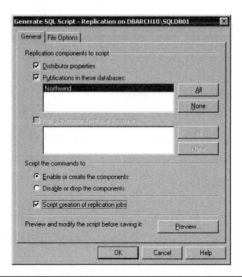

Figure 7.40　Scripting replication dialog and options via the publisher.

You can choose to have Enterprise Manager generate the creation (build up) of your data replication configuration and then have it generate the dropping (break down) of your configuration. Once you have created these scripts, update them to reflect other production scripting standards that you might have in your shop, but be certain to keep them handy for building up and breaking down replication easily.

The following is an example of some of the SQL scripts needed to generate the same data replication configuration that we just built with wizards. The full SQL script will be available as a downloadable file on the Sams website. Remember, these scripts minimize the errors we will make while supporting our data replication environments.

```
-------------------- SETUP REMOTE DISTRIBUTOR ----------------------
use master
GO
exec sp_adddistributor  @distributor = N'DBARCH20\SQLDB03',
   @password = N''
GO
-- Adding the distribution database --
exec sp_adddistributiondb  @database = N'distribution',
    @data_folder = N'C:\Program Files\Microsoft SQL Server\MSSQL\DATA',
    @data_file = N'distribution.MDF', @data_file_size = 3,
    @log_folder = N'C:\Program Files\Microsoft SQL Server\MSSQL\DATA',
    @log_file = N'distribution.LDF', @log_file_size = 1,
      @min_distretention = 0,
```

```
        @max_distretention = 72, @history_retention = 48,
            @security_mode = 0,
        @login = N'sa', @password = null
GO
----------------------- SETUP PUBLISHER/PUSH SUBSCRIPTION -------------
use master
GO
exec sp_adddistributor  @distributor = N'DBARCH20\SQLDB03',
        @password = N''
GO
-- Adding the registered subscriber --
exec sp_addsubscriber @subscriber = N'DBARCH30\SQLDB02', @type = 0,
        @login = N'sa',
        @password = N'', @security_mode = 0, @frequency_type = 64,
        @frequency_interval = 1,
        @frequency_relative_interval = 2, @frequency_recurrence_factor = 0,
        @frequency_subday = 8,
        @frequency_subday_interval = 1, @active_start_date = 0,
        @active_end_date = 0,
        @active_start_time_of_day = 0, @active_end_time_of_day = 235900,
        @description = N''
exec sp_changesubscriber_schedule @subscriber = N'DBARCH30\SQLDB02',
        @agent_type = 1,           @active_end_date = 0
GO
exec sp_replicationdboption @dbname = 'Northwind', @optname = 'publish',
        @value = 'true'
go
-- Add the publication for publisher DB --
use [Northwind]
GO
exec sp_addpublication @publication = N'Northwind2Northwind',
        @restricted = N'false',
        @sync_method = N'native', @repl_freq = N'continuous',
        @description = N'Transactional publication of Northwind database
from Publisher
        DBARCH10\SQLDB01.',
        @status = N'active', @allow_push = N'true', @allow_pull = N'true',
        @allow_anonymous = N'false', @enabled_for_internet = N'false',
        @independent_agent = N'false',
        @immediate_sync = N'false', @allow_sync_tran = N'false',
        @autogen_sync_procs = N'false',
        @retention = 336, @allow_queued_tran = N'false',
        @snapshot_in_defaultfolder = N'true',
        @compress_snapshot = N'false', @ftp_port = 21,
```

```
        @ftp_login = N'anonymous',
        @allow_dts = N'false', @allow_subscription_copy = N'false',
        @add_to_active_directory = N'false',
        @logreader_job_name = N'DBARCH10\SQLDB01-Northwind-1'

exec sp_addpublication_snapshot @publication = N'Northwind2Northwind',
        @frequency_type = 4,
        @frequency_interval = 1, @frequency_relative_interval = 1,
        @frequency_recurrence_factor = 0,
        @frequency_subday = 8, @frequency_subday_interval = 1,
        @active_start_date = 0,
        @active_end_date = 0, @active_start_time_of_day = 0,
        @active_end_time_of_day = 235959,
 @snapshot_job_name = N'DBARCH10\SQLDB01-Northwind-Northwind2Northwind-
➥1'
GO
exec sp_grant_publication_access @publication = N'Northwind2Northwind',
        @login = N'BUILTIN\Administrators'
GO
exec sp_grant_publication_access @publication = N'Northwind2Northwind',
@login = N'sa'
GO
-- Adding the transactional articles --
exec sp_addarticle @publication = N'Northwind2Northwind',
    @article = N'Categories',
        @source_owner = N'dbo', @source_object = N'Categories',
        @destination_table = N'Categories',
        @type = N'logbased', @creation_script = null, @description = null,
        @pre_creation_cmd = N'drop', @schema_option = 0x000000000000FFF3,
        @status = 16, @vertical_partition = N'false',
        @ins_cmd = N'CALL sp_MSins_Categories',
        @del_cmd = N'CALL sp_MSdel_Categories',
        @upd_cmd = N'MCALL sp_MSupd_Categories',
        @filter = null, @sync_object = null,
        @auto_identity_range = N'false'
GO
-- Adding the transactional subscription
exec sp_addsubscription @publication = N'Northwind2Northwind',
        @article = N'all',
        @subscriber = N'DBARCH30\SQLDB02', @destination_db = N'Northwind',
        @sync_type = N'automatic',
        @update_mode = N'read only', @offloadagent = 0,
        @dts_package_location = N'distributor'
GO
```

Monitoring Replication

After replication is up and running, it is important for you to monitor the replication and see how things are running. You can do this in several ways, including SQL statements, SQL Enterprise Monitor, and Windows Performance Monitor. You are interested in the agent's successes and failures, the speed at which replication is done, and the synchronization state of tables involved in replication. Other things to be watched for are the sizes of the distribution database, the growth of the subscriber databases, and the available space on the distribution server's snapshot working directory.

SQL Statements

One way to look at the replication configuration and do things like validate row counts is to use various replication stored procedures.
These include the following:

- `sp_helppublication`—Info on the publication server
- `sp_helparticle`—Article definition information
- `sp_helpdistributor`—Distributor information
- `sp_helpsubscriberinfo`—Subscriber server information
- `sp_helpsubscription`—The subscription information
- `sp_replcounters`—Shows the activity of this replication session. You can see the volume of traffic and the throughput here

```
exec sp_replcounters
go
```

yields

```
database repl_trans rate trans/sec latency (sec) etc.
Northwind 110    71.428574        2.1830001
```

For actual row count validation:

- `sp_publication_validation`—Goes through and checks the row counts of the publication and subscribers

```
exec sp_publication_validation @publication = N'Northwind2Northwind'
go
```

yields

```
Generated expected rowcount value of 53 for Territories.
Generated expected rowcount value of 58 for Suppliers.
Generated expected rowcount value of 6 for Shippers.
Generated expected rowcount value of 4 for Region.
Generated expected rowcount value of 154 for Products.
Generated expected rowcount value of 1690 for Orders.
Generated expected rowcount value of 2155 for Order Details.
Generated expected rowcount value of 49 for
EmployeeTerritories.
Generated expected rowcount value of 18 for Employees.
Generated expected rowcount value of 95 for Customers.
Generated expected rowcount value of 0 for
CustomerDemographics.
Generated expected rowcount value of 0 for
CustomerCustomerDemo.
Generated expected rowcount value of 16 for Categories.
```

Another way to monitor replication is to look at the actual data that is being replicated. To do this, first run a SELECT count (*) FROM tblname statement against the table where data is being replicated. Then verify directly if the most current data available is in the database. If you make a change to the data in the published table, do the changes show up in the replicated tables? If not, you might need to investigate how replication was configured on the server.

SQL Enterprise Manager

As you have seen, Enterprise Manager provides considerable information about the status of replication. Most of this is available via the Replication Monitor branch. In Replication Monitor, you can see the activity for publishers, agents, and the ability to configure alerts:

- Publishers—This folder contains information about publishers on the machine. By selecting any publisher on the machine, you can view information about any computers that have subscribed to the publication. This will tell you the current status and the last action taken by the subscriber.

- Agents—The Agents folder contains information about the different agents on the machine. By choosing any Agents folder, you can see the current status of that agent. Selecting an agent and double-clicking it will display the history of that agent.

- Replication Alerts—The Replication Alerts folder allows you to configure alerts to fire in response to events that occur during replication. These can activate when errors occur, or in response to success messages.

Through Enterprise Manager and Replication Monitor, you also can invoke the validate subscriptions processing to see whether replication is in sync. This is only available from the Distributor Server branch in Enterprise Manager. Under the Publishers branch of Replication Monitor, simply right-click on the publication you wish to validate. You will see the menu option to Validate Subscriptions. You can validate all subscriptions or just a particular one, as shown in Figure 7.41. After this has been invoked, the validation results can be viewed via the distribution agent history (also shown in Figure 7.41).

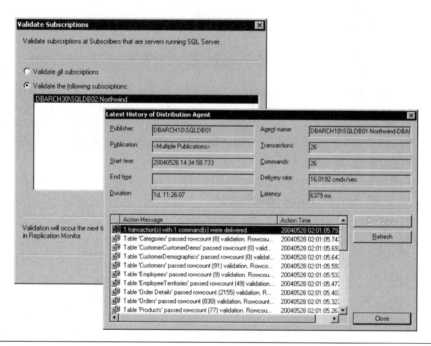

Figure 7.41   Validate subscriptions to ensure that publisher and subscriber are in sync.

The Performance Monitor

You also can use Windows NT Performance Monitor to monitor the health of your replication scenario. Installing SQL Server adds several new objects and counters to Performance Monitor:

- SQLServer:Replication Agents—This object contains counters used to monitor the status of all replication agents, including the total number running.

- SQLServer:Replication Dist—This object contains counters used to monitor the status of the distribution agents, including the latency and the number of transactions transferred per second.

- SQLServer:Replication Logreader—This object contains counters used to monitor the status of the log reader agent, including the latency and the number of transactions transferred per second.

- SQLServer:Replication Merge—This object contains counters used to monitor the status of the merge agents, including the number of transactions and the number of conflicts per second.

- SQLServer:Replication Snapshot—This object contains counters used to monitor the status of the snapshot agents, including the number of transactions per second.

Backup and Recovery in a Replication Configuration

Something that will reap major benefits for you after you have implemented a data replication configuration is a replication-oriented backup strategy. You must realize that the scope of data and what you must back up together has changed. In addition, you must be aware of what the recovery timeframe is and plan your backup/recovery strategy for this. You might not have multiple hours available to you to recover an entire replication topology. You now have databases that are conceptually joined, and you might need to back them up together as one synchronized backup.

When backing up environments, back up the following at each site:

- Publisher (published db, msdb, and master)
- Distributor (distribution db, msdb, and master)
- Subscribers (Optional subscriber db)

Maintaining a regular backup of the publisher databases and leveraging the SQL Server replication's built-in ability to reinitialize one or more subscriptions on-demand provides a simple recovery strategy.

You could further limit regular backups to your publication databases and rely on SQL Server replication scripting to provide a method for reestablishing replication if you need to restore the entire replication environment.

Another strategy includes backing up only the publisher and the distributor as long as the publisher and distributor are synchronized. This strategy allows you to restore a replication environment completely. Backing up a subscriber is optional but can reduce the time it takes to recover from a failure of the subscriber.

Always make copies of your replication scripts and keep them handy. At a very minimum, keep copies at the publisher and distributor and one more location, such as at one of your subscribers. You will end up using these for recovery someday.

Don't forget to back up master and msdb when any new replication object is created, updated, or deleted.

Back up the publication database after

- Creating new publications.

- Altering any publication property including filtering.

- Adding articles to an existing publication.

- Performing a publication-wide re-initialization of subscriptions.

- Altering any published table using a replication schema change.

- Performing on-demand script replication.

- Cleaning up merge metadata (running sp_mergecleanupmetadata).

- Changing any article property including changing the selected article resolver.

- Dropping any publications.

- Dropping any articles.

- Disabling replication.

Back up the distribution database after

- Creating or modifying replication agent profiles.

- Modifying replication agent profile parameters.

- Changing the replication agent properties (including schedules) for any push subscriptions.

Back up the subscription database after

- Changing any subscription property.
- Changing the priority for a subscription at the publisher.
- Dropping any subscriptions.
- Disabling replication.

Back up the msdb system database after

- Enabling or disabling replication.
- Adding or dropping a distribution database (at the distributor).
- Enabling or disabling a database for publishing (at the publisher).
- Creating or modifying replication agent profiles (at the distributor).
- Modifying any replication agent profile parameters (at the distributor).
- Changing the replication agent properties (including schedules) for any push subscriptions (at the distributor).
- Changing the replication agent properties (including schedules) for any pull subscriptions (at the subscriber).

Back up the master database after

- Enabling or disabling replication.
- Adding or dropping a distribution database (at the distributor).
- Enabling or disabling a database for publishing (at the publisher).
- Adding the first or dropping the last publication in any database (at the publisher).
- Adding the first or dropping the last subscription in any database (at the subscriber).
- Enabling or disabling a publisher at a distribution publisher (at the publisher and distributor).
- Enabling or disabling a subscriber at a distribution publisher (at the subscriber and distributor).

In general, you will find that even when you walk up and pull the plug on your distribution server, publication server, or any subscribers, automatic recovery works well to get you back online and replicating quickly without human intervention.

Alternate Synchronization Partners

Similar to log shipping, using alternate synchronization partners during merge replication is an option that supports continuous synchronization in the event of a failure of the primary publisher. Specifying an alternate synchronization partner for publications defined at a publisher provides a method to synchronize data changes to replicated tables with servers other than the publisher where a subscription originated. Synchronizing with alternate synchronization partners provides the ability for a subscriber to synchronize data even if the primary publisher is unavailable and increases availability greatly.

The following are requirements when using alternate synchronization partners:

- The feature is available only with merge replication.

- The alternate synchronization partner must have the data and schema required by the subscription.

- It is recommended that the publication created on the alternate server be an exact copy of the publication created on the original publisher.

- The publication properties must specify that subscribers can synchronize with other publishers.

- The subscriber must be enabled at the alternate synchronization partner so that the subscriber can synchronize data with that publisher.

- A subscription with the same attributes as the subscription at the primary publisher will be added automatically at the alternate synchronization partner.

This approach is mentioned because of its high availability capabilities. However, in practical experience, most companies have found that the added complexity of merge replication is more self-defeating than practical.

Worldwide Sales and Marketing—Scenario #2 with Data Replication

As we defined in Chapter 1, "Essential Elements of High Availability," this common business scenario is about a major chip manufacturer that has created a highly successful promotion and branding program, which results in billions of dollars in advertising dollars being rebated back to their worldwide sales channel partners. These sales channel partners must enter in their complete advertisements (newspaper, radio, TV, other) and be measured against ad compliance and logo usage and placements. If a sales channel partner is in compliance, they will receive up to 50% of the cost of their advertisement back from this chip manufacturer. There are three major advertising regions: Far East, Europe, and North America. Each region produces a huge daily influx of new advertisement information that is processed on the primary server in North America. Then for the rest of each day, the regions review compliance results and run other types of major sales reports for their region only. As you might also recall, application mix is approximately 75% online entry of advertisement events and 25% regional management and compliance reporting.

Availability:

- 24 hours per day
- 7 days a week
- 365 days a year

Planned Downtime: **3%**

Unplanned Downtime: **2%** will be tolerable

Turns out that the regional reporting and query processing is the most important (most critical) part of this application. Each region must be able to query the compliance and advertisement information in this database as they interact with their regional channel partners and provide compliance status and rebate information rapidly (including dollar figures). This often requires specialized reports that span numerous advertisement events and impact very large amounts of money. The online data entry of the advertisement information is done around the clock by third-party data entry companies and must be done directly on the central database (behind extensive firewalls and security). Performance of the OLTP portion of this application must not be sacrificed in any way.

As you can see in Figure 7.42, an optimal HA solution was chosen that basically consists of five servers servicing a global set of users. Each separate server will have basic hardware/disk redundancy, one SQL Server instance, and will be configured with SQL Server's robust "transactional" data replication implementation. This will create three regional reporting images of the primary marketing database (MktgDB). These distributed copies will alleviate the major reporting burden against the OLTP (primary database) and any one of them can serve as a warm standby copy of the database in the event of a major database problem at headquarters. Overall, this distributed architecture is easy to maintain and keep in sync, and is highly scalable. To date, there has never been a major failure that required a complete switch over to one of the subscribers. But, they are in position to do this if ever required. In addition, the performance of each reporting server has been so outstanding that each region has brought in business objects and built their own unique reporting front-end to this data.

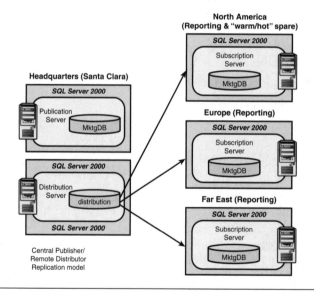

Figure 7.42   Scenario #2 HA solution using transactional data replication.

From an ROI point of view, the Sales and Marketing group calculated theirs as follows:

We had previously estimated the total incremental costs to be in the range of between **$10K and $100K**, which included

- Three new two-way servers (with 4GB RAM, local SCSI disk system RAID 10—15 new drives total) at $10K per server (one for the North American Reporting/spare server, one for Europe, and one for the Far East).

- Three MS Windows 2000 Server licenses ~ $1.5K per server.

- Two days of additional training costs for system admin personnel ~ $5K.

- Four new SQL Server licenses (SQL Server 2000—the remote distributor and three new subscribers) at $5K per server.

There are no special hardware or SCSI controllers needed to implement data replication. The total incremental cost to build this high availability solution is approximately $89,500 (total costs—as follows).

Now, let's work through the complete ROI calculation for these incremental costs along with the cost of downtime:

1. Maintenance cost (for a one-year period):

   - $5K (estimate)—Yearly system admin personnel cost (additional time for training of these personnel)

   - $24.5K (estimate)—Recurring software licensing cost (of additional HA components; [3] OS + [4] SQL Server 2000)

2. Hardware cost:

   - $30K hardware cost (of the additional HW in the new HA solution)

3. Deployment/assessment cost:

   - $20K deployment cost (develop, test, QA, production implementation of the solution)

   - $10K HA assessment cost

4. Downtime cost (for a one-year period):

   - If you kept track of last year's downtime record, use this number; otherwise produce an estimate of planned and unplanned downtime for this calculation. We estimated the cost of downtime/hour to be **$5K/Hour.**

   - Planned downtime cost (revenue loss cost) = Planned downtime hours × cost of hourly downtime to the company:

     a. 3% (estimate of planned downtime percentage in one year) × 8760 hours in a year = 262.8 hours of planned downtime

> **b.** 262.8 hours × $5K/hr (hourly cost of downtime) = $1,314,000/year cost of planned downtime.

- Unplanned downtime cost (revenue loss cost) = Unplanned downtime hours × cost of hourly downtime to the company:

> **a.** 2% (estimate of unplanned downtime percentage in one year) × 8760 hours in a year = 175.2 hours of unplanned downtime
>
> **b.** 175.2 hours × $5K/hr (hourly cost of downtime) = $876,000/year cost of unplanned downtime.

ROI totals:

- Total costs to get on this HA solution = $89,500 (for the initial year and roughly $24.5K/year for subsequent years)
- Total of downtime cost = $2,190,000 (for the year)

The incremental cost is about 4% of the downtime cost for one year. In other words, the investment of this particular HA solution will pay for itself in 18.9 hours! This is a huge ROI in a very short amount of time. And provides a great scalable and flexible platform to grow on.

After building this HA solution, the uptime goal was achieved easily. Occasionally, there were some delays in resyncing the data at each regional site (subscribers). But, overall, the users were extremely happy with performance and availability. This is a great example of knowing what your HA options are and how to minimize hardware, software, and maintenance costs. Exceptional!

Summary

Data replication is a powerful feature of SQL Server that can be used in many business situations. Companies can use replication for anything from roll-up reporting to relieving the main server from ad hoc queries and reporting. However, applying it as a high availability solution can be very effective if your requirements match well to its capability. Determining the right replication option and configuration to use is somewhat difficult, whereas actually setting it up is pretty easy. Microsoft has come a long way in this regard. As with scenario #2, if your requirements are not "extreme availability," this perhaps is one of the options you will make good use of. It is more than production-worthy, and the flexibility it offers and the overall performance is just short of incredible, incredible, incredible (replication humor for you).

CHAPTER 8

Other Ways to Distribute Data for High Availability

THE KEY TOPICS IN THIS CHAPTER ARE

- Building distributed transactions to achieve HA
- Distributed Transaction Coordinator (MS DTC)
- COM+ based distributed applications

Alternate Ways to Achieve High Availability

U p to this point, you have seen several Microsoft-based solutions that can provide varying degrees of high availability. Some, like SQL clustering, are highly transparent to the end-user. More often than not, the end-user never knows that a failure has even occurred. Other HA options such as log shipping and data replication have small amounts of non-transparency that require an end-user to reestablish the database connection that their application requires via some type of manual intervention. Not so bad, and this can be done extremely quickly, again minimizing unavailability. These techniques heavily leverage fault tolerant, shared disk management and clustered servers (SQL clustering/MSCS) and also use data redundancy techniques (log shipping and data replication). However, as an alternative, you may want to use a distributed transaction processing approach if this better matches your high availability requirements. A distributed transaction processing approach is not database oriented, but rather it is application (or service) oriented.

You can build standard client/server applications that are distributed in nature (leveraging MS DTC), or you can choose to build server side distributed applications leveraging COM+ as well. Again, this type of approach changes the high availability orientation to be application-driven, not database- or disk-oriented. The Microsoft distributed programming model consists of several technologies, including MSMQ, IIS, MS DTC, DCOM, and COM+. All of these services are designed for use by distributed applications.

A Distributed Data Approach from the Outset

For years, many application developers have decided not to rely on back-end solutions for high availability and, in fact, to "design in" a distributed data approach into their applications architecture from the start. In other words, the application design purposely distributes data (redundantly, for fail-over purposes). The distributed applications can then guarantee themselves more than one place to get to their data in the event of a single server failure. A key element to accomplishing this feat is to create units of work that span two or more database locations as part of a single database transaction (via two-phase commit [2PC] protocol) to redundantly make updates, inserts, or deletes. This is very prevalent in financial institutions that require their applications to be highly accurate and highly available.

Then, a properly designed application would be "programmed" to be aware of a failed server (data source). Figure 8.1 shows how an application could be developed to do a primary data read request against one location, and if that access fails (because the location has failed or is not accessible via the network), it would try a secondary location that had the same data. If data updates are being created (inserts/deletes/updates) at any one of the data source locations, a single distributed transaction would be used to guarantee that the updates are successful at all data locations. If one of the data locations is not available during this update, a resynchronization approach or a queuing approach can be devised that catches up any updates on the failed data location when it becomes available again.

You can design and build these types of SQL Server-based applications leveraging the distributed transaction coordinator (MS DTC). Each Microsoft SQL Server will have an associated distributed transaction coordinator on the same machine with it. For that matter, MS DTC is present on your Windows Server regardless of whether you have SQL Server installed or not.

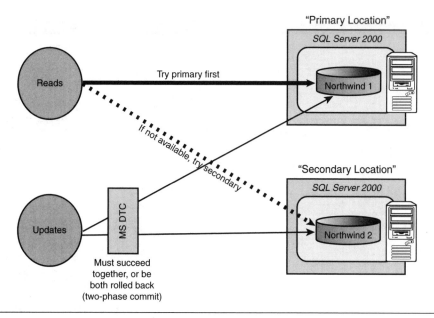

Figure 8.1   A distributed application approach for achieving HA.

The MS DTC allows applications to extend transactions across two or more instances of MS SQL Server (or other data sources) and to participate in transactions managed by transaction managers that comply with the X/Open DTP XA standard. The MS DTC will act as the primary coordinator for these distributed transactions. MS DTC ensures that all updates are made permanent in all data locations (committed), or makes sure that all of the work is undone (rolled back) if it needs to be. MS DTC is essentially brokering a multi-server transaction. Each SQL Server (or XA compliant resource) is just a resource manager for their local data.

For distributed data applications, a Unit of Work (UOW) is what is managed by MS DTC and is your design point of view. In general, a designed Unit of Work should succeed or fail together, across all resources involved (that have been enlisted) in the transaction as shown in Figure 8.2.

You can alternatively design the update portion of your application to push things to a queue using Microsoft Queue Manager (MSMQ) if any one of the database locations is not available. This is an application design decision.

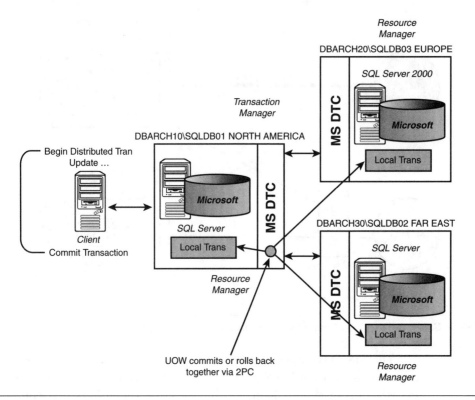

Figure 8.2   A distributed transaction across multiple SQL Servers managed by MS DTC.

It may very well be that your application has many distributed queries that do not need to be managed by MS DTC because they are read only. And, your application may only have a very small number of actual "distributed transactions" that contain updates that are few and far between. If your application has these types of processing characteristics, it might fit very well into this type of overall distributed processing model and help you achieve all of your high availability needs.

For this to happen, you must establish a way for each SQL Server to communicate with each other freely. This is done by establishing links to and from each SQL Server that will participate in a distributed architecture.

The following SQL statement is producing a list of customers from a SQL Server in North America and with a remote SQL Server in Europe. Note the four-part name for the customers table ([SQL Server\InstanceName].[database].[owner].[tableName] in the FROM clause):

```
SELECT a.CustomerID, a.CompanyName, 'North American Customers'
FROM  [DBARCH30\SQLDB02].Northwind.dbo.[customers] a -- North America
UNION ALL
select b.CustomerID, b.CompanyName, 'European Customers'
FROM [DBARCH20\SQLDB03].Northwind.dbo.[customers] b -- Europe
Go
CustomerID CompanyName
---------- ---------------------------------
VINET      Vins et alcools Chevalier              North American Customers
WARTH      Wartian Herkku                         North American Customers
WELLI      Wellington Importadora                 North American Customers
WHITC      White Clover Markets                   North American Customers
WILMK      Wilman Kala                            North American Customers
WOLZA      Wolski  Zajazd                         North American Customers
ALFKI      Alfreds Futterkiste                    European Customers
ANATR      Ana Trujillo Emparedados y helados European Customers
ANTON      Antonio Moreno Taquería                European Customers
AROUT      Around the Horn                        European Customers
BERGS      Berglunds snabbköp                     European Customers
```

It is that easy. So, let's jump into how to make this possible by first seeing how you set up access to the remote SQL Servers.

Setting Up Access to Remote SQL Servers

In order to create a SQL statement that references a distributed (remote) SQL Server from another SQL Server, you must identify the remote SQL Server to the local SQL Server. This essentially allows the SQL Servers to be linked--Microsoft has termed this "linked remote servers." As an added feature, Microsoft also allows you to setup a pre-authorized login that maps a login account created on the local server to an account created on the remote server. Now the two SQL Servers can reference each other's data objects and participate in distributed transactions.

Establishing a Link to a Remote SQL Server

Establishing a link to a remote SQL Server and establishing the proper data access is a simple process that can be done by system stored procedures (sp_addlinkedserver and sp_addlinkedsrvlogin) or via the Enterprise Manager Linked Server node under the security option. You will provide the server type ("SQL Server" in this case) and the linked server name that you are trying to establish a link to (the SQL Server name and the instance if one has been created--"DBARCH20\SQLDB03" in this example). You can also use this dialog to establish links to any OLE or ODBC compliant data source such as Access, Excel, Oracle, so on. You don't need to specify the *provider_name*, *data_source*, *location*, *provider_string, or catalog name* when you are connecting to a SQL Server 6.5 (or higher) remote data source. Figure 8.3 shows this dialog box and the tabs for the new linked server.

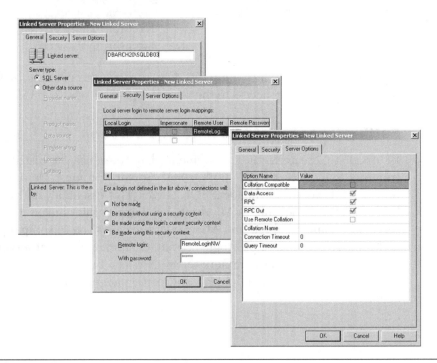

Figure 8.3   Adding a new linked (remote) server to the local SQL Server.

The system stored procedure equivalent of this dialog box starts with the sp_addlinkedserver as follows:

```
sp_addlinkedserver 'DBARCH20\SQLDB03', 'SQL Server'
go
```

You will then need to establish login IDs between the local and remote SQL Servers.

Establishing Linked Server Security

When a remote/distributed query is executed, the local SQL Server logs on to the remote SQL Server on behalf of the user. Therefore, it will be necessary to establish security between the local and remote SQL Servers. If the user's login ID and password exist on both the local and remote SQL Servers, the local SQL Server can use the account information of the user to log in to the remote SQL Server. If not (which is probably the norm), you should establish a remote login ID that has the necessary permissions at the remote SQL Server and then map all remote SQL Server accesses to use this login ID. For our example, we will create a login ID on the remote SQL Server ("DBARCH20\SQLDB03") that has been given the appropriate data access permissions in the Northwind database only. This login ID is called "RemoteLoginNW". Then, in the Security tab of the New Linked Server dialog box (Figure 8.3), we will map the local "sa" login to this remote user and also specify that all other local logins not listed in the local login list will use this same Remote Login (RemoteLoginNW login ID).

We could also have used the `sp_addlinkedsrvlogin` system-stored procedure to do the same thing. Keep in mind that `sp_addlinkedsrvlogin` or the Security tab of the New Linked Server dialog box don't "create" user accounts. They merely map a login account created on the local SQL Server to an account created on the remote SQL Server.

You can also use the `sp_helplinkedsrvlogin` system-stored procedure to quickly find out what linked server logins have been defined. Simply execute this stored procedure without parameters to see all that have been defined on a local SQL Server:

```
EXEC sp_helplinkedsrvlogin
go
Linked Server          Local Login      Is Self Mapping    Remote Login
DBARCH20\SQLDB03       NULL             0                  RemoteLoginNW
DBARCH20\SQLDB03       sa               0                  RemoteLoginNW
DBARCH30\SQLDB02       NULL             1                  NULL
```

Once you have added the linked/remote SQL Server, it appears in the tree structure under the Linked Servers node (as shown in Figure 8.4).

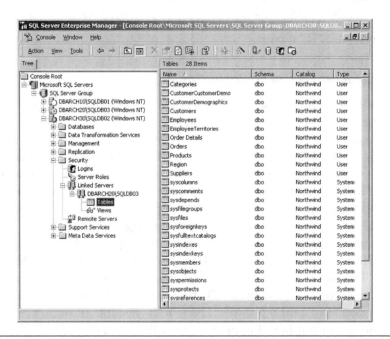

Figure 8.4   Enterprise Manager's view of a newly added linked SQL Server.

If you haven't added the linked/remote server yet, you will get an error message when you try to execute any query that has a reference to a remote SQL Server. The following distributed query was executed from the local server before the remote/linked server was added:

```
select b.CustomerID, b.CompanyName, 'European Customers'
FROM [DBARCH20\SQLDB03].Northwind.dbo.[customers] b -- Europe
Go
Server: Msg 7202, Level 11, State 2, Line 1
Could not find server 'DBARCH20\SQLDB03' in sysservers.
Execute sp_addlinkedserver to add the server to sysservers.
```

The local SQL Server has no system catalog entries that correspond to the named remote SQL Server (yet). If you added the linked/remote SQL Server but have not created the login for the linked server to use when it tries to log in to the remote SQL Server, you will get the following error message on your query attempt:

```
select b.CustomerID, b.CompanyName, 'European Customers'
FROM [DBARCH20\SQLDB03].Northwind.dbo.[customers] b - Europe
Go
Server: Msg 7314, Level 16, State 1, Line 1
OLE DB provider 'DBARCH20\SQLDB03' does not
   contain table '"Northwind"."customers"'.
The table either does not exist or the current
   user does not have permissions on that table.
OLE DB error trace [Non-interface error:  OLE DB provider
   does not contain the table:
ProviderName='DBARCH20\SQLDB03',
TableName='"Northwind"."customers"']..
```

SQL Server simply has nothing to map to on the linked/remote server side. You must resolve this by adding a valid user ID with the appropriate permissions for the linked server to use when attempting data access. If you have added the linked server but haven't set up anything on the security tab yet, you may get other error messages that reflect that no login-mapping exists or an invalid authorization has occurred.

Querying a Linked Server

When you write a distributed query (or a distributed transaction for that matter), you will be using a four-part name to refer to the linked objects. The linked server is said to conform to the IDBSchemaRowset interface--it allows for the schema information to be retrieved from the remote server. If the linked server doesn't conform to this interface, you will have to do all access using pass-through queries in the OPENDATASOURCE or OPENROWSET function. However, in most cases, you will be using this four-part name:

```
linked_server_name.catalog.schema.object_name
```

The name can be broken down as follows:

linked_server_name	The unique networkwide name of the linked server [Servername\instancename|Servername]
catalog	The catalog or database in the OLE DB that contains the object
schema	The schema or object owner
object_name	The name of the table or data object

As pointed out earlier, when this linked server is a SQL Server (6.5 or later), the four-part name will be ([SQL Server\InstanceName].[database].[owner].[tableName] for any referenced tables, views, or stored procedures. For example, if you want to use the Customers table that is owned by the database owner (dbo) in the Northwind database on the "DBARCH20\SQLDB03" linked SQL Server, you would specify:

```
[DBARCH20\SQLDB03].Northwind.dbo.[Customers]
```

Transact-SQL with Linked Servers

You can use the following Transact-SQL statements with linked servers:

- SELECT statement with a WHERE clause or a JOIN clause
- INSERT, UPDATE, and DELETE statements

You cannot use the following:

- CREATE, ALTER, or DROP statements
- An ORDER BY clause in a SELECT statement if a large object column from a linked table (other than a SQL Server table) is in the select list of the SELECT statement
- Restrictions if a linked server is defined using the OLE DB Provider for ODBC and accesses a SQL Server database:

  Tables cannot be referenced if they have one or more timestamp columns.

  Tables cannot be referenced if they have nullable char, varchar, nchar, nvarchar, binary, or varbinary columns and the ANSI_PADDING option was set OFF when the table was created.

- READTEXT, WRITETEXT, and UPDATETEXT statements

Once the linked/remote SQL Servers know about each other and have valid logins mapped, executing the query yields the desired results:

```
SELECT a.CustomerID, a.CompanyName, SalesRegion = 'North American
Customers'
FROM  [DBARCH30\SQLDB02].Northwind.dbo.[customers] a -- North America
UNION ALL
select b.CustomerID, b.CompanyName, SalesRegion = 'European Customers'
FROM [DBARCH20\SQLDB03].Northwind.dbo.[customers] b -- Europe
Go
```

```
CustomerID CompanyName                              SalesRegion
---------- -------------------------------- ------------------------
VINET      Vins et alcools Chevalier        North American Customers
WOLZA      Wolski  Zajazd                   North American Customers
ANATR      Ana Trujillo Emparedados y helados European Customers
BERGS      Berglunds snabbköp               European Customers
```

An alternative method of executing a distributed SQL query is to use the OPENQUERY syntax. Following is an example of a remote/distributed query against the "DBARCH20\SQLDB03" linked server:

```
select CustomerID, CompanyName, 'European Customers'
FROM OPENQUERY ([DBARCH20\SQLDB03],'SELECT CustomerID, CompanyName
FROM    [Northwind]..[Customers]')
Go
CustomerID CompanyName
---------- ----------------------------------------
ALFKI      Alfreds Futterkiste                      European Customers
ANATR      Ana Trujillo Emparedados y helados       European Customers
ANTON      Antonio Moreno Taquería                  European Customers
AROUT      Around the Horn                          European Customers
BERGS      Berglunds snabbköp                       European Customers
```

In addition, it is possible to execute stored procedures via a linked server. The server hosting the client connection will accept the client's request and send it to the linked server. The EXECUTE statement must contain the name of the linked server as part of its syntax:

```
EXECUTE servername.dbname.owner.procedure_name
```

The following example executes sp_helpdb for the Northwind database on the remote/linked server DBARCH20\SQLDB03:

```
exec [DBARCH20\SQLDB03].master.dbo.sp_helpdb 'Northwind'
```

Distributed Transactions

If you have decided to get into the distributed transaction business to support your high availability requirements, it will be extremely important for you to understand the distributed "unit of work" logical transaction concept. In other words, you need a way to ensure that the distributed transaction operates in the same way that a local transaction does, and that it adheres to the same ACID properties of a local transaction, across multiple servers.

Microsoft has implemented its distributed transaction processing capabilities based on the industry standard *two-phase commit protocol*. As mentioned earlier in this chapter, it utilizes the distributed transaction coordinator service (MS DTC) as the controller of this capability. This ensures the consistency of all parts of any distributed transaction passing through MS SQL Server and any referenced linked servers. The variation on the ACID test is that all sites (servers) depend on one another for completion of an update, and they must give up the site autonomy part of ACID.

Design Note

ACID (atomicity, consistency, isolation, and durability) is the acronym that describes the four primary attributes that are being enforced for any transaction by a transaction manager. These attributes are

Atomicity. In a transaction involving two or more discrete pieces of information, either all of the pieces are committed or none are.

Consistency. A transaction either creates a new and valid state of data, or, if any failure occurs, returns all data to its state before the transaction was started.

Isolation. A transaction in process and not yet committed must remain isolated from any other transaction.

Durability. Committed data is saved by the system such that, even in the event of a failure and system restart, the data is available in its correct state.

The ACID concept is described in ISO/IEC 10026-1:1992 Section 4.

In a distributed system, one way to achieve ACID is to use a two-phase commit (2PC) protocol, which ensures that all involved sites must commit to transaction completion or none do (and the complete transaction is rolled back). That is the role MS DTC takes on.

Let's examine the MS DTC architecture thoroughly.

MS DTC Architecture

In general, each Microsoft SQL Server that you want to be included in your high availability distributed transaction topology must have an associated distributed transaction coordinator (MS DTC).

As has been explained, it is MS DTC that allows your applications to extend transactions across two or more instances of MS SQL Server (and participate in transactions managed by transaction managers that comply with the X/Open DTP XA standard). Think of MS DTC as the primary coordinator for these distributed transactions. MS DTC enlists (includes) and coordinates all SQL Servers (linked servers) that are part of a single distributed transaction as is shown in Figure 8.2

SQL Server will automatically promote a local transaction to a distributed transaction when it encounters the remote server access in combination with an update request, whether or not you have explicitly started a distributed transaction. The MS DTC coordinates the execution of the distributed transaction at each participating data source and makes sure the distributed transaction completes. It ensures that all updates are made permanent in all data sources (committed), or makes sure that all of the work is undone (rolled back) if it needs to be. At all times, the states of all data sources involved are kept intact. To guarantee that this is taken care of properly, the MS DTC manages each distributed transaction using the two-phase commit protocol (2PC).

Two-Phase Commit Protocol

An MS DTC service provides two-phase commit functionality based on its ability to act as a transaction manager across one or more resource managers. A SQL Server (or other OLE DB data source for that matter) is considered a resource manager of its own data. A distributed transaction is made up of local transactions in each individual resource manager. Each resource manager must be able to commit or roll back its local transaction in coordination with all the other resource managers enlisted in the distributed transaction (again looking back at Figure 8.2). That is the transaction manager's job (MS DTC in this case). This distributed transaction is referred to as a Unit of Work (UOW). In fact, it will be given a networkwide UOW ID (unique identifier) which it will monitor and manage from. This UOW ID can be seen from the Component Services Distributed Transaction Coordinator console. Figure 8.5 shows an active distributed transaction in the DTC Transaction List. As you can see, it will have a status and a unique Unit of Work ID assigned to it.

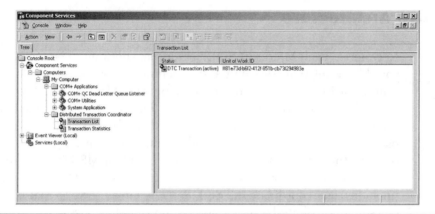

Figure 8.5   Component Services console: Distributed Transaction Coordinator – Transaction List status and UOW ID.

A distributed transaction goes through the following steps:

1. The distributed transaction is started and is assigned a unique Unit of Work ID by the controlling distributed transaction coordinator (the transaction manager) for the SQL Server.

2. Data modification statements are issued against any linked/remote servers available to and including SQL Server. These become local transactions at each linked/remote server and are controlled by the local resource manager (the DBMS engine in most cases).

3. The transaction server (MS DTC) enlists the appropriate servers into the distributed transaction.

4. Phase One (Prepare): The transaction manager sends a "prepare to commit" request to each resource manager. The resource managers, in turn, perform their local transaction commit processing to the point just before releasing the minimal locks on the affected resources. All of the resource managers communicate back to the transaction manager that they are "ready to commit."

5. Phase Two (Commit): If all the resource managers return an okay to their prepare requests, the transaction manager sends commit transaction commands to each of them. Then, each resource manager can do a final commit for the local transaction and release the locks on the held resources. The distributed transaction is complete. However, if any of the resource managers returns an error to the prepare request, the transaction manager

will send rollback commands to each of the resource managers to undo all the local transactions.

If one of the enlisted SQL Servers is unable to communicate with the transaction server, the database involved is marked as suspect. When the transaction server is "visible" again, the affected server should be restarted so that the database and the in-doubt transaction can be recovered (which is done automatically).

SQL Server Distributed Transactions

In general, an application can initiate a distributed transaction from SQL Server by doing the following:

- Starting with a local transaction and then issuing a distributed query. The transaction will automatically be promoted to a distributed transaction that is controlled by MS DTC.

- Issuing a `BEGIN DISTRIBUTED TRANSACTION` statement explicitly.

- Starting with a local transaction and then issuing a remote procedure call (SQL Server option of `REMOTE_PROC_TRANSACTIONS` must be set to "on"). Again, this will automatically be promoted to a distributed transaction.

- Allowing a SQL Server connection to participate in a distributed transaction.

Be aware that MS DTC makes use of a log file to record the outcome of all transactions that have made use of its services. By default, the DTC log file is installed in the `\System32\DTClog` directory under WIN2000. If you want it somewhere else for performance and backup/recovery purposes, specify this location at install time. It's much easier to change the location at install time than to rewire it later. Plan ahead!

Distributed Queries and Transactions for HA

There are several approaches to take when designing a highly available distributed application. Based on your data access requirements, you have some flexibility on how you handle reads versus writes (Inserts/Deletes/Updates). If your high availability requirements demand that you have read access to your data as much as possible (like with kiosk-type applications or online benefits portals) then your HA design will be focused on making sure your application can get to a secondary (distributed) database when the primary database fails. For these types of applications, updates, inserts, and deletes are typically handled in a batching mode and applied overnight against each distributed SQL Server. The reads are easily supported using the distributed query capabilities of MS SQL Server (and linked servers).

If your data access requirements demand that reads *and* writes be highly available, then we get into the distributed transaction business and must understand some of the limitations that will exist to protect the data integrity at all distributed SQL Server nodes. Basically, you will be able to read data at the primary SQL Server or the secondary SQL Server any time. For updates/inserts/deletes, you can force these to be made at both the primary or secondary SQL Server as one Unit of Work (to guarantee data integrity with no data latency) or you can have these updates/inserts/deletes queued up to an overnight batch processing queue or you can use MS Queue manager to queue up these updates/inserts/deletes for the secondary server (if it is not available for any reason). There are probably a hundred other variations on this theme. We recommend that you err on the side of data integrity and limit the updates/inserts/deletes during failed server times in order to guarantee maximum availability for the reads. But, again, your data access requirements will dictate which approach to use.

High Availability data access **Pseudo Code**

FOR READS

> Select data from SQL Server A
>
> IF connection fails (for any reason)
>
> THEN Select data from SQL Server B (distributed copy of data)

FOR UPDATES/INSERTS/DELETES

> Begin Distributed Transaction
>
> Update SQL Server A
>
> Update SQL Server B (distributed copy of data)
>
> IF Update to SQL Server A or B fails
>
> THEN Roll Back Distributed Transaction
>
> ELSE Commit Distributed Transaction

Loosely Coupled Approach Using DTS and MS Queue Manager

For the update portion of this approach, you might also decide to be a bit more loosely coupled by incorporating MS Queue manager and data transformation services (DTS). What you can do is submit your updates to be processed using DTS packages. The DTS packages utilize MS Queue managers named message queues and data transformation tasks to do all the work. The downside of using this approach is the potential for DTS failures, queue failures, and update delays. However, if one of the SQL Servers that you are trying to send distributed data to is not available, those updates can be queued up for delivery to that server. Then, when the server becomes available again, the queue will be processed until it is empty (all caught up). Figure 8.6 shows the DTS designer workspace, the queue tasks, connection tasks, and workflow to distribute updates from the customer table in Northwind on the primary SQL Server to the same table in a secondary SQL Server using the global variable messages approach.

These global variable messages can be parameterized to include the values that are being updated along with the primary key values. However, if you have numerous tables to distribute (like the entire Northwind database), this approach would not be recommended. If you only needed to distribute the updates/inserts/deletes of a couple of tables in order to meet your high availability needs, then this might work out quite nicely. And, keep in mind that to create message queue tasks, you need to first install the MSMQ client on the server.

The general DTS package setup would be

1. Create a message queue task (and named message queue in the form of *computer name\queue_type$\queue_name*—a combination that identifies the queue from which you will be reading messages).

2. Create the connections to the secondary SQL Server.

3. Create the transform data tasks that map the source table columns to the target table columns.

4. Define the workflow properties as "Join transaction if present" and "Commit transaction on successful completion of this step".

5. Create another queue to handle any logging of bad updates to this secondary SQL Server (log to a flat file or to a table in SQL Server).

6. Define a dynamic properties task to cause the package to loop.

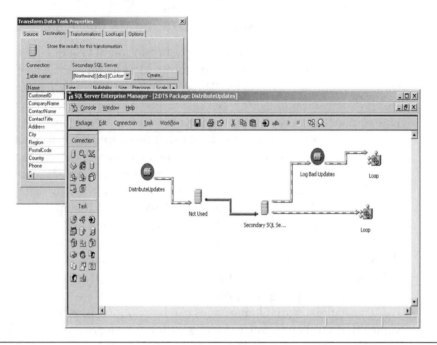

Figure 8.6   Data transformation services package setup for distributing updates to a secondary SQL Server.

You have now created the necessary data transformation services (DTS) objects, set their properties, and added them to the appropriate collections. For Visual Basic (as you can see in the following code sample), you can now use the `Execute` method of the `Package2` object to run the package (`ExecutePackageTask`, through the `Execute` and `UnInitialize` methods). This partial VB code snippet illustrates the external variables (parms) file reference and the dynamic DTS package invocation technique. Remember, this is a very loosely coupled solution but can achieve what you are looking for.

```
Private WithEvents mobjPkgEvents As DTS.Package

. . .

Private Sub RunPackage()
'Run the package stored in file C:\DTS\TestPkg\VarNWFields.dts.
Dim objPackage     As DTS.Package2
Dim objStep        As DTS.Step
Dim objTask        As DTS.Task
Dim objExecPkg     As DTS.ExecutePackageTask
```

```
On Error GoTo PackageError
Set objPackage = New DTS.Package
Set mobjPkgEvents = objPackage
objPackage.FailOnError = True

'Create the step and task. Specify the package to be run,
'and link the step to the task.
Set objStep = objPackage.Steps.New
Set objTask = objPackage.Tasks.New("DTSExecutePackageTask")
Set objExecPkg = objTask.CustomTask
With objExecPkg
    .PackagePassword = "user"
    .FileName = "C:\DTS\TestPkg\VarNWFields.dts"
    .Name = "ExecPkgTask"
End With
With objStep
    .TaskName = objExecPkg.Name
    .Name = "ExecPkgStep"
    .ExecuteInMainThread = True
End With
objPackage.Steps.Add objStep
objPackage.Tasks.Add objTask

'Run the package and release references.
objPackage.Execute

Set objExecPkg = Nothing
Set objTask = Nothing
Set objStep = Nothing
Set mobjPkgEvents = Nothing

objPackage.UnInitialize
End Sub
```

Tightly Coupled Approach Using Distributed Transactions

A tightly coupledapproach is probably the safest from a data integrity
and data latency point of view. In other words, designing your distributed queries and transactions to be contained within a unit of work is
advised. As a developer, you really don't have to change that much of
your code to take advantage of distributed transactions.

By using BEGIN DISTRIBUTED TRANSACTION instead of the usual BEGIN TRANSACTION (used for local transactions), you automatically elevate your transactions to distributed transactions. Then, all linked servers that have been defined are available to your application.

The following are two examples of distributed transactions. The first is a single update statement that references the Customers table in a linked/remote SQL Server (in fact, it is joining to this table for the source of an update). No explicit BEGIN DISTRIBUTED TRANSACTION statement was included because it was a single SQL statement and SQL Server will automatically elevate it to a distributed transaction because of the linked/remote SQL Server reference in the JOIN clause:

```
Update Customers
    set NA.ContactName = Europe.ContactName
FROM [Northwind].dbo.[Customers] AS NA
    INNER JOIN
[DBARCH20\SQLDB03].[Northwind].dbo.[Customers] AS Europe
    ON NA.CustomerID = Europe.CustomerID
```

The second example is a multi-statement unit of work that we want to succeed or fail together, which is actually updating the local table and then redundantly updating the same table at the secondary SQL server. We have decided to force this data integrity condition, since our sample application rarely does updates (it is predominantly a read-only application and the highest priority for high availability is for the reads).

```
set xact_abort on

Begin Distributed Transaction
  Update Customers
    set ContactName = 'Donald Bertucci'
  Update [DBARCH20\SQLDB03].[Northwind].dbo.[Customers]
    set ContactName = 'Donald Bertucci'
commit transaction
```

In Figure 8.7, you can take a quick peek at MS DTC transaction statistics within the Component Services console that show that a distributed transaction is currently being executed (Active is 1), there are no "in doubt" transactions, and there are currently three committed transactions (distributed transactions).

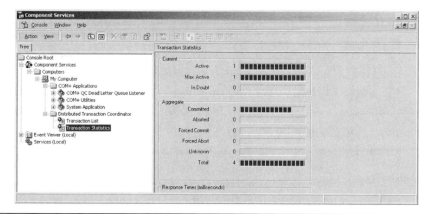

Figure 8.7   Component Services console of an active distributed transaction.

COM+ Applications for HA

COM+ is the next step in the evolution of the Microsoft Component Object Model (COM) and Microsoft Transaction Server (MTS). COM+ handles many of the resource management tasks you previously had to program yourself, such as thread allocation and security. It automatically makes your applications more scalable by providing thread pooling, object pooling, and just-in-time object activation. COM+ also helps protect the integrity of your data by providing transaction support, even if a transaction spans multiple databases over a network.

A COM+ application will support multiple users across multiple servers. In other words, you are building a distributed application, and these multiple users are going to be on different host machines from where the code runs. Users are going to access the code via the Internet or via a private network.

The COM+ application can be made scalable and can provide greater availability and reliability by deploying the application across multiple server machines. In doing this, you can balance the workload of the application and you could also provide fault tolerance by using MS cluster services on these servers.

If things go wrong, the state of the persisted data, stored in a database, from a COM+ application will be maintained if you are using distributed transactions. By design, the application state will survive accidents that can occur, such as application errors, system crashes, or network failures.

COM+ application logic will reside on server machines, not on client machines. There are three major reasons to do this:

- The client machine may not have the processing power or features needed to run the application logic. In addition, keeping the application logic on the server simplifies deployment.

- The server machines are often closer to the data, and this data is most often in a database. Because your application is accessing databases, you want to be very sensitive to the cost of database connections. By putting most of the logic on the server machines, you can share database connections and get a significant performance improvement (via connection pooling and extremely fast network backbones between servers).

- Having application logic reside on server machines keeps control of the security context with the application. You have more control over security if you maintain that security on application components running on server machines rather than on client machines.

You can design a transaction-based COM+ application to work with a resource manager and a database, which helps protect most state information. By keeping state inside a database or some other storage managed by a resource manager, you don't have to keep much state inside the actual objects your application creates. While this is a departure from a pure object-oriented model, it works well for creating distributed applications with error recovery. Application functionality is built as COM+ objects, wrapping the protocols used to communicate with other systems or technologies.

Graceful fail-over and fault tolerance are vital for mission-critical applications that require high availability. Such resilience is usually achieved through a number of hardware, operating system, and application software mechanisms.

COM+ provides basic support for fault tolerance at the protocol level. A sophisticated pinging mechanism detects network and client-side hardware failures. If the network recovers before the timeout interval, COM+ reestablishes connections automatically.

Using a referral component technique, clients can detect the failure of a component, then reconnect to the same referral component that established the first connection for them. This referral component has information about which servers are no longer available and automatically provides the client with a new instance of the component running on another machine. Applications will, of course, still have to deal with error recovery at higher levels (consistency, loss of information, and so on). And, once you have built the COM+ application, you can deploy the application across a network or server cluster. If you look back at Figure 8.7, you will see the full COM+ Applications branch that is used for deploying and monitoring COM+ applications. COM+ services span a great number of areas and comprise a rich and robust foundation for the development of applications that directly support high availability requirements.

COM+ services include

- Events
- Security
- Load balancing
- Queued components
- In memory database
- Compensating resource manager
- Administration

Summary

Using programmatic methods to achieve a high availability solution will vary in its success and complexity. I've seen shops that start their thinking as a distributed application and prefer to "design in" the high availability elements themselves. They leverage more basic fault tolerant components such as RAID for disk fault tolerance and MS cluster services for hardware/server fault tolerance. They often do not use things such as SQL clustering or replication because they have had their applications up and running for many years, long before these new HA techniques were even available for use. This is very prevalent in applications built in the financial industry.

By designing in the high availability elements (such as primary and secondary read logic and distributed transaction updates), you relieve other resources from having to provide the same or varying degrees of high availability. However, the data access requirements (type of accesses, frequency of accesses, data latency tolerances, performance, and so on) coupled with the high availability service levels you must support will quickly drive you to using a distributed data technique (like distributed transactions, distributed queries, or COM+ Applications) or to the other "canned" HA techniques such as SQL clustering, log shipping, or data replication.

CHAPTER 9

High Availability Pieced Together

THE KEY TOPICS ARE

- Putting your foundation in place
- Assembling your HA assessment team
- Scheduling the HA assessment major events
- Conducting an HA assessment
- Selecting an HA solution
- Verify the HA solution ROI

Achieving Five 9s

As you have no doubt surmised by now, evaluating, selecting, designing, and implementing the right high availability solution should not be left to the weak at heart or the inexperienced. There is too much at stake for your company in the event mistakes are made in this process. For this reason, we will, again, stress that you use your best technologists for any HA assessment you do *OR* go get some outside help that specializes in HA assessments. And get it fast.

The good news is that achieving the mythical five 9s (a sustained 99.999% availability of your application) can be done, if you follow the steps that we have outlined. In addition, you have now had a chance to thoroughly dig into the primary HA solutions from Microsoft (cluster services, SQL clustering, replication, log shipping, and distributed transaction approaches) and should be getting a feel of what these can do for you. We will combine this exposure and capability information together into a coherent step-by-step methodology for getting your applications onto the correct high availability solution. But first, a few words about the hardware and software foundation you put into place.

Foundation First

Remember, in real estate it is "location, location, location"; in HA solutions, it is "foundation, foundation, foundation." Laying in the proper hardware and software components will allow you to build most HA solutions in a solid and resilient way. As you can see in Figure 9.1, these foundation elements relate directly to different parts of your system stack.

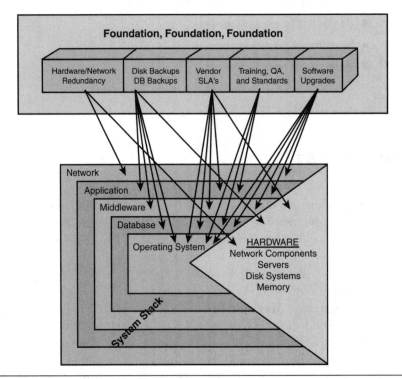

Figure 9.1   Foundation elements and their effect on different system stack components.

Specifically, these are

- Putting hardware/network redundancies into place shores up your network access and long-term stability of your servers themselves.

- Making sure all network, OS, application, middleware, and database software upgrades are always kept at the highest release levels possible (including antivirus software) affects most components in the system stack.

- Deploying comprehensive and well designed disk backups and DB backups directly impacts your applications, middleware, databases, and the stability of your operating systems.

- Establishing the necessary vendor service level agreements/contracts affects all components of the system stack (hardware and software).

- Comprehensive end-user, administrator, and developer training including extensive QA testing has a great impact on the stability of your applications, databases, and the OS itself.

Without making any further specialized HA changes, this basic foundation offers a huge degree of availability (and stability) in itself. Not necessarily five 9s, though. Adding specialized high availability solutions to this foundation allows you to push toward higher HA goals.

In order to select the "right" high availability solution, you must gather the specialized high availability detail requirements of your application. Very often, characteristics related to high availability are not considered or are neglected during the normal requirements gathering process. As you have also been advised earlier, gathering these requirements is best done by initiating a full blown Phase 0 HA Assessment project that runs through all of the HA assessment areas (these have been designed to flesh out HA requirements specifically). Then, based on the software available, the hardware available, and these high availability requirements, you can match and build the appropriate HA solution on top of your solid foundation.

If your application is already implemented (or about to be) then you will really be doing a high availability "retrofit." Coming in at such a late stage in the process may or may not limit some of the HA options you could have selected. This of course depends on what you have built. As was mentioned earlier, 90% of the HA assessments that we have done were of already "implemented" applications. We then matched up the HA solutions that best met the HA needs and that didn't result in a major rewrite of the application (not always the optimal solution, but it met or exceeded the HA requirements in all cases).

Assemble Your HA Assessment Team

If you haven't done this before, then here's what you need to do to assemble the right folks for doing an HA assessment. You have three players who have to be the kernel members of any HA assessment effort. First, the project coordinator/manager who will drive the whole thing, a lead technologist/architect who thoroughly understands HA and the technology stack at your company, and the lead business architect who understands the application inside and out and also can calculate the exact business value of the application. In addition, several other groups or representatives that cover all areas of hardware, software, security, and end-users will be tapped during the HA assessment process.

The team will look like this:

- HA project lead/Champion—The project lead that will drive all meetings, schedule all participants, and manage the day-to-day tasks.

- A system architect/data architect (SA/DA)—Someone with both extensive system design and data design experience who will be able to understand the hardware, software, and database aspects of high availability.

- A very senior business analyst (SBA)—This person must be completely versed in development methodologies and the business requirements that are being targeted by the application (and by the assessment).

- A part-time senior technical lead (STL)—A software engineer type with good overall system development skills so that they can help in assessing the coding standards that are being followed, the completeness of the system testing tasks, and the general software configuration that has been (or will be) implemented.

With participation, as needed, from

- End-users/business management
- IT system software/administration group

- IT data/database administration group
- IT security/access control group
- IT application development group
- IT production support group

Set the HA Assessment Project Schedule/Timeline

Now, get this project on the books (the calendars) of all "as needed" participants and HA project members. We would target a fast timeline for an HA assessment and selection process (easily within a two-week time window).

Here are the major events to schedule over a two-week time frame:

- Gather HA requirements (all)

  HA assessment kickoff/introduction to process (3 hours)

  HA assessment information gathering sessions—5 to 7 JAD-style assessment meetings (2 to 3 hours each) over the course of 5 days

  HA primary variables gauge (2 hours)

- Review HA assessment requirements (team/management) (2 hours)

  Sign off on these requirements (management) (1 hour)

- Selection of HA solution (team leads) (8 hours)

- Review HA solution selection and ROI (team leads/management) (2 hours)

  Sign off on HA solution selection (1 hour)

- Commit resources/project for implementation (management) (3–8 hours of planning/scheduling/resourcing time)

All time in between meetings is spent assembling the information and following up on requirements not covered in these formal JAD sessions, or meeting individually with folks not present or on follow-ups to garner information that was not provided during the formal JAD meetings. The review sessions are critical to help drive this type of assessment project to completion quickly and to get full buy-in and visibility of the findings and decisions. I personally like the formal "sign off" process following the requirements and selection events. This gives it proper teeth!

Faster timelines can be achieved, but this will depend on the complexity and state of the application being considered for high availability.

Doing a Phase 0 High Availability Assessment

Okay, we've got our team together and have scheduled the major events and meetings for the HA assessment and selection. Now you need to introduce all members to what an HA assessment is and what are the key things that you are tying to identify. You will usually present the main HA assessment ideas below during your kickoff session and explain them thoroughly, and be ready to show examples of each in the meeting. I would also recommend providing this high-level list to all members before you meet for the first time to help set the stage.

As a bonus to our readers, a sample Phase 0 HA assessment template (as a word document named "HA0AssessmentSample.doc") will be available on the Sams Publishing website for download.

The high-level information that you are seeking is

- What are the current and future characteristics of your application?
- What are your service level requirements (SLAs)?
- What is the impact (cost) of downtime?
- What are your vulnerabilities (hardware, software, human errors, and so on)?
- What is your timeline for implementing a high availability solution?
- What is your budget for a high availability solution?

In addition, you will want to drill down into as much detail as possible in the following areas:

- Analysis of the current state/future state of the application
- Hardware configuration/options available
- Software configuration/options available
- Backup/recovery procedures used
- Standards/guidelines used

- Testing/QA process employed
- Personnel administering systems assessed
- Personnel developing systems assessed

A Phase 0 HA assessment can be tackled in two major steps. Once these first two steps are completed, the selection of the "right" HA solution can be done fairly easily.

Step one explores the detailed landscape of your application and environment, and is broken down into six discreet tasks. Each task should be addressed in as much detail as is possible. Step two completes the primary variable gauge and is used to communicate the assessment findings to management and the development team. Once these first two steps are completed, the HA solution selection step can be completed.

Step 1—HA Assessment

Each task of the HA assessment is designed to identify different characteristics of your environment, your personnel, your policies, and your goals that directly relate to high availability. These tasks are

- **Task 1**—Describe the current state of the application
  - Data (data usage and physical implementation)
  - Process (business processes being supported)
  - Technology (hardware/software platform/configuration)
  - Backup/recovery procedures
  - Standards/guidelines used
  - Testing/QA process employed
  - Service level agreement (SLA) currently defined
  - Level of expertise of personnel administering system
  - Level of expertise of personnel developing/testing system
- **Task 2**—Describe the future state of the application
  - Data (data usage and physical implementation, data volume growth, data resilience)
  - Process (business processes being supported, expanded functionality anticipated, and application resilience)
  - Technology (Hardware/software platform/configuration, new technology being acquired)

- Backup/recovery procedures being planned
- Standards/guidelines used or being enhanced
- Testing/QA process being changed or enhanced
- Service level agreement (SLA) desired—Examples of real-world SLAs can be difficult to find because they are considered confidential business information, much like other contract terms. However, there are a few places where you can look. The first place to check is the agreements you have with your own vendors. Many times, the SLAs you will be able to offer are bounded by the SLAs offered by vendors on which you rely. For example, if your Internet service provider only guarantees 99% uptime, it would be impractical for you to commit to delivering 99.5% uptime. You can also check the contracts of companies similar to yours that were filed with the SEC during the initial public offering process. These contracts tend to represent the largest and most important deals, and often contain SLA terms that you can use as a benchmark.
- Level of expertise of personnel administering system (planned training and hiring)
- Level of expertise of personnel developing/testing system (planned training and hiring)

- **Task 3**—Describe the unplanned downtime reasons at different intervals (last seven days, last month, last quarter, last six months, last year)

  [NOTE: If this is a new application then this task is an estimate of the future month, quarter, six-months, and one-year intervals]

- **Task 4**—Describe the planned downtime reasons at different intervals (last seven days, last month, last quarter, last six months, last year)

  [NOTE: If this is a new application then this task is an estimate of the future month, quarter, six-months, and one-year intervals]

- **Task 5**—Calculate the availability percentage across different time intervals (last seven days, last month, last quarter, last six months, last year). Please refer back to Chapter 1, Essential Elements of High Availability, for this complete calculation.

  [NOTE: If this is a new application then this task is an estimate of the future month, quarter, six-months, and one-year intervals]

- **Task 6**—Calculate the loss of downtime
  - Revenue loss (per hour of unavailability)—As an example, in an online order entry system, look at any peak order entry hour and calculate the total order amounts for that peak hour. This will be your revenue loss per hour value.
  - Productivity dollar loss (per hour of unavailability)—As an example, in an internal financial data warehouse that is used for executive decision support, calculate the length of time that this data mart/warehouse was not available within the last month or two and multiply this times the number of executives/managers who were supposed to be querying it during that period. This would be the "productivity effect." Then multiply this by the average salary of these execs/managers. This would be a rough estimate of productivity dollar loss. This does not consider the bad business decisions they might have made without having their data mart/warehouse available and the dollar loss of those bad business decisions. Calculating a productivity dollar loss might be a bit aggressive to be included in this assessment, but there needs to be something to measure against and to help justify the return on investment. For applications that are not productivity applications, this value will not be calculated.
  - Goodwill dollar loss (in terms of customers lost per hour of unavailability)—It's extremely important to include this component. Goodwill loss can be measured by taking the average number of customers for a period of time (such as last month's online order customer average) and comparing it with a period of processing following a system failure (where there was a significant amount of downtime). Chances are that there was a drop-off of same amount that can be rationalized as goodwill loss (the online customer didn't come back to you; they went to the competition). You must then take that percentage drop-off (like 2%) and multiply it by the peak order amount averages for the defined period. This period loss number is like a repeating loss overhead value that should be included in the ROI calculation for every month.

    [NOTE: If this is a new application then this task is an estimate of the losses].

Once you have addressed the previous tasks in as much detail as is possible, you should be able to complete Step 2—the HA primary variable gauge—without much trouble.

Step 2—Primary Variable Gauge Specification

If we quickly review what these primary variables are, you should be able to specify them accurately on the primary variable gauge. The primary high availability variables are

- Uptime requirement—The goal (from 0% to 100%) of what you require from your application for this application's planned hours of operation.

- Time to recover—A general indication (from long to short) of the amount of time that can be expended to recover an application and put it back online. This could be in minutes, hours, or just in terms of long, medium, or short amount of time to recover.

- Tolerance of recovery time—Describe what the impact might be (from high to low tolerance) of extended recovery times needed to resynchronize data, restore transactions, and so on. This is mostly tied into the time to recover variable, but can vary widely depending on who the end-users of the system are.

- Data resiliency—A description of how much data you are willing to lose, and whether it needs to be kept intact (have complete data integrity, even in failure). Often described in terms of low to high data resiliency.

- Application resiliency—An application-oriented description of the behavior you are seeking (from low to high application resiliency). In other words, should your applications (programs) be able to be restarted, switched to other machines without the end-user having to re-connect, and so on?

- Degree of distributed access/synchronization—For systems that are geographically distributed or partitioned (as are many global applications), it will be critical to understand how distributed and tightly coupled they must be at all times (indicated from low to high degree of distributed access and synchronization required).

A low specification of this variable indicates that the application and data are very loosely coupled and can stand on their own for periods of time, then be resynchronized at a later date.

- Scheduled maintenance frequency—An indication of the anticipated (or current) rate of scheduled maintenance required for the box, OS, network, application software, and other components in the system stack (from often to never).

- Performance/scalability—A firm requirement of the overall system performance and scalability needed for this application (from low to high performance need). This variable will drive many of the high availability solutions that you end up with since high performance systems often sacrifice many of the other variables mentioned here (like data resilience).

- Cost of downtime ($ lost/hr)—Estimate or calculate the dollar (or euro, yen, and so forth) cost for every minute of downtime (from low to high cost). You will usually find that the cost is not a single number (like an average cost per minute). In reality, short downtimes have lower costs, and the costs (losses) grow exponentially for longer downtimes. You should also try to factor in a "good will" cost (or loss).

- Cost to build and maintain the high availability solution ($)—This last variable may not be known initially. However, as you near the design and implementation of a high availability system, the costs come barreling in rapidly and often trump certain decisions.

As you can see in Figure 9.2, you can think of each of these variables as an oil gauge or temperature gauge. You will simply place an arrow along the gauge of each variable estimating the approximate "temperature" or level of a particular variable.

Again, we have provided the reader with a sample template of the primary variable gauge and other HA representations for download (as a PowerPoint document named "HA0AssessmentSample.ppt") on the Sams Publishing website.

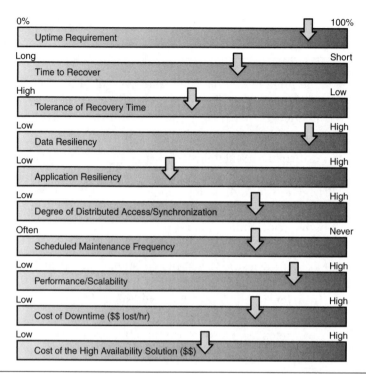

Figure 9.2   Specifying the primary variables for your application.

As you can well imagine, if we had been considering the high availability needs and characteristics since the very beginning of all development projects, we would be in a much better position to "design in" and "design for" an optimal HA solution. Let's quickly revisit how we might have integrated our high availability elements into a traditional development life cycle so that you can better understand the assessment process.

High Availability Tasks Integrated into Your Development Life Cycle

Enhancing your current development life cycle deliverables with the tailored HA deliverables depicted in Figure 9.3 is fairly easy.

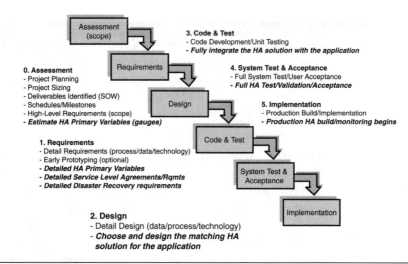

Figure 9.3   Traditional development life cycle with high availability tasks built in.

As you can see, every phase of the life cycle will have a new task or two that specifically calls out high availability issues, needs, or characteristics. For this traditional "waterfall" methodology, these included (the HA deliverables are in ***bold/italics***)

- Phase 0: Assessment (scope)
    - ***Estimate the High Availability Primary Variables (gauges)***   Using the HA primary variables gauge to do estimations is extremely valuable at this early stage in the life cycle.
- Phase 1: Requirements
    - ***Detailed High Availability Primary Variables***
    - ***Detailed Service Level Agreements/Requirements***
    - ***Detailed Disaster Recovery requirements***   Then, fully detailing the HA primary variables, defining the SLAs, and putting together the early disaster recovery requirements will position you to make well-founded design decisions and HA solution decisions in later phases.
- Phase 2: Design
    - ***Choose and design the matching High Availability solution for the application***   Phase 2 is where the HA solution that best meets your high availability requirements is selected.

- Phase 3: Code & Test
  - ***Fully integrate the High Availability solution with the application***   Each step of the way in coding and testing should include an understanding of the high availability solution that has been chosen. Unit testing may also be required on certain high availability options.
- Phase 4: System Test & Acceptance
  - ***Full High Availability Testing/Validation/Acceptance*** Full scale system and acceptance testing of the high availability capabilities must be completed without any issues whatsoever. During this phase, a determination of whether the high availability option truly meets the availability levels must be strictly measured. If it doesn't, you may have to iterate back to earlier phases and modify your HA solution design.
- Phase 5: Implementation
  - ***Production High Availability build/monitoring begins***

And lastly, you will be ready to move your application and your thoroughly tested high availability solution into production mode confidently. From this point, your system will be live and monitoring the high availability application begins.

Selecting the HA Solution

The HA selection process itself consists of evaluating your HA assessment findings (requirements) within the hybrid decision-tree evaluation technique presented in Chapter 3, Choosing High Availability (using the Nassi-Schneiderman construct). As you recall, this decision tree technique evaluates the assessment findings against the following questions:

1. What percentage of time must the application remain up during its scheduled time of operation? (The goal!)
2. How much tolerance does the end-user have when the system is not available (planned or unplanned unavailability)?
3. What is the per hour cost of downtime for this application?

4. How long does it take to get the application back online following a failure (of any kind)? (Worst case!)

5. How much of the application is distributed and will require some type of synchronization with other nodes before all nodes are considered to be 100% available?

6. How much data inconsistency can be tolerated in favor of having the application available?

7. How often is scheduled maintenance required for this application (and environment)?

8. How important is high performance and scalability?

9. How important is it for the application to keep its current connection alive with the end-user?

10. What is the estimated cost of a possible high availability solution? What is your budget?

By systematically moving through the decision tree and answering the case constructs for each question, a definitive path to a particular HA solution is attained. It's not fool-proof, but it is very good at honing in on the right HA solution that matches the requirements being evaluated. Figure 9.4 shows an example of the ASP—Scenario #1 results using this process. Remember, the answers are cumulative. All questions are relative to the answer you provided to the prior questions. The result is a "direct" path to a solution.

As you can see, the application service provider (ASP) business scenario (scenario #1) yielded a high availability selection of hardware redundancy, shared disk RAID arrays, MSCS, and SQL clustering. Having these four options together clearly met all of their requirements of uptime, tolerance, performance, and costs. The ASP's service level agreement with their customers also allows for brief amounts of downtime to deal with OS upgrades or fixes, hardware upgrades, and application upgrades. The ASP's budget was enough for a larger amount of hardware redundancy to be utilized.

The actual production implementation of this selection is depicted in Figure 9.5. It is a series of two-node SQL cluster (in an active/passive configuration) designed to support between 1 and 3 separate customer applications. This is proving to be a very scalable, high-performance, risk mitigating, and cost-effective architecture for them.

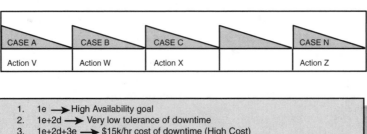

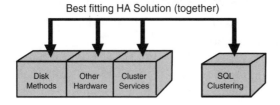

1. 1e ⟶ High Availability goal
2. 1e+2d ⟶ Very low tolerance of downtime
3. 1e+2d+3e ⟶ $15k/hr cost of downtime (High Cost)
4. 1e+2d+3e+4c ⟶ Average recovery time
5. 1e+2d+3e+4c+5a ⟶ No distributed components or synchronization
6. 1e+2d+3e+4c+5a+6b ⟶ A little data inconsistency can be tolerated
7. 1e+2d+3e+4c+5a+6b+7c ⟶ Average amount of scheduled downtime
8. 1e+2d+3e+4c+5a+6b+7c+8d ⟶ Performance is very much important
9. 1e+2d+3e+4c+5a+6b+7c+8d+9b ⟶ Connection can be re-established
10. 1e+2d+3e+4c+5a+6b+7c+8d+9b+10c ⟶ Moderate HA Cost/Good budget

Figure 9.4   ASP—Scenario #1 Nassi-Schneiderman HA questions results with the resulting HA selection.

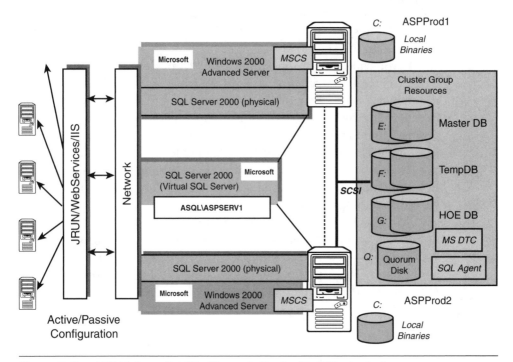

Figure 9.5   ASP high availability "live solution" with SQL clustering.

Is the HA Solution Cost Effective?

Perhaps one of the more important calculations that you will do as part of the HA assessment is determining the return on your investment (ROI). In other words, will the HA solution you pick be cost effective and how quickly will it pay for itself? The ROI for an HA solution can be estimated during the assessment process and then finalized during the HA selection process. Coming up with the downtime cost is essential to being able to measure the ROI of an HA solution. So, spend some extra time in researching what cost downtime really has for your company. If this is for a new system, use a similar application's downtime costs adjusted by what you think the new application's financial impact would be. As you recall, the HA solution's ROI can be calculated by adding up the incremental costs (or estimates) of the new HA solution and comparing them against the complete cost of downtime for a period of time (we are using one year).

Using the ASP—Scenario #1 example, we went about estimating the total costs (incremental + deployment + assessment) to get us to the selected SQL clustering high availability solution. We had to determine the downtime costs (unplanned and planned) at an hourly dollar value (for the planned hours of operation), and finally we were able to determine the percentage of these HA implementation costs as compared to the cost of downtime. This revealed that the total implementation cost of this HA solution is 41.86% of the downtime cost for one year. In other words, the investment of the HA solution will pay for itself in .41 of a year or approximately 5 months! Figure 9.6 shows this entire ROI calculation as done in Excel. The last line of the spreadsheet shows the length of time to recover the investment (your costs). This particular spreadsheet is also available on the Sams Publishing download site for this book (HAAssessment0ROI.xls).

The full ROI calculation contains these cost enumerations:

1. Maintenance cost (for a one year period):
   - $15K (estimate)—Yearly system admin personnel cost (additional time for training of these personnel)
   - $25K (estimate)—Recurring software licensing cost (of additional HA components; [5] OS + [2] SQL Server 2000)
2. Hardware Cost:
   - $205K hardware cost (of additional HW in the new HA solution)

3. Deployment/Assessment Cost:
   - $20K deployment cost (develop, test, QA, production implementation of the solution)
   - $10K HA assessment cost

4. Downtime Cost (for a one-year period):
   - If you kept track of last year's downtime record, use this number; otherwise produce an estimate of planned and unplanned downtime for this calculation. We estimated the cost of downtime/hour to be **$15K/Hour** for this ASP.
   - Planned downtime cost (revenue loss cost) = Planned downtime hours × cost of hourly downtime to the company:
     a. .25% (estimate of planned downtime percentage in one year) × 8760 hours in a year = 21.9 hours of planned downtime.
     b. 21.9 hours (planned downtime) × $15K/hr (hourly cost of downtime) = $328,500/year cost of planned downtime.
   - Unplanned downtime cost (revenue loss cost) = Unplanned downtime hours × cost of hourly downtime to the company:
     a. .25% (estimate of unplanned downtime percentage in one year) × 8760 hours in a year = 21.9 hours of unplanned downtime.
     b. 21.9 hours × $15K/hr (hourly cost of downtime) = $328,500/year cost of unplanned downtime.

ROI Totals:
- Total costs to get on this HA solution = $275,000 (for the year)
- Total of downtime cost = $657,000 (for the year)

These numbers can help push the decisions through a bit faster. That is why we go to the trouble. There is always a bean counter somewhere in your organization (or the controller themselves) who must be involved with this type of investment decision. But, just the process of having to determine a downtime cost can be a startling revelation in itself. In fact, it is very often a shocking number to most. Watch out because this can very well accelerate the whole implementation timeline once folks figure out how much money they really are losing when systems aren't available.

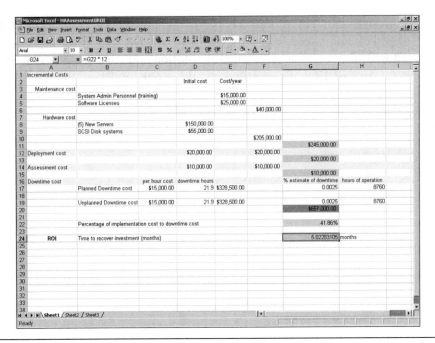

Figure 9.6   ROI calculation excel spreadsheet for ASP—Scenario #1.

Summary

Pushing through a formal HA assessment for your application, making an HA selection, and then planning its implementation puts you just shy of the actual production implementation of the HA solution. To implement the selected HA solution, just follow the detailed steps in the appropriate HA options chapters that correspond to your particular selection results (Chapter 4 for MSCS, Chapter 5 for SQL clustering, Chapter 6 for log shipping, Chapter 7 for data replication, and Chapter 8 for other distributed transaction approaches). You will be building up a test environment first, then a formal QA environment, and finally a production deployment. You will find that knowing how to implement any one of these HA options beforehand takes the risk and guessing out of the whole process. Proceeding with confidence all the way to your production implementation will hopefully be mostly anticlimatic. This is due to the fact that you have now looked at and completely thrashed through your HA requirements for this application to an excruciating level of detail. And, to top that off, you will also know how much money it will take you to achieve this HA solution and what the payback will be in terms of ROI if downtime should occur (and how quickly you will achieve this ROI). You can safely say you have considered all the essential factors in determining a high available solution and that you are fairly ready to get this HA solution into place.

CHAPTER 10

High Availability Design Issues and Considerations

THE KEY TOPICS IN THIS CHAPTER ARE

- MS HA options and design considerations
- Remote mirroring
- Stretch replication
- DB backup strategy/options
- MS Analysis Services/OLAP and HA
- Disaster recovery approach
- Other third-party alternatives

Things to Consider for High Availability

U p to this point, we have described the typical high availability paths that you can pursue that are built with Microsoft SQL Server and the Microsoft Windows Server family software. Very often, these high availability options can be implemented extremely quickly and easily. There are, however, many other things that need to be considered when building a high availability platform. This chapter will re-emphasize the primary design considerations and some common configuration options for highly available hardware, OS, and network components, and highlight critical design points for each HA option that we have described thus far. In addition, we will stress database backup and recovery strategies, describe the high availability ramifications for MS Analysis Services (MSAS) since it is also included with MS SQL Server, and identify some possible HA alternatives from third-party vendors. We would even like to spend a little time talking about worst-case scenarios that would require you to recover following a major disaster (disaster recovery). Let's start with your hardware and operating system, and work up to the primary Microsoft HA options (MSCS, SQL Server clustering, SQL Server data replication, SQL Server log shipping, and distributed transaction processing).

Hardware/OS/Network Design Considerations

We have harped quite a bit about building a solid foundation from which to build high availability. This has included defining redundant hardware components such as multiple network cards, redundant power supplies, redundant cooling fans, error correcting memory (ECC), and even redundant boxes. Spending the extra time and money to incorporate these solutions directly affects your system's availability. Whether they achieve your high availability goals by themselves is another question (to which the answer is most likely "no"). But, they can take you a long way in the right direction. These are things like

1. Regularly swapping out hardware components that reach a certain life. All hardware has a life expectancy; it is up to you to know what this expectancy is, keep track of the life expectancy of each hardware component in your systems, and schedule maintenance such as swapping old ones out and replacing them with new ones on a regular basis. As an example, let's say a moderately high quality SCSI disk has a life expectancy of three years (of continuous operation). If you have one disk failure in a RAID array in the first year of a system then you just deal with correcting that one failed drive; if you have a failure in year two or later, then this is a sign that more disks of the same age will be failing soon. You should set a plan that never allows you to get tothis second failure situation. Be proactive here. Don't wait until you start having failures to deal with this approach. If you have a servicing agreement with a vendor, make sure you define the hardware replacement schedule for them (or they should be prepared to define one based on life expectancy and usage).

2. Start with the redundancies up front. Do not wait on this. When you put your first server into service (into production), it should already be at a base high availability foundation level. As you may recall, this should start with

   - Redundant hot swappable CPUs
   - RAID or other redundant disk array systems
   - ECC memory (that is hot swappable if possible)
   - Redundant cooling fans
   - Redundant power supplies
   - UPS—uninterruptible power supplies
   - Redundant network connectors (adapters)

   We took a sampling of 10 leading highly available systems and found the following characteristics across the board:

   - Hot swappable I/O modules (network connectors and disk subsystems) on multiple channels
   - Redundant hot swappable CPU modules
   - Isolation of faulty modules capability
   - User notification through module-level LEDs and relay alarms
   - N+1 hot swappable power supplies and fans
   - Backup generators available since UPSs only have a limited lifespan

   You then combine this with multiple fault-tolerant disk arrays (RAID) and you are headed to five 9s.

3. Get OS-level and network-level software patches and upgrades applied on a very regular basis. This will guarantee that you have the most up to date fixes, security patches, OS or Network upgrades, and that the vendor (Microsoft) can support you readily. If you choose not to apply service packs, upgrades (like from Windows 2000 server to Windows 2003 server), or patches to your OS or network software for long periods of time, you are asking for trouble. I found a customer the other day that was still running NT 3.5 with SQL Server 6.0. They had a problem but Microsoft wouldn't support them because they were not on a fairly current OS and SQL Server release.

> **Design Note**
>
> Choose high availability options that potentially allow you to apply upgrades or security patches to your systems without having to bring them down. Most patches require a reboot, and an upgrade typically requires an extended period of time when no applications should be running. However, it is possible to break a cluster, upgrade/patch the standby server, rejoin the cluster, switch over, and then apply the upgrade/patch to the primary.

4. Use NAS—Network Attached Storage (or SANs) for data resiliency and data management ease. Now that accessing data via fibre level speeds is commonplace, we recommend that the robust capability offered with NAS be tapped in any high availability solution. These NAS devices can support most RAID level configurations and can expand to any storage requirement that you desire, particularly NAS devices that offer multiple channel connections (for redundancy).

5. Sizing—When sizing the system, it is important to keep in mind not only the storage capacity that is needed, but also the performance levels that must be maintained. A single disk drive can handle approximately 85 I/Os per second before latencies increase and performance begins to degrade. If the choice is a SCSI disk subsystem and it is configured with a shared volume(s) as RAID 5, it will lead to a significant number of extra I/Os during writes as well as increased write latencies due to the RAID 5 parity. So, choose your RAID levels well. Figure 10.1 shows the fault-tolerance and the I/O cost of the most often used RAID configuration levels.

6. Be proactive with monitoring tools and understand your resource utilization levels. A saturated CPU is sometimes equally as crippling as a downed server. When CPU and memory utilizations stay above 75% for prolonged periods of time, proactively plan upgrades to bring these down to an average sustained utilization of around 30%. That's about right.

7. Training on hardware/OS/network components is critical to your high availability goals. Make sure you budget and get your folks trained in all aspects of recoverability and administration in support of high availability. Not every part of a high availability solution is automated. Someone has to push the right button or administer upgrades, and so on.

RAID Level	Fault Tolerance	Logical Reads	Physical I/Os per Read	Logical Writes	Physical I/Os per Write
RAID 0	None	1	1	1	1
RAID 1 or 10	Best (Optimal for OLTP)	1	1	1	2 writes
RAID 5	Moderate (Optimal for mostly READ ONLY systems)	1	1	1	2 reads + 2 writes (that's 4 per write!)

Figure 10.1   RAID level fault tolerance and I/O costs.

8. Service level agreements with your vendors must correspond to the promised service level agreements you make with your end-users. If you have a hardware failure and your SLA with hardware vendor has a 24-hour service window, but your SLA with your end-users is 1 hour max downtime, you can be caught just sitting around waiting for your vendor to casually stroll in. This happens all too often. In addition, a comprehensive SLA with your vendors should also include keeping your hardware and software components as current as possible. Do not skimp in this area. Money may be tight, but extended downtime can quickly translate into huge money losses.

9. Network load balancing is multi-faceted in that it supports scalability along with availability. If your user base is large and growing, this is an area that you will want to expand into. Microsoft has made this fairly easy to embrace and should be designed into your larger user application implementations from the start.

10. Backup and recovery at the disk level is an extra insurance policy that many wish to pursue for highly available systems. Most NAS vendors offer high-powered disk backup mechanisms that can back up huge amounts of data in very short amounts of time. This includes leveraging mirroring techniques, writing to disk-based backup devices, traditional tape backup devices, and remote devices (via internet connections). It is critical to make sure all logically related components of a highly available system get backed up (and usually need to be done together). Then, you also need to understand and test recovering a system from its backup.

The amount of time it takes to recover dictates what backup device media you use for backups. This is very different from database backups and recovery. This will be covered later in this chapter.

Remote Mirroring

An approach that is growing in popularity is remote mirroring. Remote mirroring is a solution offered by third-party vendors that allows you to maintain a real-time mirror of your primary storage device at a remote site and to protect your data on that mirror from site destruction. In a remote mirror, redundant server hardware and a redundant storage system are maintained at the remote site (which is a bit costly). Most often, remote mirroring is accomplished over a direct IP address connection or within the confines of a virtual private network (VPN). Figure 10.2 illustrates a remote mirroring configuration.

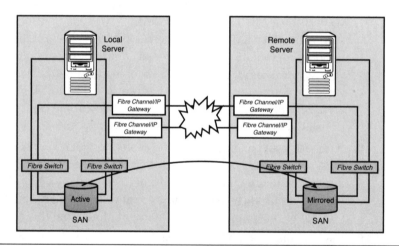

Figure 10.2   Remote mirroring in support of high availability.

A remote mirroring solution ensures absolute transactional currency and consistency for the mirrored data. If the primary server fails for any reason, the remote mirrored copy can be used in its place. It is not a completely transparent solution, but the data integrity is guaranteed to be intact. Typically, a SAN is used in each site. Each SAN is connected with fibre (if the sites are separated by less than 100 kilometers [km]) or with conventional Internet Protocol (IP) circuits with fibre channel to IP gateways. At any one time, only one of the SANs is active, updating its own local store and forwarding updates to the other SAN (the mirror). This approach is probably only valid if you can guarantee the stability of the communication lines and speed of these lines. If this communication is reliable, you will be able to build a solid fail-over site that could even cover your disaster recovery needs.

Microsoft Cluster Services Design Considerations

The things to consider with MSCS are primarily related to what you need MSCS groups to manage together or manage separately. In other words, you should plan on putting SQL Server items together, and resources that need isolated protection such as the quorum disk and MSDTC in separate groups. As you remember, a *cluster group* is a collection of logically grouped cluster resources, and may contain cluster-aware application services such as SQL Server 2000. This cluster group is sort of like a folder that has all the things you need to keep together (that you want to fail-over together). Figure 10.3 shows the basic MSCS configuration topology of a two-node cluster.

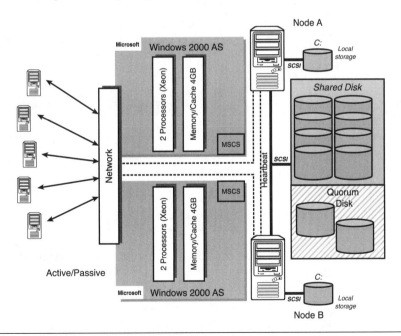

Figure 10.3   MSCS configuration topology for an active/passive two-node cluster.

As you can see in this diagram, the quorum drive should be isolated to a drive all by itself and be mirrored to guarantee that it is available to the cluster at all times. Without it, the cluster won't come up at all and you won't be able to access your SQL databases. A General rule of thumb is to isolate the quorum resource to a separate cluster group if it is possible!

Figure 10.4 shows the minimum resources controlled by Cluster Services prior to installing SQL Server clustering. These are

- Shared physical disks (quorum and data disks)
- The cluster IP address
- The cluster name itself (network name)
- Microsoft distributed transaction coordinator (MS DTC)

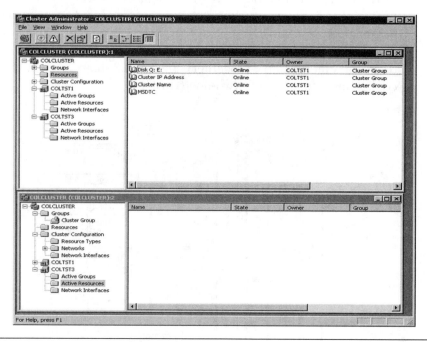

Figure 10.4   Cluster Administrator console view of the resources managed by MSCS.

SQL Server Clustering Design Considerations

SQL clustering is rapidly becoming the default high availability configuration for many organizations. But, it still should only be used when it fits your particular high availability needs. SQL clustering requires a fairly advanced set of hardware, OS, and network configuration to be in place and is fairly administrative intensive. SQL clustering is not for the faint at heart! SQL clustering builds on top of Microsoft Cluster Services and is said to be a "cluster-aware" application. In other words, MSCS manages all the resources needed to run SQL Server. If you have a SQL Server based application and your availability requirements are above 95% uptime (high and extreme availability), you are likely to be using a two, four, or more node SQL clustering configuration.

When you install a SQL Server in a clustered server configuration, you create it as a "virtual" SQL Server. In other words, a virtual SQL Server will not be tied to a specific physical server. Figure 10.5 shows a two-node cluster configuration with all of the SQL Server components identified. This "virtual" SQL Server will be the only thing the end-user will ever see (the virtual server name is VSQLDBARCH and the SQL Server instance name is VSQLSRV1).

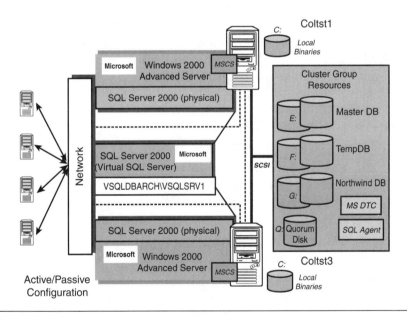

Figure 10.5   Two-node SQL clustering topology in an active/passive configuration.

From the network's point of view, the fully qualified SQL Server instance name will be "VSQLDBARCH\VSQLSRV1". Figure 10.5 also shows the other cluster group resources that will be part of your SQL clustering configuration. These, of course, are MS DTC, SQL Agent, and the shared disk where your databases will live. A SQL Agent will be installed as part of the SQL Server installation process and is associated with the SQL Server instance it is installed for. The same is true for MS DTC; it will be associated with the particular SQL Server instance that it is installed to work with (VSQLSRV1 in this case). Remember, the quorum drive should be isolated to a drive all by itself and be mirrored to guarantee that it is available to the cluster at all times. Without it, the cluster won't come up at all and you won't be able to access your SQL databases.

One or more physically separate shared disk arrays can house your SQL Server managed database files. In a SQL Server database, it is highly desirable to isolate your data files away from your transaction log files for any database that has volatility (like with OLTP systems). In addition, perhaps one of the most critical databases is a SQL Server instance is the internal shared database of TempDB. TempDB should be isolated away from your other databases and perhaps placed on some high performing disk configuration such as RAID 10. SQL Server requires TempDB to be allocated at server startup time so the location of TempDB should be protected rigorously. Do not place TempDB on a RAID 5 disk array! The write overhead is far too much for this internally used (and shared) database. In general, put your OLTP SQL Server database data/transaction log files on RAID 10 or RAID 1 (including master DB, model DB, and MSDB) and your DSS/READ Only data/transaction log files on RAID 5. As you set up SQL clustering you will also need to be aware of the following:

1. SQL Server service accounts and passwords should be kept the same on all nodes or the node will not be able to restart a SQL Server service. Use "Administrator" or, better yet, a designated account (like "cluster") that has administrator rights within the domain and on each server.

2. Drive letters for the cluster disks must be the same on all nodes (servers).

3. Create an alternative method to connect to SQL Server if the network name is offline and you cannot connect using TCP/IP. The method is to use named pipes specified as

   ```
   Default instance: \\.\pipe\sql\query
   ```

   or

   ```
   Named instance:
   \\.\pipe\MSSQL$instancename\sql\query
   ```

4. Lastly, be sure to check Microsoft's hardware compatibility list *before* you venture into building out your SQL Clustering configuration.

Figure 10.6 shows the full list of the SQL Server resources controlled by Cluster Services once SQL clustering has been setup. These are

- Physical disks (shared SCSI in this example)
    - Quorum disk (on the Disk Q: E: resource)
    - Data disk(s) (on the Disk Q: E: resource)
    - Transaction log disk(s) (on the Disk Q: E: resource)
- Cluster IP address
- Cluster name (network name)
- MSDTC
- SQL Server virtual IP address (for VSQLDBARCH virtual server)
- SQL Server virtual name (VSQLDBARCH in this example)
- SQL Server (VSQLSRV1 in this example)
- SQL Agent (for VSQLSRV1 SQL Server instance)
- SQL Full Text Service Instance (for VSQLSRV1 SQL Server instance)

Stretch Clustering

There is also a notion of *stretch clustering* that allows SQL Server transactions to be concurrently written to both the local storage system and a remote storage system. You are essentially going to be using remote mirroring, MSCS, and SQL clustering.

Stretch clustering includes most of the benefits of standard fail-over clustering but is really designed to protect the local nodes from site destruction (the local SQL clustering configuration). In particular, stretch clustering ensures absolute transactional currency and consistency to a remote SQL clustering configuration and makes fail-over virtually transparent to the client if the local SQL cluster should ever become unavailable. Consider using stretch clustering to protect against site destruction if the risk of site destruction is high, the cost of an unavailable node is high, and you require transactional currency.

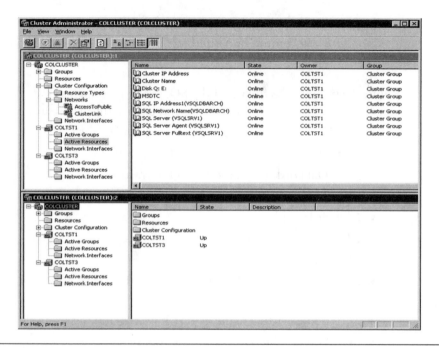

Figure 10.6   Cluster Administrator console view of the all SQL Server resources managed by MSCS.

As shown in Figure 10.7, stretch clustering maintains at least one passive (standby) server in the local MSCS cluster, in case the active server fails, and at least one passive (standby) server in the remote site. If you use Windows 2000 Datacenter Server, you can have an MSCS cluster with two local servers and two remote servers providing server redundancy in each site and fail-over in the event of site destruction. Costs of building stretch clustering configurations often eliminate this as a viable option. It is very expensive to keep entire system redundancies and maintain the dedicated communication between the local and remote sites that this demands.

SQL Server Data Replication Design Considerations

Data replication has long been used to isolate big chunks of processing (like that of reporting) away from the primary OLTP processing without having to sacrifice performance. As data replication has become hugely more stable and reliable, it has been tapped to create "warm," almost "hot" standby SQL Servers. If failures ever occurred with the primary server (publisher) in a replication topology, the secondary server (subscriber) would still be able to be used for work. In fact, it is possible for this secondary server to take over all processing from the primary server or just keep the reporting users happy (and available). When doing transactional replication in the "instantaneous replication" mode, data changes on the primary server (publisher) can be replicated to one or more secondary servers (subscribers) extremely quickly. In other words, this "instantaneous replication" mode is creating a replicated SQL Server database that is as fresh as the last transaction log entries that made it through the distribution server mechanism. Figure 10.8 illustrates a typical SQL Server data replication configuration that can serve as a basis for high availability and which also fulfills a reporting server requirement (at the same time).

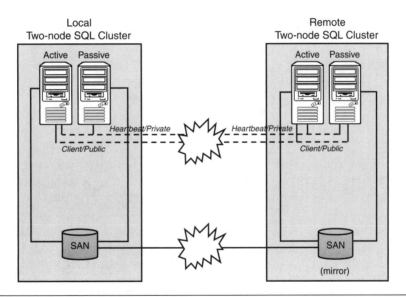

Figure 10.7 Possible "stretch clustering" configuration to support highly available systems and site destruction protection.

This particular data replication configuration is a "central publisher, remote distributor" replication model. It maximizes on isolating processing away from the primary server (publisher) including the data distribution mechanism (the distribution server) part of the replication model. There are a few things to deal with if ever the "replicate" is needed to become the primary server (take over the work from the "primary" server). Connection strings have to be changed, ODBC data sources need to be updated, and so on. But, this may be something that would take minutes as opposed to hours of potential database recovery time, and may well be tolerable to the end-users. There also exists a risk of not having all of the transactions from the primary server make it over to the replicate (subscriber). Remember, the replicated database will only be as fresh as the last updates that were distributed to it. Often, however, a company is willing to live with this small risk in favor of availability. For databases that are primarily read-only with low to medium data and schema volatility, this is a great way to distribute the load and mitigate risk of failure thus achieving high availability.

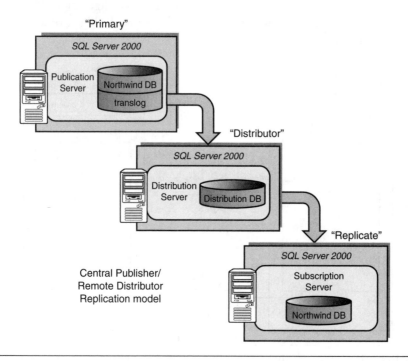

Figure 10.8   Central publisher, remote distributor replication model in support of HA.

Primary things to consider if you have chosen data replication to support your high availability solution are

- Latency between the publisher and the subscriber will deter-mine how warm or hot the subscriber will be for fail-over. Instan-taneous replication should be the default mode if you are targeting high availability.

- Backup/recovery of a replication configuration embraces the publisher, the distributor, and the subscriber.

- Impact and location of the distribution server (we recommend it be a remote distributor)!

- Schema changes in the publisher that should be in the subscriber must be factored into your data replication support plans.

- SQL Server logins/database user IDs' consistency is fairly easily administered by using DTS to synchronize the publisher and the subscriber on some type of a regular schedule (such as weekly).

- Often seed values can become an issue with columns that use identity. Very often, the subscriber will define these columns as INT columns and can receive the identity values from the publisher without issue.

- You may not want to propagate trigger code to the subscriber. But, if the subscriber is ever to take over for the publisher, the triggers will have to be added.

- The client connection switch over process in the event of failure of the publisher needs to be thoroughly described and tested.

Design Note

As an alternative to changing connection strings or ODBC data sources, you can just change settings in a DNS server and repoint the hostname to a different IP address (as long as all connections are set up using hostname instead of a fixed IP).

SQL Server Log Shipping Design Considerations

Log shipping is, perhaps, the easiest of the HA configurations to deal with from the administration point of view. Log shipping effectively replicates the data of one server (the source) to one or more other servers (the destinations) via transaction log dumps. Figure 10.9 shows a typical log shipping configuration with two destination pairs. A destination pair is any unique source/destination combination. You can have any number of source/destination pairs. This means that you can have from one to N replicated images of a database using log shipping. Then, if the source server should fail, you can upgrade one of the destination servers to become the source server. Although, you will still have to worry about the client connection changes that would be required if ever forced to use this secondary server.

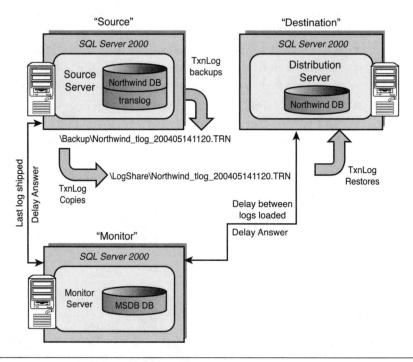

Figure 10.9   Log shipping with two destination servers and a separate monitor server.

Figure 10.9 also shows how log shipping uses a Monitor Server to keep track of what the current state of the log shipping is. If there is a breakdown in log shipping, such as the loads on the destination are not being done or taking longer than what has been set up, the monitor server will generate alerts. The primary things to consider when using log shipping for high availability are

- Understand the latency times (delays) between source and destination servers.

- If the destination server is to be used as a fail-over, it will not be available for use until it is activated for use.

- Make sure that there is ample space in the working directories for log shipping (the Backup directory and the Logshare directory). This is potentially a point of failure.

- It is a good general practice to isolate the monitor server to a separate server by itself so that this critical monitoring of log shipping is not affected if the source server or any destination servers fail.

- Understand the client connection switch over process in the event of failure of the source server. This needs to be thoroughly described and tested.

Distributed Transaction Processing Design Considerations

Distributed transaction processing as part of the application design itself changes the high availability orientation to be application driven, not database or disk oriented. The Microsoft distributed programming model consists of several technologies, including MSMQ, IIS, MS DTC, DCOM, and COM+. All of these services are designed for use by distributed applications.

You might want to design a highly available application to purposely distribute data redundantly. This type of application design can then guarantee the application more than one place to get data from in the event of a single server failure. This properly designed application would be "programmed" to be aware of a failed server (data source). Figure 10.10 shows an application that does its data access requests against one location, and if that data access fails (because the location has failed or is not accessible via the network), it would try a secondary location that had the same data. If data updates are being created (inserts/deletes/updates) at any one of the data source locations, a single distributed transaction would be used to guarantee that the updates are successful at all data locations. If one of the data locations is not available during this update, a resynchronization approach or a queuing approach can be devised that catches up any updates on the failed data location when it becomes available again.

You can design and build these types of SQL Server[nd]based applications leveraging the distributed transaction coordinator (MS DTC). Each Microsoft SQL Server will have an associated distributed transaction coordinator (MS DTC) on the same machine with it. The MS DTC will act as the primary coordinator for these distributed transactions. MS DTC ensures that all updates are made permanent in all data locations (committed), or makes sure that all of the work is undone (rolled back) if it needs to be. MS DTC is essentially brokering a multi-server transaction.

Each SQL Server (or XA compliant resource) is just a resource manager for their local data.

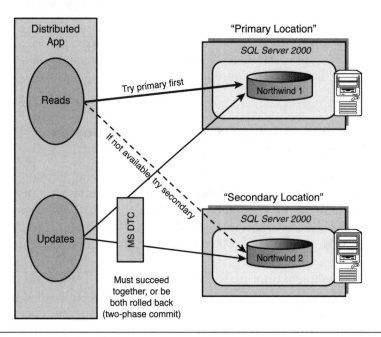

Figure 10.10 A distributed application approach for achieving HA.

In addition, you can also consider building COM+ applications. COM+ handles many of the resource management tasks you previously had to program yourself, such as thread allocation and security. And, it automatically makes your applications more scalable by providing thread pooling, object pooling, and just-in-time object activation. COM+ also helps protect the integrity of your data by providing full transactional support, even if a transaction spans multiple databases over a network. Keep in mind that COM+ application logic will reside on server machines, not on client machines.

COM+ provides basic support for fault tolerance at the protocol level. A sophisticated pinging mechanism detects network and client-side hardware failures. Using a referral component technique, clients can detect the failure of a component, and can reconnect to the same referral component that established the first connection for them. This referral component has information about which servers are no longer available and automatically provides the client with a new instance of the component running on another machine. Applications will, of course, still have to deal with error recovery at higher levels (consistency, loss of information, and so forth). And, once you have built the COM+ application, you can deploy the application across a network or server cluster.

General SQL Server File/Device Placement Recommendations

As you grow in experience with SQL Server, you might have learned the painful ramifications of placing SQL Server files on the wrong type of disk subsystem or have overloaded one disk with several competing disk write scenarios. For these reasons, it is imperative that you adopt and implement a solid placement and disk configuration plan that will not only yield high availability but also allow you to scale your applications. Figure 10.11 generalizes the type of RAID level configurations that you should target for all of your highly available system. It takes the approach of getting the highest fault tolerance without sacrificing performance. This covers both online transaction processing applications (OLTP), decision support systems (DSS—read only), and the other SQL Server databases that must be treated with care. Especially important is that of TempDB. You want to isolate this away from everything on the planet. It can be the most active database in your SQL Server instance.

File/Drive	Description	Fault Tolerance
Quorum Drive	The quorum drive used with MSCS should be isolated to a drive by itself (very often mirrored as well for maximum availability)	RAID 1 or RAID 10
SQL Server Database files (OLTP)	For OLTP (online transaction processing) systems, the database data/index files should be placed on a RAID 10 disk system.	RAID 10
SQL Server Database files (DSS)	For DSS (Decision Support Systems) systems that are primarily READ ONLY, the database data/index files should be placed on a RAID 5 disk system.	RAID 5
Temp DB	Highly volatile disk I/O (when not able to do all its work in cache)	RAID 10 or 1
SQL Server Transaction Log files	The SQL transaction log files should be on their own mirrored volume for both performance and database protection. (for DSS systems, this could be RAID 5 also.)	RAID 10 or 1
Master DB & MSDB	SQL Server system databases that are not very volatile but must be protected with high fault tolerance for maximum availability (SQL Server doesn't come up if master db is not available.)	RAID 5

Figure 10.11   SQL Server and clustering file/drive fault tolerance recommendations.

From a file placement point of view, you should adopt a strategy of isolating volatility away from each other (across controllers, or I/O channels if at all possible). Figure 10.12 illustrates this concept of spreading out the disk activity across as many devices as possible. In particular, note that transaction log files are isolated away from a particular database data files, TempDB is isolated to a drive by itself (for performance reasons and to maintain system availability), master database and MSDB are also isolated away from application databases, as is the quorum drive for MSCS. In addition, application database data files of one application that are very active can be placed with transaction log files of a different application that are not very active. The overall effect of this type of strategy is great throughput.

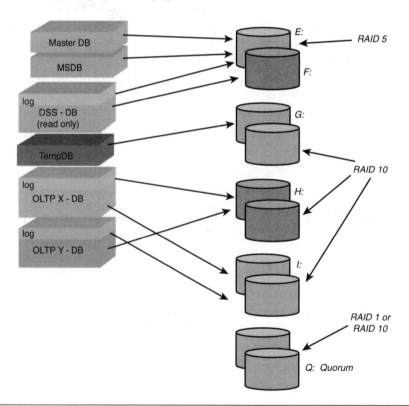

Figure 10.12   SQL Server database data and transaction log file placement recommendations.

Database Backup Strategies in Support of High Availability

Backing up and restoring databases are fundamental to any highly available implementation. The real trick is in knowing what type of backup to do and how often to do it so that your database can be recovered easily and quickly to fulfill your high availability requirements. You have two things to protect: the integrity of the data and the availability of the data. Understanding how long it takes to back up your database or to restore your database should be well known as you plan for high availability. This must also correspond closely to the service level agreements you have committed to. Having the proper backup and recovery approach in place is key to achieving these commitments. Plan your backup strategy based on the time it takes to back up *and* the time it takes to fully recover a database. It is this total time that must be considered for a system that is to be highly available. For databases that have tables with varying uses, you might want to consider a multiple file group approach that keeps tables that are read-only in one file group, huge volatile tables in another, and so on. In this way, you would only need to back up the data tables that change and not the static tables (achieving even better availability).

The good news is that there are a few varying types of database backup techniques that can be leveraged to achieve an optimal recovery strategy. There is a full database-oriented approach and a file-oriented approach. Both work well. They offer up-to-the-minute recovery, point-in-time recovery, and some degree of redundancy that allows you to recover from damaged full database backups/file backups. As you are hopefully already aware, there are four backup operations that can be used with SQL Server 2000:

- **Full database backups**—This effectively starts the logical point of recovery for most backup strategies (a full database backup or a file/file group backup). A full database backup will back up the entire database allocation, including the data portion (the database structures, indexes, database users, and so on) along with the transaction log portion of the database. This results in an exact image of the database stored in an optimized backup format that can easily be used to restore/recover from.

- **File/File group backups**—Works pretty much the same way a full database backup works, except that the transaction log portion is not backed up. You must do this as an added step to get to a recovery point that makes sense for you. However, if you are dealing with very large databases, very often the file/file group approach makes the most sense to use.

- **Transaction log backups**—Transaction log backups are the way that changes can be captured at set intervals since the last database full backup, last full file/file group backup, or the last transaction log backup (incremental log backups). These specifically back up only the "committed" portion of the transaction log. Any transaction that is still "in flight" (not completed) would not be recovered by a transaction log backup. As part of a transaction log backup, the inactive portion of the transaction log is cleared as well. Each transaction log backup essentially marks a point in time from which you can recover to.

- **Differential backups**—A differential backup makes a copy of all the pages in a database that have been modified since the last database full backup. Using this approach, backups run relatively quickly and are smaller in size than other types of backups. Moreover, differential backups may be performed while users access the database. Because of their speed and low server impact, differential backups can be made more frequently than other types of database backups, decreasing the risk of data loss.

Most database-related failures that will result in you having to do a restore are

- Server crashes—Sometimes memory or operating system related, power loss, and so on. SQL Server usually recovers automatically on its own in these cases, but there is a chance that a database will end up in a "suspect" mode.

- Corrupt or lost data—Broken page chains for a table, wrong update, delete or insert statement being executed by a user (user error), and so on. These very often require point-in-time recovery to a point just before the corruption occurred.

- Corrupt or lost database—Database becomes "suspect" or is damaged in some way. Often requires full database restoration.

- Corrupt or lost transaction log—Transaction log becomes invalid somehow. Often requires full database restoration.

- Corrupt or lost master database—This affects the SQL Server instance itself. Rebuilding a master db should be one thing you have in your arsenal, since all databases on the SQL Server instance won't be available until master is recovered properly.

- Lost SQL Server—The disk crashes, or other factors make this entire server unavailable. You will need to be able to completely recover a full SQL Server instance within a short amount of time.

Two Backup Approaches for High Availability

Your focus should be on minimizing your unavailability and, at the same time, not sacrificing data integrity or performance. For these reasons, we recommend a couple of backup approaches that leverage full backups (database or file/file group), coupled with differential and transaction log backups for the most up-to-date recovery points possible. This is a tailored hybrid backup/restore approach that promotes *fast* recovery to support your high availability needs. Also, keep in mind that SQL Server allows data to be backed up while the database remains online and accessed by users. This offers some flexibility if you are worried about what to do with your database if it must be up 24 hours a day.

The Full Database Backup Approach

Making full database backups with some periodicity (like every day or weekly—depending on the database's size and volatility) will be critical to your database's availability (actually, recoverability). The traditional full database backup approach is what most of us do (and have done since SQL Server first came out). It allows you to have up-to-the-minute and point-in-time recovery.

Up-to-the-minute recovery literally gets you recovered up to the last committed transaction in the transaction log. This is highly desirable.

Point-in-time recovery allows you to pick the point in time you wish to recover to, perhaps just before an application error messed some table's data up severely. More recently, differential database backups were added for SQL Server, which help greatly in speeding recovery because large groups of log transactions can be skipped during recovery process.

Figure 10.13 shows a typical full database backup sequence that is done daily, coupled with incremental transaction logs done on-the-hour along with a mid-day differential database backup.

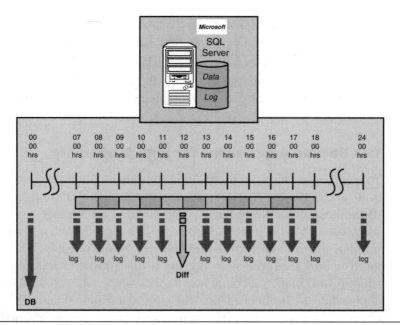

Figure 10.13   Full database backup daily schedule, with incremental transaction log dumps and a differential database backup.

Worst case recovery times are now minimized to not more than the time to restore the database from its full database backup (plus apply the differential database backup if your failure was after 1200 hours) and apply log transactions up to the point in time of the failure. This can be very fast depending on the database size and volatility. If the differential backup was invalid for any reason, you can still fully recover your database using the transaction log backups. And, vice versa, if the transaction logs are bad, you at least can recover to the differential backup point (reducing risk accordingly).

The Full File/File Group Backup Approach

With full file/file group backups, you can back up any file or file group that has been defined and at any time. There really are few restrictions here. The primary issue that comes to mind is that you cannot restore file/file group backups to a location other than the original location without first restoring the entire database. But this is rarely needed.

This type of strategy makes the most sense when you have some tables that are static (and read only) and a few that are highly volatile (and large). If these are isolated into their own files or file groups, you can selectively just back up the volatile tables (file/file groups) much more efficiently and can restore these selectively as well. The same type of backup sequencing and scheduling should be employed that was illustrated in Figure 10.13, but the need to do full database dumps is no longer needed. Best rule of thumb is to back up logically related tables and indexes together. Then, the same differential backup approach is used at the file/file group level (with all the same advantages). Great!

Design Note

We often use the special backup device of NUL to test out our backups. It will actually back up your database but not write the backup anywhere (it goes to the NUL device). It does allow you to accurately see the number of pages processed of both your data and log portions of the database, and the amount of time of the backup process so you can better plan your recovery (and availability). Below is an example of using the DISK = 'NUL' technique:

```
BACKUP DATABASE Northwind to DISK = 'NUL'
Go
Processed 320 pages for database 'Northwind',
      file 'Northwind' on file 1.
Processed 1 pages for database 'Northwind',
      file 'Northwind_log' on file 1.
BACKUP DATABASE successfully processed 321 pages in 0.365
      seconds (7.187 MB/sec)
```

To translate the pages processed into the actual disk space that it will occupy simply multiply the pages by 8192 bytes per page (for example, 321 pages * 8192 bytes/page = 2,629,632 bytes or 2.6MB backup file size).

And, once you have run a BACKUP command using the NUL device, SQL Server still thinks that a normal backup has occurred. So, don't forget to start the backup sequence again (for real) with a full database backup (or full file/file group backup) to a valid backup device before you go live with these strategies.

Parallel Striped Backup

SQL Server 2000 also allows you to backup a database to multiple devices in parallel, resulting in a striped backup set. You might want to pursue this type of backup strategy if you need super fast full database backups. We have not seen this used in practice because of the limitations it has on restoration. All striped backup devices must be restored together and if any one of them is damaged, the whole set is invalid. And, with the faster and faster disk drives that are available today, the speed of disk access has become less of the bottleneck.

Split-Mirror Backups (Server-less Backups)

The split-mirror or server-less backup business is intended to garner much higher database availability by providing an extremely rapid database backup and restore capability. And, with nearly instantaneous split-mirror restores of large amounts of data, you can keep your system online and available almost continuously. Split-mirror backups also help greatly to reduce the resource utilization on your server that would normally be needed to do scheduled backups. In addition, split-mirrored backups are also easily tapped to create copies of your primary database that can be used for reporting or even for fail-over if needed. This is not triple mirroring though. Triple mirroring is a purely hardware only solution at the disk-subsystem level.

To use split-mirror backup and restore capabilities, your database will have to leverage customized hardware and software from leading disk subsystem vendors such as EMC, Veritas, HP, and others. Be forewarned: There is usually a hefty price tag to this technology. These specialized offerings usually contain at least RAID 10 mirrored disks and volume management software that interacts directly with SQL Server.

The disk subsystem illustration in the top of Figure 10.14 shows the starting point of a split-mirror configuration (which is not split yet). In this case, it is a RAID 10 mirrored configuration that is mirroring to two mirrored volume sets (Mirrored Set and Second Mirrored Set) in the same disk subsystem. All SQL Server disk writes are being fully mirrored from the primary set to both mirror sets simultaneously. This, in itself, is a very high fault-tolerant configuration. To turn this into a split-mirror backup, you will "split" off the second mirrored set to become a snap shot of the primary set that can be synchronized later. So, at the time of this split, you are giving up a mirror, but gaining a database snapshot to provide you with faster backup and recovery capabilities (for high availability).

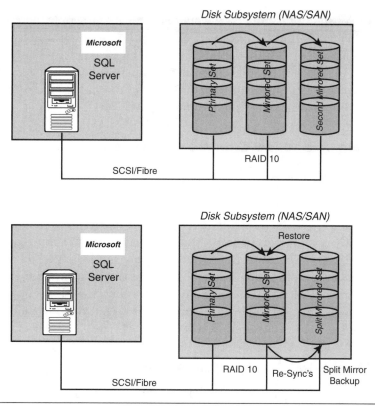

Figure 10.14   Split-Mirrored backup approach for higher database availability.

In Figure 10.14 (at the bottom), you can see the second mirrored set that gets split off. This is often referred to as a business continuance volume or a split-mirrored set. The vendor's software utility will issue a SQL Server native level backup of the database and will store it on the split-mirrored set. During this backup process, writes to the physical disks are suspended to eliminate torn pages (partially written pages to a mirror) but reads are still possible. And, the splitting itself is really fast. Once the split-mirrored backup is complete, writes at the physical disk level are resumed. This split-mirrored backup is completely usable in any way you want. It can be the basis of a fail-over, used for archiving, or for reporting. You can choose to re-synchronize this split-mirror with the primary mirror (basically a re-mirroring) and do a split-mirror restores (at the SQL Server database level).

If you do a split-mirrored restore, SQL Server will be able to read the split-mirrored set immediately and write to all mirrored sets, the net effect being that the database becomes available almost instantaneously.

Following the restore, you would also be able to apply incremental log backups to your database as needed (and these are usually applied very quickly depending on the time between log backups).

You should be able to do numerous full database backups during normal operating hours to guarantee up-to-date database images and maximum availability (minimum recovery times).

Volume Shadow Copy Service (VSS)

If you haven't heard by now, Windows Server 2003 comes with a Volume Shadow Copy Service that is, as its name suggests, a volume-oriented shadowing capability. It has been integrated with SQL Server via a component named SQLWriter. It is essentially like a split-mirror but done at the OS level rather than via specialized hardware. Combined, you will be able to do full database backups (with snapshot) via the VSS service and then separately apply transaction logs to the point in time you want to recover to. Slowly, backup and recovery (of even SQL Server databases) is being brought out to the operating system level for single point of management (this is long overdue).

Monitoring/Verifying Backups

If you are serious about database backup and recovery, you will want to monitor and verify the backups that are being made. I've lost count of the number of times that I went to restore a backup and it was unreadable for a variety of reasons. There is both a database integrity check and a backup integrity check (for both data and transaction log dumps) that you can execute as part of your regular maintenance plans (or as a separate offline process). This can save the day if the integrity check just catches one bad transaction log backup or one bad full database backup. Figure 10.15 shows both the verify database integrity option and the verify backup integrity option as part of your database maintenance plan. Performance issues of these integrity checks may preclude you from making them part of the maintenance plan, but they should be run regularly somehow.

In addition, activating alerts to notify support personnel when backups fail, transaction logs are filling up, or integrity is in question is an essential part of maintaining high availability. Figure 10.16 shows the integrated capability of SQL Server to completely support an alert and notification process in the event of these types of problems.

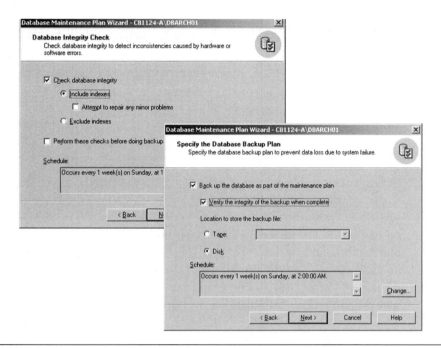

Figure 10.15   "Check Database Integrity" and "Verify the Integrity of the Backup when Completed" options of a database maintenance plan.

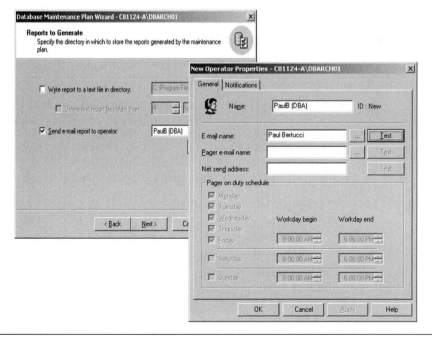

Figure 10.16   Alert and notification setup and testing for the primary SQL Server issues during backup and integrity verification.

- Is a "clustered" pair of high-end IBM servers on the AIX 5.1 operating system platform using HACMP capabilities in an active/active mode (see Figure 10.19)

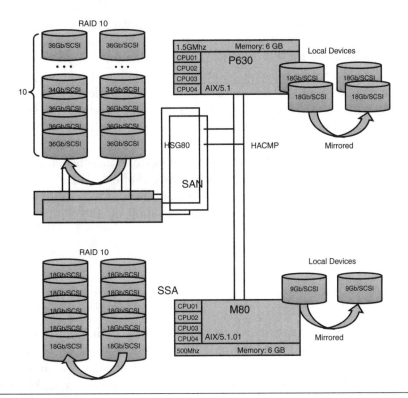

Figure 10.19 IBM/DB2 Clustered Server configuration supporting a 99.999% high availability requirement.

As you can also see in Figure 10.19, High Availability Cluster Multi-Processing (HACMP) is IBM's software for building highly available clusters on IBM Scalable POWERParallel systems and/or a combination of pSeries systems. It is supported by a wide range of IBM pSeries systems, including the new p690, storage systems, and network types. HACMP builds on the inherent reliability of the hardware to provide greater uptime for applications, and enables upgrades and reconfiguration without interrupting operations. This example utilizes the IBM Serial Storage Architecture (SSA) to share a network attached storage device (SAN) for all of the database and application files. In the event of a system failure (like if the P630 should fail), the HACMP automatically

If you do not define these notifications, you are putting your company at risk.

Disaster Recovery Planning

Speaking of putting your company at risk, if you haven't considered a major disaster or defined a disaster recovery plan, you are doing just this. Disasters come in many flavors. Perhaps it is just a hardware failure of a single server, a power outage, a fire, a tornado, an earthquake, or a terrorist act. Very often a disaster recovery (DR) plan will be devised, but never tested. The mandate we would put on you would be to devise a highly efficient disaster recovery plan in support of your high availability needs and then *test it* completely! Make sure it considers all aspects of completely being able to come up in an alternate location as smoothly, quickly, and with as little data loss as possible. Defining a disaster recovery plan can be a tedious job because of the potential complexities of your high availability configuration. But, keep in mind, a disaster recovery plan *is* part of your high availability configuration (or at least it should be). It should also be part of your decision process of picking the high availability solution in the first place.

The Overall Disaster Recovery Approach

In general, there will be a handful of things that need to be put together (defined and executed upon). These are

1. Create a disaster recovery execution tasks/run book. This will include all steps to take to recover from a disaster and cover all system components that need to be recovered.

2. Arrange for or procure a server/site to recover to. This should be a configuration that can house what is needed to get you back online.

3. Guarantee that a complete database backup/recovery mechanism is in place (including offsite/alternate site archive and retrieval of databases)

4. Guarantee that an application backup/recovery mechanism is in place (like COM+ apps, web services, other application components, and so on).

5. Make sure you can completely re-create and resynchronize your security (MS Active Directory, domain accounts, SQL Server Logins/passwords, and so on). We call this *security resynchronization readiness*.

6. Make sure you can completely configure and open up network/communication lines. This would also include routers configured properly, IP addresses made available, and so on.

7. Train your support personnel on all elements of recovery. You can never know enough ways to recovery a system. And, it seems that a system never recovers the same way twice.

8. Plan and execute an annual or bi-annual disaster recovery simulation. The one or two days that you do this will pay for itself a hundred times over if a disaster actually occurs. And, remember, disasters come in many flavors.

Many organizations have gone to the concept of having "hot" alternate sites available via stretch clustering or log shipping techniques. Costs can be high for some of these advanced and highly redundant solutions.

The Focus for Disaster Recovery

On the more practical side (dollar-wise), if you create some very solid, time-tested mechanisms for re-creating your SQL Server environment, they will serve you well when you need them most. The things to focus on for disaster recovery are

- Always generate scripts for as much as possible (anything that was created using a wizard, enterprise manager, and so on). These scripts will save your rear end (can I say that?). These should include
  - Complete replication buildup/breakdown scripts
  - Complete database creation scripts (DB, tables, indexes, views, and so on)
  - Complete SQL login, database user IDs, and password scripts (including roles and other grants)
  - Linked/remote server setup (linked servers, remote logins)
  - Log shipping setup (source, target, and monitor servers)
  - Any custom SQL Agent tasks

- Backup/restore scripts
- Potentially other scripts, depending on what you have built on SQL Server

- Make sure you document all aspects of SQL database maintenance plans that are being used. This includes frequencies, alerts, email addresses being notified when errors occur, backup file/device locations, and so on.

- Document all hardware/software configurations used:
  - Leverage the sqldiag.exe for this (described in the next section)
  - Record what accounts were used to start up the SQL Agent service for an instance and MS distributed transaction coordinator (MS DTC) service. This is especially important if using distributed transactions and data replication.
  - My favorite set of SQL Server information that I script and record for a SQL Server instance are
    - `select @@SERVERNAME`—Will provide the full network name of the SQL Server and instance.
    - `select @@SERVICENAME`—Will provide the registry key under which Microsoft SQL Server is running
    - `select @@VERSION`—Provides the date, version, and processor type for the current installation of Microsoft SQL Server
    - `exec sp_helpserver`—Provides the server name, the server's network name, the server's replication status, the server's identification number, collation name, and time-out values for connecting to, or queries against, linked servers
    - `exec sp_helplogins`—Provides information about logins and the associated users in each database
    - `exec sp_linkedservers`—Returns the list of linked servers defined in the local server
    - `exec sp_helplinkedsrvlogin`—Provides information about login mappings defined against a specific linked server used for distributed queries and remote stored procedures

- exec `sp_helpremotelogin`—Provides information about remote logins for a particular remote server, or for all remote servers, defined on the local server

- exec `sp_server_info`—Returns a list of attribute names and matching values for Microsoft SQL Server

- exec `sp_helpdb` `dbnamexyz`—Provides information about a specified database or all databases. This includes the database allocation names, sizes, and locations.

- exec `sp_spaceused`—Provides the actual database usage information of both data and indexes in a database.

- Get the current SQL Server configuration values by running `sp_configure` (from Query Analyzer). Here are the results of running `sp_configure` with `show advanced option` specified:

```
USE master
EXEC sp_configure 'show advanced option', '1'
RECONFIGURE
go
EXEC sp_configure
Go
```

name	minimum	maximum	config_value	run_value
affinity mask	-2147483648	2147483647	0	0
allow updates	0	1	0	0
awe enabled	0	1	0	0
c2 audit mode	0	1	0	0
cost threshold for parallelism	0	32767	5	5
Cross DB Ownership Chaining	0	1	0	0
cursor threshold	-1	2147483647	-1	-1
default full-text language	0	2147483647	1033	1033
default language	0	9999	0	0
fill factor (%)	0	100	0	0
index create memory (KB)	704	2147483647	0	0
lightweight pooling	0	1	0	0
locks	5000	2147483647	0	0
max degree of parallelism	0	32	0	0
max server memory (MB)	4	2147483647	2147483647	2147483647
max text repl size (B)	0	2147483647	65536	65536

max worker threads	32	32767	255	255
media retention	0	365	0	0
min memory per query (KB)	512	2147483647	1024	1024
min server memory (MB)	0	2147483647	0	0
nested triggers	0	1	1	1
network packet size (B)	512	65536	4096	4096
open objects	0	2147483647	0	0
priority boost	0	1	0	0
query governor cost limit	0	2147483647	0	0
query wait (s)	-1	2147483647	-1	-1
recovery interval (min)	0	32767	0	0
remote access	0	1	1	1
remote login timeout (s)	0	2147483647	20	20
remote proc trans	0	1	0	0
remote query timeout (s)	0	2147483647	600	600
scan for startup procs	0	1	1	1
set working set size	0	1	0	0
show advanced options	0	1	1	1
two digit year cutoff	1753	9999	2049	2049
user connections	0	32767	0	0
user options	0	32767	0	0

- Disk configurations, sizes, and current size availability (use standard OS directory listing commands on all disk volumes that are being used).

- Capture the sa login password and the OS Administrator password so that anything can be accessed and anything can be installed (or re-installed).

- Document all contact information for your vendors:
    - Microsoft support services contacts (for example, list all support agreements such as Premier Product support services)
    - Storage vendor contact info
    - Hardware vendor contact info
    - Offsite storage contact info (to get your archived copy fast)

- Network/telecom contact info
- Your CTO, CIO, and other senior management contact
- CD-ROMs available for everything (SQL Server, service packs, operating system, utilities, and so on)

Documenting Environmental Details Using SQLDIAG.EXE

One good way to get a complete environmental picture is to run the SQLDIAG.exe program provided with SQL Server 2000 on your production box (that you would have to re-create on an alternate site if a disaster occurs). It can be found in the "Binn" directory where all SQL Server executables are (C:\Program Files\Microsoft SQL Server\MSSQL$YourSqlInstance\Binn). It will show you how the server is configured, all hardware and software components (and their versions), memory sizes, CPU types, operating system version and build info, paging file info, environment variables, and so on. If you run this on your production server periodically, it will serve as a good environment documentation to supplement your disaster recovery plan. Open a DOS command prompt and change directory to the SQL Server BINN directory. Then, at the command prompt run SQLDIAG.exe.

```
C:\Program Files\Microsoft SQL Server\MSSQL$SQLInstance\Binn> sqldiag
```

The results will be written into a text file named SQLDIAG.TXT at the root (c:\ by default or the SQL Server log directory) and contain a verbose snapshot of everything that relates to SQL Server (in one way or another). The following is an abbreviated sample of what you will see:

```
[System Summary]
Registry Information
--------------------
SOFTWARE\Microsoft\MSSQLServer\Client\ConnectTo:
------------------------------------------------
DSQUERY:     DBNETLIB
DBARCH6000\CORE650NET:     DBMSSOCN,DBARCH6000\CORE650NET
\\DBARCH6000\CORE650NET:     DBMSSOCN,\\DBARCH6000\CORE650NET

SOFTWARE\Microsoft\MSSQLServer\Client\DB-Lib:
---------------------------------------------
```

```
AutoAnsiToOem:    ON
UseIntlSettings:   ON


SOFTWARE\Microsoft\MSSQLServer\Setup:
-----------------------------------


Version Information
-------------------
ntwdblib.dll:    8.00. 194
ssmsad60.dll:    N/A
ssmsde60.dll:    N/A
ssmsrp60.dll:    N/A
ssmsso60.dll:    N/A
ssmssp60.dll:    N/A
ssmsvi60.dll:    N/A
ssnmpn60.dll:    N/A
dbmsadsn.dll:    08.00.9030
dbmsdecn.dll:    N/A
dbmsrpcn.dll:    08.00.9030
dbmssocn.dll:    7.00.819
dbmsspxn.dll:    7.00.819
dbmsvinn.dll:    08.00.9030
dbnmpntw.dll:    08.00.9030
sqlsrv32.dll:    3.81.9042
Item  Value
OS Name  Microsoft Windows 2000 Professional
Version  5.0.2195 Service Pack 4 Build 2195
OS Manufacturer  Microsoft Corporation
System Name  SQLDB01
System Manufacturer  XYZ
System Model  XYZ
System Type  X86-based PC
Processor  x86 Family 6 Model 9 Stepping 5 GenuineIntel ~1594 Mhz
BIOS Version  Insyde Software MobilePRO BIOS Version 4.00.00
Windows Directory  C:\WIN2K
System Directory  C:\WIN2K\system32
Boot Device  \Device\Harddisk0\Partition1
Locale  United States
User Name  C81124-A\Administrator
Time Zone  Pacific Daylight Time
Total Physical Memory  1,048,048 KB
Available Physical Memory  703,756 KB
Total Virtual Memory  3,569,232 KB
```

```
Available Virtual Memory  2,961,300 KB
Page File Space  2,521,184 KB
Page File  C:\pagefile.sys
[Environment Variables]
[Services]
[Startup Programs]
so on..
```

Again, we suggest that this be done on a regular basis and compared with prior executions to guarantee that you know exactly what you have to have in place in case of disaster.

Plan and Execute a Complete Disaster Recovery test

Plan and execute a complete disaster recovery (DR). This is serious business and many companies around the globe set aside a few days a year to do this exact thing. This test should include:

- Simulate a disaster.
- Record all actions that get taken.
- Time all events from start to finish. Sometimes this means there is someone standing around with a stopwatch.
- Hold a post-mortem following the DR simulation.

Many companies tie the results of the DR simulation to the IT group's salaries (their raise percentage). This is more than enough motivation for IT to get this drill right and to perform well. And, it is critical to correct any failures or issues that occurred. The next time might not be a simulation.

Software Upgrade Considerations

We can't stress the importance of keeping your application and infrastructure software up to date. Many companies are moving to a network-deployed push model for software upgrades and fixes. This guarantees that all connected components in their infrastructure (servers, routers, workstations, and so on) are as up to date as possible at all times. If you are in a 24x7x365 uptime requirement for an application, finding downtime to upgrade or apply fixes might be a little difficult. It is less difficult if you are using a multi-server clustered configuration that permits you to take a server offline (out of the cluster), apply service packs to it, and then rejoin the cluster. Keep these types of options in mind when making that final high availability solution choice. Here are the basics:

- Plan on downtime (if possible)—This can usually be negotiated during your end-user SLA definition time. The value of planned downtime for software/hardware maintenance is huge. You don't need much time, but plan for it. The planned downtime doesn't count against your high availability percentage performance measurement.

- Be aggressive about applying upgrades—If possible, use a network-deployed push model to periodically upgrade servers and workstations. Or, selectively plan on at least monthly upgrades as part of your planned downtime maintenance (if you have planned downtime). This also covers application software, middleware, and database software. Some of these won't have frequent updates or upgrades, but you must stay current on these. If you have problems with any of these software components, you will get better support from the software vendor if you are on the latest release.

- Antivirus software—Make sure you have antivirus software in place and it is active at all times but probably not have it scanning your database files due to the performance impact. (I'm not sure there are any exceptions to this rule any more. Even at the time of this chapter's writing, a major "attack" virus has been hitting servers and workstations around the world.)

- Close backdoors—Make sure you have closed all backdoors (ports, and so forth) that are not being used, make sure you have some type of firewall is in place (hardware or software), and turn off things such as anonymous FTP accounts.

- Configuration snapshots—Make periodic snapshots of the configuration you have and the release levels of all software components in our high availability solution (you can use SQLDIAG.EXE for this if you want). Suggest this be done at least twice a year, if not quarterly. Be proactive here, it will also keep you honest on all software upgrades that are needed.

- Automatic Updates—Microsoft has an option to automatically update Windows but we recommend that this be turned "off."

So, leave on the notification of new updates, but turn off the automatic installation option. You need control over what update to apply and when to apply it.

- Vendor agreements—Get all vendor agreements in place in the form of current software licenses, renewable software support agreements. This should include a service level agreement with the vendors that corresponds to your service level agreement that you will have with your end-users (and matches your high availability requirements).

All of these items have a direct effect on high availability. Consider them carefully.

High Availability and MS Analysis Services/OLAP

Building business intelligence (BI) applications that utilize Microsoft SQL Server 2000 Analysis Services (MSAS) may be the most rapidly expanding area within SQL Server-based systems. Up until recently, OLAP applications were primarily developed with classic availability needs to support (5 days per week, 8 a.m. to 5 p.m. uptime requirements). However, in recent years, a higher and higher percentage of analysis services-based implementations have vaulted to near extreme availability requirements (to the point that many OLAP applications are now needed 24 hours a day, 365 days of the year). This is partly due to the improved decision capability that can be attained from OLAP applications (and with MS Analysis Services leading the way). Many fortune 5000 companies around the world have very key OLAP/MSAS applications up and running now that directly influence huge business and financial decisions continuously. If these OLAP applications become unavailable for any extended period of time, enormous financial losses from unresearched decisions could occur. These ramifications provide much fuel to fully integrate MS Analysis Services into a solid high availability framework from the start.

The purpose of OLAP is to provide for an online reporting environment that can support various end user reporting requirements. These OLAP applications are usually created by complex extraction, cleansing, and aggregation processes from multiple operational systems (ODSs) into multi-dimensional or star schema data marts or data warehouses with full hierarchical level drill down capabilities. These OLAP applications must also provide full querying, reporting, and complex analysis capabilities to guarantee that the critical business decisions of an organization can be serviced properly. And most importantly, these OLAP applications must be extremely reliable, fast, and highly available (near 100% uptime).

Cubes are created by preprocessing aggregations (pre-calculated summary data) that reflect the desired levels within dimensions and support the type of querying that will be done. These aggregations provide the mechanism for rapid and uniform response times to queries. All queries are utilizing either these aggregations, the cube's source data, a copy of this data on the MSAS, a client cache, or a combination of these sources. In some complex data situations, you may want to create cubes with little to no aggregates and then run usage-based optimization so that the aggregates that get designed match the user's query patterns. A single analysis server can manage many cubes.

A cube is defined by the measures and dimensions that it contains. Each cube dimension can contain a hierarchy of levels to specify the natural categorical breakdown that users need to drilldown into for more details.

You can write custom client applications using Multidimensional Extensions (MDX) with OLE DB for OLAP (using Pivot Table Services) orActiveX Data Objects Multidimensional (ADO MD) which is built on OLE DB for OLAP, or you can use a number of third-party OLE DB for OLAP-compliant tools. MDX is the multidimensional expression in SQL that enables you to formulate complex multidimensional queries.

Every cube has a schema from which the cube draws its source data. A cube contains a series of partitions. Each partition uses a fact table. In the simple case there is only one partition per cube, but in many large production implementations, partitioning is used extensively. Not only can each partition in a cube have a different data source, it can have different storage methods (one partition MOLAP; one ROLAP) and it can have different aggregates (you may have a lot of aggregates for the current month partition, but little or no aggregates for history five years ago). The central table in a schema is the fact table that will yield the cube's data measures. The other tables in the schema are the dimension tables that are the source of the cube dimensions. A classic star-schema data warehouse design will have this central fact table along with multiple dimension tables.

It has been found that highly available OLAP/MSAS systems increase the end-users' acceptance of this type of system and the data it delivers. If the OLAP data is unavailable, end-users may find it easier to interpret offline data on their own rather than waiting for the OLAP application to come back up. In addition, if the system is always available, end-users make decisions using the integrated analysis tools that you have painstakingly built into your OLAP/MSAS application, which yields more accurate, well-founded results, by design.

When designing for highly available OLAP/analysis services systems, you must be keenly aware of things like

- Outages for dimension maintenance—If the dimensions in your OLAP cubes contain updates to data, then realignment of things such as customers, products, or sales will cause downtime during reprocessing.

- Processing windows—When normal nightly processing is done, query response times and query data scopes can be affected during incremental processing of partitions. In some cases, a cube partition will be completely unavailable during full processing of that partition. However, as long as the dimension structure remains the same, doing a full process of a partition may not cause the cube to become unavailable. The processing is done in a shadow folder and then switched when processing completes.

- OLAP storage mechanism—MSAS supports three OLAP storage methods, providing flexibility to the data warehousing solution and enabling powerful partitioning and aggregation optimization capabilities. These OLAP storage methods are MOLAP, ROLAP, and HOLAP. Choosing the right storage mechanism to best support your high availability requirement will be necessary very early on. Both ROLAP and HOLAP will result in Analysis Services having to make direct queries against another system (the source RDBMS, or the aggregate RDBMS). If one of those systems becomes unavailable, so does your Analysis Services server. It can be argued that to reduce dependencies and increase availability you should use the MOLAP storage method for your partitions.

- Upstream data availability—A critical operational issue in a production OLAP/MSAS application is to guarantee the availability of the feeder systems (the providers of the detail operational data). A thorough understanding of data context, data latency, and data integrity from these upstream systems is essential.

- Usage-based optimization—Running the Usage-Based Optimization Wizard on a regular basis to add new aggregations based on changing query patterns can increase the total number of aggregations, which in turn would increase processing times and might ultimately exceed the length of the nightly processing window.

OLAP Cubes Variations

Cubes can be regular, virtual, or local cubes (as shown in Figure 10.17). Slight variations on this theme are linked cubes and real-time cubes. The following list explains these cubes in more detail:

- Regular cubes—Regular cubes are based on real tables or views for their data source, will have aggregations, and will occupy physical storage space of some kind. If a data source that contributes to cubes partition changes, it must be reprocessed.

- Virtual cubes—Virtual cubes are logical cubes based on one or more regular cubes (or linked cubes). Similar to relational views, virtual cubes use the aggregations of their component regular cubes, in which case storage space is not needed.

- Linked cubes—Linked cubes are based on regular cubes defined and stored on another analysis server. Linked cubes also use the aggregations (and storage) of the regular cube they reference.

- Local cubes—Local cubes are entirely contained in portable files (tables) and can be browsed without a connection to an analysis server. They do not have aggregations. This is really like being in "disconnected" mode.

- Real-time cubes—These are regular cubes that have dimensions or partitions that have been enabled for "real-time OLAP." In other words, real-time cubes receive updates dynamically from the data sources that are defined in their dimensions/partitions.

- Write-enabled cubes—These are cubes in which updates (writes) are allowed and can be shared back with the data sources.

MSAS supports three OLAP storage methods, providing flexibility to the data warehousing solution and enabling powerful partitioning and aggregation optimization capabilities. These OLAP storage methods are MOLAP, ROLAP, and HOLAP.

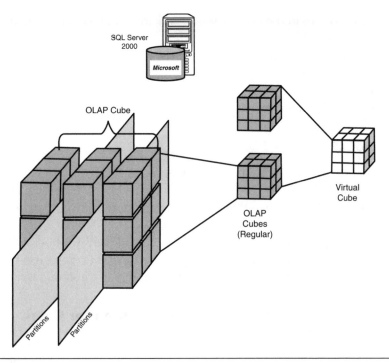

Figure 10.17 The MSAS cube representations — regular OLAP cubes, partitions, and virtual cubes.

MOLAP

Multidimensional OLAP (MOLAP) is a storage approach in which cubes are built directly from OLTP data sources or from operational databases and stored in a native Microsoft OLAP format. No zero-activity records are stored (zero-activity records occur when an original value is zeroed out but the record remains in the database; it will be included in the count of records and affects other calculations like sums and so on).

The dimension keys in the fact tables are compressed, and bitmap indexing is used. A high-speed MOLAP query processor retrieves the data.

ROLAP

Relational OLAP (ROLAP) uses fact data in summary tables in the OLTP data source to speed retrieval. The summary tables are populated by processes in the OLTP system and are not downloaded to MSAS. The summary tables are known as materialized views and contain various levels of aggregation, depending on the options you select when building data cubes with MSAS. MSAS builds the summary tables with a column for each dimension and each measure. It indexes each dimension column and creates an additional index on all the dimension columns.

HOLAP

MSAS also implements a combination of MOLAP and ROLAP called hybrid OLAP (HOLAP). Here, the facts are left in the OLTP data source (RDBMS), and aggregations are stored in the native Microsoft OLAP format on the MSAS server.

However, keep in mind that when using MSAS, both ROLAP and HOLAP require more storage space because they don't use the storage optimizations of the pure MOLAP-compressed implementation.

Recommended MSAS Implementation for High Availability

If your requirements are clearly pushing you into implementing your MSAS environment to support high availability, we would recommend that you consider the following:

- Leverage NLB if possible—If you have a large number of MSAS end-user requests to be serviced, more than one server can be configured with the network load balancing settings and loaded with a copy of the latest OLAP data to fulfill these requests (as depicted in Figure 10.18). Availability at the analysis server level is maintained because network load balancing detects when a server that is not responding to network requests and dynamically removes it from the NLB cluster. The remaining nodes pick up the load of the unresponsive server to service the end-user requests.

- OLAP Storage mechanism for HA—MOLAP is recommended because the data is self-contained in the Analysis Services data folder and can easily be moved from any processing server to the analysis servers. To ensure 100 percent availability of the OLAP facility, you need a mechanism that allows multiple versions of the data to be spread out among the members of a cluster. The data must be independently configured and controlled along with the server being converged into the network load balancing cluster. If you use ROLAP or HOLAP, a single relational database contains (at minimum) the fact data and possibly the aggregates. This complicates the movement of data, because you must copy both relational databases and data files throughout the cluster.

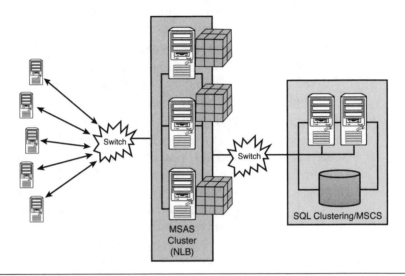

Figure 10.18   Leveraging multiple NLB clustered analysis servers and SQL clustering for high availability.

- Windows Clustering—At a very minimum, you will be implementing your Analysis Services and SQL Server within a Windows clustered configuration (MSCS) so that all files needed by the master copy of Analysis Services and SQL Server are completely managed by the cluster. This offers a very stable base platform from which to build varying degrees of high availability.
- RAID configuration for Analysis Services:
  - For the best performance with full recoverability, use RAID 10.
  - RAID 5 for the Analysis Services data folder (because the data is mostly read-only).
  - Use RAID 0 (just disk striping) for the Analysis Services temp folder. The temp folder does not require recoverability. It is used only for cube or partition processing.

- Controller and disk technologies:
    - Use a controller that supports hot standby disks that are automatically added to the RAID set if a disk failure occurs.
    - Use fibre-channel RAID controllers whenever possible. Small Computer System Interface (SCSI) is acceptable for mid-range systems, but not for large RAID or system area network (SAN) configurations.
    - Consider using SAN technology to obtain snapshots of data (to move data from staging to production). This greatly reduces time required to copy OLAP database files—which tend to be large (greater than 50GB).
- The master copy of the OLAP data is stored in the data storage location managed by cluster services. If multiple NLB configured servers are being used, the local disks on these front-end servers will store the operational versions of the OLAP data. This approach guarantees that there is a master copy of the OLAP data and instantiating any load-balanced servers with copies is relatively easy to do and easily managed. After any new copy of the OLAP data is placed on the front-end servers, an update job can easily change the location of the data folder referenced. Now keep in mind that with a master copy of the OLAP data being managed within a cluster, it is easy to add a new analysis server to the front-end NLB cluster. The analysis server is required only to copy the data and add the host to the cluster—then the server is up and running extremely rapidly. Because every analysis server contains its own data, they are not dependent on any outside resource. Performance is consistent, and there is no single point of failure anywhere in the cluster.
- Data Staging—Design a high performance data staging capability that will feed your MSAS environment affectively. OLAP applications integrate data from many data sources. Make sure your data staging capability has the disk and CPU resources to handle the data and processing to continuously populate the OLAP/MSAS system.
- SQL clustering—Use SQL clustering for your SQL Server portion of your system. This would include the staging data capabilities that are usually present in an OLAP processing

configuration. SQL clustering offers the highest fail-over capability for SQL Server-based processing. In addition, this should be at least a two-node SQL cluster in an active/passive mode.

- If you use the NLB clustered configuration you will not be able to use the *writeback* data capabilities of your OLAP cubes. In this one configuration case, the multi-dimensional data must be read-only.

These OLAP/MSAS focused recommendations will yield a highly available platform for your OLAP end-users. Once you get these basic elements in place, the staging of any data updates and managing database size growth will quickly take over as the bigger challenge within your OLAP/MSAS deployments.

Alternative Techniques in Support of High Availability

As you consider and evaluate all of the primary high availability options that are available to you, you often realize that you might only need one portion of an application to be highly available, or that a Microsoft solution isn't optimal. Better understanding what third-party high availability alternatives are available in the marketplace can be time well spent. In addition, understanding intermediate techniques to utilize (like using DTS packages to dynamically create redundant data) as an early step to achieving some degree of high availability may help you mitigate your current risk and exposure. And, seeing what other vendor technical architectures look like (like an IBM high availability configuration) is a good contrast and learning exercise to go through. The next few sections dive into some of these alternative ideas, and third-party offerings.

Data Transformation Service (DTS) Packages Used to Achieve HA

For those of us who have been using DTS for many years to do major data conversions, data loads, and data migrations, it is very clear that DTS packages could be used to create fail-over database environments. This was not listed as a primary solution for high availability, but is a solution nonetheless. DTS packages can be a short-term solution to start creating viable alternate sites without much effort and result in a first step in achieving some level of high availability capability. The thing to keep in mind is that the packages that are created with DTS will be issuing native insert and bulk insert calls and not using page level techniques that are present with log shipping and other methods. There is also a processing impact to the source server. For these reasons, we keep it as an idea, and not as a viable, easily managed high availability solution.

Have You Detached a Database Recently?

Another crude (buy extremely powerful) method to create a snapshot of a database (for any purpose, even for backup and recovery) is to simply detach the database and attach it in another location (pretty much anywhere). There will be some downtime during the detach time, the compressing of the database files (the .mdf and .ldf), some time during the data transfer of these files (or single zipped file) from one location to another, some uncompress time, and the final attach time (seconds). All in all it is a very reliable way to move an entire database from one place to another. What we are suggesting is that all methods of backup and recovery be considered when dealing with high availability. This is crude, but fairly fast and extremely safe. To give you an example of what this takes, a database that is about 30GB can be detached, compressed, moved to another server across a network (with a 1GB backbone), uncompressed, and attached in about 10 minutes. Make sure your administrators know they can do this in a pinch. This is probably not a good high availability solution to advertise though.

Third-party Alternatives to High Availability

Third-party alternatives to replication, mirroring, and synchronization approaches of support high availability are fairly prevalent. Companies such as Veritas, Computer Associates, and others lead the way with very viable, but often expensive solutions. However, many are bundled with their disk subsystems (which make them easy to use and manage, out-of-the-box). In a recently published survey (June 2004) of alternatives to Microsoft Clustering, several very strong solutions were identified. Some of the better ones included

- Veritas (www.veritas.com)—Veritas storage and clustering products for Windows. The Veritas clustering solutions provide protection against application and database downtime. These include

- VERITAS Cluster Server
- VERITAS Cluster Server Traffic Director
- VERITAS CommandCentral Availability
- VERITAS Global Cluster Manager

The Veritas replication solutions can create duplicate copies of data across any distance for data protection. These include

- VERITAS Storage Replicator
- VERITAS Volume Replicator

- SteelEye Technologies (www.steeleye.com)—The SteelEye Life-Keeper family of data replication, high availability clustering, and disaster recovery products are for Linux and Windows environments. These are all certified solutions (on a variety of other vendor products) across a wide range of applications and databases running on Windows and Linux, including mySAP, Exchange, Oracle, DB2, SQL Server.

- LEGATO software (www.legato.com)—Co-StandbyServer and Automated Availability manager. The LEGATO Automated Availability (AA) family of products includes capabilities required to manage system's performance and to automate recovery from failures. LEGATO AA also automates data mirroring and replication, to enable data consolidation, migration, distribution, and preservation through failures and disasters.

- Computer Associates (www.ca.com)—BrightStor High Availability. This product incorporates file-system replication, rapid fail-over replication, and process-monitoring technology from CA's Unicenter enterprise-management solution.

  - BrightStor High Availability Manager provides maximum availability for mission-critical applications. Data stored on a primary server is replicated in real-time to a secondary server, which can be located on a LAN or WAN. Whether hardware failure or natural disaster, BrightStor High Availability Manager automatically detects critical problems with the primary server and immediately switches activity to the secondary server, allowing you to continue working with virtually no interruption. BrightStor High Availability Manager lessens the risk to your vital business systems and maintains access to server-based applications such as databases and email—even if systems suffer damage or service outages.

- BrightStor Data Availability Solutions provide complete end-to-end storage protection for all critical business storage assets from the laptop to the mainframe. CA solutions provide complete integrated support for server-less backup, snapshot technology, complete devices support and full application/database support. These solutions provide comprehensive cross-platform backup/recovery, disaster recovery, data replication, and hierarchical storage management.

Our recommendation is that if you are already a customer of one of these vendors you should look at these solutions, since they may be available with a product you already are using. This is a starter list for those interested in high availability solutions that are Microsoft compatible and offer non-Microsoft compatibility as well. This is not a comparison of high availability solutions, but rather an invitation to look at other high availability solutions that might fit your needs.

IBM/DB2 High Availability Example

Just to keep us honest, we thought it would be a good idea to share a typical high availability configuration of a competing product (and company). One of our customers has recently put a lot of time and money in building out a very good high availability solution for their most critical application (their order entry system). They churn between 6,000 and 8,000 orders per day with an average order value of about $550.00 (USD). That's $4.4 million a day. They run nationwide warehouses in all North American time zones translating into 12 hours (720 minutes) per day, 6 days per week uptime requirements. So, that's on average 11.11 orders per minute or a cost of downtime of approximately $6,111.11 dollars per minute. It adds up quickly.

In their business, all orders are either taken by phone directly or via the web. The system must be up 99.999% of the time, which would classify this as an "extreme" availability requirement.

The underlying database engine is DB2 and the overall high availability configuration is as follows:

- Application database is highly partitioned to segregate static tables from volatile tables

- Full database backups (with incremental log backups) are done

- A very resilient NAS disk subsystem consisting of RAID 10 multiple stripped and mirrored volumes is in place

switches the control of the application and access to the database to the secondary server (the M80 server).

The amazing part of this story is that the front-end has been built using C# (and VS.NET). In other words, this is a .NET framework implementation that is using DB2 as the database engine on an AIX backend set of clustered servers. It is equally interesting to note that all development for this extreme availability system was done using Microsoft SQL Server followed by porting the schema, stored procedures, and functions to DB2 after user acceptance was completed. The port to DB2 was done entirely because the customer already owned the big AIX iron and the licenses to DB2 (they have been true blue for 30 years). This porting to DB2 in no way meant that SQL Server 2000 couldn't handle this type of application. In fact, the performance benchmarks we did reflect equal performance capabilities and equal high availability coverage. But, the customer demanded that it be on DB2. We, however, keep the user acceptance version (that was built on MS SQL Server 2000) alive and well on their site "just in case."

Summary

There are perhaps thousands of considerations that must be dealt with when building a viable production implementation, let alone one that needs to be highly available. You would be well advised to make the extra effort of first properly determining which highly available solution matches your application's needs, then to switch focus to what is the most effective way to implement that chosen high availability solution. There are critical design decisions that need to be addressed for each high availability solution. If, for example, you choose data replication to support your HA needs, you must determine the right type of replication model to use (like a central publisher and remote distributor), what the schema limitations might be, the fail-over process that needs to be devised, and so on. Understanding the characteristics of your highly available data will also drive the RAID level configurations that need to be used, number of controllers, controller types, network topologies, and the proper database backup/recovery techniques to use.

Disaster recovery planning and execution must also be made part of your high availability implementation from start to finish. Considering this upfront *before* you have selected your high availability solution is critical to your success.

This chapter also described some other high availability perspective on processing capabilities such as Microsoft Analysis Services (MSAS/OLAP). There is a huge proliferation of new MSAS/OLAP applications that have high availability requirements.

NOTE Another depiction of MSAS and high availability issues can be found in a paper titled "Improved Web Connectivity in Microsoft SQL Server 2000 Analysis Services" by Dennis Kennedy and Dave Wickert of Microsoft Corporation available at www.microsoft.com.

In addition, understanding that there other vendors (other than Microsoft) with very sound high availability alternatives should allow you to mix and match your capabilities depending on any existing (or intended) vendor relationship.

You must get the design basics down first for all of these high availability solutions. Then fine-tune your designs to achieve the optimal availability results.

CHAPTER 11

High Availability and Security

- Applying security standards and sound techniques to your HA environment (with well thought out roles and permissions schemes)

- Creating schema-bound views to protect tables from being changed or dropped accidentally (to minimize these types of inadvertent failures)

- Security considerations for each major HA option (MSCS, SQL clustering, log shipping, and data replication)

Security Breakdowns' Effect on High Availability

The subject of security and high availability are rarely considered in the same breath. However, having built numerous (and varying) types of high availability solutions, it became apparent that one Achilles' heel was always present—that of properly planning, specifying, managing, and protecting the security related portions to these high availability solutions.

In other words, time after time, application failures and the need to recover an application from a backup were related to security breakdowns of some kind. In general, nearly 23% of application failures or applications that become inaccessible can be attributed to security related factors. Examples of various security related breakdowns that can directly affect the availability of an application are

- Data in tables are deleted (updated or inserted) by users that shouldn't even have update/delete/insert privileges on a table, rendering an application unusable (unavailable).

- Database objects in production are accidentally dropped by developers (or sysadmins), completely bringing down an application. Oops!

- The wrong Windows accounts are used to start services for log shipping or data replication, resulting in SQL Agent tasks not being able to communicate with other SQL Servers to fulfill transaction log restores, monitor server status updates, and process data distribution in data replication.

- Hot standby servers are missing local database user IDs that resulted in the application being inaccessible by a portion of the user population.

Unfortunately, these and other types of security-related breakdowns are often neglected in any high availability planning, but often contribute to large amounts of "unavailability."

General Security Comments

To guard against any type of unauthorized access or untimely data manipulation that affects the data integrity of your application, the usual precautions of firewalls, virus software, and a complete and well-orchestrated user id and permissions scheme should be in place. Most applications are now tied into LDAP directories that are able to authenticate and authorize use of both data and functionality (via roles and other properties in the LDAP directory). You must keep the virus software detection profiles up to date, the LDAP directory in sync with your database level permissions, and make sure that no other points of failure (or points of corruption) exist in your environment. These basic protections directly affect your systems availability!

Much can be done in the early stages of planning and designing your high availability solutions to prevent this from happening altogether. You can take general object permissions and roles approach or object protection approaches that use constraints or schema-bound views. Even more thorough testing of your applications or better end-user training on their applications can reduce data manipulation errors on the database that the application uses. One or more of these methods can be used to directly increase your applications' availability.

Using an Object Permissions and Roles Method

The first line of defense for making sure someone doesn't drop (or alter) a table, view, stored procedure, or other object accidentally is to make sure that you create an administering user id (like MyDBadmin) other than sa and then explicitly grant these user ids specific CREATE permissions (such as CREATE TABLE, CREATE VIEW, and so on). At a minimum, you will be able to tightly control object creations by a small set of authorized users. You can create an administering user id or you can assign the appropriate roles to individual Windows logins (for better audit tracking and less sharing of passwords). These approaches will translate directly into reducing errors of this kind.

Securing via a Set User ID or Windows Account

An example of granting object rights to an individual login/user id is

```
GRANT CREATE TABLE TO [MyDBadmin]
```

This MyDBadmin user (can be a Microsoft SQL Server login or you can use existing Microsoft Windows user accounts) can now create and drop tables in the current database. Any user in the dbcreator or sysadmin server roles can also create and drop tables. Your company's group responsible for object maintenance in production will only be given the MyDBadmin user id to use, not sa. To get a quick verification of what grants exist for a user you can run the sp_helprotect system stored procedure. An example might be

```
EXEC sp_helprotect NULL, 'MyDBadmin'
```

Result set:

Owner	Object	Grantee	Grantor	ProtectType	Action	Column
.	.	MyDBadmin	dbo	Grant	Create Table	.

Securing via Created Roles

Another approach is to create a "role," assign the object permissions to this role, and then add a user id to this role. An example of this would be to create a role called `ManageMyDBObjects`, grant the `CREATE TABLE` permissions to this role, and then add a user id as a member of this role:

```
EXEC sp_addrole 'ManageMyDBObjects'
GRANT CREATE TABLE to ManageMyDBObjects
EXEC sp_addrolemember 'ManageMyDBObjects', 'MyDBadmin'
```

This will have the same net effect as granting to an individual user id, but is much easier to manage at the role level. We can also look at the protections for all statement level permissions (s option) in the current database using the sp_helprotect system stored procedure:

```
EXEC sp_helprotect NULL, NULL, NULL, 's'
```

Results in

```
Owner Object Grantee                 Grantor ProtectType Action        Column
----- ------ ----------------------- ------- ----------- ---------     ------
.     .      MyDBadmin               dbo     Grant       Create Table  .
.     .      ManageMyDBObjects       dbo     Grant       Create Table  .
```

Securing via Fixed Server Roles or Database Roles

You can also tap into the fixed server roles such as `dbcreator`, `sysadmin`, or use the database role `db_ddladmin`. Once you create a user id in SQL Server (or want to use any Windows account), simply grant that user (or Windows account) the role you wish them to have. An example of this is to grant the `MyDBadmin` user id the fixed role of `sysadmin`:

```
EXEC sp_addsrvrolemember 'MyDBadmin', 'sysadmin'
```

As you may know, the ability to grant and revoke permissions via the GRANT and REVOKE commands depends on which statement permissions are being granted and the object involved. The members of the `sysadmin` role can grant any permission in any database. Object owners can grant permissions for the objects they own. Members of the `db_owner` or `db_securityadmin` roles can grant any permission on any statement or object in their database.

Statements that require permissions are those that add objects in the database or perform administrative activities with the database. Each statement that requires permissions has a certain set of roles that automatically have permissions to execute the statement. For example

- The CREATE TABLE permission defaults to members of the sysadmin, db_owner, and db_ddladmin roles.
- The permissions to execute the SELECT statement for a table default to the sysadmin and db_owner roles, and the owner of the object.

There are some Transact-SQL statements for which permissions cannot be granted. For example, to execute the SHUTDOWN statement, the user must be added as member of the serveradmin or sysadmin role, whereas dbcreator can execute ALTER DATABASE, CREATE DATABASE, and RESTORE operations.

Taking a thorough, well-managed approach to permissions and access (user ids and what roles they have) will go a long way toward keeping your systems intact and highly available.

Object Protection Using Schema-Bound Views

Another easy to implement method to combat against tables being accidentally dropped in production by developers or system administrators is to use schema-bound views. This is accomplished by creating views on all production tables that you don't want dropped accidentally, using the "with schemabinding" option. The net effect is that a table cannot be dropped until the view is dropped first. This behavior results from the dependency that you are explicitly creating between the view and the table (the "with schemabinding" option). This is a nice safety net that is easy to use and manage. If you are using products like ERWin to generate all schema for your databases, creating an ERWin template that automatically generates this schema-bound view is trivial.

An example of an ERWin script template that creates schema-bound views automatically follows:

```
/*  ERWin Template: PROTECT_SBV
### Date ####### By ############# Comment ####
#   08/01/2004   P Bertucci     Created    #
################################################
Generated View: dbo.PROTECT%TableName_SBV
*/
```

```
/* DROP PROC dbo.PROTECT%TableName_SBV*/
IF OBJECT_ID('dbo.PROTECT%TableName_SBV' ) IS NOT NULL
BEGIN
     DROP VIEW dbo.PROTECT%TableName_SBV
     PRINT  '<<< DROPPED VIEW dbo.PROTECT%TableName_SBV >>>'
END
go


CREATE VIEW PROTECT%TableName_SBV
WITH SCHEMABINDING
AS
BEGIN
   SELECT %ForEachAtt(,",
          ")
          {%AttFieldName}
   FROM %TableName
END
go
IF OBJECT_ID('dbo.PROTECT%TableName_SBV') IS NOT NULL
  PRINT '<<< CREATED VIEW dbo.PROTECT%tableName_SBV >>>'
ELSE
  PRINT '<<< FAILED CREATING VIEW dbo.PROTECT%TableName_SBV >>>'
```

Basic Schema-bound Views with Primary Key Column Only

The easiest way to create a schema-bound view to help prevent accidentally dropping tables in production databases is to create a basic view for each table that has the table's primary key column only. The following is a sample table that can be created in the Northwind database in SQL Server:

```
Use Northwind
go
CREATE TABLE [CustomersTest] (
     [CustomerID] [nchar] (5)  NOT NULL ,
     [CompanyName] [nvarchar] (40)  NOT NULL ,
     [ContactName] [nvarchar] (30)  NULL ,
     [ContactTitle] [nvarchar] (30)  NULL ,
     [Address] [nvarchar] (60)  NULL ,
     [City] [nvarchar] (15)  NULL ,
     [Region] [nvarchar] (15)  NULL ,
     [PostalCode] [nvarchar] (10) NULL ,
```

```
     [Country] [nvarchar] (15)  NULL ,
     [Phone] [nvarchar] (24)  NULL ,
     [Fax] [nvarchar] (24)  NULL ,
     CONSTRAINT [PK_CustomersTest] PRIMARY KEY  CLUSTERED
     (    [CustomerID]
     )  ON [PRIMARY]
) ON [PRIMARY]
```

This table has no outright protection to prevent it from being dropped by any user id that has database creator or object owner rights (like sa). By creating a schema-bound view on this table that will reference at least the primary key column of the table, we can completely block a direct drop of this table. In fact, to drop this table will now require that the schema-bound view be dropped first (making this a formal two-step process, which will drastically reduce failures of this nature in the future). You might think that this is a pain (if you are the DBA), but this type of approach will pay for its built in overhead time and time again.

Creating a view that is schema-bound will require that you use the WITH SCHEMABINDING statement in the view. Below is an example of how we would do this for the just created CustomerTest table:

```
CREATE VIEW [dbo].[NODROPPK_Customers]
WITH SCHEMABINDING
AS
SELECT [CustomerID] FROM [dbo].[CustomersTest]
```

Don't worry, you will not be creating any GRANTs on this view since its sole purpose is to protect the table.

If you now try to drop the table, you will be rudely prohibited as the following example shows:

```
DROP TABLE   [dbo].[CustomersTest]
```

Resulting in the error:

```
Server: Msg 3729, Level 16, State 1, Line 1
Cannot DROP TABLE 'dbo.CustomersTest' because it is being
referenced by object 'NODROPPK_Customers'.
```

Great! You have effectively and painlessly added an extra level of protection to your production system, which will directly translate into higher availability.

To look at all objects that depend on a particular table, you can use the sp_depends system stored procedure. As you can see, it shows the view we just created and any other dependent objects that may exist:

```
EXEC sp_depends N'CustomersTest'
```

This results in

```
In the current database, the specified object is referenced by the
    following:
name                            type
--------------------------      --------
dbo.NODROPPK_Customers   view
```

Another example of a widely used table is that of the Customer table in the Northwind database. As you can see, there are numerous object types that depend on this table:

```
EXEC sp_depends N'Customers'
```

This results in

```
In the current database, the specified object is referenced by the
    following:
name                                    type
-----------------------------------     --------
dbo.Customer and Suppliers by City      view
dbo.CustOrderHist                       stored procedure
dbo.Invoices                            view
dbo.Orders Qry                          view
dbo.Quarterly Orders                    view
dbo.Sales Totals by Amount              view
```

Keep in mind that this initial method does not prohibit other types of changes to a table's schema (that can be done using an ALTER statement). The next section will describe how to take this approach a bit further to embrace schema changes that would also cause your application to become unavailable.

Full Table Structure Protection (All Columns Specified in the Schema-bound View)

Building on the schema-bound view approach a bit further, you can also protect from many table structure changes by listing all columns in the base table in the Select list in the schema-bound view. This essentially provides column-level schema-binding, which means that any changes to the bound columns will be restrictive. This will prevent the altering of any schema-bound column in a table (either the datatype, nullability, or dropping of the column). It does not prohibit you from adding a new column, though. So this must be understood from the start. The following is an example of creating a schema-bound view that lists all columns in the referenced table and then various ALTERs attempted on this table:

```
CREATE VIEW [dbo].[NOALTERSCHEMA_Customers]
WITH SCHEMABINDING
AS
SELECT [CustomerID], [CompanyName], [ContactName], [ContactTitle],
       [Address], [City], [Region], [PostalCode], [Country],
       [Phone], [Fax]
FROM [dbo].[CustomersTest]
```

Then when we try to change the datatype and nullability of an existing column this operation will fail (as it should):

```
ALTER TABLE [dbo].[CustomersTest] ALTER COLUMN [Fax] NVARCHAR(30)
NOT NULL
```

This results in the failure message of

```
Server: Msg 5074, Level 16, State 3, Line 1
The object 'NOALTERSCHEMA_Customers' is dependent on column 'Fax'.
Server: Msg 4922, Level 16, State 1, Line 1
ALTER TABLE ALTER COLUMN Fax failed because one or more objects access
    this column.
```

If we try to drop an existing column from the table we get a similar message:

```
ALTER TABLE [dbo].[CustomersTest] DROP COLUMN [Fax]
```

This results in the failure message of

```
Server: Msg 5074, Level 16, State 3, Line 1
The object 'NOALTERSCHEMA_Customers' is dependent on column 'Fax'.
Server: Msg 4922, Level 16, State 1, Line 1
ALTER TABLE DROP COLUMN Fax failed because one or more objects access
    this column.
```

This is a fairly safe method of protecting your applications from inadvertent table alters that can render your application useless (and effectively "unavailable"). All of these schema-bound methods are designed to minimize the human errors that can and will take place in a production environment.

Design Note

If you have any Foreign Key constraints defined on a table (Declarative Referential Integrity—DRI), this too will protect the table from being dropped. However, do not rely on this alone. Many tables don't necessarily have foreign key constraints defined on them. To take a quick look at any foreign keys that a table may have you can use the sp_fkeys system stored procedure as follows:

```
EXEC sp_fkeys @pktable_name = N'Customers'
go
Results in (abbreviated result set):
FK_NAME                              PKCOLUMN_NAME
---------------------------------    -------------
FK_CustomerCustomerDemo_Customers    CustomerID
FK_Orders_Customers                  CustomerID
```

If you try to drop a table that has a foreign key constraint, you will receive the following error:

```
USE Northwind
go
DROP TABLE  [dbo].[Customers]
go
Server: Msg 3726, Level 16, State 1, Line 1
Could not drop object 'dbo.Customers' because it is referenced by
a FOREIGN KEY constraint.
```

Proper Security in Place for HA Options

Aside from the common infrastructure security protections that have been discussed already, there are often security breakdowns and other miscues directly associated with the major high availability options. As you will see, each HA option has its own set of problems and areas to consider from a security point of view. A good example of possible security miscues is not specifying the correct startup service account (Windows login/domain account) for the SQL Agent that is needed to distribute transactions for data replication. This section will highlight and re-enforce these types of issues and considerations so that you can head them off before you attempt to build any one of these complete HA options.

MSCS Security Considerations

As part of building up a viable MSCS configuration, you must make sure that you have done one of the following:

- Identified (or defined) a domain to be a member of
- Configured all nodes that will be part of the cluster to be domain controllers in the same domain
- Created a domain account that will be used by cluster services (like "cluster" or "clusterAdmin") with appropriate permissions
- Created a private network available for the Heartbeat communication (this is not really a true security consideration, but is a private communication line between all of the servers that are to be clustered)

To configure the cluster service on a Windows server, the account you use must have administrative permissions on each node. In other words, this is the domain user account that will start the cluster service (as you can see in Figure 11.1) and is used to administer the fail-over cluster. Make this account a member of the Administrators local group on each node of the fail-over cluster.

All nodes in the cluster must be members of the same domain and able to access a domain controller and a DNS Server. They can be configured as member servers or domain controllers. If you decide to configure one node as a domain controller, you should configure all other nodes as domain controllers in the same domain as well. It is not acceptable to have a mix of domain controllers and member servers in a cluster.

The private network that you want to use for the internal communication between the nodes in the cluster should be set up with the option of Enable This Network for Cluster Use and specify that this network is to be for Internal Cluster Communications Only (Private Network) as illustrated in Figure 11.2.

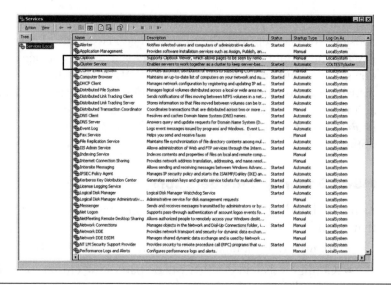

Figure 11.1 Using the domain account to start the cluster service (log on as).

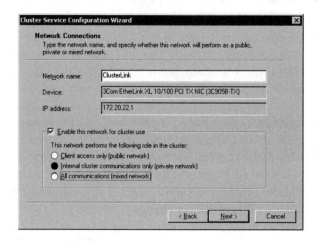

Figure 11.2 Specifying that this network is enabled for cluster use and is to be used for internal cluster communications only.

SQL Clustering Security Considerations

As you know, SQL clustering is built on top of Microsoft Cluster Services (MSCS), and SQL Server is "cluster aware." This allows SQL Server and all related resources to be managed as resources within Cluster Services and to fail over. For this reason, all of the security setup and configuration that you have done for MSCS must be done *before* you start installing a SQL clustering configuration. Then, there are only a couple more security related items that will need to be set up to successfully install SQL clustering. These are

- Create domain user accounts for SQL Server and SQL Server Agent services
- Make sure you have configured MS DTC as an cluster resource

A SQL Agent will be installed as part of the SQL Server installation process and is associated with the SQL Server instance it is installed for. The same is true for MS DTC; it will be associated with the particular SQL Server instance that it is installed to work with. By default, the MS DTC service will start with a local system account. This local system account must be given full permissions to the DTCLOG folder.

During the installation process of the virtual SQL server, you must be prepared to identify the user account that will be starting the services associated with SQL Server (SQL Server itself, SQL Agent, and optionally, SQL Full Text Search service). SQL Server service accounts and passwords should be kept the same on all nodes or the node will not be able to restart a SQL Server service. You can use Administrator, or better yet a designated account (like `Cluster` or `ClusterAdmin`) that has administrator rights within the domain and on each server (member of the Administrators local group on any node in the cluster). Figure 11.3 shows each of the described security related points that can cause failure in a SQL clustering configuration.

Log Shipping Security Considerations

Log shipping effectively replicates the data of one server (the source) to one or more other servers (the destinations) via transaction log dumps. By definition, that means that more than one SQL Server instance will be potentially used as the primary database server. Effectively, each of these source/destination pairs should be equal (from a security point of view at the very least). In order for log shipping to work well, a few things must be considered during the setup and implementation time:

- Copy the source SQL Server user IDs must be copied to any destination SQL Servers securely.
- Verify the login being used to start the SQL Server Agent for each SQL Server instance.

- Create the appropriate network share on the primary server for log shipping files.
- Make sure you create the `log_shipping_monitor_probe` login/user id that will be used by the monitor server (unless you are using Windows Authentication).
- Create cross-domain log shipping trusts.

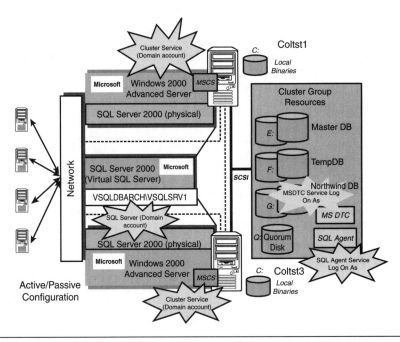

Figure 11.3 SQL clustering security breakdown points.

The user IDs and the permissions associated with the source SQL Server database must be copied as part of log shipping. They should be the same at all servers that will be destinations for log shipping. If you are going to create the database on the destination servers first, you can use the special Data Transformation Services (DTS) task to transfer logins from the source server to the destination server. This works very well.

Make sure that the source and each destination SQL Server instance have their corresponding SQL Server Agent running, since log shipping and monitoring tasks will be created on each SQL Server instance and won't get executed unless their SQL Server Agent is running. The login that you use to start the MS SQL Server and SQL Server

Agent services must have administrative access to the Log Shipping plan jobs, the source server, and the destination server. These accounts are usually the same account and are best created as Domain accounts. The user who is setting up log shipping must be a member of the SYSADMIN server role, which gives them permission to modify the database to do log shipping.

You will need to create a network share on the primary server where the transaction log backups will be stored. This is done so that the transaction log backups can be accessed by the log shipping jobs (tasks). This is especially important if you use a directory that is different from the default backup location. This would take the form

```
"\\SourceServerXX\NetworkSharename"
```

The log shipping Monitor Server is usually (and is recommended to be) a separate SQL Server instance. The log_shipping_monitor_probe login is used to monitor log shipping. Alternatively, Windows Authentication can also be used. If you use the log_shipping_monitor_probe login for other database maintenance plans, you must use the same password at any server that has this login defined. What is actually happening is the log_shipping_monitor_probe login is used by the source and destination servers to update two log shipping tables in the MSDB database—thus the need for cross-server consistency.

Very often, the network share becomes unavailable or disconnected. This will result in a copy error to the destination transaction log backup directory (share). It's always a good idea to verify that these shares are intact, or establish a procedure to monitor them and re-create them if they ever are disconnected. After you have re-established this share, log shipping will be able to function fully again.

Make sure your logins/user ids are defined in the destination server. Normally, if you intend the destination to act as a fail-over database, you will be regularly synchronizing the SQL server logins and user ids anyway. The special Data Transformation Services (DTS) task to transfer logins from a source server to a destination server should be used. Double check that each login has the proper role that was present in the source database. This is probably the place that causes the most headaches during a primary role change (getting the logins sync'd, that is). Figure 11.4 illustrates each of the security breakdown points of log shipping that have been mentioned previously and shows the login/ids synchronization process that can be executed with DTS.

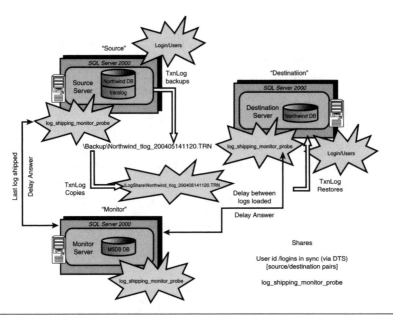

Figure 11.4   Log shipping security breakdown points (from source to destination pairs and the Monitor Server).

And, last but not least, if you are log shipping a database from a SQL Server in one domain to a SQL Server in another domain, you will have to establish a two-way trust between the domains. This can be done with the Active Directory domains and trusts tool within the Administrator tools option. The downside of using two-way trusts is that it opens up a pretty big window of trusting for SQL Server and any other Windows-based application. Most log shipping is done within a single domain to maintain as tight a control as possible.

Data Replication Security Considerations

The security considerations within the different data replication models can be a bit complex sometimes. However, a standard approach to replication can all but eliminate any issues you might ever have. Start by thinking through the entire data replication flow from publisher, to distributor, to subscribers.

When you first start setting up your replication configuration for high availability, you will likely use the replication tools option within Enterprise Manager (as opposed to just the replication system-stored procedures). Microsoft has figured that you will start here as well and has proactively started to plot your future actions. They start by actively querying what account is being used to start up the SQL Server Agent service. This is a built-in check to verify that you have the right login with the correct authorization at every step of the way. Microsoft is truly trying to get security started off on the right foot. It is your job to answer the call by supplying the right scheme to your replication solution. And, it's not really that hard.

In general, the places that are cause for concern from the security point of view for data replication are

- SQL Server Agent service startup accounts on each node of a replication topology
- All Replication Agents functioning with proper accounts
- All replication setup and grant authorizations
- Correctly authorized data and schema transfers for data synchronization/snapshot processing
- Logins/user ids synchronized between publisher and subscriber (if used as a hot spare for fail-over)

As described earlier, Enterprise Manager looks at what account is defined to start the SQL Server Agent service itself. This is critical because all replication agents are initiated via the SQL Server Agent service. If this is down or has not been started with the appropriate account, replication doesn't occur.

You will need to make sure that a duly authorized account is used that is a member of the `sysadmin` server role. Figure 11.5 shows the stiff warning that Enterprise Manager issues when you start the replication wizard (when it has detected that the SQL Server Agent login for startup is not a member of the `sysadmin` server role).

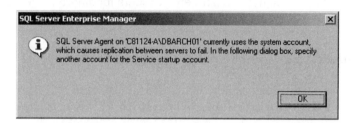

Figure 11.5 Enterprise Manager warning for which account is going to be used to start the SQL Server Agent service.

The best approach for data replication is to use one designated account for all replication oriented setup. This should be an account named `Repl_Administrator` that is defined on each SQL Server instance that will be involved in the replication topology and that is a member of the sysadmin server role. Then, another account named `SQL_Administrator` (not `sa`) should be created that is used for the overall SQL Server Agent processing and startup, which should also be a member of the sysadmin server role. Create this same `SQL_Adminstrator` account in all SQL Server instances and use it to start all SQL Server Agents consistently. In fact, this is best done as a domain account. This way, you can have pretty tight account and password control at the SQL Server Agent services level and at the detail replication agent levels. Remember, the SQL Server Agent is used for many things in SQL Server land, so you don't want to use a login that is just oriented toward replication to start it. However, you will want to use the `Repl_Administrator` account (domain account) as the owner of all replication agents in your topology. If you ever undo replication, you can also remove the `Repl_Administrator` account; that will guarantee replication won't work (a nice undo safety net).

Keep in mind that from the time of setting up remote distributors, enabling publishers and distributors, registering subscribers, and eventually to subscribing to a publication, there are numerous security interactions that must work perfectly. Below is an abbreviated list of the many system-stored procedures that get executed while configuring and enabling replication. Each require a login and password as part of their execution parameters and will, in turn, create agents (and tasks that an agent will execute).

CAUTION Being consistent with accounts and passwords is critical to your stability. Do not use different accounts for different agents; keep it consistent.

```
exec sp_adddistributor  @distributor = N'DBARCH20\SQLDB03',
     @password = N'xyzpassword'
exec sp_adddistributiondb  @database = N'distribution',
     @login = N'Repl_Administrator', @password = N'xyzpassword'
exec sp_addsubscriber @subscriber = N'DBARCH30\SQLDB02', @type = 0,
@login = N'Repl_Administrator', @password = N'xyzpassword'
```

```
exec sp_grant_publication_access @publication = N'Northwind2Northwind',
    @login = N'BUILTIN\Administrators'
exec sp_grant_publication_access @publication = N'Northwind2Northwind',
@login = N'Repl_Administrator'
```

As you may recall from Chapter 7, "Microsoft SQL Server Data Replication," the replication agents that get created are the snapshot agent, the log reader agent, the distribution agent, and several miscellaneous agents that do history cleanup and other work. Figure 11.6 illustrates most of these replication agents and the owning account that you should have them set up with. All agents should be configured to be owned (and executed) by this Repl_Administrator account.

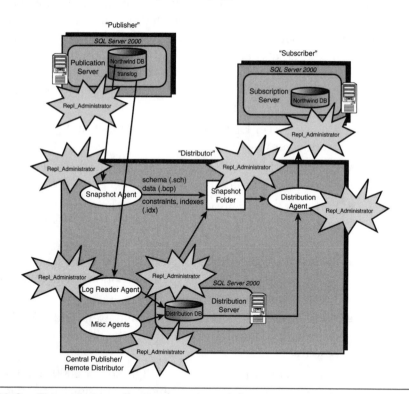

Figure 11.6 The various replication agents and the accounts that will be needed to ensure a secure and stable replication configuration.

Taking this simple and standardized account management approach will really make replication work in your environment and creates a stable high availability result.

General Thoughts on Database Backup/Restore, Isolating SQL Roles, and Disaster Recovery Security Considerations

As was emphasized in Chapter 10, "High Availability Design Issues and Considerations," and throughout this book, you should make a concerted effort to ensure that you can back up and recover your databases on a moment's notice. Very often (and usually at three in the morning, it seems), a system administrator is asked to restore a database because of some type of failure or database corruption. This system administrator's ability to recover can be dependent on whether they have the rights to recover a database or not. It is your job to make sure the mechanisms for database backup and recovery are well tested and are completely up-to-date. This should include having created system administrator accounts that are members of the sysadmin fixed server role or, at a minimum, have created an account that has the db_backupoperator database role so that your system administrators can backup a database.

Many organizations will isolate different SQL Server accounts for specialized purposes such as

- Manage server logins—must be a member in the securityadmin fixed server role

- Creates and Alters Databases—an account that is a member of the dbcreator fixed server role

- Performs any activity in SQL Server. The permissions of this role span all of the other fixed server roles—this is the sysadmin fixed server role

- Adds and removes linked servers, and executes some system stored procedures, such as sp_serveroption—a member in the serveradmin fixed server role

- Adds or removes Windows groups and users, and SQL Server users in the database—a member in the db_accessadmin database role

- Manages roles and members of SQL Server 2000 database roles, and manages statement and object permissions in the database—a member in the db_securityadmin database role

- Adds, modifies, or drops objects in the database—a member in the db_ddladmin database role

- Performs the activities of all database roles, as well as other maintenance and configuration activities in the database. The permissions of this role span all of the other fixed database roles—a member of the db_owner database role

From a disaster recovery point of view, make sure you can completely re-create and resynchronize your security from the ground up (MS Active Directory, domain accounts, SQL Server Logins/passwords, and so on). This includes making sure that someone has access to the sa password if necessary. We call this *security resynchronization readiness*. And, as part of this readiness, you need to completely test this recovery (one or more times a year)!

Summary

We have devoted a full chapter to security considerations and how security affects high availability because of years of past experience failing in this area. Lessons are often "hard lessons" when it comes to systems that are highly available, and much anguish can be avoided if enough attention and planning is given to the security ramifications up front. We have outlined the key security points that can become mismanaged or broken for each HA option presented in this book and a few general security techniques that can be applied to all of your production implementations. Most of the SQL scripts that were illustrated in this chapter can be downloaded from the Sams website for this book (HASecurityScripts.sql).

Many of the security techniques described in this chapter are common sense methods such as preventing tables from being dropped in production by using a schema-bound view approach. Others are more standards and infrastructure oriented, such as using domain accounts for clustering, and common SQL accounts for data replication or starting SQL Server Agent services. But they all add up to stability and minimizing downtime. Getting these types of security practices into place in your environment will allow you to achieve or exceed your high availability goals much more easily.

CHAPTER 12

Future Directions of High Availability

THE KEY TOPICS IN THIS CHAPTER ARE

- Barriers to high availability addressed in Yukon (SQL Server 2005)
- Other industry directions with high availability

Microsoft Stepping Up to the Plate

Microsoft has slowly been moving in the direction of trying to make SQL Server (and the Windows operating system) as continuously available as possible for as many of its options as possible. Remember, they are competing with the Unix/Linux-based worlds that have offered (and achieved) much higher uptime levels for years. Whether it is the SQL Server RDBMS engine itself, or any of the surrounding services such as Analysis Services, Notification Services, and Reporting Services, each have taken big steps towards higher availability.

What is also becoming evident is that there are several fundamental areas within SQL Server and Windows that will continue to be the cornerstone of high availability (they will live on and prosper). These include Microsoft Cluster Services, any of the transaction log-based options such as data replication and log shipping (however, log shipping will take on a different life as something called *database mirroring*, which we will explain a little later in this chapter), and SQL clustering. And, to top that off, Microsoft is taking great strides in the areas of online maintenance operations (online restores, online index creates, and so on), as well as leaping into the realm of one or more virtual server machines (with Virtual Server 2005) that will not bring down a physical server that houses them.

For the right here and now, any of the systems that you design and build within the current high availability options from Microsoft (Windows 2000/2003 family and SQL Server 2000) will be supported for years to come. When future releases become available, there will be upward compatibility with the options you have used and definitive upgrade paths to follow to achieve higher availability levels (if you need them). Think of this as expanding the reach of your high availability capabilities into areas that were not supported very well in the past and raising your high availability goals to higher levels than you could have supported before (like raising uptime from three 9s to five 9s by simply upgrading to the Yukon/SQL Server 2005 release).

At the time of writing this book, Yukon (SQL Server 2005) was just winding down beta 1 and ramping up a more widespread beta 2. At Microsoft, beta 2s are the last shakeout times and essentially contain what will be part of the general product. Very little changes from beta 2 to the general released product are anticipated. What is not known is how long beta 2 will have to be in place. Since Microsoft has officially named Yukon "SQL Server 2005," it is assumed that the product will be released sometime in 2005. It is looking like this release will be in the later part of quarter two or the early part of quarter three. In the meantime, do not stop planning and deploying your high availability systems. You would probably not be deploying your high availability systems on SQL Server 2005 anyway, because it will take time for you to acquire this product and then roll it out within your organization. In addition, you do not have the luxury to wait. Every minute of downtime you have today translates into losses that you cannot well afford.

What's Coming in Yukon for High Availability?

In general, Yukon (Microsoft SQL Server 2005) is shifting very strongly to a goal of providing a database engine foundation that can be highly available seven days a week, 365 days a year. Microsoft's sights are set on being able to achieve five 9s with almost anything that is built within its four walls. We will list a few of the most significant enhancements and new features of Yukon later in this chapter. However, this author is only looking at beta software, and what actually ships in the final product build has yet to be determined.

Enhancements in Fail-over Clustering (SQL Clustering)

Still, the cornerstone of SQL Server fail-over is SQL clustering (or often termed *SQL fail-over clustering*). Built on top of Microsoft Cluster Services, this fail-over capability provides a server-wide solution that has fewer and fewer restrictions and whose stability and reliability is unmatched. The primary enhancements to fail-over clustering in Yukon are

- Increases in the number of nodes in a SQL cluster—you will be able to create a SQL Cluster of up to eight nodes on Windows 2003 Data Center and up to four nodes on Windows 2003 Enterprise Edition.
- Ability to do unattended cluster setup—instead of having to use wizards to set up SQL clustering, it will be possible to use the "Unattended cluster setup" mode. This is very useful for fast re-creation or remote creation of SQL clustering configurations.
- Full SQL Server 2005 Services as cluster managed resources—all SQL Server 2005 services, including the following, will be cluster aware:
  - SQL Server DBMS engine
  - SQL Server Agent
  - SQL Full Text Search
  - Analysis Services
  - Notification services
  - Reporting services
  - Service broker

With these enhancements, you can extend this fault-tolerant solution to embrace more SQL Server instances and *all* of SQL Server's related services. This is a big deal since things like Analysis Services previously had to be handled with separate techniques to achieve near high availability (as we outlined in Chapter 10, "High Availability Design Issues and Considerations"). Not anymore: Each SQL Server service will be cluster aware!

Database Mirroring for Fail-over

The newest fail-over option with SQL Server is database mirroring. Database mirroring essentially extends the old log shipping feature of SQL Server 2000 and creates an automatic fail-over capability to a "hot" standby server. In other words, this is being billed as creating a fault-tolerant virtual database that is an "instant" standby (ready for use in less than three seconds). This new capability was once being referred to as Real-Time Log Shipping (RTLS). At the heart of this database mirroring is the new "copy-on-write" technology (which means that transactional changes are shipped to another server as the logs are written. And, all logged changes to the database instance become immediately available for copying to another location).

With database mirroring, if the principal SQL Server should fail, a feature called "transparent client redirect" is able to detect this failure and switch to the mirrored database without the application knowing. This is database-level fault-tolerance (unlike SQL clustering, which embraces the full SQL Server instance).

Basically, as shown in Figure 12.1, a database mirroring system requires three servers that are running SQL Server 2005, and each server has a specific architectural role: the "principal," the "mirror," and the "witness."

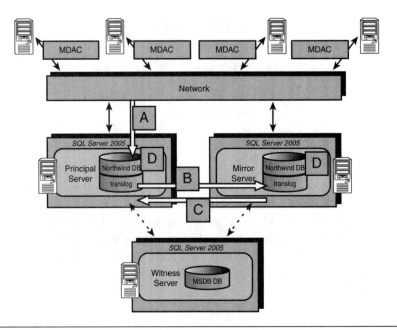

Figure 12.1   SQL Server 2005—synchronous mirrored database architecture.

The principal database is on the server that applications connect to and where transactions are processed (arrow A). The mirror database is the target of transaction log records (arrow B), which can be applied either synchronously or asynchronously. The mirror database exists in a state that does not allow direct read access to the data. In other words, you cannot be connected to the mirror for any reason—it is in constant restore mode. It can only be connected to if it becomes the principal.

As transaction log records are generated on the principal database, utilizing the copy-on-write technology, the transactions are continuously replayed at the mirror database, producing a state in which the mirror is normally behind the principal only by the amount of time it takes to replay the log written in a single log write. Once the transaction log entry is written on the mirror, an acknowledgement of this write is provided back to the principal (arrow C). This essentially provides an intact duplicate of the data at a point in time (but without a full two-phase commit server providing transactional consistency across servers and databases). As with this and prior versions of SQL Server, once the transaction is written to the log (log write ahead), it is a valid transaction and the data pages can be written any time (as depicted by the letter D in Figure 12.1). Both the principal and the mirror are in the same state (right down to their caches).

The witness server (shown at the bottom of Figure 12.1) is an arbiter within the architecture, providing the tie-breaking "vote" in determining which server is the principal and which is the mirror. Two servers in the architecture must agree in order for a server to be designated as the principal, and it then becomes the target of all transactions. The server that is the witness is only needed in instances where automatic fail-over is needed. It is possible to lose the witness server and still be fully fault-tolerant.

From a client application point of view, the fail-over from one server to the next is automatic and nearly instantaneous. This fast and automatic client switch is possible because when the client first connects via the Microsoft Data Access Component (depicted as MDAC in Figure 12.1), MDAC will cache both the principal SQL Server name and the mirror name. In this way, the client has everything it needs to know to redirect its connection if it needs to (hence the term *transparent client redirect*).

As part of database mirroring, you automatically are able to synchronize changes in both directions. In the event that the principal should ever fail and the application fails over to the mirror, the mirror then becomes the principal server. When the failed server comes back online, it is designated the mirror and transaction log records from the principal are applied to it to bring it into synchronization with the state of the database at that point in time (in reverse direction from the original configuration).

Microsoft also says that you should expect a fail-over (a switch from the principal to the mirror) to complete in less than 3 seconds (or less depending on the transaction volumes). This is nearly 10 to 20 times faster than SQL fail-over clustering, which can take up to 60 seconds or more. A great feature of database mirroring is that it works on standard server hardware and requires no special storage or controllers (in contrast to SQL clustering's very restrictive hardware compatibility requirements).

The copy-on-write technology that is used for database mirroring also enables another capability called *database snapshots*. Remember, the mirrored database is not available for data access directly, but its data can be made available for any number of purposes (like for reporting) by creating a database snapshot (as illustrated in Figure 12.2).

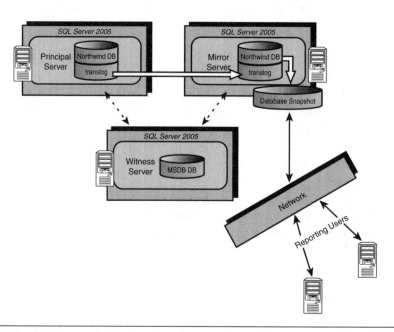

Figure 12.2   Utilizing a database snapshot against a mirrored database for reporting.

The downside of database snapshots is just that: They are snapshots and are pretty much out of date as soon as the first new transaction hits the mirrored database system. However, by making snapshots at regular intervals, your reporting users can be kept fairly happy.

Combining Fail-over and Scale Out Options

SQL Server 2005 pushes combinations of options to achieve higher availability levels. A prime example of this would be to combine data replication with database mirroring to provide maximum availability of your data, scalability to your users, and fault-tolerance via fail-over potentially at each node in the replication topology. By starting with the publisher and perhaps the distributor, you make them both database mirror fail-over configurations. Figure 12.3 shows a possible data replication and database mirroring configuration (database mirroring the publisher and database mirroring the distributor).

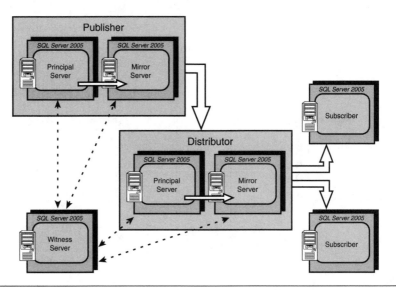

Figure 12.3 Rolling out database mirroring fail-over within data replication for scalability, availability, and fault-tolerance.

Building up a combination of both options together is essentially the best of both worlds—the super low latency of database mirroring for fault-tolerance and high availability (and scalability) of data through replication.

Data Access Enhancements for Higher Availability

Other areas that Yukon has made great strides in for higher availability is that of maximizing data access. In other words, Microsoft is directly attacking several operations that previously required the table or whole database to be offline. For several critical database operations (such as recovery operations, restores, indexing, and others), Microsoft has either made the data in the database available earlier in the execution of an operation or made the data in the database completely available simultaneously with the operation. The primary areas addressed are

- Fast recovery—A new faster recovery option will directly improve availability of SQL Server databases. Administrators will be able to reconnect to a recovering database after the transaction log has been rolled forward (and before the roll-back processing has finished). Figure 12.4 illustrates how Microsoft will make a SQL Server 2005 database available earlier as compared with SQL Server 2000.

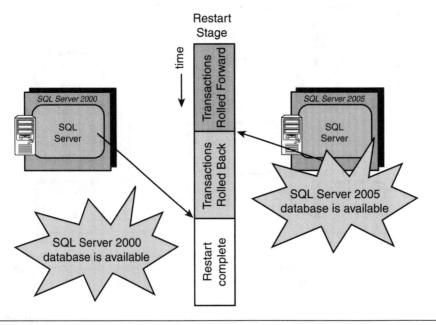

Figure 12.4 SQL Server 2005 database becomes available earlier then the database is recovering (fast recovery).

In particular, a database in SQL Server 2005 will become available when committed transaction log entries are rolled forward (termed "redo") and no longer have to wait for the "in flight" transactions to be rolled back (termed "undo").

- Online restore—With SQL Server 2005, database administrators will be able to perform a restore operation while the database is still online. Online restore improves the availability of SQL Server because only the data being restored is unavailable; the rest of the database remains online and available to users. In addition, the granularity of the restore has changed to be at the file group level and even at the page level if needed. The remainder of the database would remain available.

- Online indexing—The online index option will allow concurrent modifications (updates, deletes, and inserts) to the underlying table or clustered index data and any associated indexes during index creation time. For example, while a clustered index is being rebuilt, you can continue to make updates to the underlying data and perform queries against the data.

- Database snapshot (this was referred to as database ViewPoint for a while, but that term is used in the mobile Windows CE world)—SQL Server 2005 allows for the generation and use of a read-only, stable view of a database. The database snapshot is created without the overhead of creating a complete copy of the database or having completely redundant storage. A database snapshot is simply a reference point of the pages used in the database (that is defined in the system catalog). When pages are updated, a new page chain is started that contains the data pages that were changed since the database snapshot was taken, as illustrated in Figure 12.5.

As the original database diverges from the snapshot, the snapshot will get its own copy of original pages when they are modified. The snapshot can even be used to recover an accidental change to a database by simply reapplying the pages from the snapshot back to the original database.

The copy-on-write technology that is used for database mirroring also enables the database snapshots. Once a database snapshot is created on a database, all writes will check the system catalog of "changed pages" first; if not there, the original page is copied (using the copy-on-write technique) and is put in a place for reference by the database snapshot (since this snapshot must be kept intact). In this way, the database snapshot and the original database share the data pages that have not changed.

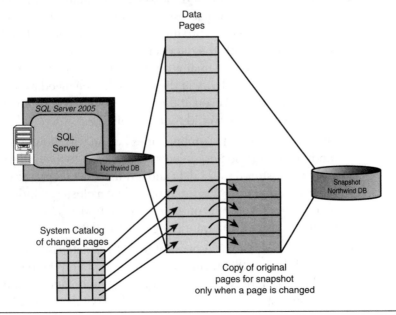

Figure 12.5   Database snapshots and the original database share pages and are managed within the system catalog of SQL Server 2005.

- Data partitioning improvements—Data partitioning will be enhanced with native table and index partitioning that essentially allow you to manage large tables and indexes at a lower level of granularity. In other words, a table can be defined that identifies distinct partitions (like by date or a range of key values). This effectively defines a group of data rows that are unique to a partition. These partitions can be taken offline, restored, or loaded independently while the rest of the table is available.

- Addition of a snapshot isolation level—A new snapshot isolation (SI) level will be provided at the database level. With SI, users will be able to access the last committed row using a transactionally consistent view of the database. This capability will provide greater scalability and availability by not blocking data access of this previously unavailable data state. This new isolation level will essentially allow data reading requests to see the last committed version of data rows even if they are currently being updated as part of a transaction (that is, they see the rows as they were at the start of the transaction without being blocked by the writers, and the writers are not blocked by readers, as the readers do not lock the data). This new isolation level is probably best used for databases that are read-mostly (with few writes/updates) due to the potential overhead in maintaining this isolation level.

- Dedicated administrator connection—SQL Server 2005 will introduce a dedicated administrator connection that administrators can use to access a running server even if the server is locked or otherwise unavailable. This capability will enable administrators to troubleshoot problems on a server by executing diagnostic functions or Transact-SQL statements without having to take the server down.

High Availability from the Windows Server Family Side

To enhance system uptimes, there have also been numerous system architecture enhancements in Windows 2000 and 2003, such as improved memory management and driver verification, that directly reduce unplanned downtime. New file protection capabilities prevent new software installations from replacing essential system files and causing failures. Additionally, Windows device drivers and operating system files have been digitally signed by Microsoft to ensure their quality. A Microsoft digital signature is your assurance that a particular file has met a certain level of testing, and that the file has not been altered or overwritten by another program's version of the same device driver. Looking forward to Windows 2005 and as x86 server platforms have continued to make dramatic improvements in price-to-performance value, software technologies have evolved to help businesses more effectively harness that improved performance in a manageable way. Virtual machine technology (Virtual Server 2005) is one such technology.

Microsoft Virtual Server 2005

Virtual Server 2005 is the cost-effective virtual machine solution designed on top of Windows Server 2003 to increase operational efficiency in software testing and development, application migration, and server consolidation scenarios. Virtual Server 2005 is designed to increase hardware efficiency, help boost administrator productivity, and is a key Microsoft deliverable toward their Dynamic Systems Initiative (eliminating reboots of servers—that directly affects downtime!). As you can see in Figure 12.6, the host operating system—Windows Server 2003—manages the host system itself (at the bottom of the stack).

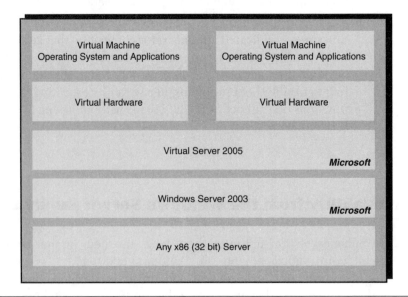

Figure 12.6 Microsoft Virtual Server 2005 server architecture.

Virtual Server 2005 provides a Virtual Machine Monitor (VMM) virtualization layer that manages virtual machines, providing the software infrastructure for hardware emulation. As you move up the stack, each virtual machine consists of a set of virtualized devices, the virtual hardware for each virtual machine.

A guest operating system and applications run in the virtual machine—unaware, for example, that the network adapter they interact with through Virtual Server is only a software simulation of a physical Ethernet device. When a guest operating system is running, the special-purpose VMM kernel takes mediated control over the CPU and hardware during virtual machine operations, creating an isolated environment in which the guest operating system and applications run close to the hardware at the highest possible performance.

Virtual Server 2005 is a multithreaded application that runs as a system service, with each virtual machine running in its own thread of execution; I/O occurs in child threads. Virtual Server derives two core functions from the host operating system: The underlying host operating system kernel schedules CPU resources, and the device drivers of the host operating system provide access to system devices. The Virtual Server VMM provides the software infrastructure to create virtual machines, manage instances, and interact with guest operating systems. An example of leverage Virtual Server 2005 capabilities would be to use it in conjunction with your Disaster Recovery needs.

Virtual Server 2005 and Disaster Recovery

Virtual Server 2005 enables another form of server consolidation through disaster recovery. Rather than maintaining redundancy with costly, physical servers, customers can use Virtual Server 2005 to back up their mission-critical functionality in a cost-effective way by means of virtual machines. The Virtual Machine Monitor (VMM) and Virtual Hard Disk (VHD) technologies in Virtual Server 2005, coupled with its comprehensive COM API, can be used to create similar fail-over functionality as standard, hardware-driven disaster recovery solutions. Then, customers can use the Virtual Server COM API to script periodic duplication of physical hard disks containing vital business applications to virtual machine VHDs. Additional scripts can switch to the virtual machine backup in the case of catastrophic failure. In this way, a failing device can be taken offline to troubleshoot, or the application or database can be moved to another physical or virtual machine. Moreover, because VHDs are a core Virtual Server technology, they can be used as a disaster recovery agent, wherein business functionality and data can be easily archived, duplicated, or moved to other physical machines.

Other Industry Trends in High Availability

Third-party hardware innovations continue to lead the way in evolving high availability. Microsoft will not go into the hardware business (I don't think), so look for most of the major hardware vendors to be pushing heavily into "blade" and other "hot swappable" hardware architectures for years to come. This will also be much more tightly tied to the virtual machines approach (and the virtual server) so successfully utilized in the Unix world.

Disk/media vendors are quickly gobbling up horizontally compatible companies and combining their expertise to provide more reliable and available content platforms. An example of this was when EMC recently bought Documentum and then rolled out a completely integrated fault-tolerant and highly available document management system.

Disaster recovery is rapidly evolving to become an outside service rather than an in-house capability. Within the coming years, there will be numerous subscription models for any size company to subscribe to that can be used in the event of a disaster. This will include remote and secure distribution of a company's data and applications that can be switched on in a moment's notice.

General pods (or grids) of computing will slowly take over many organizations' data processing needs. IBM is pushing "on demand" centers for companies that need extended virtual processing capabilities in a moment's notice. Intel is building server farms around the world to position itself to accommodate a global move to outsourced computing, and many other companies are building up variations on this theme (such as Oracle and HP). And, most Application Service Providers (ASP) vendors simply list high availability as the minimum capability that they offer.

Summary

The crux of high availability is in laying a fundamentally sound foundation that you can count on when failures occur. Then, when failures do occur, determining how much data loss you can tolerate, how much downtime is possible, and what this downtime is costing you are all part of understanding your high availability picture.

The future seems to be improving greatly in all of the foundation levels' support for high availability. This includes

- Cheaper and more reliable hardware components that are highly swappable

- The advent of virtual server capabilities (with Windows Virtual Server 2005) to insulate software failures from affecting hardware

- Enhancements that Microsoft is making to SQL Server 2005 that address availability square in the face

The critical enhancements to the cornerstone availability capabilities of SQL clustering will help this fault-tolerant architecture grow more reliable for years to come. The big bonuses come with the new features of database mirroring as another fault-tolerant solution at the database level along with the new database snapshots feature to make data more available to more users more quickly than the older methods of log shipping.

And last but not least, the enhancements to the everyday operations of restores, restarts, partitioning, indexing, and the new snapshot isolation level all directly affect availability in one or more ways. We will still have to wait a bit before these new technologies are available and considered stable, but our high availability future is getting brighter and more easily achievable for even the smallest application of the smallest company.

Index

NUMBERS

2PC (two-phase commit protocol)
 distributed queries, 285-286
 distributed transactions, 282-283,
  286, 290
   DTS/MS Queue Manager,
    287, 289
   SQL servers, 285
4-node clustering topologies, 124-125
8-node clustering topologies, 124-125

A

acceptable availability, 13
access
 data access, enhancements
  (Yukon), 398-401
 distributed, 16
 remote SQL servers, 275
accounts
 administration (clusters), 101
 Repl_Administrator, 386
 SQL_Administrator, 386
 users, Windows, 371
ACID (atomicity, consistency, isolation,
 and durability), 282
active/active clustering, 97, 128

active/passive clustering, 97, 127
active/passive MSCS mode, 45
ActiveX Data Objects Multidimensional
 (ADO MD), 354
addresses, IP (Internet Protocol)
 clustering, 101, 139-140
 MSCS networks, 99-100
administration
 log shipping implications, 170-171
 user ids, 371
administration accounts (clusters), 101
administrative permissions, nodes, 104
ADO MD (ActiveX Data Objects
 Multidimensional), 354
Agent History Clean Up agent, 224
agents
 data replication, 217
  Agent History Clean Up, 224
  distribution, 222-223
  Distribution Clean Up, 224
  Expired Subscription Clean
   Up, 224
  log reader, 221-222
  merge, 223-224
  Reinitialize Subscription
   Having Data Validation
   Failures, 224
  Replication Agents Checkup,
   225
  snapshot, 218-221

distribution, 228-229
log reader, 229
merge, 230
snapshot, 228-230
alerts
Backup Alerts, 180
log shipping, 169, 180-181
Out of Sync, 180
anonymous subscriptions, 215-216
anti-virus software, 352, 370
application resiliency, 16
application service provider (ASP), 25-26
clustering scenario, 161-164
hybrid selection method (solution assessment), 66-74
applications
assessing, design approaches, 22-24
avoiding failure, 42-44
cluster aware, 92-93
clustering, 20
COM+
distributed transaction processing, 332
distributed transactions, 291-293
fault tolerance, 332
high availability business scenarios
ASPs (application service providers), 25-26
investment portfolio management, 27
life at risk-classified applications, 27-28
sales/marketing, 26-27
architects (assessment teams), 298
architecture, 403
arrays
disks (clustering), 134
shared nothing disk, 96
arrows, assessment (Primary Variable gauges), 59-60

articles
data replication, 201-206
stored procedure executions, 204-205
ASP (application service provider), 25-26
clustering scenario, 161-164
hybrid selection method (solution assessment), 66-74
assessing applications, design approaches, 22-24
assessing solutions, process, 53-55
step 1, 54-59
step 2, 54, 59-60
step 3, 54, 60
adding HA elements, 88
cost justification, 86-88
hybrid selection method, 61-86
ROI (Return on Investment), 86-88
step 4, 54-55
assessments (HA)
assembling teams, 298-299
Phase 0
development life cycle tasks, 306-308
required information, 300
Step 1, 301-304
Step 2, 304-306
templates, 300
project schedule/timeline, 299-300
atomicity, consistency, isolation, and durability (ACID), 282
authentication, log shipping, 181, 383
autonomy, data replication, 226-227
availability
blanket approaches, 9
business scenarios
ASPs (application service providers), 25-26
investment portfolio management, 27

life at risk-classified
applications, 27-28
sales/marketing, 26-27
calculating, 10-12
design approaches, 18-20
assessments, 22-24
built-in, 21-22
iterative, 22
SLAs (service level
agreements), 24-25
Microsoft technologies, 28-30
overview, 5-10
system stacks, 6-7
variables, 7-9, 15-17
availability continuum
acceptable availability, 13
downtimes, planned/unplanned,
13-14
extreme availability, 12
high availability, 12
marginal availability, 13
standard availability, 12

B

Backup Alerts, 180
BACKUP command, 339
backups
data replication, monitoring,
261-264
design considerations, 319
differential backups, 336, 338
file/file group backups, 335,
338-339
full database backup, 335-338
monitoring/verifying, 342-344
parallel striped backups, 339
split mirror backups (server-
less backups), 340-342

transaction log backups,
336-338
VSS (Volume Shadow Copy
Service), 342
differential, 336-338
file/file groups, 335, 338-339
foundation component options, 33
full database backup, 335-338
NUL, 339
parallel striped, 339
split mirror (server-less backups),
340-342
transaction log, 336-338, 383
.BCP extension, 219
betas, 392
binaries, cluster installations, 143
blade architecture, 403
blanket high availability, 9
built-in design approach (high
availability), 21-22
business continuance volumes, 341
business scenarios, high availability, 25
ASPs (application service
providers), 25
investment portfolio management,
27
life at risk-classified applications,
27-28
sales/marketing, 26-27

C

cache, RAID (Redundant Array of
Independent Disks), 37
calculating
availability, 10-12
goodwill loss, 303
loss, downtime, 303
central publisher replication model,
207-208

central publisher, remote distributor replication model, 197, 208-210, 327

central subscriber replication model, 210

charts, Nassi-Schneiderman, 63-65

CLB (component load balancing), 120

Client Test program, 152, 155-159

ClusSvc event sources, 137-138

cluster aware applications, 92-93

cluster groups, 321

Cluster Service Configuration Wizard, 106

Cluster Services, 136-138, 151

cluster-managed disks, 141

clustering. *See also* MSCS (Microsoft Cluster Services
- 4-node topologies, 124-125
- 8-node topologies, 124-125
- active/active, 97, 128
- active/passive, 97, 127
- administration accounts, 101
- applications, 20
- ASP (application server provider) scenario, 161-164
- Client Test program, 152, 155-159
- configurations, 131
    - *Cluster Service, 136-138*
    - *database files, 133-135*
    - *disk arrays, 134*
    - *network interfaces, 135*
    - *quorum drives, 133*
    - *RAID levels, 132-133*
    - *shared disks, 132*
- domain controllers, configuring, 379
- fail-over, Yukon, 393
    - *database mirroring, 394-397*
    - *scalability, 397*
    - *virtual servers, 102*
- four-node, 97
- groups, 101

hybrid selection method (solution assessment), 61

IBM/DB2 Clustered Server example, 364-366

installing, 142
- *cluster-managed disks, 141*
- *instances, 138, 141*
- *IP (Internet Protocol) addresses, 139-140*
- *nodes, 141*
- *server binaries, 143*
- *server licensing, 143*
- *server resources, 145-147*
- *server user accounts, 143*
- *servers, 138*
- *service packs, 144*

IP addresses, 101

MS DTC (Microsoft Distributed Transaction Coordinator), configuring, 130-131

MSAS (MS Analysis Services), 359

names, 101

nodes, 45
- *evicting, 161*
- *failure, 148-149, 152*
- *recovery, 160-161*

operating system requirements, 92

removing, 152-153

resources, 101, 129, 132

setup issues, 160

SQL, 29, 46-47
- *design considerations, 322-325*
- *hybrid selection method (solution assessment), 61*
- *MSAS (MS Analysis Services), 360*
- *security considerations, 380-381*
- *virtual servers, 323*

status, 115

stretch, design considerations, 325-326

topologies, 106

two-node, 128

column-level schema-binding, 376-378

columns, primary key (schema-bound views), 374-376

COM+ applications

distributed transaction processing, 332

distributed transactions, 291-293

fault tolerance, 332

comclust.exe file, 130

commands, BACKUP, 339

component load balancing (CLB), 120

components

foundation

backup options, 33

hardware options, 32

operating system options, 33

server isolation options, 34

standards/procedures options, 34

testing options, 34

training options, 34

vendor agreement options, 33

hot-swappable, 32

Computer Associates website, 363-364

configurations

clustering, 131

Cluster Service, 136, 138

database files, 133-135

disk arrays, 134

network interfaces, 135

quorum drives, 133

RAID levels, 132-133

shared disks, 132

disk controllers (MSCS), 98

disks (MSCS), 98-99

domain controllers (clusters), 379

MS DTC (Microsoft Distributed Transaction Coordinator), 130-131

networks (MSCS), 99-101

Configure Publishing, Subscribers, and Distribution Wizard, 235

conflict resolvers, 224

connections, dedicated administrator (Yukon), 401

constraints, foreign key (dropped tables), 378

content platforms, developing, 404

continuum (availability)

acceptable availability, 13

downtimes, planned/unplanned, 13-14

extreme availability, 12

high availability, 12

marginal availability, 13

standard availability, 12

copy-on-write technology, 394-395

cost effectivity, selecting, 311-312

CREATE permissions, 371

Create Publication Wizard, 241

Cubes, OLAP (online analytical processing), 356

HOLAP (hybrid OLAP), 358

MOLAP (multidimensional OLAP), 357

partitions, 354

ROLAP (relational OLAP), 357

D

data

distributed transaction processing, 271

ACID (atomicity, consistency, isolation, and durability), 282

COM+ applications, 291-293

MS DTC (distributed transaction coordinator), 272, 283-290
MSMQ (Microsoft Queue Manager), 273
remote SQL servers, 274-281
resource managers, 283
step-by-step process, 284-285
two-phase commit protocol (2PC), 282
UOW (Unit of Work), 273, 282-283
real-enough time, 226
data access, enhancements (Yukon), 398-401
data blocks, striping, 37
data distribution methods (data replication), 227-228
data latency, log shipping, 50, 169-170
data loads, database load states, 177-178
data partitioning, Yukon, 400
data replication, 29, 47-49. *See also* log shipping
   agents, 217
      Agent History Clean Up, 224
      distribution, 222-223
      Distribution Clean Up, 224
      Expired Subscription Clean Up, 224
      log reader, 221-222
      merge, 223-224
      Reinitialize Subscription Having Data Validation Failures, 224
      Replication Agents Checkup, 225
      snapshot, 218-221
   articles, 201-206
   data autonomy, 226-227
   data distribution methods, 227-228
   defined, 197-198

   design
      consideration, 326-329
      user requirements, 232-234
   distribution database, 216-217
   distribution servers, 200
   example, 265-268
   fail-over, warm standby (subscriber), 252
   hybrid selection method (solution assessment), 61
   latency, 226-227
   merge replication, 230-232
   models, 206
      central publisher, 207-208
      central publisher with remote distributor, 208-210
      central subscriber, 210
      multiple publishers, 211
      multiple subscribers, 211
      publishing subscriber, 210
      subscribers, updating, 212-213
   monitoring
      backup/recovery, 261-264
      Performance Monitor, 261
      SQL Enterprise Manager, 259-260
      SQL statements, 258-259
      synchronization, 264
   NLB (Network Load Balancing), warm standby (subscriber), 252-254
   overview, 195-197
   publication servers, 199
   publications, 201
   ROI (Return on Investment), 266-268
   scripting replication, 254-257
   security considerations, 384-387

setup, 234
    distributors, enabling,
        235-239
    publications, creating,
        241-245
    publishers, 239-241
    subscriptions, creating,
        246-251
    snapshot replication, 228-229
    subscription servers, 200
    subscriptions, 214-216
    timing, 226-227
    transactional replication, 229-230
data resiliency, 16
data staging, MSAS (MS Analysis
    Services), 360
Data Transformation Services (DTS),
    170, 226, 361-362, 382
    setting up, 287
    two-phase commit protocol (2PC),
        287-289
database files (clustering), 133-135
database load states, log shipping,
    177-178
Database Maintenance Plan Wizard, 173
    alerts, 180-181
    common errors, 183-184
    database load states, 177-178
    database primary roles, 178
    destination databases, 175-177
    initializing databases, 178
    monitoring, 181-183
    network share locations, 175
    Northwind database, 174-175
    scheduling log shipping, 179
database mirroring, 171, 391, 394-397
database roles, 372-373
database snapshots, 396, 399-400
databases
    destination, log shipping, 175-177
    detaching, 362

distribution, data replication,
    216-217
failures, 336-337
full backup, 335-338
initializing (log shipping), 178
Northwind, log shipping setup,
    174-175
primary roles, log shipping, 178
store-and-forwarded, 216
TempDB, 134, 324
decision-tree approach, hybrid selection
    method (solution assessment), 63-65
Declarative Referential Integrity (DRI),
    378
dedicated administrator connection,
    Yukon, 401
design
    backup strategies
        differential backups, 336-338
        file/file group backups, 335,
            338-339
        full database backup, 335-338
        monitoring/verifying, 342-344
        parallel striped backups, 339
        split mirror backups (server-
            less backups), 340-342
        transaction log backups,
            336-338
        VSS (Volume Shadow Copy
            Service), 342
    Computer Associates website,
        363-364
    considerations, 315
        backup/recovery, 319
        data replication, 326-329
        distributed transaction
            processing, 331-333
        hardware, 316-320
        log shipping, 329-331
        MSCS (Microsoft Cluster
            Services), 321-323

networks, 317-319
operating systems, 317-318
remote mirroring, 320-321
security/upgrades, 318
servers, 317
SQL clustering, 322-325
stretch clustering, 325-326
transactional replication, 327
data replication, user requirements,
    232-234
databases, detaching, 362
disaster recovery
    focus, 345-349
    overall approach, 344-345
    planning, 344
    SQLDIAG.EXE file, 349-351
    testing, 351
DTS (Data Transformation
    Service), 361-362
file/device placement, 333-334
IBM/DB2 Clustered Server
    example, 364-366
LEGATO website, 363
log shipping implications, 170-171
MSAS (MS Analysis Services),
    353-361
OLAP (online analytical
    processing), cubes, 353-356
    HOLAP (hybrid OLAP), 358
    MOLAP (multidimensional
      OLAP), 357
    partitions, 354
    ROLAP (relational OLAP),
      357
software upgrades, 351-353
SteelEye Technologies website, 363
Veritas website, 362
designing high availability, 18-20
    assessments, 22-24
    built-in, 21-22

iterative, 22
SLAs (service level agreements),
    24-25
destination databases, log shipping,
    175-177
destination pairs, 329
destination servers, log shipping, 168
detaching databases, 362
development life cycles, tasks (Phase 0),
    306-308
devices, placement recommendations,
    333-334
DHCP (Dynamic Host Configuration
    Protocol), MSCS networks, 100
differential backups, 336-338
disaster recovery (DR)
    focus, 345-349
    Microsoft Virtual Server 2005, 403
    overall approach, 344-345
    planning, 344
    remote capabilities, 404
    security considerations, 388-389
    SQLDIAG.EXE file, 349-351
    testing, 351
disk arrays (clustering), 134
disk controllers, configuring (MSCS), 98
disk devices, checking (MSCS), 105
disk space, log shipping, 175
disks
    cluster-managed, 141
    configuring (MSCS), 98-99
    drive letters (MSCS), 98
    hybrid selection method (solution
      assessment), 61
    quorum
      majority note sets (MSCS),
        120-123
      MSCS (Microsoft Cluster
        Services) installations, 104
      Windows 2003 (MSCS),
        120-123

shared
  clustering, 132
  MSCS, 96
shared nothing arrays, 96
distributed access, 16
distributed queries, two-commit phase
  protocol (2PC), 285-286
Distributed Transaction Coordinator
  (DTC), 226, 272, 283
  two-phase commit protocol (2PC),
    283, 286, 290
    DTS/MS Queue Manager,
      287-289
    SQL servers, 285
  UOW (Unit of Work), 273
distributed transaction processing, 271
  ACID (atomicity, consistency,
    isolation, and durability), 282
  COM+ applications, 291-293
  design considerations, 331-333
  MS DTC (distributed transaction
    coordinator), two-phase commit
    protocol (2PC), 272, 286, 290
    DTS/MS Queue Manager,
      287-289
    SQL servers, 285
  MSMQ (Microsoft Queue
    Manager), 273
  remote SQL servers, 274
    access, setting up, 275
    links, creating, 276-277
    queries, 279-280
    security, 277-279
    Transact-SQL statements,
      280-281
  resource managers, 283
  step-by-step process, 284-285
  two-phase commit protocol (2PC),
    282
  UOW (Unit of Work), 273, 282-283

distributed transactions, 29, 51, 62, 227
distribution, data distribution methods
  (data replication), 227-228
distribution agent, 222-223, 228-229
Distribution Clean Up agent, 224
distribution databases, data replication,
  216-217
distribution servers, data replication, 200
Distributor Server, 260
distributors, enabling (data replication),
  235-239
domain controllers, configuring
  (clusters), 379
downtime
  availability continuum, 13-14
  calculating loss, 58-59, 303
  costs of, 6, 17
  planned, 7-8
  recoverable, 9
  unplanned, 8-9
DR. *See* disaster recovery
DRI (Declarative Referential Integrity),
  378
drive letters, disks (MSCS), 98
drives, quorum, 97, 133
dropped tables, foreign key constraints,
  378
DTA (Data Transformation Service),
  361-362
DTC (Distributed Transaction
  Coordinator), 226
DTCSetup.exe file, 130
DTS (Data Transformation Services),
  170, 226, 382
  setting up, 287
  two-phase commit protocol (2PC),
    287-289
Dynamic Host Configuration Protocol
  (DHCP), MSCS networks, 100

E-F

Enterprise Manager, SQL data
    replication, 259-260
errors, log shipping, 183-184
ERWin templates, 373-374
events, ClusSvc event sources, 137-138
evicting nodes (clustering), 161
executions, stored procedures, 204-205
Expired Subscription Clean Up agent,
    224
extensions
        .BCP, 219
        MDX (Multidimensional
            Extensions), 354
        .SCH, 219
extreme availability, 12

fail-over, 96
        active/passive clustering, 127
        nodes (clustering), 148-149, 152
        stretch clustering, 325
        testing (clustering), 155-159
        virtual servers, 102
        warm standby (subscriber)
                converting to publishers, 254
                NLB (Network Load
                    Balancing), 254
                scenarios, 252-253
        Windows 2003 (MSCS), 120-123
fail-over clustering, Yukon, 393
        database mirroring, 394-397
        scalability, 397
fail-over servers, log shipping, 50
fault tolerance
        COM+ applications, 292, 332
        mirroring, 34-36
        RAID (Redundant Array of
            Independent Disks), 34-42
file extensions
        .BCP, 219
        .SCH, 219

file group backups, 335, 338-339
file retention periods (transaction logs),
    179
files
        backups, 335, 338-339
        comclust.exe, 130
        database (clustering), 133-135
        DTCSetup.exe, 130
        placement recommendations,
            333-334
        SQLDIAG.EXE, 349-351
filtering articles (data replication),
    201-206
Five 9s, 13, 295-296
fixed server roles, 372-373
foreign key constraints (dropped tables),
    378
formatting partitions (MSCS), 98
foundation, hardware/software, 296-298
foundation components
        backup options, 33
        hardware options, 32
        operating system options, 33
        server isolation options, 34
        standards/procedures options, 34
        testing options, 34
        training options, 34
        vendor agreement options, 33
four-node clustering, 97
full database backup, 335-338
future releases, 392

G-H

gauges, Primary Variable (step 2 solution
    assessment), 59-60
goodwill loss, calculating, 303
groups, clusters, 101

HA assessments
  assembling teams, 298-299
  Phase 0
    development life cycle tasks,
      306-308
    required information, 300
    Step 1, 301-304
    Step 2, 304-306
    templates, 300
  project schedule/timeline, 299-300
HA solutions
  cost effectiveness, 311-312
  selecting, 308-309
HACMP (High Availability Cluster
  Multi-Processing), 365
hardware
  design considerations, 316-320
  foundation component options, 32
  hybrid selection method (solution
    assessment), 61
  requirements, MSCS (Microsoft
    Cluster Services), 93-95
Hardware Compatibility List (HCL)
  website, 95
hardware foundations, 296-298
hardware/software stacks, 32
HCL (Hardware Compatibility List)
  website, 95
heartbeats (nodes), fail-over, 96
high availability, 12
  blanket approaches, 9
  business scenarios
    ASPs (application service
      providers), 25-26
    investment portfolio
      management, 27
    life at risk-classified
      applications, 27-28
    sales/marketing, 26-27
  cost of, 17

design approaches, 18-20
  assessments, 22-24
  built-in, 21-22
  iterative, 22
  SLAs (service level
    agreements), 24-25
  Microsoft technologies, 28-30
  overview, 5-10
  system stacks, 6-7
  variables, 7-9, 15-17
  virtual servers, 102
High Availability Cluster Multi-
  Processing (HACMP), 365
HOLAP (multidimensional OLAP), 358
horizontal filtering, articles, 201-202
hot swappable architecture, 403
hot swappable components, 32
hot swapping, 8
hybrid decision-tree evaluation, HA
  solutions, 308-309
hybrid OLAP (HOLAP), 358
hybrid selection method (solution
  assessment), 61
  ASP (application service provider),
    66-74
  decision-tree approach, 63-65
  investment portfolio, 78-81
  life at risk-classified application,
    82-86
  sales/marketing, 74-78

I

IBM/DB2 Clustered Server, example,
  364-366
IDs
  administering user, 371
  SCSI, 98
immediate transactional consistency, 226
immediate updating (subscribers), 212

index, online (Yukon), 399
initializing databases (log shipping), 178
installations
    clustering, 142
        cluster-managed disks, 141
        instances, 138, 141
        IP (Internet Protocol)
            addresses, 139-140
        nodes, 141
        server binaries, 143
        server licensing, 143
        server resources, 145-147
        server user accounts, 143
        servers, 138
        service packs, 144
    MSCS (Microsoft Cluster
        Services), 102-103
        disk devices, checking, 105
        nodes, administrative
            permissions, 104
        pre-installation, 104-105
        quorum disks, 104
        step 1, 106 113, 116
        step 2, 116-118
        system logs, checking, 104
instantaneous replication, 327
IP (Internet Protocol) addresses
    clustering, 139-140
    clusters, 101
    MSCS networks, 99-100, 113
iterative design approach (high
    availability), 22

J-K-L

join filtering articles, 204

latency
    data replication, 226-227
    data, log shipping, 169-170

latent transactional consistency, 226
LDAP, 370
LEGATO website, 363
licenses, foundation component options,
    33
licensing agreements, Microsoft, 139
licensing servers, cluster installations,
    143
linked OLAP cubes, 356
links, remote SQL servers, 276-277
load balancing
    CLB (component load balancing),
        120
    NLB (Network Load Balancing)
        MSCS (Microsoft Cluster
            Services), 118-120
        subscriber failover, 254
local OLAP cubes, 356
log reader agent, 221-222, 229
log shipping, 29, 49-51
    administration implications,
        170-171
    alerts, 169
    authentication, 181
    data latency, 169-170
    database mirroring, 391
    deleting, 187
    design considerations, 329-331
    design implications, 170-171
    destination servers, 168
    disk space, 175
    example, 191-193
    functions, 167
    hybrid selection method (solution
        assessment), 62
    monitor servers, 168
    overview, 167-169
    ROI example, 191-193
    security considerations, 381-384
    servers, primary roles, 188-189

setup, Database Maintenance Plan
Wizard, 173
alerts, 180-181
common errors, 183-184
database load states, 177-178
database primary roles, 178
destination databases,
175-177
initializing databases, 178
monitoring, 181-183
network share locations, 175
Northwind database, 174-175
scheduling log shipping, 179
setup
properties, 184-185
properties, monitor servers,
186
server instances, 172-173
servers, 171
system stored procedures, 189-190
Yukon, 171
Log Shipping Monitor, 186
login IDs, remote SQL servers, 277

M

maintenance, scheduled, 16
majority note sets (quorum disks),
120-123
manual synchronization, 219
marginal availability, 13
MDAC (Microsoft Data Access
Component), 395
MDX (Multidimensional Extensions),
354
memory, RAID (Redundant Array of
Independent Disks), 37
merge agent, 223-224, 230

merge replication, 228
conflict resolution, 232
functions, 231
preparations, 230-231
Microsoft
beta, 392
high availability technology, 28-30
licensing agreement, 139
Microsoft Cluster Services (MSCS), 28,
45, 128-130
4-node topologies, 124-125
8-node topologies, 124-125
active/active clustering, 97
active/passive clustering, 97
cluster status, 115
design considerations, 321-323
disk controllers, configuring, 98
disks, 98-99
fail-over, 96
four-node clustering, 97
hardware requirements, 93-95
installing, 102-103
disk devices, checking, 105
nodes, administrative
permissions, 104
pre-installation, 104-105
quorum disks, 104
step 1, 106-113, 116
step 2, 116-118
system logs, checking, 104
IP addresses, 113
networks
configuring, 99-101
private, 111-112
public, 111
requirements, 93-95
NLB (Network Load Balancing),
118-120
nodes, heartbeats, 96
operating systems, 93-95, 101-102

overview, 91-93
partitions, formatting, 98
quorum drives, 97
security considerations, 379
shared disks, 96
split-brain scenarios, 96
SQL clustering, 46-47
times slices, 96
topologies, 106
Windows 2003, 120-123
WINS (Windows Internet Naming
  Service), 101
Microsoft Component Object Model
  (COM), COM+ applications, 291-293
Microsoft Data Access Component
  (MDAC), 395
Microsoft Distributed Transaction
  Coordinator (MS DTC), configuring,
  130-131
Microsoft Queue Manager (MSMQ), 273
Microsoft Virtual Server 2005, 401-403
Microsoft Windows authentication, log
  shipping, 181
mirroring, 34-36
  Database Mirroring, 171, 391,
    394-397
  remote mirroring, design
    considerations, 320-321
  triple, 340
models, data replication, 206
  central publisher, 207-208
  central publisher with remote
    distributor, 208-210
  central subscriber, 210
  multiple publishers, 211
  multiple subscribers, 211
  publishing subscriber, 210
  subscribers, updating, 212-213
modes, 177
MOLAP (multidimensional OLAP), 357

monitor servers, log shipping, 168, 186,
  330, 383
monitoring
  backups, 342-344
  data replication
    backup/recovery, 261-264
    Performance Monitor, 261
    SQL Enterprise Manager,
      259-260
    SQL statements, 258-259
    synchronization, 264
  log shipping, 181-183, 186
MS Analysis Services (MSAS), 353-361
MS DTC (Distributed Transaction
  Coordinator), 272, 292
  configuring, 130-131
  two-phase commit protocol (2PC),
    283, 286, 290
    DTS/MS Queue Manager,
      287-289
    SQL servers, 285
  UOW (Unit of Work), 273
MS Queue Manager, two-phase commit
  protocol (2PC), 287-289
MS SQL Server 2000, 29
MSAS (MS Analysis Services), 353-361
MSCS (Microsoft Cluster Services), 28,
  45, 128-130
  4-node topologies, 124-125
  8-node topologies, 124-125
  active/active clustering, 97
  active/passive clustering, 97
  cluster status, 115
  design considerations, 321-323
  disk controllers, configuring, 98
  disks, 98-99
  fail-over, 96
  four-node clustering, 97
  hardware requirements, 93-95

installing, 102-103
  disk devices, checking, 105
  nodes, administrative
    permissions, 104
  pre-installation, 104-105
  quorum disks, 104
  step 1, 106-113, 116
  step 2, 116-118
  system logs, checking, 104
IP addresses, 113
networks
  configuring, 99-101
  private, 111-112
  public, 111
  requirements, 93-95
NLB (Network Load Balancing),
  118-120
nodes, heartbeats, 96
operating systems, 93-95, 101-102
overview, 91-93
partitions, formatting, 98
quorum drives, 97
security considerations, 379
shared disks, 96
split-brain scenarios, 96
SQL clustering, 46-47
times slices, 96
topologies, 106
Windows 2003, 120-123
WINS (Windows Internet Naming
  Service), 101
MSCS Setup Wizard, 104
MSCS Wizard, 106
MSMerge_contents table, 232
MSMQ (Microsoft Queue Manager), 273
Multidimensional Extensions (MDX),
  354
multidimensional OLAP (MOLAP), 357
multiple publisher replication model,
  211
multiple subscriber replication model,
  211

N

n-tier infrastructures (NLB), 120
naming
  clusters, 101
  virtual servers, 142
NAS (Network Attached Storage), 318
Nassi-Schneiderman charts
  HA solutions, selecting, 308-309
  hybrid decision-tree approach
    (solution assessment), 63-65
Network Attached Storage (NAS), 318
network deployed push model, software
  upgrades, 351-352
network interfaces (clustering), 135
Network Load Balancing (NLB)
  MSAS (MS Analysis Services), 358
  MSCS (Microsoft Cluster
    Services), 118-120
  subscriber failover, 254
network share locations, log shipping,
  175
networks
  configuring (MSCS), 99-101
  design considerations, 317-319
  private (MSCS), 111-112
  public (MSCS), 111
  requirements, MSCS (Microsoft
    Cluster Services), 93-95
NLB (Network Load Balancing)
  MSAS (MS Analysis Services), 358
  MSCS (Microsoft Cluster
    Services), 118-120
  subscriber failover, 254
node failure (clustering), 148-149, 152
nodes
  4-node clustering topologies,
    124-125
  8-node clustering topologies,
    124-125
  administrative permissions, 104

clustering, 128, 141
evicting (clustering), 161
heartbeats, 96
recovery (clustering), 160-161
two-node clustering, 128
NORECOVERY mode, 177
Northwind database, log shipping setup,
174-175
NUL (backups), 339

O

objects
SQLServer:Replication Agents, 261
SQLServer:Replication Dist, 261
SQLServer:Replication Logreader,
261
SQLServer:Replication Merge, 261
SQLServer:Replication Snapshot,
261
OLAP (online analytical processing), 353
cubes, 356
HOLAP (hybrid OLAP), 358
MOLAP (multidimensional
OLAP), 357
partitions, 354
ROLAP (relational OLAP),
357
focus, 355-356
on demand virtual processing, 404
online analytical processing (OLAP), 353
cubes, 356
HOLAP (hybrid OLAP), 358
MOLAP (multidimensional
OLAP), 357
partitions, 354
ROLAP (relational OLAP),
357
focus, 355-356

online index, Yukon, 399
online restore, Yukon, 399
operating systems (OSs)
design considerations, 317-318
foundation component options, 33
MSCS (Microsoft Cluster
Services), 101-102
requirements, 92-95
options, 31
data replication, 47-49
distributed transactions, 51
fault tolerance
mirroring, 34-36
RAID (Redundant Array of
Independent Disks), 34-42
foundation components
backup, 33
hardware, 32
operating systems, 33
server isolation, 34
standards/procedures, 34
testing, 34
training, 34
vendor agreements, 33
log shipping, 49-51
MSCS (Microsoft Cluster
Services), 45
server instance isolation, 42-44
SQL clustering, 46-47
OSs (operating systems)
design considerations, 317-318
foundation component options, 33
MSCS (Microsoft Clustering
Services), 101-102
requirements, 92-95
Out of Sync alerts, 180

P

parallel striped backups, 339
parity, 39
partitions
    data, Yukon, 400
    formatting (MSCS), 98
    OLAP (online analytical
        processing) cubes, 354
performance, 17
Performance Monitor, data replication,
  261
permissions
    administrative, nodes, 104
    CREATE, 371
    statements, 373
Phase 0 HA assessment, 55
    development life cycle tasks,
        306-308
    required information, 300
    resources, 56
    Step 1, 301-304
    Step 2, 304-306
    tasks, 56-59
    templates, 300
planned downtime, 7-8, 13-14
platforms, content, 404
point-in-time recovery (full database
  backups), 337
polling Cluster Services, 151
pre-installations, MSCS (Microsoft
  Cluster Services), 104-105
primary high availability variables,
  304-305
primary key columns (schema-bound
  views), 374-376
primary roles
    changing (servers), 188-189
    databases, log shipping, 178

primary variables gauges
    Step 2 (Phase 0 HA assessment),
        59-60, 304-306
    templates, 305
principal servers, 395
private networks (MSCS), 111-112
procedures/standards, foundation
  component options, 34
processing
    distributed transaction processing,
        design considerations, 331-333
    on demand virtual processing, 404
    snapshot agents, 220-221
programs, Client Test, 152, 155-159
project coordinator/manager (assessment
  teams), 298
project lead/Champion (assessment
  teams), 298
project schedules, setting (assessments),
  299-300
protocols
    DHCP (Dynamic Host
        Configuration Protocol), MSCS
        networks, 100
    IP (Internet Protocol) addresses,
        113, 139-140
    two-phase commit (2PC)
        distributed queries, 285-286
        distributed transactions,
        282-286, 289-290
public networks (MSCS), 111
publication servers, data replication, 199
publications
    creating (data replication), 241-245
    data replication, 201

publisher
  central publisher replication model,
    207-208
  central publisher with remote
    distributor replication model,
    208-210
  publishing subscriber replication
    model, 210
publishers
  configuring (data replication),
    239-241
  converting subscribers to (failover),
    254
  enabling (data replication), 239-241
  multiple publisher replication
    model, 211
publishing subscriber replication model,
  210
pull subscriptions, 214, 246
push subscriptions, 215, 246

Q-R

quality assurance, foundation component
  options, 34
queries
  distributed, two-commit phase
    protocol (2PC), 285-286
  remote SQL servers, 279-280
Queue Manager (MS), two-phase
  commit protocol (2PC), 287-289
queued updating (subscribers), 213
quorum disks
  majority note sets (MSCS), 120-123
  MSCS (Microsoft Cluster Services)
    installations, 104
  Windows 2003 (MSCS), 120-123
quorum drives, 97, 133

RAID (Redundant Array of Independent
  Disks), 34-42
  cluster configurations, 132-133
  MSAS (MS Analysis Services), 359
RAID 0 striping (without parity), 37-38
RAID 0+1, 41
RAID 0/1, 41
RAID 01, 41
RAID 1 mirroring (with duplexing),
  38-39
RAID 5, 36
RAID 5 block-level striping (with
  distributed parity), 39-40
RAID 10, 41
real-enough time data, 226
Real-Time Log Shipping (RTLS), 171,
  394
real-time OLAP cubes, 356
recoverable downtime, 9
recovery
  data replication, monitoring,
    261-264
  design considerations, 319
  disaster recovery
    focus, 345-349
    Microsoft Virtual Server
      2005, 403
    overall approach, 344-345
    planning, 344
    remote capabilities, 404
    security considerations,
      388-389
    SQLDIAG.EXE file, 349-351
    testing, 351
  nodes (clustering), 160-161
  point-in-time (full database
    backups), 337
  tolerance, 15
  up-to-the-minute (full database
    backups), 337
  Yukon, 398-399

Redundant Array of Independent Disks (RAID), 34-42
regular OLAP cubes, 356
Reinitialize Subscription Having Data Validation agent, 224
relational OLAP (ROLAP), 357
releases, 392
remote disaster recovery, 404
remote mirroring, design considerations, 320-321
remote SQL servers, 274
    access, setting up, 275
    links, creating, 276-277
    security, 277-280
    Transact-SQL statements, 280-281
replication. *See also* data replication
    central publisher, remote distributor, 197, 327
    instantaneous, 327
    merge, 228-232
    scripting, 254-257
    snapshot, 227-229
    snapshot with updating subscribers, 227
    transactional, 196, 223, 227-230, 327
    transactional with updating subscribers, 227
Replication Agents Checkup agent, 225
Replication Monitor, 259
Repl_Administrator accounts, 386
resiliency, 16
resource managers, distributed transactions, 283
resources
    clustering, 101, 129, 132
    Phase 0 (step 1 solution assessment), 56
    servers (clustering), 145-147
    SQL Server, 325
restore, online (Yukon), 399

restoring database failures, 336-337
ROI (Return on Investment) calculation
    ASP (application server provider), clustering scenario, 162-164
    data replication, 266-268
    HA solutions, cost effectiveness, 311-312
    log shipping example, 191-193
ROLAP (relational OLAP), 357
roles
    database, 372-373
    fixed server, 372-373
    MSCS networks, 100
    primary, changing (servers), 188-189
RTLS (Real Time Log Shipping), 171, 394

S

scalability, 17, 397
scaling out, 118
.SCH extension, 219
scheduled maintenance frequency, 16
scheduling
    log shipping, 179
    setting (assessments), 299-300
schema-bound views, 373
    column-level, 376-378
    primary key columns, 374-376
scripting replication, 254-257
SCSI IDs, 98
security
    administering user ids, 371
    anti-virus software, 352
    CREATE permissions, 371
    data replication, 384-387
    design considerations, 318
    disaster recovery, 388-389

LDAP, 370
log shipping, 381-384
MSCS (Microsoft Cluster Service), 379
overview, 369-371
remote SQL servers, 277-279
roles, 372-373
schema-bound views, 373
    column-level, 376-378
    primary key columns, 374-376
SQL clustering, 380-381
virus software, 370
Windows user accounts, 371
security resynchronization readiness, 345, 389
senior business analysts (assessment teams), 298
senior technical leads (assessment teams), 298
server binaries, cluster installations, 143
server licensing, cluster installations, 143
server user accounts, cluster installations, 143
server-less backups (split mirror backups), 340-342
servers
    cluster installations, 138
    design considerations, 317
    destination, log shipping, 168
    distribution, data replication, 200
    Distributor Server, 260
    fail-over, log shipping, 50
    instance isolation
        application failures, 42-44
        foundation component options, 34
    instances, log shipping setup, 172-173
    log shipping setup, 171
    Microsoft Virtual Server 2005, 401-403

Monitor, log shipping, 168, 186, 330, 383
MS SQL Server 2000, 29
nodes, 45
primary roles, changing, 188-189
principal, 395
publication, data replication, 199
remote SQL, 274
    access, setting up, 275
    links, creating, 276-277
    queries, 279-280
    security, 277-279
    Transact-SQL statements, 280-281
resources (clustering), 145-147
SQL, two-phase commit protocol (2PC), 285
subscription, data replication, 200
virtual, 102, 131, 142, 323
witness, 395
service level agreements (SLAs)
    availability continuum, 12
    design approaches, 24-25
    Phase 0 HA assessments, 302
service packs, cluster installations, 144
services, Yukon clustering, 393
shadowing, VSS (Volume Shadow Copy Service), 342
shared disks, 96, 132
shared nothing disk arrays, 96
sharing network share locations, log shipping, 175
shipping, log shipping, 29, 49-51
    administration implications, 170-171
    alerts, 169
    authentication, 181
    data latency, 169-170
    database mirroring, 391
    deleting, 187
    design considerations, 329-331

design implications, 170-171
destination servers, 168
disk space, 175
example, 191-193
functions, 167
hybrid selection method (solution
   assessment), 62
monitor servers, 168
overview, 167-169
ROI example, 191-193
security considerations, 381-384
servers, primary roles, 188-189
setup, Database Maintenance Plan
   Wizard, 173
     alerts, 180-181
     common errors, 183-184
     database load states, 177-178
     database primary roles, 178
     destination databases,
       175-177
     initializing databases, 178
     monitoring, 181-183
     network share locations, 175
     Northwind database, 174-175
     scheduling log shipping, 179
setup
     properties, 184-185
     properties, monitor servers,
       186
     server instances, 172-173
     servers, 171
system stored procedures, 189-190
Yukon, 171
SI (snapshot isolation) levels, Yukon, 400
site autonomy, 226
sites. *See* websites
SLAs (service level agreements)
   availability continuum, 12
   design approaches, 24-25
   Phase 0 HA assessments, 302

snapshot agent, 218, 228-230
   processing, 220-221
   synchronization, 219
snapshot isolation (SI) levels, Yukon, 400
snapshot replication, 227-229
snapshot replication with updating
   subscribers, 227
software
   anti-virus, 352
   hardware/software stacks, 32
   upgrading, 351-353
   virus, 370
software foundations, 296-298
software scaling, 118
solution assessment, process, 53
   step 1, 54-59
   step 2, 54, 59-60
   step 3, 54, 60
     adding HA elements, 88
     cost justification, 86-88
     hybrid selection method,
       61-86
     ROI (Return on Investment),
       86-88
   step 4, 54-55
solutions (HA)
   cost effectiveness, 311-312
   selecting, 308-309
split mirror backups (server-less
   backups), 340-342
split-brain scenarios (MSCS), 96
SQL Agents, 132, 323, 381
SQL clustering, 29, 46-47
   design considerations, 322-325
   hybrid selection method (solution
     assessment), 61
   MSAS (MS Analysis Services), 360
   security considerations, 380-381
   virtual servers, 323
SQL Enterprise Manager, data
   replication, 259-260

SQL Server 2005. *See* Yukon

SQL Server Configuration Wizard, 156

SQL servers
  authentication, log shipping, 181
  remote, 274
    access, setting up, 275
    links, creating, 276-277
    queries, 279-280
    security, 277-279
    Transact-SQL statements,
      280-281
  resources, 325
  two-phase commit protocol (2PC),
    285

SQL Setup Wizard, 153

SQL statements, data replication,
  258-259

SQLDIAG.EXE file, 349-351

SQLServer:Replication Agents object,
  261

SQLServer:Replication Dist object, 261

SQLServer:Replication Logreader
  object, 261

SQLServer:Replication Merge object,
  261

SQLServer:Replication Snapshot object,
  261

SQL_Administrator accounts, 386

stack components, high availability, 6-7

stacks, hardware/software, 32

standard availability, 12

standards/procedures, foundation
  component options, 34

STANDBY mode, 177

statements
  permissions, 373
  SQL data replication, monitoring,
    258-259
  Transact-SQL, remote SQL
    servers, 280-281

status, clusters, 115

SteelEye Technologies website, 363

Step 1 (Phase 0 HA assessment), 54-55,
  301-304
  resources, 56
  tasks, 56-59

Step 2 (Phase 0 HA assessment), 54,
  59-60, 304-306

step 3 (solution assessment process), 54,
  60
  cost justification, 86-88
  HA elements, adding, 88
  hybrid selection method, 61
    ASP (application service
      provider), 66-74
    decision-tree approach, 63-65
    investment portfolio, 78-81
    life at risk-classified
      application, 82-86
    sales/marketing, 74-78
  ROI (Return on Investment), 86-88

step 4 (solution assessment process),
  54-55

store-and-forward databases, 216

store-and-forward distribution model,
  197

stored procedures
  executions, 204-205
  systems (log shipping), 189-190

stretch clustering, design considerations,
  325-326

striping data blocks, 37

subscribers
  central subscriber replication
    model, 210
  multiple subscribers replication
    model, 211
  publishing subscriber replication
    model, 210
  snapshot replication, 227
  transactional replication, 227
  updating, 212-213
  warm standby failover, 252-254

subscriptions
    anonymous, 215-216
    creating (data replication), 246-251
    pull, 214, 246
    push, 215, 246
    servers, data replication, 200
    warm standby failover, 253-254
summary tables, ROLAP (relational OLAP), 357
synchronization
    data replication, monitoring, 264
    distributed access, 16
    manual, 219
    security resynchronization readiness, 345
    snapshot agents, 219
system architect/data architect (assessment teams), 298
system logs, checking (MSCS installations), 104
system stacks, high availability, 6-7
system stored procedures, log shipping, 189-190

T

tables
    dropped, foreign key constraints, 378
    MSMerge_contents, 232
    summary, ROLAP (relational OLAP), 357
    triggers (data replication), 233-234
tasks
    development life cycles (Phase 0), 306-308
    Phase 0 (step 1 solution assessment), 56-59
technologists (assessment teams), 298

technology, Microsoft (high availability), 28-30
TempDB database, 134, 324
templates
    ERWin, 373-374
    Phase 0 HA assessment, 300
    primary variable gauges, 305
testing
    disaster recovery, 351
    fail-over (clustering), 155-159
    foundation component options, 34
time slices, 96
timelines, setting (assessments), 299-300
timing data replication, 226-227
tolerance, recovery time, 15
topologies, clustering, 106, 124-125
training, foundation component options, 34
Transact-SQL statements
    permissions, 373
    remote SQL servers, 280-281
transaction logs
    backups, 336-338, 383
    file retention periods, 179
transactional replication, 196, 223, 227-230, 327
transactional replication with updating subscribers, 227
transactions
    distributed, 29, 51, 62, 227
    distributed transaction processing, 271
        ACID (atomicity, consistency, isolation, and durability), 282
        COM+ applications, 291-293
        design considerations, 331-333
        MS DTC (distributed transaction coordinator), 272, 283-290

MSMQ (Microsoft Queue Manager), 273
remote SQL servers, 274-281
resource managers, 283
step-by-step process, 284-285
two-phase commit protocol (2PC), 282
UOW (Unit of Work), 273, 282-283
transparent client redirect, 394-395
triggers, tables (data replication), 233-234
triple mirroring, 35, 340
troubleshooting
    applications, avoiding failure, 42-44
    log shipping, 183-184
    nodes (clustering), 148-149, 152
    unplanned downtime, 8-9
two-node clustering, 106, 128
two-phase commit processing (2PC), 226
    distributed queries, 285-286
    distributed transactions, 282-283, 286, 290
        DTS/MS Queue Manager, 287-289
        SQL servers, 285

U-V

unattended cluster setup (Yukon), 393
Unit of Work (UOW), 273, 282-283
unplanned downtime, 8-9, 13-14
UOW (Unit of Work), 273, 282-283
up-to-the-minute recovery (full database backups), 337
updating subscribers, 212-213

upgrading
    design considerations, 318
    software
        design considerations, 351-353
        network deployed push model, 351-352
uptime, 7-8
user accounts
    cluster installations, 143
    Windows, 371

variables
    high availability, 7-9, 15-17
    primary high availability, 304-305
vendor agreements, foundation component options, 33
verifying backups, 342-344
Veritas website, 362
vertical filtering, articles, 201-202
VHD (Virtual Hard Disk), 403
ViewPoint. *See* database snapshots
views, schema-bound, 373-376
Virtual Hard Disk (VHD), 403
Virtual Machine Monitor (VMM), 402-403
virtual OLAP cubes, 356
virtual processing, on demand, 404
Virtual Server 2005 (Microsoft), 401-403
virtual servers, 102, 131, 142, 323
virus software, 370
VMM (Virtual Machine Monitor), 402-403
VSS (Volume Shadow Copy Service), 342

W-X

warm standby
    subscribers, failover
        converting to publishers, 254
        NLB (Network Load
            Balancing), 254
        scenarios, 252-253
    subscriptions, failover, 253-254
waterfall design approach (high
    availability), 21-22
websites
    Computer Associates, 363-364
    HCL (Hardware Compatibility
        List), 95
    LEGATO, 363
    SteelEye Technologies, 363
    Veritas, 362
Windows 2003
    fail-over, 120-123
    quorum disks (MSCS), 120-123
Windows Authentication, log shipping,
    383
Windows Components Wizard, 113
Windows Internet Naming Service
    (WINS), 101
Windows user accounts, 371
WINS (Windows Internet Naming
    Service), 101
witness servers, 395
wizards
    Cluster Services Configuration, 106
    Configure Publishing, Subscribers,
        and Distribution Wizard, 235
    Create Publication, 241
    Database Maintenance Plan, 173
        alerts, 180-181
        common errors, 183-184
        database load states, 177-178
        database primary roles, 178
        destination databases,
            175-177
        initializing databases, 178
        monitoring, 181-183
        network share locations, 175
        Northwind database, 174-175
        scheduling log shipping, 179
    MSCS, 106
    MSCS Setup, 104
    SQL Server Configuration, 156
    SQL Setup, 153
    Windows Components, 113
write-enabled OLAP cubes, 356

Y-Z

Yukon (SQL Server 2005)
    beta, 392
    data access enhancements, 398-401
    data partitioning, 400
    database snapshot, 399-400
    dedicated administrator
        connection, 401
    fail-over clustering, 393
        database mirroring, 394-397
        scalability, 397
    fast recovery, 398-399
    log shipping, 171
    online index, 399
    online restore, 399
    services (clustering), 393
    snapshot isolation (SI) levels, 400

Microsoft Windows Server System Series

Books in the **Microsoft Windows Server System Series** are written and reviewed by the world's leading technical authorities on Microsoft Windows technologies, including principal members of Microsoft's Windows and Server Development Teams. The goal of the series is to provide reliable information that enables administrators, developers, and IT professionals to architect, build, deploy, and manage solutions using the Microsoft Windows Server System. The contents and code of each book are tested against, and comply with, commercially available code. This series should be an invaluable resource for any IT professional or student working in today's Windows environment.

TITLES IN THE SERIES

Paul Bertucci, *Microsoft SQL Server High Availability*, 0-672-32625-6 (Sams)

Peter Blackburn and William R. Vaughn, *Hitchhiker's Guide to SQL Server 2000 Reporting Services*, 0-321-26828-8 (Addison-Wesley)

William Boswell, *Learning Exchange Server 2003*, 0-321-22874-X (Addison-Wesley)

Bill English, Olga Londer, Shawn Shell, Todd Bleeker, and Stephen Cawood, *Microsoft Content Management Server 2002: A Complete Guide*, 0-321-19444-6 (Addison-Wesley)

Don Jones, *Managing Windows® with VBScript and WMI*, 0-321-21334-3 (Addison-Wesley)

Sakari Kouti and Mika Seitsonen, *Inside Active Directory, Second Edition: A System Administrator's Guide*, 0-321-22848-0 (Addison-Wesley)

Shyam Pather, *Microsoft SQL Server 2000 Notification Services*, 0-672-32664-7 (Sams)

For more information please go to www.awprofessional.com/msserverseries